The Official ebaY™ Bible

THE OFFICIAL

eBaY™

BIBLE

■ The Newly Revised and Updated Version of
the Most Comprehensive eBay How-To Manual
for Everyone from First-Time Users to eBay Experts

THIRD EDITION

JIM "GRIFF" GRIFFITH

GOTHAM
BOOKS

GOTHAM BOOKS
Published by Penguin Group (USA) Inc.
375 Hudson Street, New York, New York 10014, U.S.A.
Penguin Group (Canada), 90 Eglinton Avenue East, Suite 700, Toronto, Ontario M4P 2Y3, Canada
(a division of Pearson Penguin Canada Inc.); Penguin Books Ltd, 80 Strand, London WC2R 0RL, England;
Penguin Ireland, 25 St Stephen's Green, Dublin 2, Ireland (a division of Penguin Books Ltd); Penguin Group
(Australia), 250 Camberwell Road, Camberwell, Victoria 3124, Australia (a division of Pearson Australia
Group Pty Ltd); Penguin Books India Pvt Ltd, 11 Community Centre, Panchsheel Park, New Delhi – 110
017, India; Penguin Group (NZ), 67 Apollo Drive, Rosedale, North Shore 0745, Auckland, New Zealand
(a division of Pearson New Zealand Ltd.); Penguin Books (South Africa) (Pty.) Ltd, 24 Sturdee Avenue,
Rosebank, Johannesburg 2196, South Africa

Penguin Books Ltd, Registered Offices: 80 Strand, London WC2R 0RL, England

Published by Gotham Books, a division of Penguin Group (USA) Inc.

First printing, August 2007
10   9   8   7   6   5   4   3   2

Gotham Books and the skyscraper logo are trademarks of Penguin Group (USA) Inc.

LIBRARY OF CONGRESS CATALOGING-IN-PUBLICATION DATA

Griffith, Jim.
    The official eBay Bible : the newly revised and updated version of the most comprehensive eBay how-to
manual for everyone from first-time users to eBay experts / Jim "Griff" Griffith. — 3rd ed.
        p. cm.
    Includes index.
    ISBN 978-1-592-40301-1 (hardcover)
    1.   eBay (Firm) 2.   Internet auctions. 3.   Electronic commerce—Management. 4.   New business
enterprises—Computer networks. I.   Title.
HF5478.G75 2007
658.8'7—dc22   2007013239

Printed in the United States of America
Set in Sabon with Frutiger

While the author has made every effort to provide accurate telephone numbers and Internet addresses at the
time of publication, neither the publisher nor the author assumes any responsibility for errors, or for changes
that occur after publication. Further, the publisher does not have any control over and does not assume any
responsibility for author or third-party Web sites or their content.

To the millions of eBay members
who have helped make eBay what it is today

CONTENTS

Acknowledgments   xv
Introduction   xvii

Section One—Buying the eBay Way!   1

1. Let's Get Started   3

- The eBay Phenomenon   3
- Registering on eBay, Step-by-Step   9
- User ID and Password Selection Tips   11
- Terms of Use and Your Privacy   13
- Changing Your Contact Information   17
- Changing Your User ID, E-mail Address, or Password   19
- Troubleshooting Registration Problems   21
- Opening a PayPal Account   22

2. The eBay Web Site   29

- Navigating the eBay Web Site—a Road Map   29
- The eBay Navigation Bar   29
- The Sign In Page   36
- Navigating the eBay Home Page   38
- Navigating the Site Map, Categories, and Item Description Page   40
- eBay Categories   41

- My eBay   53
- Your eBay Account   68
- The Feedback Forum   78
- Reading Feedback   78
- Leaving Feedback   84
- Feedback Protocol   85

3. Shopping on eBay—Find It!   93

- What Can I Buy on eBay?   93
- Browsing eBay   96
- Searching eBay   118
- Title Search   120
- Search Tips   127
- Search Command Chart   129
- Advanced Searching Options   134

4. Shopping on eBay—Buy It!   151

- Before You Bid or Buy—a Safe Trading Checklist   160
- What Type of Payment Does a Seller Accept?   183
- Online Payments—The Safest Way to Buy on eBay   189
- We've Found It . . . We've Checked It Out . . . Let's Buy It!   190
- Bidding   191
- Sniping   200
- Multiple Item Bidding—How It Works   211
- Buy It Now—How It Works   214

5. Shopping at eBay—Pay for It!   221

- Completing the Transaction   222
- Contact the Seller   230
- Ask the Seller a Question   231
- Payment Options   232
- Online Payment Services   233
- Managing Bids and Purchases with My eBay   237
- Leaving Feedback for the Seller   242

6. Other Bidding and Buying Options and Considerations   243

- eBay Express   244

- Half.com 247
- Buying Big Stuff at eBay 248
- eBay Motors—Cars, Trucks, Boats, and So On 249
- Real Estate 253
- International Buying 256
- Searching International eBay Sites 258
- More on Currency 260
- Buying Locally 264

7. eBay Guidelines, Rules, and Help for Buyers 267

- eBay Buyer Guidelines and Rules 267
- A Buyer Trust and Safety Checklist 271
- Avoid Questionable or Prohibited Activity 272
- eBay Rules for Buyers 272
- Special Retraction Rules 274
- Shill Bidding 276
- Unpaid Items (UPIs) 276
- Feedback Offenses 277
- Reporting Questionable Activity or Items 278
- Dispute Resolution 279
- Resolving a Difficult Transaction 280
- How to Get Help on eBay 289
- eBay Education 291

Section Two—Selling the eBay Way! 301

1. Selling Setup, Step-by-Step 305

- Following the Steps 305
- Setting Up an eBay Seller's Account 306
- Opening a Premier- or Business-Level PayPal Account 317
- Research Your Item 323
- Completed Listings Search 323

2. Creating and Editing Digital Pictures of Your eBay Item 331

- What Are Digital Pictures? 331
- Do I Need Digital Pictures of My eBay Item? 332
- Taking the Picture—Selecting a Method 332

- What to Look For in a Digital Camera 334
- Taking the Picture—Setting Up the Item 335
- Picture-Taking Tips 345
- Editing Digital Pictures (Using Software) 355
- Griff's Pixel Guidelines 366
- Saving and Archiving Your eBay Digital Pictures 368

3. Writing a Description and Packing the Item 373

- A Simple and Thorough Description 374
- Packing—Do It Right! 380
- The eBay Sell Your Item Form 388
- Selecting a Category 390
- Setting the Show/Hide Options 395
- Describe Your Item 399
- Adding Pictures 401
- eBay Picture Services 401
- Picture Options 413
- Writing a Description 415
- Cut, Copy, and Paste 416
- Formatting Your Description with the Description Editor 423
- Selecting a Selling Format 430
- Selling Format: Online Auction 431
- Reserve Price 433
- Buy It Now 433
- Quantity and Duration 434
- Selling Format: Fixed Price 436
- Payment Methods You Accept 440
- Shipping Calculator 442
- Buyer Requirements 451
- Return Policy Considerations 453
- Promote and Review Your Listing 454
- Recommendations For Your Listings 462
- Preview Your Listing 462
- Fees 466
- Selling Troubleshooting 471
- Second Chance Offer 479

4. After the Sale — 481

- Invoicing the Buyer — 482
- Accessing PayPal Payments — 492
- Leaving Feedback — 496
- Shipping — 498
- Crating and Freighting Large Items — 509
- International Shipping Considerations — 512

5. eBay Business Tips and Tools — 515

- Business Structures for eBay Sellers — 516
- The Advantages of Incorporation vs. Sole Proprietorship — 517
- Costs of Incorporation — 518
- A Few Words About Taxes — 518
- eBay Main Street — 520
- What to Sell? — 521
- Be Gone, Inefficient Markets . . . eBay to the Rescue! — 526
- Finding Product — 527
- Trading Assistants — 533
- Your Business Location — 535
- Selling from Your Home — 535
- Your Office Equipment — 538
- Bookkeeping — 539
- Using Auction Management Tools — 546
- Keeping Track of Your Listings Using My eBay for Low-Volume Sellers — 546
- eBay Seller Tools For High-Volume Sellers — 547
- Turbo Lister — 547
- Selling Manager (Basic and Pro) — 551
- Blackthorne Basic and Pro Versions — 554
- eBay Stores — 556
- eBay Cross Promotions Tool — 560
- eBay Sales Reports — 563
- Promoting Your eBay Business with Your About Me Page — 568
- Growing Your eBay Business — 569
- The eBay PowerSeller Program — 571
- Successful Business Practices — 573
- Special Selling Considerations — 580
- Selling to the World — 582

6. HTML for eBay Sellers 587

- What Is HTML? 588
- What Exactly Are Web Pages? 588
- What Is the Web? 589
- What Is a Web Browser? 590
- Creating an HTML-Formatted eBay Description from Scratch ... 591
- HTML Tags 610
- HTML Character Entities 626
- Hyperlinks 629
- The Image Tag 635
- Table Tags 638
- Other HTML Tags 643

7. Advanced Image Hosting Solutions 649

- eBay Listings and Digital Pictures—Advanced Solutions ... 649
- Pictures on a Web Page—How Does That Work? 650
- Digital Picture Hosting (Image Hosting) 655
- eBay's Picture Manager 682

8. Help! 687

- Trust and Safety for Sellers 687
- Questionable or Prohibited Practices and Activities 688
- Bidding Offenses—Shill Bidding 692
- Feedback 692
- Unpaid Items 692
- Listing Violations 694
- eBay and PayPal Buyer Protection 696
- Listing Copyrighted or Trademarked Items on eBay 697
- The eBay VeRO Program (Verified Rights Owners) 698
- Listing Brand-Name and Copyright-Protected Items on eBay . 699
- Appealing VeRO Actions 700
- Dispute Resolution 701
- How to Get Assistance at eBay 702
- On-site Help 702
- My eBay 703
- Getting Help from Other eBay Members 704

- Live Help   709
- Contacting eBay Customer Support   712
- eBay Radio   714

Glossary   719
Index   731

ACKNOWLEDGMENTS

I would like to thank the following: Pierre Omidyar and Jeff Skoll for throwing me that lifesaver back in 1996; my esteemed eBay colleagues Henry Gomez—whose support was crucial in getting this project off the ground—and Brad Williams for his guidance; Lisa Shotland and Jim Davis; Joni Evans and Jay Mandel at William Morris; Lauren Marino, Erin Moore, Jessica Sindler, and William Shinker at Gotham Books, for showering me with their expertise, advice, and counsel; my friends Patti Louise Ruby, Matt England, Rodney Hill, John Tillinger, Chris Byrne, Rob Stanger, Joan Wing, Mary Lou Song, Marsha Collier, Michael Kaiser, and Josh Lewis for their support and encouragement; Mike Winslow, for standing by me during the rough and lean early days. Howie Miller, George Morgan, and Michael Johnson, for their friendship and support during the creation of this third edition.

Very special thanks to the following eBay members who contributed their tips, tricks, and stories: Craig M. Keller Sr., Craig Knouse, Tim Heidner, Tom Reddick, Tim Burnett, Julie Douglas, Pam Withers, Heather Luce, Mike Ford, Leah Lestina, Karen Gray, Anita Leather, Melissa Fiala, Brenda Bienlein, Robert Sachs, Barry Lamb, Peter Cini, Deanna Rittel, Keri Lyn Shosted, Classic Moments Video, Dave Rayner, Mike Driscoll, Chris Spencer, Pat Fulton, Peter Becker, and Erik Holcomb.

INTRODUCTION

On the morning of May 10, 1996, a friend sent me an e-mail. At the time, I was living in Vermont, dividing my day between administrative duties for a nonprofit arts organization known as The Carving Studio, some residual mural painting left over from my once-flourishing decorative painting business, and buying, building, and reselling computers.

I was going broke.

My online friend knew I was searching for a hard-to-find memory chip. He had just stumbled upon a new Web site called eBay, where he had discovered that the very part I needed was for sale there in an auction format. I immediately clicked the URL he had copied into the body of the e-mail and found myself at a plain, gray-background Web site with a logo on the top of the page that announced "AuctionWeb—eBay Internet."

With a little easy searching, I soon found the chip and put in a bid of $15. (Two days later, I would win the auction for $10—a bargain.) I had finally found the part for which I had been looking. Excited by my find, I was soon exploring the rest of the site, looking for more treasure on which to bid, when I came across a page called "The AuctionWeb Bulletin Board."

The original eBay chat board was nothing fancy—just a simple message board where anyone could submit a text-only post for the rest of the world to read and to which anyone else could post a response.

I watched for a few hours as new eBay users posted their questions and a few regular eBay experts provided answers. Here were a group of friendly buyers and sellers having a grand time chatting and sharing expertise—a genuine online community! Unable to resist the fun, I jumped in and started posting my own eBay-related questions, making the acquaintance of other regular posters and learning a lot about buying and selling on eBay. Within weeks and with the help of generous eBay chat denizens, I had mastered the finer points of buying and selling and started answering questions like a seasoned eBay pro.

The ultimate pro, AuctionWeb creator Pierre Omidyar, usually stopped by the chat board in the evenings to say hello and chat about new features he was considering for his "hobby" site. He would even answer a few queries about listing procedures or policies. I was immediately struck by Pierre's good-natured chatting style, encyclopedic computer knowledge, and genuine concern for eBay users.

During the next few weeks, inspired by Pierre, I slowly patched together my own online persona, "Uncle Griff"—a hybrid of Miss Manners, Dame Edna Everage, and Maude from the 1971 cult film *Harold and Maude*, along with a bit of Norman Bates thrown in for balance.

Uncle Griff's primary mission on the chat board—besides chewing the online scenery—was to establish and maintain decorum and civility by dint of his own exemplary online behavior and slightly weird sense of humor. With the torch of his perfect manners held aloft, Uncle embarked on a valiant crusade to lead the huddled eBay chat board masses out of the darkness of messy, tear-ridden misunderstandings—which often escalated into all-out flame wars—onto the lofty plateau of polite and productive eBay discussion.

For a while, it was great fun, but although the Uncle Griff avatar was outwardly a jolly and well-adjusted—if somewhat bizarre—old coot, in truth, my off-line life was coming apart, and by late September, with savings depleted and no prospect of gainful employment in sight, I sank into a severe and paralyzing depression.

I thought it was a typical male midlife crisis, but it proved to be much more serious. I would later learn that I had been suffering from regular bouts of clinical depression for most of my life, but just like many sufferers of this pernicious disease, I had proudly resisted acknowledging or addressing my condition.

Unable to rouse myself out of bed, Uncle Griff unceremoniously disappeared one day from the AW Bulletin Board.

After a few weeks, with the support of concerned friends, therapy, and medication, I was able to return one morning to my studio. My landlord, an understanding man, had been patient about the back rent, but not so the utility companies. The studio heat and electricity had been shut off.

Standing alone in my cold, dark space, I considered my options. Although technically "on the mend," I would still need a job in order to crawl out of debt and pull my life together. But who in his right mind would ever hire an under-educated, middle-aged, previously-self-employed-now-flat-broke gentleman with a very left-of-center sense of humor?

It was the low point of my life. Then the phone rang.

"Hello?"

"Hello, is Uncle Griff there?"

"Who wants to know?"

"This is Jeff Skoll from eBay. Pierre is here with me. We are looking for Uncle Griff."

I remember thinking that I must have not paid my AuctionWeb bill.

"Uncle? Where have you been?"

"I had, uh . . . a cold. Is something wrong?"

"No, not at all. We were concerned. We've been watching Uncle Griff's antics for the last few months. We really think he's terrific. Then he just disappeared. We don't want Uncle to disappear again, so we were wondering if we could pay you to keep him around."

I was speechless.

"Uncle? You still there?"

"Work for eBay?"

"Are you interested?"

Interested? Jeff and Pierre had thrown me a life preserver. I found my voice and I grabbed the opportunity before they changed their minds.

"Yes, I am interested!"

The rest is a blur. We settled on a fair hourly wage, worked out a schedule of sorts, and by the end of the call, I was eBay's first official customer-support rep—answering e-mails and chatting on the boards, and all from West Rutland, Vermont.

More than ten years, and a lot of changes, later, I am still with eBay, except that my job title has changed to "Dean of eBay Education" and I am living in California instead of Vermont. Although I now travel around the country and the world spreading the word about eBay to the experienced and the uninitiated, I am still teaching others how to use eBay every other weekend at one of our eBay University seminars. (More on eBay University later in this book.) And, although I am no longer officially with Customer Support, I have never stopped answering e-mails. In fact, here is my e-mail address: griff@ebay.com. E-mail me if you ever need a hand with your eBay buying or selling.

EBAY CHANGED MY LIFE—IT CAN CHANGE YOURS!

It sounds like a cliché, but it's absolutely true—eBay changed my life. eBay has changed or enhanced the lives of literally millions of folks who, like me, stumbled one day upon this incredible revolutionary Web site and, as either buyers or sellers or both, found themselves suddenly taking control of their lives in ways they had never imagined were possible.

Over the past ten years, through e-mail and face-to-face, literally hundreds of eBay members have shared their own awe-inspiring eBay stories with me. Some of these stories are brief tales of the Good Samaritan who helped someone get started with her auctions. Others border on the miraculous—how finding eBay helped salvage a career or a business on the verge of collapse and ruin. People have met on eBay and were later married. One woman bought her entire wedding on eBay.

Others who once felt they were too incompetent or just plain too dumb to ever learn how to get online were motivated by the eBay juggernaut to finally master that damnable computer their son or daughter had given them, and were soon buying and selling along with the other millions of registered eBay users.

Today, more than two hundred million buyers and sellers around the world have jumped on the eBay train. An impressive number indeed, but by my reckoning that leaves several hundred million still unaccounted for.

Are you one of them?

- Do your friends and relatives all use eBay and you want to join in the fun, but the very thought of computers gives you the willies?
- Have you heard the buzz and checked out eBay once or twice but were overwhelmed by the sheer number of items for sale on the eBay Web site?
- Are you are currently selling at eBay but you want to improve your eBay skills with more tips, tricks, and eBay seller secrets?

If any of the above fit your situation, then this book is for you.

By combining the eBay knowledge I have garnered since 1996, the tips and tricks of other savvy eBay experts, and the incredible tales of people whose lives have been changed forever by eBay, I've put together this comprehensive how-to manual for using eBay—one that I hope will inspire you to take those first steps toward successful eBay buying and selling, and reward you with the confidence and the satisfaction that comes from learning and applying, firsthand, a new and exciting set of skills.

Do you like to buy? I'll take you step-by-step through the eBay registration process and show you how to effectively browse and search the eBay site with lots of information on how to bid and buy safely both for yourselves and your families.

Do you want to sell? I'll show you how to take better digital pictures and write professional item listings and you will learn how to put together a new eBay business and promote it effectively.

Don't think you can do it? Think again.

Over the last decade, I've witnessed thousands of folks just like you get the "eBay knack," and all it took was encouragement, a little humor, and step-by-step instructions in plain English.

I know you can do it! I have great confidence in you.

What are we waiting for? There's treasure to discover.

Let's get started!

The Official eBaY™ Bible

SECTION

1

Buying
the eBay Way!

Let's Get Started

You are about to enter a wondrous universe called eBay—a place where you can hunt for and buy treasure, sell the contents of your attic, or maybe finally follow that old dream of yours and start your own online business—all the while meeting and chatting with other eager eBay traders in your hometown, in your state, or from halfway around the globe. But first, a little history . . .

The eBay Phenomenon

Shopping!

Whether it's at garage sales or malls, through mail-order catalogs or the Shopping Channel, in Middle Eastern souks, at auctions, bazaars, swap meets, or flea markets, or even in the stock market, we humans love to shop. Shopping and acquiring are basic to human nature. We can't get enough of them. Our uniquely human passion for barter and trade is what sets us apart from the rest of the animal kingdom. In fact, we've been bartering goods since before recorded history, so it's no surprise that some of the earliest surviving examples of human writing—Sumerian cuneiform V-shaped impressions on clay tablets—are receipts.

There have been watershed moments in the history of human commerce, starting with the invention of the wheel, agriculture, water-powered mills, and currency, through the creation of the first steam engines, assembly lines, and flight, but in the 1990s a completely new conduit for commerce appeared—one so revolutionary in scope that in just a few short years, it changed forever the way that humans traded with one another.

The Internet provided anyone with a computer and a telephone line access to a rapidly growing universe of millions of Web sites from around the globe offering a staggering array of information, news, entertainment, and most important, goods.

At first, the Internet was considered suitable only for the exchange of information through e-mail and bulletin boards, but in 1993, with the creation of the graphics-capable World Wide Web, the idea of the Internet as a venue for commerce took hold, especially as the first trickle of Internet pioneers grew overnight into a virtual stampede of new users. Where there are people, there's trading.

In the early summer of 1995, the commercial and social potential of the Internet was on the mind of Pierre Omidyar, a computer programmer living and working in San Jose, California.

Before 1995, most commercial Web sites were just online variations of the off-line merchant-customer model where a single company offered merchandise for sale at a set cost. These Web sites were only slightly more exciting than mail-order catalogs. But Pierre had an idea. Why not create a Web site where buyers and sellers could trade directly with each other, much like an old-time flea market, using an auction format?

The concept was simple. The World Wide Web could provide a market "space" where sellers could list items and where buyers could browse for and buy these items, just like a flea market—except where the traditional flea market was limited to one geographical location, the Web was truly worldwide in scope. This would be real Internet trading—people trading with other people online, through their computers, from the comfort of their homes, from anywhere around the world.

Working alone and in his spare time (he had a day job, after all), it took Pierre only a few weeks to complete a design and write the software that would run his new Web site.

The actual design of the site was simple.

Using a unique e-mail address as an identifier, anyone with something to sell could, through their home computer and an Internet connection, upload an item description and title to the site. Anyone who visited the site and found the item—either by searching with keywords or by browsing the list of item titles in various categories—could then submit a bid for that item.

Bids would be accepted by a proxy system; that is, instead of having to sit on the listing to rebid every time someone outbid him, the bidder could instead submit a maximum bid amount—the highest amount he was willing to pay—and the system behind the Web site would execute his maximum bid on his behalf, protecting his interest until either the auction ended or another bidder submitted a bid amount higher than the first bidder's proxy. It was a simple but brilliant and efficient way to import the traditional auction format into this new medium.

The most brilliant aspect of all: The buyer and seller would complete the transaction without the direct involvement of the Web site! The seller would send payment instructions to the high bidder, and the high bidder would send payment. The seller would then mail or deliver the item to the high bidder.

Pierre called his new Web site "AuctionWeb—eBay Internet." The AuctionWeb site went "live" on Labor Day in 1995. Pierre's only initial marketing effort was to post a simple announcement that month on Usenet:

```
From: Pierre Omidyar <pierre@shell1.best.com>
Subject: SHOPPING: Free Interactive Web Auction
Date: 1995/09/27

AuctionWeb
----------

  "The most fun buying and selling on the web!"

  * Run your own auction
  * Bid on existing auctions
  * New listings added daily!
  * Fast, fun, and FREE!

  * AuctionWeb doesn't sell anything - we just provide the service.

Try it out!

  <URL:http://www.ebay.com/aw/>

--
Pierre Omidyar    Home page: http://www.ebay.com/pierre.shtml
pierre@ebay.com   Free Web Auction:   http://www.ebay.com/aw/
```

(The AuctionWeb name was dropped in favor of just eBay in September 1997.)

The first eBay site was totally devoid of fancy graphics, colors, icons, or logos. It was as visually thrilling as a gray paper box:

5

```
Auction Web
        [Menu]  [Listings]  [Buyers]  [Sellers]  [Search]  [Contact/Help]  [Site Map]
```

Welcome to today's online
marketplace...

...the market that brings
buyers and sellers together
in an honest and open
environment...

Welcome to eBay's
AuctionWeb.

Welcome to our community. I'm glad you found us. AuctionWeb is dedicated to bringing together buyers and sellers in an honest and open marketplace. Here, thanks to our auction format, merchandise will always fetch its market value. And there are plenty of great deals to be found!

Take a look at the listings. There are always several hundred auctions underway, so you're bound to find something interesting.

If you don't find what you like, take a look at our **Personal Shopper**. It can help you search all the listings. Or, it can keep an eye on new items as they are posted and let you know when something you want appears. If you want to let everyone know what you want, post something on our wanted page.

If you have something to **sell**, start your auction instantly.

Join our community. Become a registered user. Registered users receive additional benefits such as daily updates and the right to participate in our user feedback forum and the bulletin board.

Please **read on** about the AuctionWeb vision...

What Does the Word *eBay* Mean?

Earlier on in Pierre's career, he made a trip to Sacramento to incorporate all of his current and future business endeavors under a single holding company using a favorite name—Echo Bay. However, much to Pierre's disappointment, the clerk at the state office informed him that someone else had already incorporated a California business using Echo Bay. Thinking fast, Pierre came up with eBay.

The clerk checked. The name eBay had not yet been incorporated.

The rest is history.

In the months immediately following the launch, a few hundred people stumbled across eBay and began listing items for bid—at first mostly computer parts, used items, and a smattering of collectibles.

Throughout 1996, news about Pierre's little Web site began to spread across the Internet. Each day, more and more sellers came to eBay, liked what they saw, and added their merchandise to the expanding list of items for bid. The increasing number and variety of items brought more curious buyers looking for a possible bargain. As more items were sold, even more sellers would come to AuctionWeb and list even more items, bringing even more new buyers and so on, until the number of eBay users began to expand at a remarkable rate.

By the fall of 1996, there were close to ten thousand registered users on eBay.

In May 1997, the one millionth item was sold on eBay (a Sesame Street Big Bird figure).

For the first two years, the astonishing growth in both eBay members and eBay items was due entirely to word of mouth. By the end of 1998, there were more than 2 million registered eBay users. Sellers were listing 3.4 million items per month.

In 1998, eBay went public. This new American pastime—buying and selling on eBay—had attracted the attention of not only Wall Street but the general public as well. By 1999, eBay—the brand—was recognizable enough to be a regular feature of David Letterman's Top Ten List and a punch line in *The New Yorker* cartoons. eBay had become a bona fide cultural phenomenon.

The number of registered users grew to 10 million by the end of 1999, and eBay sellers were listing nearly 10 million items a month. By the end of 2001, the number of eBay users stood at over 40 million, with eBay sellers each month listing a staggering 31 million items.

Starting in earnest in early 2000 and continuing to the present, the eBay Inc. team, led by CEO Meg Whitman, has extended the eBay reach across the globe as new language and culturally distinct eBay Web sites were opened in Britain, Australia, France, Italy, South America, Korea, and mainland China.

Today, the trading statistics are astonishing. On eBay . . .

Someone buys a Corvette every hour.
A diamond ring is purchased every two minutes.
Thirteen CDs are sold every minute.
A digital camera sells every forty seconds.
One article of clothing is sold every three-quarters of a second.

Looking back, given the extraordinary timing, the brilliant simplicity of the idea and the business model, and how seamlessly it fit the promise of the Internet, the birth and subsequent phenomenal success of eBay now seem to have been inevitable. Pierre's vision of a Web site for person-to-person trading was an idea whose time had clearly arrived. But that's not the entire picture.

A person-to-person trading site is nothing without the people who do the trading. eBay's success and popularity are due in large part to the dedication and hard work of those individual buyers and sellers who use it every day. These folks make up the core of the eBay Community.

That's the story of eBay so far. It's most definitely not the end of the tale. From Pierre's simple idea—a Web site trading outpost—eBay has grown into the biggest human commerce phenomenon of the last hundred years of trading.

eBay, the Internet, and computers can be overwhelming at first, especially for those of us older folks who didn't have the good fortune to grow up surrounded by the information revolution of computing. However, with just a little perseverance, you will master eBay in no time.

Before we begin, here's eBay member Craig M. Keller Sr. with some words of encouragement:

Uncle Griff,

I am one of those "older farts." . . . I wanted nothing, and I mean nothing, to do with computers, when we first got them in at work. I fought and fought against using them. When in 1999 due to a serious illness I was forced to leave work and retire, my daughter (bless her heart) said that she was going to e-mail me a joke or cartoon every day on my wife's computer and that I had to read it.

One day, my wife came home from her job and said that if while I was reading my joke of the day, I wanted to check out the neatest site, try www.ebay.com. Well, let me tell you, my whole life changed on that day. I found a whole new world out there in cyberspace, and I have learned not only great things to buy, but I now do quite a bit of selling. . . .

Believe you me, without eBay to go to each day, I would have sooner or later went out of my mind after being forced to stay at home.

I have had an operation, in 2001, that now lets me pretty much do everything I used to do before the illness, but I'll never give up eBay.

Craig did it. So can you!
In order to begin you will need:

✔ A computer
✔ An Internet connection
✔ An e-mail account

If you have all three, you are ready. If you don't have all three yet, you will need to purchase or borrow a computer and subscribe to an Internet service provider (like AOL or Earthlink). Once you are online, it's easy to obtain an e-mail account. Your ISP will provide you with one, or you can obtain a free e-mail account from services such as MSN (Hotmail), Yahoo, or Google.

Registering on eBay, Step-by-Step

THE COMPLETE PROCESS

You will need to register on eBay to bid or buy, sell, or use the other various eBay features such as feedback or chat. Even though you don't need to be registered to browse for treasure at eBay, you might as well create your eBay registration sooner rather than later.

Registering on eBay is fairly straightforward, with three simple steps:

1. Fill in your information (name, address, etc.) and choose your eBay User ID and password.
2. Agree to the eBay User Agreement and Privacy Policy.
3. Receive confirmation e-mail and confirm your registration.

To begin, go to the eBay home page, *www.ebay.com*, and look for the "register" links on the top of the page.

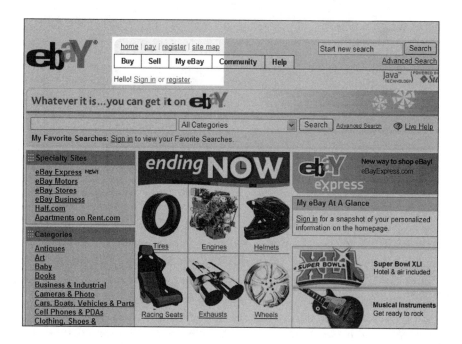

This will bring you to Step 1 of the three-step registration process.

Step 1—Enter Information

On this page, enter your contact information.

> First and last name
> Street address
> City
> State (from the drop-down list)
> Zip code
> Country
> Primary phone number
> Secondary phone number
> E-mail address

Register: Enter Information Help

1 **Enter Information**   2. Check Your Email

Register now to bid, buy, or sell on any eBay site worldwide. It's easy and **free**. Already registered? Sign in now.

👁 Live help - Chat online with a Customer Support representative.

Your Personal Information - All fields are required

Want to register as a business?

First name _____   Last name _____

Street address
_____
_____

City
_____

State / Province   Zip / Postal code   Country or Region
–Select–   ▼   _____   United States   ▼

Primary telephone
(___) ___ - ___ ext.: ___
Telephone is required in case there are questions about your account.

Email address
_____
Valid email address is required to complete registration. Example: myname@yahoo.com

Re-enter email address
_____

Your privacy is important to us
eBay does not rent or sell your personal information to third parties without your consent.
To learn more, read our privacy policy.

Your address will be used for shipping your purchase or receiving payment from buyers.

TRUST℮

GRIFF TIP! If you are planning on running a business on eBay and you currently have a business name, click the link for "Want to register as a business?" This will provide you with an extra field where you can enter your business name and change your registration type from "personal" to "business." If you don't currently have a business name, continue setting up your registration as a personal type. You can change your registration type from personal to business at any time in the future when you are ready.

Contact Information—Tips

As a part of registration, you agree to provide correct and valid contact information. This information is not available to anyone except the winning buyer or seller in a successful closed eBay transaction, and then only your phone number is provided (not your name or address) and only by manual request, never automatically. In addition, the information on file is never sold or rented to another party. (View eBay's privacy policy at *http://pages.ebay.com/help/policies/privacypolicy.html*.)

You may provide a P.O. box for an address, and you may provide a dedicated voice mail or pager number for a primary phone number.

At the bottom of the same page, enter your valid e-mail address (twice, to make sure you type it correctly), your choice of eBay User ID and password, and select a secret question and answer. (If you forget your password, you'll be asked the secret question and you'll need to answer the question correctly to receive a new password.)

```
Your User ID and Password - All fields are required

Create an eBay User ID
[                              ]  [ Check Availablility of User ID ]
Your User ID identifies you to other eBay users. Learn more about eBay User IDs.

Create password
[                    ]
6 character minimum See tips.

Re-enter password
[                    ]

Secret question                    Secret answer
[Pick a suggested question...  ▼]  [            ]
You will be asked for the answer to your secret question if you forget your password.

Date of birth
[--Month-- ▼] [--Day-- ▼]  Year [      ]
You must be at least 18 years old to use eBay.

Terms of use and your privacy - All fields are required
☐ I agree to the following:
  • I accept the User Agreement and Privacy Policy.
  • I may receive communications from eBay and I understand that I can change my notification preferences at any time in My eBay.
  • I am at least 18 years old.

[ Continue > ]
```

Choosing an eBay User ID and Password—Tips

Your eBay User ID is the unique "handle" by which all other eBay members will recognize you on the site. Your User ID will show up on the pages of your items for sale, next to your bids, on your feedback profile, on your About Me page, and anywhere you chat online at eBay. Since this is your official handle (you may actually become famous by this User ID), it is crucial that you create one that is absolutely perfect for you. First, some facts:

User IDs:

- May contain letters (a-z), numbers (0–9), and/or some symbols
- Must be at least two characters long
- Can't contain spaces
- Can't be obscene, be profane, or violate eBay's guidelines
- Can't be an e-mail address or Web address
- Can't be the same as another seller's eBay Store name

Things you can't include in an eBay User ID:

- The @, &, ', <, or > symbols
- URLs (example: *xyz.com*)
- Consecutive underscores: "__"
- An underscore ("_"), dash ("-"), or period (".") at the beginning of a User ID
- Spaces or tabs
- The word *eBay* (only eBay employees may use "eBay" in their User IDs)
- The letter *e* followed by numbers.

One more tip: Because spaces are not allowed in an eBay User ID, use a hyphen to represent a space.

If you are primarily a bidder, you may want to create an eBay User ID that reflects your buying passions. For example, if you collect balls of string, a good ID might be "ballofstringlover001" or something similar.

If you are a seller, choose something that hints at your business. If your business name is Say It with Widgets, then perhaps "sayitwithwidgets" would be a good choice. (Do not use "*www.sayitwithwidgets.com*," as the system is set to reject any User ID that is a Web site address.)

Whatever you choose, do keep it easy to remember. Complicated combinations of letters and numbers are not easy to remember, and if you are a seller, this can be an obstacle for your future eBay customers. Shorter User IDs are easier to notice and recall.

Avoid tricky punctuation. If you attempt to create a User ID and it comes back as already in use, you may find that by adding a period at the end it will go through. However, as a seller, you could end up with confused bidders who think you are someone else. Your User ID should be as identifiable and memorable as possible.

Every User ID on eBay is displayed in lowercase, regardless of how you type it in the box. Certain combinations of letters and numbers in lowercase can look ambiguous in a viewer's Web browser, so avoid User ID choices that include directly adjacent combinations of the letters *I* and *L* and the numeral *1*. Also avoid choices that include directly adjacent combinations of the letter *O* and the numeral *0*.

You cannot use your e-mail address as your eBay User ID. Initially, it was possible to do so, but this policy was changed in 2001. This no-e-mail-address-for-a-User-ID policy was implemented to discourage bulk e-mail senders from using software to harvest the eBay site for new e-mail addresses to add to their spam lists. Although the policy cannot completely prevent e-mail harvesting, it has made it more difficult for harvesters to do so.

A Word About Passwords . . .

Never use an obvious word or phrase as a password! For example, don't use a common name or your eBay User ID. The best passwords are a combination of random letters and numbers. Another solution is to use a word or words that have special meaning to you, then surround them with numbers that also relate to something in your life, maybe the first phone number you can recall for your family. Either way, avoid writing the password down unless you positively cannot memorize it. If you must write it down, store it in a secure, safe place such as a locked or safe-deposit box.

Like eBay User IDs, eBay passwords are always reduced to lower case. Therefore, to avoid confusing yourself, use only lowercase in your password.

TERMS OF USE AND YOUR PRIVACY

To use the eBay site, you must first agree to the eBay User Agreement and Privacy Policy. Take a few moments to read through them and print them out (by clicking the links for "User Agreement and Privacy Policy").

If you have never registered with an online service, you may be unfamiliar with user agreements (also known on other Web sites as Terms of Service agreements).

User agreements are binding contracts. They list the dos and don'ts for you, the registered user, and for eBay. The eBay User Agreement is extensive and comprehensive. If you read it carefully, you will get a clear picture of the responsibilities, activities, and conduct eBay expects from all registered members.

GRIFF TIP! Never take a Web site's user agreement for granted, including ours. The information contained in the user agreement can prove invaluable later on. You can always review the text of the eBay User Agreement by clicking the Help link on the top of the eBay home page. Type the phrase "user agreement" into the Search Help box. On the next page, click the link for "User Agreement."

You also must check the boxes for "I am 18+ years old" and "I understand that eBay may e-mail or notify me." Once you have done so, click the button "I Agree to these terms."

Once you have finished entering all the requested information, click the "Continue" button.

Step 2—Confirm Your E-mail

This screen informs you that you need to check your e-mail.

I used a free Yahoo e-mail account to register, so I will open my web-based Yahoo e-mail for officialebaybible01@yahoo.com.

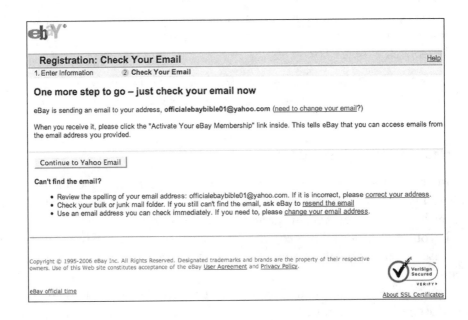

Here is the eBay registration confirmation e-mail in my Yahoo In Box:

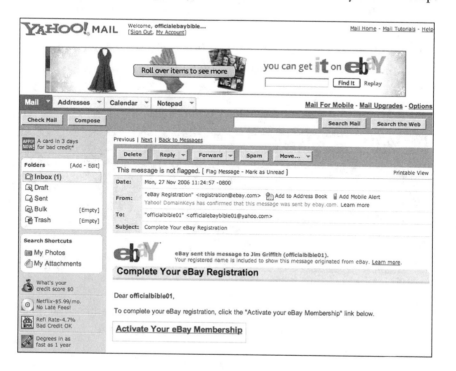

I open it and click on the button for "Activate Your eBay Membership."

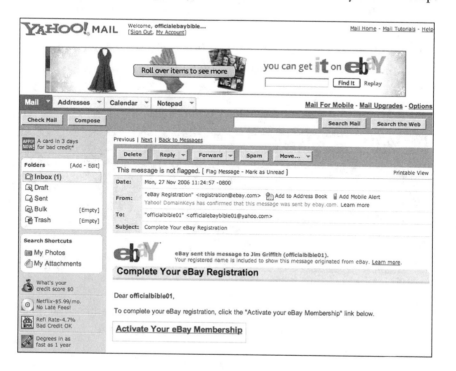

And the registration process is complete!

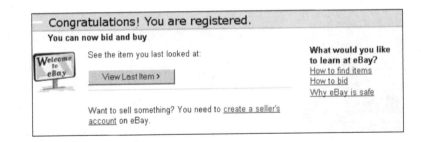

(And eBay even reminds me of the last item I viewed! Clever, huh?)

GRIFF TIP! If your e-mail doesn't display clickable links, you can go directly to the User ID and Password page by going to the eBay Site Map:

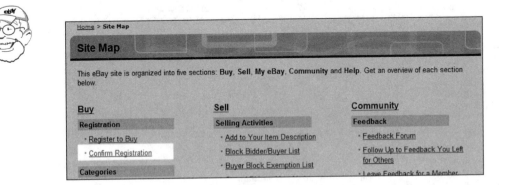

On the Site Map, look for the link "Confirm registration" under the section Registration in the top left column of links.

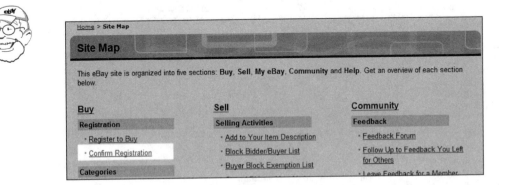

This will take you to the following page, where you can enter your e-mail address and the confirmation code contained in the confirmation e-mail.

Changing Your Contact Information

Should you someday move to a new address, you will need to change the address for your eBay registration information.

You can change your contact information by going to your My eBay page. The link for "My eBay" can be found on the top of any eBay page.

Click the link. If you are not currently signed in, you will be prompted for your eBay User ID and password. Enter them and click the "Sign in securely" button.

Once you are on your My eBay page, look on the left-hand side of the page for the link "Personal Information," under "My Account."

Here you will find three sections: Personal Information, Address Information, and Financial Information. Each component has a "change" link to the far right of its row. For example, let's change our address information. Under the section for Address Information, locate the link "Change" to the right of the Registration Address section.

On the next page, make the necessary changes and click the "Change registration information" button.

```
Enter Your Registration Information
E-mail address    officialebaybible01@yahoo.com        ( change your e-mail address)
User ID           officialbible01                       ( change your User ID)
                  First Name     M.I.   Last Name
Name              James          J      Griffith
Address           [                                   ]
                  [                                   ]
City              San Jose
State             California
Postal Code (Zip) 95116
Country           United States                         ( change your Country)
Primary
telephone         ( 408 )        -        ext.:
Secondary
telephone         (     )        -        ext.:
(optional)
Gender (optional) Unspecified
```

Registration date: Nov-27-06 11:24:56 PST
Last change to registration or feedback: Nov-28-06 08:27:07 PST

Click [change registration information] to submit your changes.

Click [clear form] to reset the form to the original values and start over.

Review the information to make sure it is accurate. If you are satisfied, click the "Submit" button.

```
Review and confirm your contact information
Full name        James J Griffith       OK
Address          151 S20th St           OK
City             San Jose               OK
State            CA                     OK
Zip Code         95116                  OK
Country          United States          OK
Primary phone #  (408) 286-4199         OK
```

Click the Back button on your browser if you want to change any of the listed information.

Click [submit] to commit your changes.

Your new contact information is now recorded.

Changing Your User ID, E-mail Address, Password, and Other Information
Use the other "Edit" links to change your account type, User ID, password, secret question, About Me page, and e-mail address.

Changing your eBay User ID, e-mail address, or password is nearly as easy as changing your contact information. However, there are some important points you need to know about each.

Changing Your User ID—Tips

When you change your User ID, your old User ID becomes "locked" for thirty days, after which anyone can claim it. Therefore, you should give serious consideration to any changes you make to your current User ID, since once it is abandoned, you may not be able to get it back.

You can only change your eBay User ID once every thirty days.

Each time you change your eBay User ID, a special icon will appear next to your new eBay User ID for thirty days. This alerts other members that you are either a brand-new eBay member or have recently changed your User ID.

Other eBay members will still be able to locate you through a search of your old User ID anytime during the first thirty days. After that, any search on your old User ID will return a "no such user" type error message until and if such time as someone "claims" your old User ID for his or her own.

Changing Your E-mail Address

You can change the e-mail address for your registration at any time and as often as you like. However, you cannot change it to one that is currently or was previously registered at eBay. If the system rejects your choice of a new e-mail address, you probably registered it sometime in the past and forgot that you had done so.

Important: Never register a new account in order to change your e-mail address! If you have established a good feedback profile (more on feedback later) and a noted presence as a seller or a bidder, you will not be able to move your feedback from the old account to the new account. Instead, use "My eBay" to change the e-mail address for your current, established account.

Changing Your eBay Password

Although you should not need to change your eBay password, in some cases doing so is prudent. For example, if you suspect that someone has obtained or deciphered your password, or if you believe you may unwittingly have supplied it to a stranger, you should change it immediately. Again, choose a password that is not obvious. (Don't use your pet's name.) Create a combination of random letters and numbers. Memorize it to avoid having to write it down. If you must write it down, store it somewhere safe and secure, a bank safe-deposit box, for example.

TROUBLESHOOTING

I Forgot My User ID or Password!

It happens. Maybe you registered a while back and don't recall your User ID or password. Don't panic. There is a quick and easy process for obtaining a forgotten eBay password. Click the "Sign in" link at the top of any eBay page.

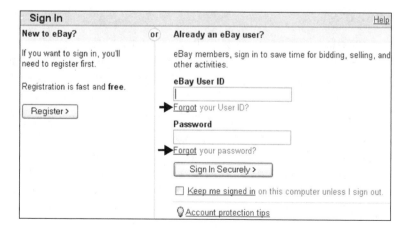

On the Sign In page, look for the links "Forgot your password?" and "Forgot your User ID?"

Click either one and follow the instructions from there.

Opening a PayPal Account

If you are planning on shopping or selling on eBay, you really need a PayPal account. Not surprisingly, PayPal is the preferred payment method of a majority of eBay buyers and sellers.

There is no time like the present, so let's open one now!

WHAT IS PAYPAL?

Founded in 1998 and acquired by eBay in October 2002, PayPal enables any individual or business with an e-mail address to securely, easily, and quickly send and receive payments online. PayPal's service builds on the existing financial infrastructure of bank accounts and credit cards and utilizes the world's most advanced proprietary fraud prevention system allowing customers around the globe to make safe, real-time payments.

PayPal has quickly become a global leader in online payment solutions, with 100 million account members worldwide. Available in 103 countries and regions around the world, buyers and sellers on eBay, online retailers, online businesses, and traditional off-line businesses are transacting with PayPal.

PayPal has received close to twenty awards for technical excellence from the Internet industry and the business community at large—most recently the 2003 Webby Award for Best Finance Site and the 2003 Webby People's Voice Award for Best Finance Site.

WHY PAYPAL?

PayPal lets you send a payment to any eBay seller (or online merchant) who accepts PayPal using your PayPal balance, a credit card, or a bank account as a funding source. However, unlike using a credit card directly with a merchant, the PayPal seller never obtains or sees sensitive financial details such as your credit card's number, expiration date, or CVV code, or your bank account number.

On the flip side, if you are an eBay seller, PayPal lets you accept payment from credit cards, bank accounts, and PayPal funding sources without having to set up a costly and cumbersome merchant account with a credit card issuer.

Best of all, PayPal is the fastest way of sending and receiving money.

If you buy or sell on eBay, you really must have a PayPal account!

To open a PayPal account, go to *www.paypal.com* and click the "Sign up" link:

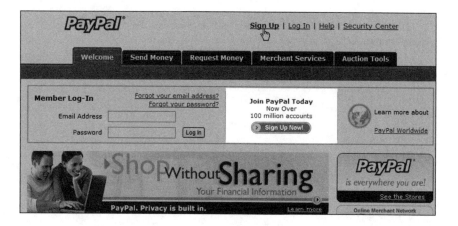

The first step is to select an account type. If you like to shop online and will probably never sell on eBay, then a Personal Account will work for you. A Premier account is the ideal account type for selling and shopping on eBay. If you are not certain which account type is right for you, settle for a Personal Account for now. You can easily upgrade a personal account at any time.

Select the country or region where you live and click the "Continue" button.

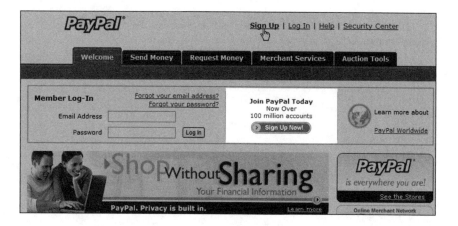

23

On the next screen, enter the requested information.

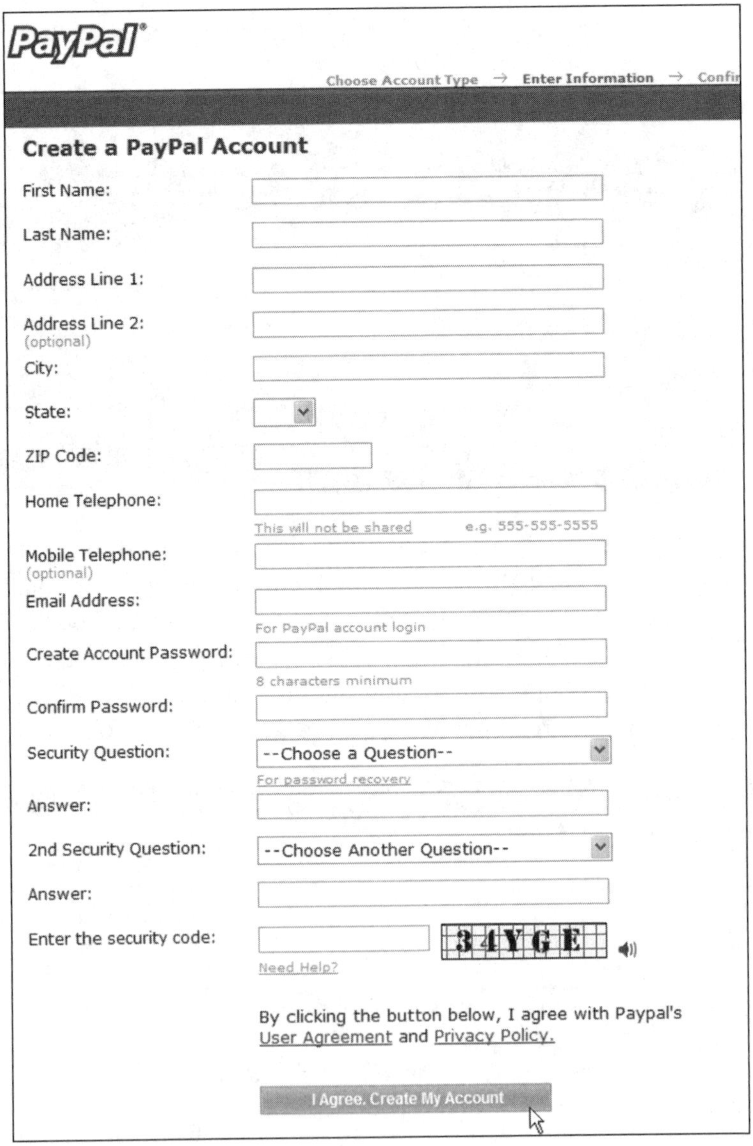

PayPal®

Choose Account Type → **Enter Information** → Confir

Create a PayPal Account

First Name:

Last Name:

Address Line 1:

Address Line 2:
(optional)

City:

State:

ZIP Code:

Home Telephone:

This will not be shared   e.g. 555-555-5555

Mobile Telephone:
(optional)

Email Address:

For PayPal account login

Create Account Password:

8 characters minimum

Confirm Password:

Security Question: --Choose a Question--

For password recovery

Answer:

2nd Security Question: --Choose Another Question--

Answer:

Enter the security code: 34YGE

Need Help?

By clicking the button below, I agree with Paypal's
User Agreement and Privacy Policy.

I Agree. Create My Account

Click the "Sign up" button. Then go to your e-mail application to check for the PayPal confirmation e-mail. Follow the instructions to complete the process.

ADDING BANK ACCOUNT AND CREDIT CARDS TO YOUR PAYPAL ACCOUNT

In order to send payments from a bank account or credit card to another PayPal member through PayPal, you need to add at least one funding source and ideally, two (a bank account and a credit card).

You can add up to eight bank accounts and eight credit cards to your PayPal profile. Each will then be available to you in PayPal as a possible funding source for sending payments. To add a bank account or credit card, log in to your PayPal account, click the "Profile" tab, and then click the "Bank Accounts" link under Financial Information.

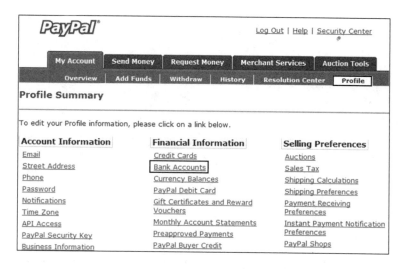

Click the "Add" button.

Enter the information as requested and click the "Continue" button.

My Account	Send Money	Request Money	Merchant Services	Auction Tools
Overview	Add Funds	Withdraw	History	Resolution Center	Profile

Add a Bank Account in the United States

Secure Transaction

PayPal protects the privacy of the your financial information regardless of your payment source. This bank account will become the default funding source for most of your PayPal payments, however you may change this funding source when you make a payment. Review our education page to learn more about PayPal policies and your payment-source rights and remedies.

The safety and security of your bank account information is protected by PayPal. We protect against unauthorized withdrawals from your bank account to your PayPal account. Plus, we will notify you by email whenever you deposit or withdraw funds from this bank account using PayPal.

Country: United States

Bank Name: [   ]

Account Type: ⦿ Checking
⦾ Savings

U.S. Check Sample

MEMO

⑂211554465⑂ 0012 1456874801⑆

Routing Number   Check#   Account Number

⑂ (9 digits) ⑂   (3-17 digits) ⑆

Routing Number: [   ] (9 digits)
Is usually located between the ⑂ symbols on your check.

Account Number: [   ] (3-17 digits)
Typically comes before the ⑆ symbol. Its exact location and number of digits varies from bank to bank.

Re-enter Account Number: [   ]

[Continue] [Cancel]

To add a credit card, follow the steps above but click the "Credit Cards" link under Profile instead of "Bank Accounts." Repeat each step for adding up to eight bank accounts and eight credit cards.

CONFIRMING A BANK ACCOUNT IN PAYPAL

In order to transfer funds from your bank account to your PayPal account or perform electronic funds transfers, PayPal requires that you confirm your bank account. Confirming your bank account proves that you are the account's true owner. This confirmation process serves to protect your bank account and PayPal account from unauthorized use. You should confirm at least one bank account in your profile. In the Profile > Bank Accounts page, click the "Confirm" link for the bank account you have selected to confirm and follow the instructions from there.

You are now ready to use your PayPal account to purchase items on eBay (and at thousands of Web sites around the world).

Note the "Overview" tab for your account:

My Account	Send Money	Request Money	Merchant Services	Auction Tools

Overview	Add Funds	Withdraw	History	Resolution Center	Profile

Premier Account Overview - United States

Name: Jim Griffith
Email: jimgriff@sover.net   [Add email]
Status: Verified (79)

PayPal Account Balance [View Limits]

Currency ?	Account Balance ?
U.S. Dollar:	$0.00 USD
Currently Earning:	5.02%*

Recent Activity | All Activity | Items Won ebY $ = PayPal Preferred Cashback

File	Type	To/From	Name/Email/Phone	Date	Status	Details	Action	Amount	Fee
☐	Payment	To	OutletShirts	Jan. 12, 2007	Completed	Details		-$188.02 USD	$0.00 USD
☐	Transfer	From	Bank Account	Jan. 12, 2007	Completed	Details		$188.02 USD	$0.00 USD
☐	Payment	To	MING YU	Jan. 11, 2007	Completed	Details		-$158.50 USD	$0.00 USD
☐	Transfer	From	Bank Account	Jan. 11, 2007	Completed	Details		$158.50 USD	$0.00 USD
☐	Payment	To	Helen Lew	Jan. 10, 2007	Completed	Details	Check Shipment	-$24.95 USD	$0.00 USD
☐	Transfer	From	Bank Account	Jan. 10, 2007	Completed	Details		$24.95 USD	$0.00 USD
☐	Payment	To	saleinstore	Jan. 9, 2007	Completed	Details		-$108.25 USD	$0.00 USD
☐	Transfer	From	Bank Account	Jan. 9, 2007	Completed	Details		$108.25 USD	$0.00 USD

On the Overview page, you can view all your past transactions. Later, in Section Two of this book, we will outline how to use your PayPal account as an eBay seller. You will want to remember this Overview page so keep it in mind.

The eBay Web Site

Navigating the eBay Web Site—a Road Map

The eBay Web site is big. No, that's not quite accurate. The eBay Web site is ginormous. Not counting the nearly 50 million separate pages for each item listed on eBay, there are hundreds of other pages containing virtual warehouses of information about eBay, so finding your way around eBay can sometimes be daunting.

But don't despair. You will find navigating eBay is a snap once you have a good grasp of how certain eBay Web pages are grouped together, what they contain, and how they are interconnected.

Let's start with the most basic navigation tool, the eBay Navigation Bar.

THE EBAY NAVIGATION BAR

The eBay Navigation Bar is found on the top of nearly every eBay Web page.

Think of the eBay Navigation Bar as your personal signpost showing you the route and direction to every single possible place on eBay you might wish to visit.

Whenever you are lost or are searching for a particular area of the eBay Web site, use the navigation bar and the various hyperlinks above it to quickly get your bearings.

These are the hyperlinks on the top of the eBay Navigation Bar:

home | pay | register | site map

These links point to important Web pages on eBay:

Home (the eBay home page)
Pay (the PayPal home page)
Register
Site Map

These links, and the pages to which they lead, are examined in greater detail later on in this chapter.

Below the links are the boxes that make up the eBay Navigation Bar. Each of these boxes will take you to the respective main page for Buy, Sell, My eBay, Community, and Help. In addition to taking you to the main topic page, clicking "Community" will expand the eBay Navigation Bar down one level to display the sub-navigation bar for that topic.

The "Buy" link takes us to the Buy portal page. This page contains sections for Search, Browse Categories, My eBay At A Glance, Buying Resources, and other helpful views.

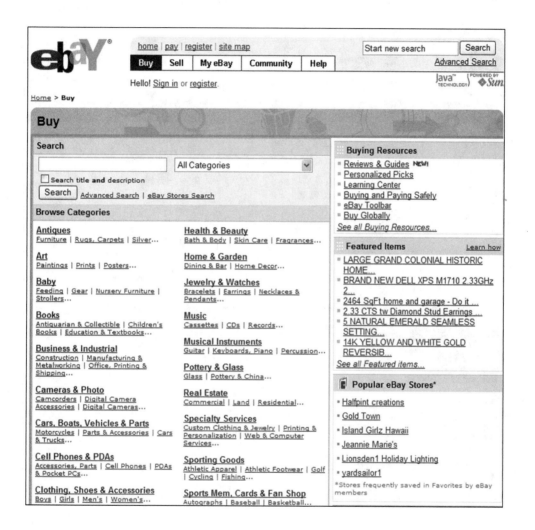

The "Sell" link leads to the Sell Hub page. From here, you can begin the process of creating an eBay listing or you can check the sections for "Decide what to sell" and "Prepare to sell" (both of which you should keep in mind for later when you post your first item listings on eBay).

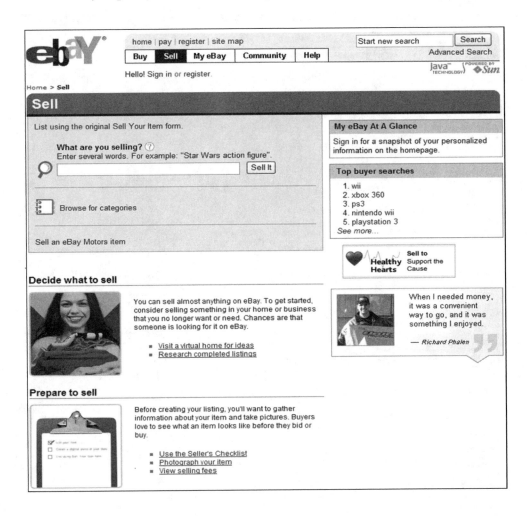

My eBay was mentioned earlier, but let's come back to it. Click the "My eBay" box on the top of the page.

We'll explore My eBay in greater depth later.

The "Community" link directs you to the Community portal page, which contains all the links related to the eBay Community.

The "Feedback forum" link takes you to the hub page for everything related to eBay feedback.

Under "Connect," you will find links to eBay MyWorld, discussion boards, groups, Answer Center, eBay blogs, and chat rooms. We will take a closer look at all of these sections later in the book, but feel free to explore them now.

GRIFF TIP! Pay special attention to the links for Discussion Boards, including links to nearly a hundred different online discussion boards focused on specific topics.

Discussion Boards

eBay's discussion boards are a great place to find information on everything from art to travel. Browse the discussion boards below and see what you discover.

Community Help Boards

About Me Pages
Auction Listings
Bidding
Buyer Central: Professional Buying
Checkout
eBay Blogs Help NEW!
eBay Express NEW!
eBay My World NEW!
eBay Stores
eBay Wiki NEW!
Escrow/Insurance
Feedback
Half.com
International Trading
Live Auctions
Miscellaneous
My eBay
Packaging & Shipping
PayPal
Photos/HTML
Policies/User Agreement
Registration
Reviews & Guides NEW!
Search
Seller Central
Skype
Technical Issues
Trading Assistant
Trust & Safety (SafeHarbor)

eBay Tools Boards

eBay Board Usage Policy explanation
Accounting Assistant & Record Keeping
Blackthorne Basic/SA Basic
Blackthorne Pro/SA Pro
eBay Marketplace Research and Sales Reports
eBay Picture Services and Picture Manager
eBay Toolbar
File Exchange
Selling Manager
Selling Manager Pro
Turbo Lister

Category Specific Discussion Boards

Animals
Antiques
Art & Artists
Bears and Plush
Book Readers
Booksellers
Business & Industrial
Children's Clothing Boutique
Clothing, Shoes & Accessories
Coins & Paper Money
Collectibles
Comics
Computers, Networking & I T
Cooks Nook
Country/Rural Style
Custom Made Items and Services NEW!
Decorative & Holiday
Disneyana
Dollhouses and Miniatures
Dolls
Dolls Artists and Limited Edition NEW!
eBay Motors
Handmade/Custom Clothing for Kids
Health & Beauty
Historical Memorabilia
Hobbies & Crafts
Home & Garden
Jewelry & Gemstones
Mid-Century/Modern
Motorcycle Boulevard
Movies & Memorabilia
Music & Musicians
Needle Arts & Vintage Textiles
Outdoor Sports
Photography
Pottery, Glass, & Porcelain
Products & Accessories for Infants NEW!
Science & Mystery
Scrapbooking
Shoes, Purses, and Fashion Accessories
Sports Cards, Memorabilia & Fan Shop
Toys & Hobbies
Victorian/Edwardian
Vintage
Vintage Clothing & Accessories
Watches, Clocks & Timepieces

When you need targeted help for a very specific issue, these online discussion areas are the best source of valuable information on eBay. Why? Because the discussion boards are frequented by thousands of expert eBay buyers and sellers who are always happily eager to share their expertise with other members, especially new members like you.

And besides, this is the very same place where Uncle Griff got his start all those years ago! The format may have changed and expanded, but the community spirit is still alive and well there.

The News section contains links to all the eBay news-related pages, for example, the general and system announcement boards, calendar events, and The Chatter, which was formerly our newsletter and is now our official eBay blog.

Finally, my favorite navigation bar link, "Help." This link will lead you directly to the eBay Help page portal.

We discuss eBay Help in depth at the end of Section Two, but you should note these pages now for access later. Help contains the answer to all commonly asked eBay questions. If you are stumped for an answer, try Help first by either entering a keyword into the box provided or scanning and reading through the various Help subtopics below the Search Help section.

THE SIGN IN PAGE

Although you don't need to supply an eBay User ID and password to view current items or item categories or to search for current items using keywords (Title Search), you will need to supply your User ID and password to bid, buy, list an item, search for a completed listing, or visit your My eBay page. To reduce the need to enter your User ID and password over and over, you will need to sign in.

To sign in, just click the "Sign in" link on the top of any eBay page.

home	pay	register	site map

| Buy | Sell | My eBay | C |

Hello! Sign in or register.

This will take you to the eBay Sign In page.

Sign In   Help

| New to eBay? | or | Already an eBay user? |

If you want to sign in, you'll need to register first.

Registration is fast and free.

[Register >]

eBay members, sign in to save time for bidding, selling, and other activities.

eBay User ID

Forgot your User ID?

Password

Forgot your password?

[Sign In Securely >]

☐ Keep me signed in on this computer for one day, unless I sign out.

💡 Account protection tips
Be sure the Web site address you see above starts with https://signin.ebay.com/

Enter your eBay User ID and password in the boxes provided. To keep yourself signed in indefinitely, check the box "Keep me signed in on this computer unless I sign out." Then click the "Sign in securely" button.

Now you won't have to reenter your eBay User ID and password each time you bid on or list an item, leave feedback, or use your My eBay page.

One other important, often-overlooked, feature of the Sign In page: Notice the links for "Forgot your User ID?" and "Forgot your password?" If you ever do forget either one, you can always retrieve it by clicking on the appropriate "Forgot" link.

GRIFF TIP! You can change your sign-in preferences using your My eBay page. We discuss the My eBay page in depth later on in this chapter.

NAVIGATING THE EBAY HOME PAGE

Go to *http://www.ebay.com*. Many eBay members make the eBay home page their browser's start or home page so that it is the first Web page they see when they start their Web browser.

The basic layout of the eBay home page currently looks something like this:

The eBay home page includes a section for searching by keyword at the very top of the page, a link for "Register," and a link to the eBay Featured Items (covered in more depth in a following chapter). At the bottom of the home page there are links to third-party services and partners.

There's also a series of text links at the bottom of the page:

Argentina | Australia | Austria | Belgium | Brazil | Canada | China | France | Germany | Hong Kong | India | Ireland | Italy | Korea | Malaysia | Mexico | Netherlands | New Zealand | Philippines | Poland | Singapore | Spain | Sweden | Switzerland | Taiwan | United Kingdom

Feedback Forum | eBay Toolbar | Downloads | Gift Certificates | PayPal | Jobs | Affiliates | Developers | The eBay Shop

About eBay | Announcements | Learning Center | Security & Resolution Center | Policies | Government Relations | Site Map | Help

These may come in handy someday, especially Security Center (also indicated as the Security & Resolution Center), so remember where you saw them. One of my favorites is the About eBay page.

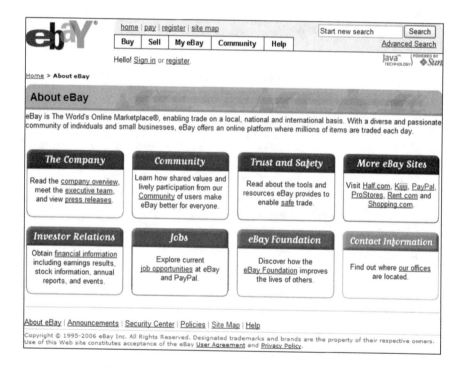

Visit this page to read recent eBay press releases as well as to learn more about eBay Inc., the eBay Foundation, the eBay Community, and current job openings at eBay. (Who knows? Maybe you will find the perfect job!)

NAVIGATING WITH THE EBAY SITE MAP

Although not the prettiest page at eBay, the eBay Site Map is definitely one of the most helpful. Nearly every page on the eBay site can be reached by a link on this page. Think of the Site Map as your eBay index page. If you are ever unable to find a certain eBay page using other navigation methods, don't give up! Try looking on the Site Map. If it's an eBay page, it's probably on this list.

I make it a habit to stop at this page first whenever I can't find a certain eBay Web page. I am usually able to find it again starting from the Site Map!

NAVIGATING THE EBAY CATEGORIES— CATEGORY HIERARCHY

There are more than 55,000 separate eBay categories. To make navigating them easy, all of them are arranged in a hierarchy structure according to topic.

There is more than one way to view the eBay category hierarchy. The most obvious and most popular method is to start from the list of top categories in the left-hand column on the eBay home page.

The links listed under "Categories" represent the top-level categories of the eBay category hierarchy.

Navigating eBay's category hierarchy is a breeze. By clicking any one of these top-level categories, you are directed to that category's home page, where you can find a list of links for subcategories related to the top-level category. For example, here is a partial view of the home page for the Clothing, Shoes & Accessories category.

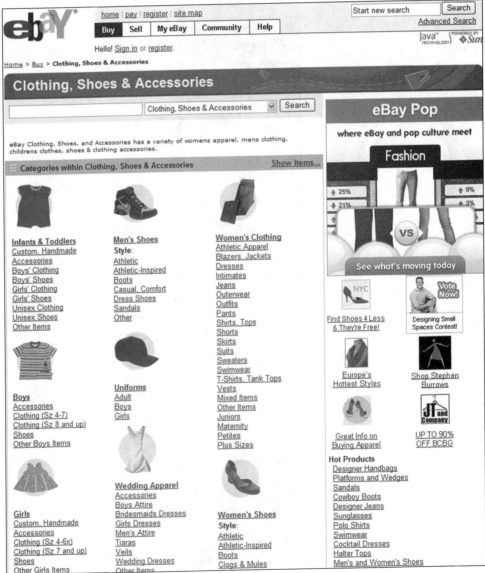

From here, you can navigate to any of the various Clothing, Shoes & Accessories subcategories, related categories, or popular searches for the category. Let's click the subcategory "Heels, Pumps" under the category Women's Shoes.

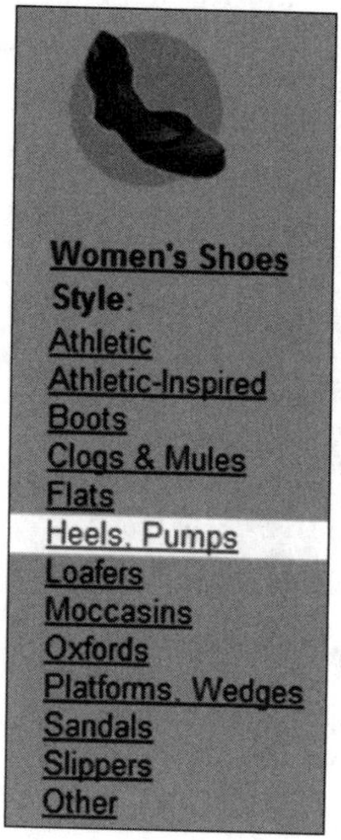

Women's Shoes
Style:
Athletic
Athletic-Inspired
Boots
Clogs & Mules
Flats
Heels, Pumps
Loafers
Moccasins
Oxfords
Platforms, Wedges
Sandals
Slippers
Other

From here, you can start browsing through the category for women's heels and pumps.

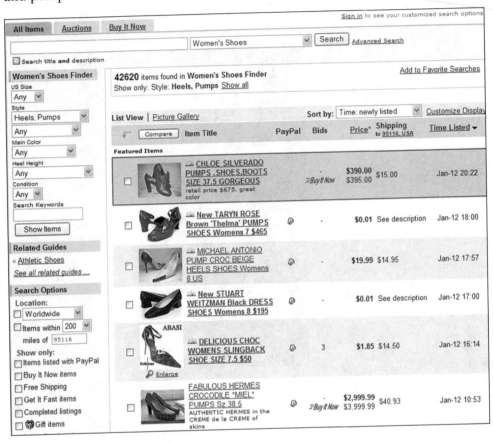

GRIFF BROWSING TIP! The Heels, Pumps subcategory page above shows that there are 42,620 items currently listed within this subcategory. It would take several hours to scroll through that many items looking for that special pair of shoes.

You can easily filter these 42,620 items by selecting one or more options from the drop-down lists in the box Women's Shoes Finder. For example, let's select "6.5" in the US Size drop-down list.

This reduces the number of displayed items to 3,533 that match your shoe size!

We'll dive deeper into the finer points of searching eBay in the next chapter.

If you plan on revisiting this or any other category, you may want to make it one of your Favorite Categories in My eBay (see the My eBay section later in this chapter for more information about My eBay Favorites).

VIEW ALL CATEGORIES

Under each of the many main categories on the home page, there are numerous subcategories, all grouped together by type, brand name, or make. Here's a quick way to view all top- and sub-level subcategories:

Click Buy on the eBay Navigation Bar.

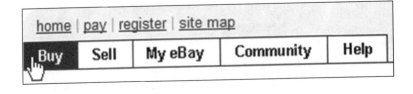

Scroll down the page and click the link for "See all categories . . ."

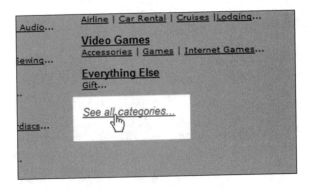

This displays the All Categories page. You can also customize the display of this page for Category, Item Type, and Item Status, as well as filter the results to show the number of items in each category or the actual category numbers.

All Categories

[Search titles & descriptions]

☐ Search titles & descriptions

Browse Categories

Category [All Categories ▾] Format [All Items ▾] Listings [All Active ▾] Location [Available on: eBay.com ▾] [Show]

⦿ Show number of items in category ◯ Show category numbers

Antiques (203901)
Antiquities (Classical, Amer.) (7359)
Architectural & Garden (12783)
Asian Antiques (32097)
Books, Manuscripts (3382)
Decorative Arts (32680)
Ethnographic (3931)
Furniture (14999)
Maps, Atlases, Globes (10555)
Maritime (4024)
Musical Instruments (644)
Primitives (13081)
Rugs, Carpets (15178)
Science & Medicine (1975)
Silver (31516)
Textiles, Linens (11699)
Other Antiques (7998)
See all Antiques categories...

Art (228598)
Digital Art (1840)
Drawings (4539)
Folk Art (6019)
Mixed Media (1956)
Paintings (48988)
Photographic Images (8013)
Posters (32338)
Prints (99292)
Sculpture, Carvings (9831)
Self-Representing Artists (11691)
Other Art (3054)
Wholesale Lots (1037)
See all Art categories...

Computers & Networking (475090)
Apple, Macintosh Computers (11566)
Desktop & Laptop Components (53526)
Desktop & Laptop Accessories (113002)
Desktop PCs (6795)
Drives, Controllers & Storage (39513)
Laptops, Notebooks (17981)
Monitors & Projectors (7153)
Networking (65476)
Printers (12157)
Printer Supplies & Accessories (67433)
Scanners (1795)
Software (62559)
Technology Books (6499)
Vintage Computing Products (2814)
Other Hardware & Services (6821)
See all Computers & Networking categories...

Consumer Electronics (387372)
Car Electronics (43175)
DVD Players & Recorders (8380)
Digital Video Recorders, PVR (1108)
Gadgets & Other Electronics (31873)
GPS Devices (10127)
Home Audio (41910)
Home Theater in a Box (2074)
Home Theater Projectors (4435)
MP3 Players & Accessories (136465)
Portable Audio (18675)
Radios: CB, Ham & Shortwave (19314)
Satellite Radio (4923)
Satellite, Cable TV (11657)

Music (430771)
Accessories (5460)
Cassettes (8490)
CDs (255181)
Digital Music Downloads (302)
DVD Audio (642)
Records (154521)
Super Audio CDs (287)
Other Formats (4019)
Wholesale Lots (1869)
See all Music categories...

Musical Instruments (181191)
Brass (4132)
DJ Gear & Lighting (8299)
Electronic (3119)
Equipment (2504)
Guitar (65828)
Harmonica (1309)
Instruction Books, CDs, Videos (8914)
Keyboard, Piano (7764)
Percussion (12905)
Pro Audio (26189)
Sheet Music, Song Books (18531)
String (10848)
Woodwind (9579)
Wholesale Lots (279)
Other Instruments (991)
See all Musical Instruments categories...

Pottery & Glass (271602)
Glass (97926)
Pottery & China (173676)

You can navigate from here to any of the top-level category home pages (sometimes referred to as Category Portal pages). For example, click on the link "See all Antiques categories . . ." to display that category's portal page.

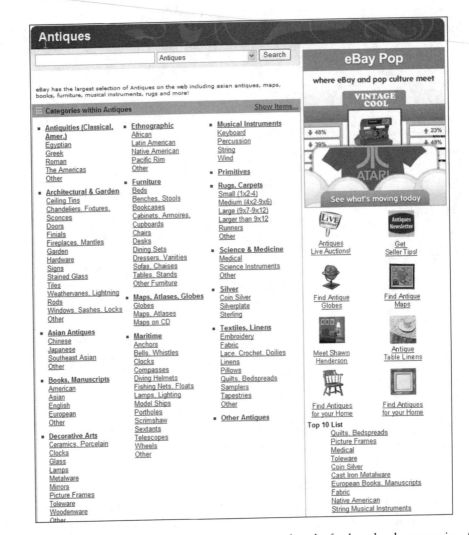

The Antiques portal page displays a smorgasbord of related subcategories, for example, Antiquities, Architectural & Garden, Furniture, Rugs, Carpets, and so on.

The All Categories page is an excellent way to search for those sublevels in the category hierarchy that contain items of interest to you.

NAVIGATING THE EBAY ITEM DESCRIPTION PAGE

We've seen how browsing through categories can take us to specific subcategories where we can more easily find particular treasure that piques our interest. On eBay, all items are displayed in a list. In the next screen shot, we are looking at a category list for Antiques > Rugs, Carpets.

(Later we will cover search lists that look almost exactly like category lists. Item titles are displayed the same way in both.)

Each item title in a category list is a clickable link. To view an individual item, you simply click on the item title wherever it appears in a category or search list. I searched through the Rugs, Carpets category pages and found this intriguing gallery picture and title:

Clicking on the title will open up the Item Description page for that particular item.

A typical Item Description page looks like this:

Shipping, payment details and return policy

Ships to
United States

Country: United States ▾		
Shipping and Handling	**To**	**Service**
US $70.00	United States	UPS Ground
1 to 6 business days*

*Sellers are not responsible for service transit time. This information is provided by the carrier and excludes weekends and holidays. Note that transit times may vary, particularly during peak periods.

Shipping insurance
US $5.00 Optional

Seller's payment instructions
Paypal payments to be made to pakobel@pakobel.com. To pay through credit card please go to www.pakobel.com For Checks and MoneyOrder please send the payment to Pakobel 13651 SW 143 Ct#103 Miami, FL 33186

Seller's return policy:

Item must be returned within: 3 Days	Refund will be given as: Money Back
Return Policy Details:	100% Refund Return Policy: 1) For items not as advertised, you can contact anytime within 2 days of delivery. Your full amount, including the shipping you paid with it, will be refunded; 2) Return shipping is not included; 3) If we are contacted after 2 days but within 7 days of delivery, the shipping and 20% restocking fee will be deducted from the refund; 4) Returns on basis of colors are not accepted

Sales tax
Seller charges sales tax for items shipped to: FL* (7.000%).
* Tax applies to subtotal + S&H for these states only

Payment methods accepted

- PayPal
  MasterCard VISA AMEX DISCOVER eCHECK
- Personal check
- Money order/Cashiers check
- Other - See Payment Instructions for payment methods accepted
- Visa/MasterCard, American Express
Learn about payment methods.

Ready to bid?   help

Rare Vegetable Afghan Chobi Large Rug 10x8

Item title:	Rare Vegetable Afghan Chobi Large Rug 10x8
Starting bid:	US $0.99
Your maximum bid:	US $ [ ] (Enter US $0.99 **or more**)

[Place Bid >] You will confirm in the next step.

eBay automatically bids on your behalf **up to** your maximum bid.
Learn about bidding

There are six sections to every Item Description page:

> Title
> Meet the seller
> Description
> Shipping, payment details, and return policy
> Payment methods accepted
> Ready to bid?

The Title section of the Item Description page, directly under the bar containing the item's title, is where you find the basic information about the item, such as the current high bid, time and date of the listing's closing, bid history, and seller's location. The title may also contain a subtitle if the seller opted for this feature. If applicable, it may also show a Buy It Now button if the seller has made the item available for immediate purchase, and the quantity available (if more than one).

The Meet the Seller section displays the seller's feedback stats and history with eBay. There are also links for sending questions to the seller or adding the seller to your Favorite Sellers list. It may also show a link to the seller's eBay Store (if she has one) and an indication of PayPal Buyer Protection (if the seller is offering it).

The Description section is just below the Title section. The seller provides everything that appears in this section, including text, pictures, and any fancy layout or graphics. There is no limit to how much text or how many pictures a seller can include within the Description section.

Underneath Description, you will find the Shipping, Payment Details and Return Policy section, which displays the seller's shipping terms (carriers, costs, and delivery times) for this item. Note that most experienced sellers on eBay restate this information within their item description.

The Payment Methods Accepted section outlines exactly what types of payment the seller accepts. Again, smart sellers repeat this information within their item description.

Finally, the Ready to Bid? or Ready to Buy? section is where you either enter the amount of your bid or, if the seller provided a Buy It Now option for instant purchase, simply buy the item outright without bidding.

If I think I might want to bid on an item later, I can add it to my Watch list. The link for adding the item to my Watch list is toward the top of the Item Description page.

I click the "Watch this item" link and the display changes to:

Where is the item actually being "watched"? In My eBay!

My eBay

No other page on eBay provides such a fantastic array of services for the eBay buyer or seller as My eBay.

From your My eBay page, you can keep track of all your current and recent bidding and selling; items on your Watch list; your feedback; your eBay favorite searches, sellers, and stores as well as your eBay e-mail notice preferences, your account setup, your contact information, and your custom My eBay preferences as well.

To go to your My eBay page, simply click the link for My eBay located on the top of any eBay page.

(If you have not signed in yet, you will be prompted to do so.)

Your My eBay page will look something like mine (minus the item-listing details, of course):

(Note the listing for the item that I just added to my Watch list. More on this later . . .)

The important My eBay navigation links are located under the section My eBay Views on the left-hand side of the page. They include My Summary, All Buying, All Selling, All Favorites, and My Account.

NOTE: Remember these links! You will need them to access important information and procedures. Do you need to change your e-mail address or User ID? Have you moved and now need to change your contact information? Every aspect of your eBay activity or information can be accessed, viewed, and, if applicable, edited, augmented, or deleted from your My eBay page.

Since I am primarily a buyer (who regularly sells), I tend to use the All Buying, All Favorites, and My Account sections of My eBay the most.

Let's explore the various sections of the All Buying page for my regular User ID, uncle_griff. (Note: You can customize the display of your page and shuffle each section's place on the page.)

BUYING REMINDERS

This summarizes all your buying activity, including how many items you need to pay for, how many items you are watching, and how many feedbacks (more on feedback later) you need to leave. This is a helpful tool for keeping up with all your buying obligations.

ITEMS I'M BIDDING ON

All of your current bids will appear in this section, with each item on a separate row. One of the best uses of this section is to check your maximum bid amounts.

In addition, any auctions where you are a bidder but have been outbid will show the bid amount in red as an alert so that you can consider a new bid.

BUYING TOTALS

Shows all your current bidding activity, including which ones are currently high bids, and the cost of all your current winning bids. This section also shows the quantity and the total of all your won bids.

ITEMS I'VE WON

GRIFF TIP! You have powerful display customization options for My eBay right at your fingertips. Just locate the section's "Customize" link.

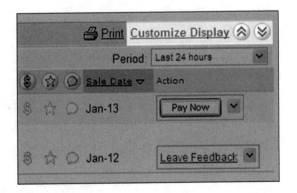

Clicking it allows you to add or subtract fields to the current section as well as change the way the section is displayed.

Customize Items I've Won

Available Columns
- Start Price
- My Max Bid
- Shipping Cost
- Purchased On

Columns To Display
- Qty
- Sale Price
- Total Price
- Paid*
- Feedback Left*
- Feedback Received*
- Sale Date

Move

Seller ID/Seller Email, Title, Sale Date and Action are required columns and cannot be moved.

*Legend: $ Paid ☆ Feedback Left ○ Feedback Received

Display: seller by their: [Email Address ▾]
Email addresses will be displayed for 14 days after a transaction ends.

☐ My Notes ☐ eBay Notes
☐ Pictures

[25 ▾] items per page
This setting does not apply to the My Summary page.

Custom Period: Show items for last [0] days (60 days max)

[Save] Restore Defaults | Cancel

Select from the list of available column headers to delete or add columns to your view. You can also alter the way the section displays.

I have customized My eBay to show the fields for the quantity, the sale price, the total price (with shipping), and the sale date for each item I have won. In addition, there is the field "Action," which, when clicked, displays a drop-down list of available actions that the buyer can take. In this case, I can either leave feedback or pay for an item.

Items I've Won (3 items, 1 in time period) 🖨 Print Customize Display ⊗ ⊗
Show: **All** | Awaiting Payment (1) | Awaiting Feedback (1) Period: Last 24 hours ▾

☐ Seller Email/ ID	Qty	Sale Price	Total Price $ ☆ ○	Sale Date ▾	Action
☐ fitz... (brent111@aol.com) (9685 ☆)	2	$65.00	– $ ☆ ○	Jan-13	[Pay Now ▾]
Timex Men's I-Control "Turn n Pull" Alarm Indiglo Watch (300069201781)					
	1	$32.50	– $ ☆ ○	Jan-12	[Leave Feedback ▾]
Timex Indiglo Men's I-Control "Turn n Pull" Alarm Watch (300069792999)					

I need to pay for the two watches I bought earlier today. I click the "Pay Now" button and follow the links through to PayPal to complete payment. We will explore the quick and easy PayPal payment process later in this section, but for now, I want to show how My eBay indicates the payment status for an item. Notice the icons to the left of the "Pay Now" button:

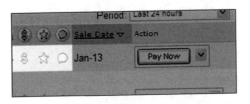

These icons indicate payment and feedback status for that listing (depending on the type of icon or whether it is grayed out or full black). Once I have paid for the item, the payment icon goes from grayed out to full.

ITEMS I DIDN'T WIN

Items I Didn't Win (4 items)				Print Customize Display
Show: All | Second Chance Offers (0)				Period: Last 60 days
☐	Sale Price	My Max Bid	Bids	End Date ▽	Action
☐ antique rug - turkish anatolian kilim					
	$261.00	$256.00	8	Jan-08	View Similar Items
☐ O399: Pair of Vinage Japanese scroll. Great two Cranes.					
	$203.50	$189.00	11	Jan-05	Visit Seller's Store
☐ Japanese Hanging scroll : The bamboo of summer #L433					
	$338.00	$333.00	15	Jan-01	View Similar Items
☐ OLD ANTIQUE ROOMSIZED TURKISH CARPET 9' x 11'					
	$1,125.00	$1,100.00	14	Dec-17	View Similar Items
Remove Add Note				Undo Remove: Select an option

The saddest place on the whole page, this section displays items where you were a bidder but were outbid and subsequently the auction closed. (I really, really, really wanted that pair of vintage Japanese scrolls but I forgot to rebid. Curses!) This section is helpful in that you can use the links to the right of the item title to view that seller's other current items.

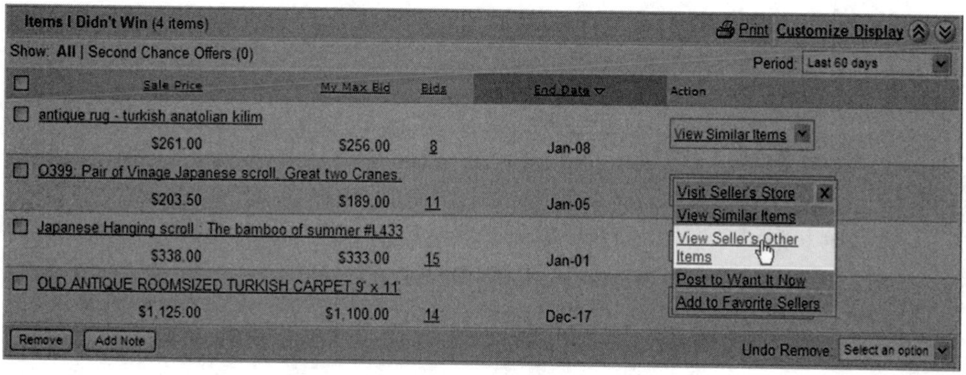
Items I Didn't Win (4 items)
Print Customize Display
Show: All | Second Chance Offers (0)
Period: Last 60 days
Sale Price
My Max Bid
Bids
End Date
Action
antique rug - turkish anatolian kilim
$261.00
$256.00
8
Jan-08
View Similar Items
0399: Pair of Vinage Japanese scroll. Great two Cranes.
$203.50
$189.00
11
Jan-05
Visit Seller's Store
View Similar Items
View Seller's Other Items
Post to Want It Now
Add to Favorite Sellers
Japanese Hanging scroll : The bamboo of summer #L433
$338.00
$333.00
15
Jan-01
OLD ANTIQUE ROOMSIZED TURKISH CARPET 9' x 11'
$1,125.00
$1,100.00
14
Dec-17
Remove
Add Note
Undo Remove
Select an option

ITEMS I'M WATCHING

Finally, we reach one of my favorite features, the Items I'm Watching section of My eBay.

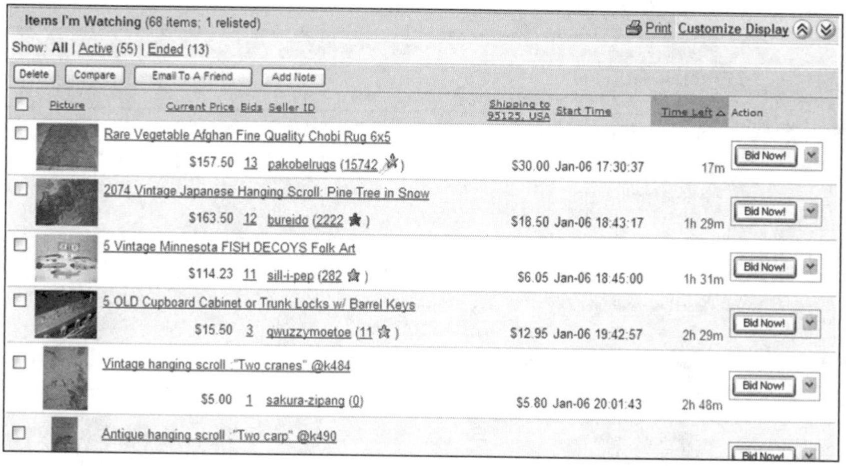
Items I'm Watching (68 items; 1 relisted)
Print Customize Display
Show: All | Active (55) | Ended (13)
Delete
Compare
Email To A Friend
Add Note
Picture
Current Price
Bids
Seller ID
Shipping to 95125, USA
Start Time
Time Left
Action
Rare Vegetable Afghan Fine Quality Chobi Rug 6x5
$157.50 13 pakobelrugs (15742)
$30.00 Jan-06 17:30:37
17m
Bid Now!
2074 Vintage Japanese Hanging Scroll: Pine Tree in Snow
$163.50 12 bureido (2222)
$18.50 Jan-06 18:43:17
1h 29m
Bid Now!
5 Vintage Minnesota FISH DECOYS Folk Art
$114.23 11 sill-i-pep (282)
$6.05 Jan-06 18:45:00
1h 31m
Bid Now!
5 OLD Cupboard Cabinet or Trunk Locks w/ Barrel Keys
$15.50 3 qwuzzymoetoe (11)
$12.95 Jan-06 19:42:57
2h 29m
Bid Now!
Vintage hanging scroll :"Two cranes" @k484
$5.00 1 sakura-zipang (0)
$5.80 Jan-06 20:01:43
2h 48m
Bid Now!
Antique hanging scroll :"Two carp" @k490

Now you have a better idea of what type of treasure I hunt on eBay.

When I find intriguing items that I may wish to bid on later, I add the item to my My eBay Watch list by clicking the "Watch this item in My eBay" link on the right side of the item Title bar (as described earlier in this chapter).

You can watch up to one hundred items at a time, and you can delete items from your Watch list by checking the box to the left of the item number and then clicking the "Delete" button.

You can go directly to an item on your Watch list by clicking the item title or the "Bid now!" button for that item on the right of the item title.

The other columns display the current bid amount for the item and the start time and time left.

GRIFF TIP! Worried you might forget to bid on an item you are watching? Have no fear! eBay can remind you that a watched item is about to end by sending you an e-mail reminder, Instant Message alert, or SMS text message on your cell phone. To configure each delivery method, go to My eBay > My Account > eBay Preferences. Click the link for "Show" for "Notification delivery" under the Notification Preferences bar.

My eBay

Hello, **uncle_griff** (1264 ★) 📁 me

· Love it brand new? **eBay** express

My eBay Views

My Summary

All Buying
- Watching (68)
- Bidding
- Best Offers
- Won (1)
- Didn't Win (4)
- Personalized Picks

Selling Manager Pro
- Inventory (15)
- Scheduled
- Active (1)
- Unsold
- Sold
  - Awaiting Payment
  - Awaiting Shipment
  - Paid & Shipped
  - Archived
- Reporting
- Picture Manager
- Automation Preferences
Marketing Tools NEW!

Want It Now

My Messages

All Favorites
- Searches
- Sellers
- Categories

My Account
- Personal Information
- Addresses
- Preferences
- Feedback
- PayPal Account
- Half.com Account
- Seller Account
- Subscriptions

Preferences   Show all

Use Preferences to change your eBay settings for email, payment, selling, etc.
To view your preferences, click the "Show" link.

Notification Preferences

Notification Delivery   Show
Edit your delivery preferences for email, SMS & instant messaging notifications.

Buying Notifications   Show
Edit your buying notifications preference and set your watched or outbid items for email and instant messaging.

Selling Notifications   Show
Edit your selling notifications preferences.

Other Transactions and Notifications   Show
Edit your other transaction notifications preferences.

Newsletters, Promotions and Event Notifications   Show
Edit your newsletters, promotions, and event notifications preferences.

Legal and Policy Notifications   Show
Edit your legal and policy notifications preference.

Selling Preferences

Sell Your Item form and listings   Show
Edit your Sell Your Item form preferences and other listing preferences.

Payment from buyers   Show
Edit Checkout, PayPal, and other payment options you offer buyers.

Enable Checkout through your ProStores Web store   Show
Allow buyers to pay for their eBay items in your ProStores Web store.

Shipping and discounts   Show
Offer shipping discounts on combined purchases, UPS shipping rate options, etc.

Promoting Similar Items on eBay Pages and Emails   Show
Promote your items in emails and on item pages.

Edit any of the separate features by clicking the "Edit" link for each. To configure instant message alerts, click the "Subscribe" (or "Unsubscribe") link.

Notification Preferences		
Notification Delivery		Hide
Registered email address	jim█████@█████.net	Edit
Preferred format for emails	⦿ HTML emails (include pictures and graphics)	
	◯ Text-only emails	
	[Apply]	
Mobile phone number for SMS alerts	██████████	Edit
PIN:	****	
Delivery Time	Anytime when alert occurs	
Watched Item Setting	30 minutes before the auction ends	
Instant message (IM) alerts	Through your AOL account	Unsubscribe

Next click the "Show" link next to Buying Notifications.

Notification Preferences	
Notification Delivery	Show
Edit your delivery preferences for email, SMS & instant messaging notifications.	
Buying Notifications	Show
Edit your buying notifications preference and set your watched or outbid items for email and instant messaging.	
Selling Notifications	Show
Edit your selling notifications preferences.	

Click the "Edit" link to change any of the settings for Buying Notifications.

Notification Preferences		
Notification Delivery		Show
Edit your delivery preferences for email, SMS & instant messaging notifications.		
Buying Notifications		Hide
Watched item ending reminder	Email, Instant Messaging	Edit
Watched item daily list	Not subscribed	
Watched item emails for relisted items	Not subscribed	
Bid confirmation	Not subscribed	
Outbid	Email	
Winning buyer	Email	
Non-winning bidder	Not subscribed	
Second Chance Offer	Email	
Personalized New Item Updates	Not subscribed	
Daily buying status	Not subscribed	
Want It Now reminder	Not subscribed	

As a constant eBay bidder, I would be lost without the My eBay All Buying page. If you are primarily a bidder, I urge you to make this page one of your favorite places and visit it every time you come to eBay.

ALL SELLING

The My eBay All Selling page is similar to the All Buying page except that instead of tracking bids and purchases, it tracks an eBay seller's pending, current, and completed selling.

We cover the My eBay All Selling page in greater depth in Section Two of the book. For now, just keep it in mind.

WANT IT NOW

Want It Now is eBay's online version of the traditional "wanted" feature familiar to anyone who has ever scanned a newspaper's Wanted section. With Want It Now, you can post your request for specific items you seek. The post is placed in the Want It Now area. Sellers can then scan through the posts and send a response to posters with any matching eBay listings.

We will delve into Want It Now in greater detail in a later chapter.

MY MESSAGES

eBay recently created a secure, internal messaging system called My Messages. Every registered eBay member has a My Messages Inbox.

My eBay Views						
My Summary						
All Buying						
• Watching (68)						
• Bidding						
• Best Offers						
• Won (1)						
• Didn't Win (4)						
• Personalized Picks						
All Selling						
• Scheduled						
• Selling (1)						
• Sold						
• Unsold						
• Picture Manager						
Marketing Tools NEW!						
Want It Now						
My Messages						
All Favorites						
• Searches						
• Sellers						
• Categories						
My Account						
• Personal Information						
• Addresses						
• Preferences						
• Feedback						
• PayPal Account						
• Half.com Account						
• Seller Account						
• Subscriptions						
My Reviews & Guides						
Dispute Console						

My Messages

← Back to My eBay

My Messages
All Unread
All Flagged

My Folders (Edit)
• Inbox
• Sent
• From Buyers
• From eBay
• From Sellers

Create Message
Archive

Contacts
Find & Contact a Member
Contact Us

Related Links
My Messages Help
Search for Items
Feedback Forum
eBay Policies
How to Detect Spoof Email
Report an Unpaid Item
Report an Item Not Received
eBay Toolbar

Inbox (1-10 of 20 messages | 0 unread)   Refresh Customize My Messages

From: All   Period: All

Flag	From	Subject	Received ▽	Expires	Status
☐	eBay PowerSeller	PowerSeller Notification	Jan-11	Jan-25	
☐	fitz...	Re: Message from eBay Member Regarding Item #300066064379	Jan-11	Feb-10	
☐	eBay	eBay Sales Reports Plus Subscription Confirmation	Jan-09	Mar-10	
☐	eBay	eBay Invoice for Monday, January 1, 2007	Jan-04	Mar-05	
☐	eBay Seller Central	A Message from Bill Cobb: eBay.com and eBay Motors Fee Adjustments	Jan-03	Feb-02	
☐	eBay Customer Support	Thank You for Your Report (Community Watch) (KMM240450355V93536L0KM)	Jan-02	Mar-03	
☐	eBay	SB NOTICE: eBay Auction 230035255042 Cancelled - Results Null and Void	Jan-02	Mar-03	
☐	fabricelite	Re: Message from eBay Member Regarding Item #320019820819	Jan-01	Jan-31	
☐	oldworldmerchants	Re: Question for item #230071586622 - Solid Oak Double Manor Bookcase Removable Shelving	Dec-30	Jan-29	
☐	fabricelite	Re: Message from eBay Member Regarding Item #320019820819	Dec-28	Jan-27	

Delete   Mark as: --Select--   Move to: --Folder--

Legend: Messages: 📑 Flagged   ✉ Unread   📭 Read   📬 Responded to   📨 Forwarded

Back to top

Page 1 of 2   Go to page [   ] Go
← Previous 1|2 Next →

All eBay Inc messaging as well as messages from and to other members will show up here. Although all official e-mails from eBay and eBay members will also show up in your regular e-mail application, you should make it a habit to check My Messages for all eBay related correspondence. Why? The reason is best expressed in a Griff Tip!

GRIFF TIP! Well, it's more a rule of thumb than a tip. There are crooks out there who will attempt to steal your identity and money by sending you spoofed e-mail that appears to come from eBay or PayPal (see "spoof" and "phishing" in the index for more information). How do you know if an e-mail is legit or not? Simple. If an e-mail isn't in your My Messages inbox, it isn't a legitimate eBay e-mail. Trust only e-mail messages that show up in My Messages!

ALL FAVORITES

The next My eBay page is All Favorites, which is definitely my favorite!

My eBay

My eBay Views	Hello, officialbible01 (0)

My Summary

All Buying
- Watching (1)
- Bidding
- Best Offers
- Won
- Didn't Win
- Personalized Picks

All Selling
- Scheduled
- Selling
- Sold
- Unsold (1)

Marketing Tools NEW!

Want It Now

My Messages (8)

All Favorites
- Searches
- Sellers
- Categories

My Account
- Personal Information
- Addresses
- Preferences
- Feedback
- Seller Account
- Subscriptions

My Reviews & Guides

Dispute Console

Item counts delayed. Refresh

Related Links

PayPal
Buyer's Guide
Shop eBay Stores
Global Trade
Search for Items
Download Tools
Buying Resources
Selling Resources
Dispute Console
more...

All Favorites

My Favorite Searches (4 searches)   Add new Search

Show: All | Searches (4) | Want It Now Searches (0)

Name of Search △	Search Criteria	Email Settings	Action
Chromatics	chromatics Category: Fragrances > Men, Sort: Newly Listed	Not receiving emails	Sign up for Emails
Fish Decoys	fish (decoy,decoys) Sort: Newly Listed	Not receiving emails	Sign up for Emails
Hanging Scrolls	hanging (scroll,scrolls) Category: Antiques > Asian Antiques, Sort: Newly Listed	Not receiving emails	Sign up for Emails
Turkish Rug	turkish oriental (rug,carpet) Category: Antiques, Sort: Ending First	Not receiving emails	Sign up for Emails

Delete   Search items will be emailed to: officialebaybible01@yahoo.com

Back to top

My Favorite Sellers (2 sellers)   See Top Picks from Favorite Sellers | Add new Seller or Store

Seller / Store △	Added	Subscriptions (Email Sent)	Action
beachbadge (2689 ⭐) me Top 1,000 Reviewer Beachbadge's FIRE and ICE Beach Hut	Jan-13-07	Pending	Edit Preferences
uncle_griff (1264 ⭐) me Uncle Griff's Closet View Seller's Items on Half.com	Jan-13-07	Pending	Edit Preferences

Delete   Add Note   Edit Sellers Preferences   Favorite Sellers Top Picks will be sent to:
officialebaybible01@yahoo.com   Bi-Weekly ▾ Save

Back to top

My Favorite Categories (2 categories)   Add new Category

My Favorite Categories	Action
Health & Beauty:Fragrances:Men:Other Brands All Active	Starting Today	Ending Today	Ending Within 5 Hours	--
Antiques:Rugs, Carpets:Large (9x7-9x12) All Active	Starting Today	Ending Today	Ending Within 5 Hours	--

Delete

Back to top

On this page, you can:

- Select up to four favorite categories to display
- Save up to one hundred favorite title searches for easy access
- Have eBay automatically run these searches for you and notify you by e-mail when new matching items have been listed
- Create a list of your favorite sellers or stores

Since my My eBay Favorites page is rather full, I have broken it up into separate screens to better illustrate each section.

All Favorites: Searches

You can add up to one hundred Favorite Searches to My eBay. To add a Favorite Search to your list, click on the link "Add new search" on the top right-hand side of the table.

To delete a search, check the box next to it and click the "Delete" button. We delve deeper into the intricacies of Search (both creating and saving) in a later chapter.

All Favorites: Sellers and Stores

To add up to fifty new favorite sellers or eBay Store IDs to this list, click the link for "Add new seller or store" and follow the instructions.

All Favorites: Categories

You can add categories to your Favorite Categories list by clicking the "Add new category" link.

Select the category from the series of boxes.

To delete categories from the list, check the box next to the category you wish to delete and click the "Delete" button.

MY ACCOUNT

Make special note of this section of My eBay. If you ever have to change anything about your eBay registration, go to this page. This includes your User ID, password, e-mail address, contact information, credit card on file, and About Me page.

The top-level My Account link displays a quick access portal to a seller's PayPal and eBay account information.

We explore these pages in greater detail in Section Two of this book, "Selling the eBay Way." Below the My Account link are links for:

Personal Information
Addresses
Preferences

Feedback
Seller Account
Subscriptions

Personal Information

Clicking this link displays the Personal Information page, which contains sections for your personal, address, and financial information.

Under the section labeled Personal Information, you will find links for editing the main components of your eBay Registration, including your User ID (which you can change once every thirty days), password, password hint, e-mail addresses, wireless e-mail address, and your About Me page.

The next section of the Personal Information page—Address Information—contains links for changing your billing or shipping addresses.

The last section of the Personal Information page—Financial Information—provides links for adding or changing your checking and credit/debit card on file for your eBay Seller's Account.

Addresses

You have up to three addresses on file on eBay: a registration address, a payment address (for receiving mailed payments), and a primary shipping address (to which sellers will ship purchases).

You can change these addresses at any time by clicking the appropriate "Change" link and following the instructions.

Preferences

The Preferences page contains four sections:

Notification Preferences
Selling Preferences
Member-to-Member Communication Preferences
General Preferences

My eBay

My eBay Views

My Summary

All Buying
- Watching (1)
- Bidding
- Best Offers
- Won
- Didn't Win
- Personalized Picks

All Selling
- Scheduled
- Selling
- Sold
- Unsold (1)
- **Marketing Tools** New!

Want It Now

My Messages (8)

All Favorites
- Searches
- Sellers
- Categories

My Account
- Personal Information
- Addresses
- Preferences
- Feedback
- Seller Account
- Subscriptions

My Reviews & Guides

Dispute Console

Item counts delayed. Refresh

Related Links

PayPal
Billing FAQ
Paying Fees
eBay Fees
Search for Items
Dispute Console
more...

Hello, **officialbible01** (0)

Deal Finder
Great Last-Minute Deals!

Preferences   Show all

Use Preferences to change your eBay settings for email, payment, selling, etc.
To view your preferences, click the "Show" link.

Notification Preferences

Notification Delivery   Show
Edit your delivery preferences for email, SMS & instant messaging notifications.

Buying Notifications   Show
Edit your buying notifications preference and set your watched or outbid items for email and instant messaging.

Selling Notifications   Show
Edit your selling notifications preferences.

Other Transactions and Notifications   Show
Edit your other transaction notifications preferences.

Newsletters, Promotions and Event Notifications   Show
Edit your newsletters, promotions, and event notifications preferences.

Legal and Policy Notifications   Show
Edit your legal and policy notifications preference.

Selling Preferences

Sell Your Item form and listings   Show
Edit your Sell Your Item form preferences and other listing preferences.

Payment from buyers   Show
Edit Checkout, PayPal, and other payment options you offer buyers.

Enable Checkout through your ProStores Web store   Show
Allow buyers to pay for their eBay items in your ProStores Web store.

Shipping and discounts   Show
Offer shipping discounts on combined purchases, UPS shipping rate options, etc.

Promoting Similar Items on eBay Pages and Emails   Show
Promote your items in emails and on item pages.

Logos and branding   Show
Display your logo and send customized emails to buyers.

Buyer requirements   Show
Block certain eBay users from buying your items.

eBay Express   Show
Include qualifying items on eBay Express.

Ask seller a question   Show
Customize what is displayed on the Ask a Question page.

Member-to-Member Communication Preferences

Skype preferences   Show
Link your Skype account to eBay and edit your Skype preferences.

General Preferences

Searching and buying   Show
Display your recently viewed items and searches while you shop.

My eBay   Show
Customize how you'd like information displayed in My eBay.

Reviews & Guides   Show
Display Reviews & Guides icon.

Third-party authorizations   Show
Authorize third parties to act on your behalf.

Other general preferences   Show
Customize other preferences.

Under Notification Preferences, you can turn the feature on or off that allows you to receive e-mails from eBay, along with special promotions, newsletters, and event notifications. Finally, you can view and edit your legal and policy notifications from eBay.

From Seller Preferences, you can change critical components for selling on eBay, including your Sell Your Item form preferences, your payment, eBay Checkout, shipping, and shipping discount preferences.

You can also change how your items are promoted in e-mails and on eBay item pages and how your logo is displayed on your listings and in e-mails to buyers.

Note for later the links for setting your buyer requirements and your eBay Express and Ask Seller a Question preferences. These will come in very handy in Section Two.

With Member-to-Member Communication Preferences, you can link your Skype account to your eBay listings as well as edit your Skype preferences. For more on Skype, check the index for "Skype."

Finally, General Preferences lets you set all of your other preferences.

By utilizing all of the above and configuring each preference to your liking, you can tailor and customize your eBay experience to suit your tastes and needs.

Feedback

Whenever two people trade with each other on eBay, either or both can leave a short, public, indelible comment for the other person indicating their satisfaction (or lack thereof) with their trading partner.

These comments are called feedback. All eBay members have a Feedback Profile, which can easily be viewed simply by clicking the number in parentheses next to their eBay User ID.

We discuss the intricacies of eBay feedback in a later section. For now, note that the My eBay feedback page displays recent feedback left for you with the most recent on the top of the list. (You will be so proud the day you get your first feedback. I have heard from new members who wept with joy when they got theirs. We have some very emotional members.)

My eBay

My eBay Views	Hello, **uncle_griff** (1264 ★) 📄 me			Review It Now Read user reviews.

My Summary

All Buying
- Watching (72)
- Bidding
- Best Offers
- Won
- Didn't Win (4)
- Personalized Picks

Selling Manager Pro
- **Inventory** (15)
- Scheduled
- Active (1)
- Unsold
- Sold
  - Awaiting Payment
  - Awaiting Shipment
  - Paid & Shipped
  - Archived
- Reporting
- Picture Manager
- Automation
- Preferences

Marketing Tools New!

Want It Now

My Messages (1)

All Favorites
- Searches
- Sellers
- Categories

My Account
- Personal Information
- Addresses
- Preferences
- Feedback
- PayPal Account
- Half.com Account
- Seller Account
- Subscriptions

Would you like to leave feedback for **all** your items at once?

[Leave Feedback] | Go to Feedback Forum to reply or follow up on feedback.

Recent Feedback (View all feedback)

Comment	From	Date/Time	Item #
Very quick payment! A very good customer!	Seller: jiejiejie (362 ★)	Jan-11-07 20:19	(Private)
AAAAAAAAAAAAAAAAAAAAAAAAAAAAAAAAAAAAAAAAAAAAAAAAAAAAAAAAAAAAAAAAAAAAAAAAAAAAAAAAA	Seller: 9321jackie (3491 ★)	Jan-08-07 14:40	140070647270
excellent transaction. thank you	Seller: dvd-42 (345 ★)	Jan-08-07 10:46	180068573111
Fast payment, great communication, fast and friendly emails.	Seller: agvgera (1440 ★)	Jan-05-07 06:15	220049162211
Great transaction, come back anytime!	Seller: agvgera (1440 ★)	Jan-05-07 06:14	220052099673

Back to top

Items Awaiting Feedback (40 items)

Title	User ID	Sale Date ▽	Action		
O700: Vintage Japanese scroll, Crane, Pine, Sun. (230074766948)	katuragi_jp (2994 ★)	Jan-12-07 20:24:11	Leave Feedback	☆	○
Timex Indiglo Men's I-Control "Turn n Pull" Alarm Watch (300059792999)	fitz... (9686 ★)	Jan-12-07 16:55:55	Leave Feedback	☆	○
Timex Men's I-Control "Turn n Pull" Alarm Indiglo Watch (300069201781)	fitz... (9686 ★)	Jan-12-07 16:55:33	Leave Feedback	☆	○
B841:Chinese Scroll Painting of Fish by Ni Zan (260072749117)	jiejiejie (362 ★)	Jan-11-07 17:36:07	Leave Feedback	☆	⊕
Ormonde Jayne ORRIS NOIR EDP - 5 ml spray SAMPLE (190053304535)	helena14_99 (1258 ★)	Jan-10-07 12:20:34	Leave Feedback	☆	○
On Truth : Harry Frankfurt (Hardcover, 2006) (340135428846)	xianxian-half (1199 ★)	Jan-09-07 22:31:38	Leave Feedback	☆	○
BACKGROUND by Jil Sander 2.5 COLOGNE SPRAY MENS NEW (140072910647)	singerandray (4516 ★)	Jan-09-07 15:30:58	Leave Feedback	☆	○
1918 Japanese Hanging Scroll, Crow on Persimmon Tree (140067221928)	bureido (2222 ★)	Jan-07-07 19:30:00	Leave Feedback	☆	○
Timex Men's "Turn n Pull" Alarm Watch - Blue Face (300066064379)	fitz... (9686 ★)	Jan-07-07 14:58:30	Leave Feedback	☆	○

On this same page, you can view the feedback you need to leave by individual transaction.

GRIFF TIP! One extremely important tool on this page bears highlighting. Click the "Leave feedback" button on the top of the My eBay feedback page to leave feedback in bulk.

My eBay

My eBay Views	Hello, **uncle_griff** (1264 ★) 📄 me

My Summary

All Buying
- Watching (72)
- Bidding

Would you like to leave feedback for **all** your items at once?

[Leave Feedback] | Go to Feedback Forum to reply

On the Feedback Forum: Leave Feedback page, you can find an individual feedback comment by searching with a User ID or item number. In addition, you can view all of your recent transactions from the past ninety days where you were either the buyer or the seller and have not yet left the other party feedback.

Feedback Forum: Leave Feedback help

[_____] [Find Feedback]

Enter a User ID or Item Number

Rating other members by leaving feedback is a very important part of transactions on eBay.

Please note:
- Once left, you cannot edit or retract feedback; you are solely responsible for the content.
- It's always best to keep your feedback factual; avoid making personal remarks.
- Feedback can be left for at least 90 days following a transaction.
- If you have a dispute, contact your trading partner to try and resolve the dispute before leaving feedback.

You have 37 transactions for which to leave feedback. Showing 1 - 25 below.

Seller:	buyitnow_here (8668 ☆) me 📷	Single Transaction Form
Item:	COTTON DESERT SAND COMBAT TEE T SHIRT TOP 2XL NEW (330012984100) Ended: Oct-21-06 23:33:43 PDT	
Rating:	○ Positive ○ Neutral ○ Negative ◉ I will leave feedback later	
Comment:	[_____]	80 characters left.

Seller:	vintageparfum (6813 ☆) me	
Item:	TIFFANY COLOGNE FOR MEN CONCENTREE SPRAY 1.7oz (180054392885) Ended: Nov-23-06 10:32:18 PST	
Rating:	○ Positive ○ Neutral ○ Negative ◉ I will leave feedback later	
Comment:	[_____]	80 characters left.

Seller:	fastcashl (1395 ★)	
Item:	SONY DVP-CX860 300+1 DVD/CD PLAYER W/REMOTE & MANUAL!!! (110058334203) Ended: Nov-23-06 14:13:32 PST	
Rating:	○ Positive ○ Neutral ○ Negative ◉ I will leave feedback later	
Comment:	[_____]	80 characters left.

Seller:	scrappydog1 (52 ★)	
Item:	SuperScope PSD230 CD Player /w Tempo & Key Control (180055151711) Ended: Nov-27-06 09:51:18 PST	
Rating:	○ Positive ○ Neutral ○ Negative ◉ I will leave feedback later	
Comment:	[_____]	80 characters left.

Just scroll down this page and enter feedback comments for each completed transaction.

This little-known and little-used feature not only makes leaving feedback an easy task as opposed to a confusing chore, it also prevents your forgetting to leave feedback for a deserving buyer or seller.

Do make a note of this feature for later reference. This and the fine art of leaving and receiving feedback are examined in depth later in this chapter.

PayPal and Half.com Accounts

These link provide a handy and fast way to access your PayPal and Half.com accounts.

Half.com is an eBay-owned site where you can buy and sell certain types of items, including books, CDs, DVDs, and some electronic devices. More on Half.com in Section Two.

Seller Account

From here, you can view your most recent eBay invoice and your account status as well as change the settings for your automatic monthly invoice payment method (credit/debit card, bank account, or manual). If you elect to pay your monthly invoices manually and you have a PayPal account (as well you should!), you can pay your current balance with PayPal at any time by clicking the button provided.

Seller Account is covered in greater depth in Section Two.

Subscriptions

eBay provides a roster of services that are available on a monthly subscription basis. Most are for sellers, and they are all covered in depth in Section Two.

My Reviews & Guides

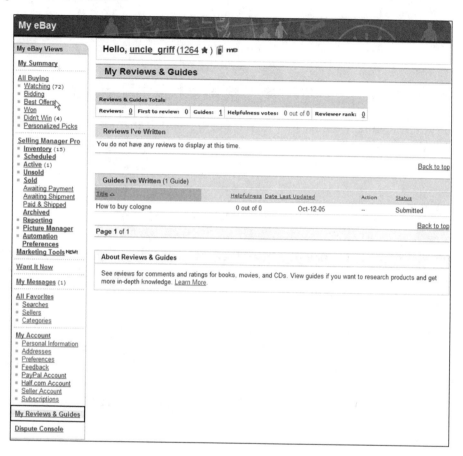

In the last few years, eBay has added many features for members to create and post their own content on the site. The Reviews and Guides feature lets an eBay member post his or her own product reviews for and guides to just about anything you can think of. All of this content is searchable by the most popular search engines and thus provides for more exposure for both the member's content and also by default, the seller's listings on the site.

To write, edit, and submit a review or a guide, click the "Learn More" link under "About Reviews & Guides." Follow the instructions from there.

About Reviews & Guides

See reviews for comments and ratings for books, movies, and CDs. View guides if you want to research products and get more in-depth knowledge. Learn More.

Dispute Console

If you ever find yourself in a dispute with another member (and I hope you don't), the Dispute Console is where you can view the current status of a dispute case.

The Feedback Forum

To the first pioneering eBay buyers and sellers back in late 1995 and early 1996, the infant eBay Web site proved to be a nearly perfect trading platform where individuals could trade with each other directly through the age-old tradition of the auction format.

An enterprising new eBay seller could set up listings in a matter of minutes, and within days that seller would be completing successful transactions, usually with a buyer whom she had never met. As eBay's founder, Pierre Omidyar, stated on the old Web site, it was all truly based on trust. A seller trusted that a high bidder would honor her bid and send payment, and a buyer trusted a seller to send him the merchandise.

The system had one glaring deficiency: After an eBay sale was completed, the buyer and seller had no mechanism for telling the world how the transaction had gone. You could complete many transactions, but no one else at eBay would know that you were someone who could be trusted based on your prior successful transactions.

And so it was that within about six months after the introduction of eBay/ AuctionWeb, Pierre created a system where members could leave comments about other eBay members from whom they had bought or sold.

READING FEEDBACK

Simply put, the eBay Feedback Forum is a mechanism whereby a registered eBay member can leave a public comment about any other registered eBay member. All feedback left for a member can be viewed by clicking the number in parentheses next to that member's User ID wherever the User ID appears.

uncle_griff (1264 ★) me

You can also view feedback for a member by clicking on the "Advanced search" link on the upper right-hand corner of any eBay page

and then clicking the link "Find a member."

Enter that member's User ID in the box provided and click the Search button. This will take you to a page showing the member's feedback number next to her User ID.

Either way will take you to that member's Feedback Profile. Here is my Feedback Profile:

Member Profile: uncle_griff (1264 ★) me

Feedback Score:	1264
Positive Feedback:	99.9%
Members who left a positive:	1264
Members who left a negative:	1
All positive feedback received:	1633

Learn about what these numbers mean.

Recent Ratings:

		Past Month	Past 6 Months	Past 12 Months
⊕	positive	30	139	245
⊘	neutral	0	0	0
⊖	negative	0	0	0

Bid Retractions (Past 6 months): 0

Member since: May-20-96
Location: United States
· ID History
· Items for Sale
· Visit my Store
· Add to Favorite Sellers
· View My World page
· Learn more About Me
· View my Reviews & Guides

Contact Member

Feedback Received | From Buyers | From Sellers | Left for Others

1644 feedback received by uncle_griff (0 ratings mutually withdrawn)

Page 1 of 66

Comment	From	Date / Time	Item #
Very quick payment! A very good customer!	Seller jiejiejie (362 ★)	Jan-11-07 20:19	Private
AAAAAAAAAAAAAAAAAAAAAAAAAAAAAAAAAAAAAAAAAAAAAAAAAAAAAAAAAAAAAAAAA	Seller 9321jackie (3492 ★)	Jan-08-07 14:40	140070647270
excellent transaction. thank you	Seller dvd-42 (345 ★)	Jan-08-07 10:46	180068573111
Fast payment, great communication, fast and friendly emails.	Seller agvgera (1440 ★)	Jan-05-07 06:15	220049162211
Great transaction, come back anytime!	Seller agvgera (1440 ★)	Jan-05-07 06:14	220052099673
Fast payment, great communication, fast and friendly emails.	Seller agvgera (1440 ★)	Jan-05-07 06:14	220054736710
Honest & Trustworthy buyer. Thanks :)	Seller fabricelite (193 ★)	Jan-04-07 16:47	320019820819
Quick payer. Would do biz. with again. AAA+++	Seller jag-luvr (97 ★)	Jan-04-07 12:11	290065845798
Superb BUYER! Instant Payment! Flawless Sale. Highly Recommend! AAAAA+++++	Seller skeetermax (21995 ☆)	Jan-02-07 02:04	120067388723
Great buyer. Quick payment and great communication. A+	Seller azsmells (71 ★)	Dec-31-06 10:06	140067907036
·*·. 10 ·*·. STAR ·*·. EBAYER ·*·. PERFECT ·*·. Thank You!	Seller lotusinthemoonlight (9094 ★)	Dec-30-06 21:16	120061129059

The Feedback Profile page consists of two parts: Member Profile and Feedback Received (a paginated list of all the comments ever left for that member). The list of left comments can be sorted by All Feedback Received, From Buyers, From Sellers, and Left for Others.

Three important facts about eBay feedback:

1. From the beginning of the Feedback Forum, there have been three types of comments from which a member can select: positive, neutral, and negative. A colored icon to the left of the feedback comment indicates the comment type: green for positive, gray for neutral, and red for negative. Besides the type of comment, a member can also type a comment of up to eighty characters.

2. Everyone starts out at eBay with a feedback rating of zero. Each positive feedback comment left for another member increases his feedback rating (the number in parentheses) one point. Each negative decreases his rating one point. A neutral comment does not count for or against a person's feedback rating.

3. The same user can increase or decrease another user's feedback score only one point in either direction. A user can leave successive comments for the same user (if he has future transactions with that person), and those comments could be a combination of positive and negative, but they will not move the other user's feedback score up or down more than one point.

HOW TO READ A MEMBER'S FEEDBACK PROFILE

Here is the Member Profile for my eBay registration:

Member Profile: uncle_griff (1264 ★) me 🏠

Feedback Score:	1264	Recent Ratings:				Member since: May-20-96
Positive Feedback:	99.9%		Past Month	Past 6 Months	Past 12 Months	Location: United States
Members who left a positive:	1264	⊕ positive	30	139	245	▪ ID History
Members who left a negative:	1	⊙ neutral	0	0	0	▪ Items for Sale ▪ Visit my Store
All positive feedback received:	1633	⊖ negative	0	0	0	▪ Add to Favorite Sellers ▪ View My World page
Learn about what these numbers mean.		Bid Retractions (Past 6 months): 0				▪ Learn more About Me ▪ View my Reviews & Guides

Contact Member

Since May 20, 1996, I have received a total of 1,633 positive comments in my feedback profile, but my actual feedback score is only 1,264. How is that? Though it is possible to leave multiple comments for each transaction one has with a specific member, an eBay member can only increase another eBay member's feedback score once. Any subsequent feedback left for that member will not raise that member's score. Thus the difference between the total received and the actual feedback score shown is the sum of positive comments left by repeat buyers or sellers. I have about 368 comments that were left by repeat buyers or sellers. Though the comments for these 368 positive feedbacks are displayed chronologically within the long list of feedback comments, they do not count toward my total score.

I received one negative (way back in 1996).

A member's Feedback Profile tells you many things about that member, for example, when she became an eBay member and the country from which she registered.

Also, the Recent Ratings section breaks down how many of what type of comment the member has received in the past one, six, and twelve months.

Notice the mention of Bid Retractions. Any bids retracted in the last six months will be listed on a page accessible via the Bid Retraction link. If the member has not retracted bids in the last six months, the text will be static (no link).

On the right-hand side of the Profile section, there are four links: "ID history" (where you can view any previous User IDs used for this account), "Items for sale," "Visit my Store," and "Learn more about me" (which leads to my About Me page if I have previously created one).

Finally, there is a "Contact member" button for sending the member an e-mail through the eBay e-mail system.

A Little eBay Feedback History Trivia

In its original incarnation, the ability to leave a comment for another eBay member was unrestricted. You could leave a comment for anyone just to tell the rest of the world just how wonderful he or she was. Unfortunately, it was also possible to leave unlimited negative comments for another eBay member, deserved or not. Although the majority of community members maintained only the highest standards of conduct on the Feedback Forum, a few bad apples did cause innocent eBay members some major headaches.

For a short time, eBay implemented a remedy for this problem that effectively wiped out all scores by any suspended eBay member. The comments remained but the type was changed from negative or positive to neutral.

Still, this remedy proved to be only a partial panacea. Since fairness dictated that all of the feedback, both positive and negative, left by a suspended member be changed to neutral, many eBay members would wake up one day to find their feedback score had decreased overnight.

eBay members came up with the best solution: limit the ability to leave feedback to only the buyer and the seller of a closed listing.

Feedback Comments

Below the Member Profile section, one finds all of the feedback comments left for that member.

By default, comments are displayed twenty-five per page. You can change the number of comments displayed per page by scrolling down to the bottom of the first page of comments and selecting from the options provided.

The numbers in the row are the individual pages of twenty-five comments each. You can navigate to any of these pages by clicking the page number. In addition, there are links here for "Leave feedback" and "Reply to feedback received."

Let's break down the information contained within one feedback comment.

The comment above was left by har1986 on April 3, 2002, at 8:12 Pacific Standard Time. The comment was about item 707217972. You can view the item itself by clicking the item number, but the link is clickable for only ninety days from the close of the listing. "Seller" indicates that the person leaving the comment was the seller for this transaction.

Another feature of the feedback system allows members to follow up on feedback left for them or that they left originally. Here's an example of a feedback in my profile where the seller posted a follow-up:

In addition, the person who left the comment can also respond to the recipient's response. This allows for some back-and-forth between two parties.

LEAVING FEEDBACK

A buyer or seller can leave feedback for any eBay member with whom he has a closed eBay transaction. There are two ways to begin: from the Closed Item page and from My eBay. How to leave feedback using My eBay is described earlier in this chapter in the "My eBay" section.

Leaving Feedback from the Closed Item Page

The Closed Item page is simply the item page for a closed listing. You can reach a Closed Item page via the item number, from your completed item list in Search as Bidder or Seller, or from your My eBay All Buying page.

The Title section of every eBay Closed Item page has a link to leave feedback for the other party in the closed transaction:

> **IQUITOS BY:ALAIN DELON 3.4 OZ NIB**
>
> ✓ This item has been paid through PayPal.
>
> [Leave Feedback >]
>
> To let other eBay users know what your experience has bee
>
> **Find more items from the same seller. Bid o**

The link will appear only if you are the signed-in buyer or seller of the item.

THE IMPORTANCE OF FEEDBACK

All eBay members place enormous importance on their feedback. At eBay, feedback is considered by most to be the currency of an eBay member's reputation. Feedback promotes accountability and good trading ethics among all eBay members, buyers and sellers alike.

Feedback Protocol—Who Goes First?

For most members, leaving feedback is a crucial duty. However, there is no set protocol regarding who should leave feedback first. In fact, leaving feedback is and always will be voluntary.

Ideally, the seller leaves it for the buyer once the seller has received the buyer's payment. The buyer never leaves feedback until she has received the item. Over the past few years, I have noticed that many sellers will not leave feedback for a buyer until the buyer has done so for them. It really doesn't matter who leaves feedback first as long as someone does so.

GRIFF TIP! Sellers! If your policy is to not leave feedback for a buyer until the buyer has left feedback for you, don't post your policy in your item description. No matter how politely you word such a policy, a buyer will always interpret it as, "Leave me a negative and you get one back!" This will turn off many buyers, one of whom may have been the ideal buyer or bidder for your item!

Keep a Civil Tongue

The vast majority of all eBay transactions end with satisfied buyers and sellers. However, if by some chance you need to leave a less-than-positive comment, don't do so in anger. Remember that feedback left cannot be removed (except under specific, severely defined, and limited circumstances outlined later). It never pays to leave a belligerent comment. State your case clearly and concisely. A good rule of thumb: Never post a feedback comment you would be ashamed to show your mother.

Positive Feedback

If you do your homework and bid with trusted eBay sellers who provide professional, easy-to-understand, comprehensive item descriptions, payment/shipping terms, secure methods of payment such as PayPal, and clear photos of their items, all of your eBay transactions should be flawless. Let the world know by leaving your trading partner a glowing positive feedback.

eBay member Craig Knouse provided a few examples of simple but concise positive comments:

"Item was even better than described. I'm very pleased with this deal."

"Thanks again, I'll be happy to refer more eBay customers to you in the future."

"Thanks for the opportunity to buy this outstanding item. You really made my day!"

"I was very impressed by this seller's professionalism and commitment. Thanks!"

And I love this comment someone left for me:

⊕ MY MAILMAN HAD FLAMES COMING OUT OF THE BACK OF HIS SHOES. FASTEST PAYMENT EVER!

And if you'll indulge me for a second, the following comment I left for a seller (who sold me a wonderful Timex Indiglo wristwatch) I believe may be the only palindrome feedback ever left on eBay (prove me wrong!):

⊕ Look ma! I won! Olga's Timex emits a 'glo!' Now I am 'kool!'

A few tips:

- Use all of the eighty character spaces. With a little ingenuity, you can get a lot of praise and information into eighty spaces. Try abbreviating wherever possible for example, use "thank u" for "thank you" and save two valuable spaces.

- Leave out punctuation. It takes up valuable space from the 80-character-limit-space that is better served with actual words.
- Avoid using any part of a member's contact information, such as name or phone number.
- Never post an e-mail address or Web address in a feedback comment.

Negative Feedback—the Last Resort

Your eBay transaction didn't go as smoothly as you hoped. The item arrived broken or was not as described. The seller used soiled packing materials. The bidder or seller hasn't responded to your e-mails. The item or payment is late in arriving. The receipt shows that the shipping cost was a lot less than what the seller charged you.

Stop. Take a deep breath. The world is not a perfect place. Sometimes things go awry. Sometimes sellers make mistakes.

Only leave negative feedback as a last resort. What's key to avoiding a potential nasty situation? Communication! On eBay, communication is crucial. Before pulling the negative feedback trigger, e-mail the other party and, using all the diplomatic skills you possess, try to work out a solution. Let her know your concerns.

The item arrived broken? Many sellers buy insurance as a habit. Contact the seller via e-mail. Let him know, in a polite, nonaccusing manner, that the item arrived damaged.

The item isn't as described? Even those sellers who state "no returns" will exhibit more flexibility if you state your case with respect and with no aggression.

The packing materials were soiled or the packing was imperfect? Let the seller know your feelings in a polite and helpful e-mail.

Your bidder or seller hasn't responded? A faulty e-mail system or address could be the culprit. Request the contact information (phone number) of the other party and give him a call.

The item or payment has not yet arrived? E-mail the seller or buyer and let her know. No delivery system is perfect.

You feel you were overcharged for shipping? Let the seller know (again, in a polite e-mail) and perhaps suggest that she state her shipping terms more explicitly in her descriptions so that bidders will not be unpleasantly surprised by the higher-than-necessary shipping costs. (And of course, in the future, you will always determine shipping costs before you bid.)

The rule of thumb is to never jump to conclusions. Get the facts first.

When communicating with another member with whom you may be on the brink of a dispute, always be polite. Nine times out of ten, you will find that diplomacy, civility, and tact are more effective at resolving difficulties than a hasty negative comment.

If all of the above fail and you have to leave negative feedback as a last resort, keep in mind what longtime eBay member Tim Heidner (just_ducky) has to say about leaving negative feedback:

1. Never, under any circumstances, leave feedback when you are angry. Take a break and think about what you want to say. Don't be a hothead. It can scare away future users.
2. Don't embellish. Stick to the facts.
3. Keep it within your transaction. Don't bring up other problems this person has had. You don't know the circumstances regarding other feedback left for this person. It might not be true.
4. Don't use profanity. We are adults. Profanity is immature and solves nothing.
5. Be respectful. Remember, this is still a human being. It is possible to leave negative feedback in a respectful way.

Communication is a two-way street. How you say something may tell a story about someone else, but it could speak volumes about you.

The majority of feedback left at eBay is positive, but occasionally a buyer or seller may not be pleased with his trading partner's behavior and will let the world know with a neutral or negative comment. In most cases where someone has left a negative comment, the other party will usually respond in kind.

Over the past five years, I have fielded many an e-mail from an unhappy eBay member who is distraught to have received what he believes to be an undeserved negative comment. A retaliatory negative feedback may sting at first, but it is a necessary risk that all eBay members must assume if feedback is to work as originally and currently intended.

Feedback is a public record between you and your trading partner. If you are a good eBay buyer or seller, your feedback will reflect that clearly to all who view it, even if your feedback contains the occasional negative comment. That one recent negative may glare out at you, but in the eyes of other eBay members, it doesn't change your previous string of positive comments, and that is what counts: the sum total of all your comments.

I hear from many eBay members who flatly tell me they will never leave a negative comment, no matter how well deserved, for fear of receiving a negative in kind. These eBay members are more concerned with keeping their feedback unblemished. On first consideration, who could blame them? However, there is a dangerous flaw in this strategy.

Feedback is not a beauty contest. If you have an unpleasant experience with another eBay member and you do not leave appropriate feedback for fear of retaliation, you may keep your own feedback lily-white, but you are doing a grave disservice to the rest of the eBay Community. There are two important reasons for always leaving appropriate feedback.

One: You could be the victim. You read a feedback profile of another eBay member and decide, based on their total lack of negatives, to go ahead and bid on her item. Subsequently, you discover that the seller is not very customer-oriented and is prone to anger and rudeness in her e-mails to you. Wouldn't you have appreciated a warning about this seller's rudeness? Why did no one leave a previous feedback alerting you to this seller's lack of good business manners? Because people were afraid that if they did, the seller would leave a negative in kind for them. The outcome? This seller's bad business practices go unmentioned, and you are unaware of them until it is too late.

Two: Appropriate feedback is corrective. People really are basically good. It's true. Still, sometimes it is up to us to help bring out this innate goodness, especially for those buyers or sellers whose eBay activity could use some gentle correction. By leaving constructive critical feedback that is neutral or, when necessary, negative, you help educate and, hopefully, reform the buyer or seller so that she can learn from the experience.

EBAY MEMBER TIP! Not all sticky situations call for negative feedback. You have to use common sense and good judgment. Tom Reddick (treddick), an eBay member since 1998, makes a good point regarding when not to leave negative feedback: "As a buyer I have received a few things that were not as described but the losses were small and I did not leave a negative feedback. And I did not get any in return. It is important to leave feedback to warn others in serious situations, but it is also smart to consider the long-term consequences of racking up lots of negatives because you 'negged' someone over a small oversight or a misunderstanding over a three-dollar item."

EBAY INC. AND FEEDBACK

eBay will not edit or change a feedback comment under any circumstances. No exceptions. Don't even think about it. That's why it is so important to make sure you leave comments carefully, especially negative comments.

eBay will, however, remove a feedback comment, but only under very specific circumstances.

In addition, if the two parties in a transaction agree, they can have feedback withdrawn. Mutually withdrawn feedback comments remain in view, but their point count is neutralized. An eBay notation explaining that the feedback was mutually withdrawn will be displayed with the comment.

To view the Feedback Removal and Withdrawal policies and instructions, click on the "Help" link on the top of any eBay Web page. Then click the link "Help topics."

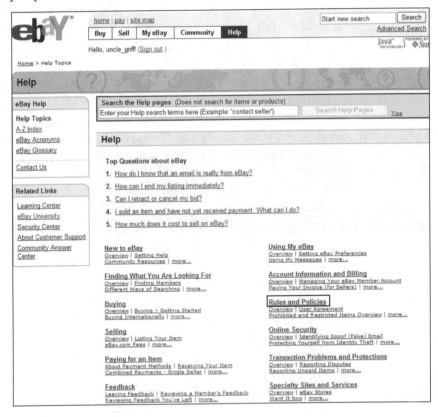

Scroll down to the "Rules and policies" link, and then click on "Feedback withdrawal and removal."

Rules and Policies

Top Questions about Rules and Policies

1. How can I report an item that appears to be violating eBay rules and policies?
2. Why was my account suspended?
3. What are the rules and policies for listing items for sale on eBay?
4. I sold an item and have not yet received payment. What can I do?
5. What is VeRO and why was my item ended because of it?

eBay Rules and Policies - Overview

Rules for Buyers
Rules for Buyers Overview | Unpaid Item Policy
Invalid Bid Retraction Policy | more...

Rules for Everyone
Rules for Everyone - Overview | Community Content Policy
Discussion Boards Usage Policy | more...

Rules about Intellectual Property
35 mm, 70 mm Movie Prints | Academic Software
Authenticity Disclaimers | more...

Privacy
eBay Privacy Policy | Appendix to the Privacy Policy

Trust and Safety Tutorials

Rules for Sellers
Rules for Sellers - Overview | Listing Policies for Sellers - Overview
Accepted Payment Policy | more...

Prohibited and Restricted Items
Prohibited and Restricted Items - Overview | Alcohol
more...

Feedback
Feedback Policies - Overview | Feedback Abuse, Withdrawal and Removal
Feedback Extortion | more...

Identity
Identity Overview | False or Missing Contact Information
Invalid or Dead Email Addresses | more...

This page contains important detailed rules and guidelines regarding how to leave feedback.

ANOTHER AMAZING EBAY TESTIMONIAL

Before we move on, take a look at this post to one of the eBay chat boards, by eBay member auntiem:

Sincere Gratitude and Heartfelt Thanks

auntiem71 (176)

I just wanted to tell you how thankful I am for eBay. My husband had a severe stroke seven years ago, at age forty-four. It left him with aphasia/apraxia and comprehension difficulties. He had all but closed himself off to the world. He was afraid people would laugh at him and think he was stupid. I bought a computer a few years ago, hoping he would try to use it. Well, after months of failed attempts, he finally mastered the basics. In the meantime, I had gotten "hooked" on eBay through my brother-in-law. I started selling some of my dolls to make some extra money. My husband eventually learned to navigate eBay also, a slow process for him. It has been many months now and he has become quite a pro!

He had been an automotive machinist, so naturally our house is packed with car parts. He decided he wanted to start selling his "treasures" on eBay! He gets the parts ready and gives me the information and I type up the auctions for him.

Here is the part I am grateful for. He has started talking to people, is more outgoing, and has confidence in himself! He realizes that he is not worthless just because he cannot get the words out of his mouth or that he takes a long time to do something that other people finish in a short time. He has always been excellent where cars are concerned, and now knows he still has this knowledge and always will. Thank you, everyone, for listening to me. I just needed to express my thanks.

3

Shopping on eBay—Find It!

What Can I Buy on eBay?

Well, what are you looking for?

eBay seller Linda Huffman (eBay User ID lindyfrommindy) found a small wooden beer sign at a local yard sale. After she dragged it home, her husband nixed her plan to hang it in their family room. She put it aside in her "to be eBayed" pile.

"I finally got around to photographing it and listing it and I was surprised at the interest in this corny Pabst Blue Ribbon sign."

She was most pleased when the winning bidder contacted her with profuse thanks. He had been searching everywhere (Internet, yard sales, flea markets, etc.) for a long time for this particular sign.

"His dad had owned one just like it and for years it had decorated their family's basement until it was destroyed in a fire. His dad had passed away, and being able to have this memento of his childhood in his own home now was very important to him. The money I made selling this item was small, but knowing I had reunited someone with an item they valued more than money was priceless."

Just about anything you can imagine is probably available right now, this very minute, on eBay. From the old stalwarts, collectibles and computers, to clothing, jewelry, cameras, farm machinery, real estate, houses, cars, planes, boats, event tickets, services, and so on . . . you can find it on eBay.

In just a few minutes of random browsing on eBay, I found all the items shown on these two pages.

A 1960 Cadillac

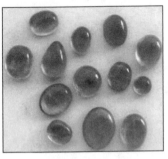

13 Colombian emeralds

A complete computer system

A used ten-burner commercial Garland restaurant stove

A new men's Armani suit

A new cello

A new glass chess set

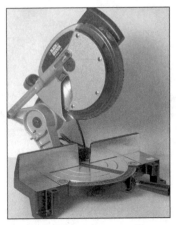

A new Black & Decker miter saw

A John Deere bucket loader

A Lalique vase

Lucille Ball's childhood home in upstate New York

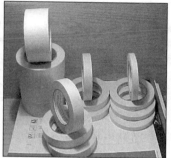

A box of brand new masking tape rolls

A pet-door kit

A new Pierre Cardin luggage set

A fifties pink poodle suitcase

If you can think of it (and it's legal), you can probably find it on eBay. A while back, I received an e-mail from an eBay member named Julie who actually found almost everything for her wedding on eBay!

Let me tell you a little about myself. I am a working mom. My fiancé works and has two kids and so do I. . . . I started going to eBay because of the great deals my fiancé and I got on computer parts for my whole family. . . . I want this day to be so special. I plan to keep everything for the girls when they get married. We even found real champagne glasses on eBay. . . . Most of what I bought I got from eBay. . . . I bought a wedding topper on eBay that cost $25 including shipping. It was completely custom-made . . . the prettiest cake topper I have ever seen. The seller runs her business off of eBay. . . . My wedding is going to be totally elegant. I owe my thanks to all the people who I have purchased things from. . . . One deal early in the game changed everything about the wedding. . . . I was bidding on four bridesmaid dresses . . . in the auction [the seller] stated that they were a pastel blue. Well, when I got them, they were a pastel green. She did offer to take them back. I had already bid on some other high-dollar things in dark blue based *off of the dresses. Anyway, my fiancé and I discussed this problem and I was busy sending out e-mails frantically the next day to the auctioneers. I didn't know if I was going to be able to have these good people change the color from blue to green but I had to try. . . . Our wedding colors are now emerald green and white. . . . I have met some wonderful friends . . . on eBay. . . . eBay has been very good to me and my fiancé is impressed with the deals that I have made.*

Of course, the trick is, like Julie, to know how to find what you are looking for. With over 25 million items up for bid or sale at any given moment, finding that special object (like an entire wedding) can seem a formidable task. However, by utilizing some or all of the following helpful tips, you'll be an expert eBay searcher in no time!

To begin, there are two primary methods of finding items on eBay—browsing and searching.

Browsing eBay

By "browsing," I mean the Internet equivalent of old-fashioned window-shopping, much like taking a leisurely stroll through a mall or the old downtown of your hometown, scanning the windows of the shops, not exactly sure what it is you are looking for but hoping that something will catch your eye. Or maybe you have a pretty good idea of the type of item you want, so you focus on specific stores offering this type of item.

Browsing on eBay is much the same thing. A buyer can browse on eBay two ways: through eBay Categories and through eBay Stores.

BROWSING THE EBAY CATEGORIES

All items on eBay are placed somewhere in the eBay category hierarchy (see chapter 2). As of this writing, there are thirty-one top-level categories (and five specialty categories). The folks at eBay don't usually add more top-level categories, but new subcategories are always showing up, based primarily on eBay buyer and seller requests.

Let's say you are looking to buy something old and rare. You can start your search from the eBay home page by clicking on the link "Antiques" in the category list.

This will bring you to the Antiques category home page.

Antiques

| | Antiques ▾ | Search |

eBay has the largest selection of Antiques on the web including asian antiques, maps, books, furniture, musical instruments, rugs and more!

Categories within Antiques   Show Items...

- **Antiquities (Classical, Amer.)**
  Egyptian
  Greek
  Roman
  The Americas
  Other

- **Architectural & Garden**
  Ceiling Tins
  Chandeliers, Fixtures, Sconces
  Doors
  Finials
  Fireplaces, Mantles
  Garden
  Hardware
  Signs
  Stained Glass
  Tiles
  Weathervanes, Lightning Rods
  Windows, Sashes, Locks
  Other

- **Asian Antiques**
  Chinese
  Japanese
  Southeast Asian
  Other

- **Books, Manuscripts**
  American
  Asian
  English
  European
  Other

- **Decorative Arts**
  Ceramics, Porcelain
  Clocks
  Glass
  Lamps
  Metalware
  Mirrors
  Picture Frames
  Toleware
  Woodenware
  Other

- **Ethnographic**
  African
  Latin American
  Native American
  Pacific Rim
  Other

- **Furniture**
  Beds
  Benches, Stools
  Bookcases
  Cabinets, Armoires, Cupboards
  Chairs
  Desks
  Dining Sets
  Dressers, Vanities
  Sofas, Chaises
  Tables, Stands
  Other Furniture

- **Maps, Atlases, Globes**
  Globes
  Maps, Atlases
  Maps on CD

- **Maritime**
  Anchors
  Bells, Whistles
  Clocks
  Compasses
  Diving Helmets
  Fishing Nets, Floats
  Lamps, Lighting
  Model Ships
  Portholes
  Scrimshaw
  Sextants
  Telescopes
  Wheels
  Other

- **Musical Instruments**
  Keyboard
  Percussion
  String
  Wind

- **Primitives**

- **Rugs, Carpets**
  Small (1x2-4)
  Medium (4x2-9x6)
  Large (9x7-9x12)
  Larger than 9x12
  Runners
  Other

- **Science & Medicine**
  Medical
  Science Instruments
  Other

- **Silver**
  Coin Silver
  Silverplate
  Sterling

- **Textiles, Linens**
  Embroidery
  Fabric
  Lace, Crochet, Doilies
  Linens
  Pillows
  Quilts, Bedspreads
  Samplers
  Tapestries
  Other

- **Other Antiques**

- **Show all Antiques categories...**

By starting your browsing on the Antiques home page, you have reduced the number of items to browse from the more than 100 million total items available on eBay to about 200,000 items that were specifically listed by sellers in the Antiques categories. Note: The seller determines under which category her item will appear when she lists the item.

The Antiques home page contains subcategories for specific types of antiques. Select and click on a link for a subcategory of your choice and you will be directed to "page one" for all items that are currently listed under that subcategory. For example, I like to search for Oriental rugs, so I would click on the "Rugs, carpets" link and start my browsing from there.

Let's dissect this page.

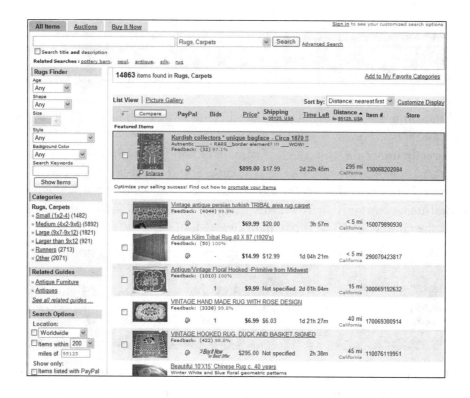

The most prominent features are the three tabs on the top of the page: "All Items," "Auctions," and "Buy It Now." The default view is for All Items. Clicking the "Auctions" tab will display only those listings that are listed as auctions. Clicking the "Buy It Now" tab will display only those listings where the seller has listed the item as either an auction with a Buy It Now option or a straight, no-auction, fixed-price listing.

This feature is a boon to the many eBay buyers who prefer to skip the auction listings and shop only for those items that they can buy immediately.

Over the tabs are a series of links showing the location of the subcategory Rugs, Carpets in the overall category hierarchy.

Back to Antiques Overview   Home > Buy > Antiques > **Rugs, Carpets**

All Items   **Auctions**   **Buy It Now**

You can move up the hierarchy by clicking any of the links. We'll stay with Rugs, Carpets for now.

Directly under the subcategory name you will find a search box where you can enter keywords to search within the category. (The mechanics of a search are discussed in depth in the next section of this chapter.) Under that is the number of total items currently listed in this category. When this screen shot was captured, the number of New Today items was 14,863.

Related Searches : pottery barn, wool, antique, silk, rug

Rugs Finder   **14863** items found in **Rugs, Carpets**

Age
Any
Shape   List View | Picture Gallery

To the right of the page is a drop-down box for selecting one of six sort options, four for time and two for price. The time sort options are "Ending soonest" followed by "Newly listed," "Ending today," and "New today." The price sorts are "Lowest first" and "Highest first." There is also sort for "Distance: nearest first."

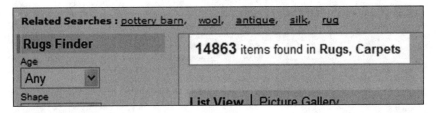

"Ending soonest" shows the category sorted by the chronological order of their listing, with those about to end on the top.

"Newly listed" shows all items in the category, sorted by newest items first.

"Ending today" displays only those items that are slated to end in the next twenty-four hours, sorted by the oldest first.

"New today" shows only those items listed in the last twenty-four hours, with the newest first.

The two price sorts order the items by either lowest price or highest price. Note that the price used is either the current bid or, if there are no bids on the item, the starting bid. The obvious choice for many shoppers is "Price: lowest first," but there are instances when "Price: highest first" is ideal—for example, categories where the lowest-priced items are accessories for an item you seek and not the actual item itself.

"Distance: nearest first" sorts the list of items by nearest first based on your zip code and the zip code of the seller. This sort is an excellent way to find items located in your town or city. For example, if you are looking for a big piece of furniture or equipment, then you can sort the list by "Distance: nearest first." Most of these items can be picked up instead of shipped, saving you lots of money on shipping. In addition, some (but not all) sellers may be willing to let you inspect the item in person before placing a bid or making a Buy It Now purchase.

Scroll down to the bottom of this category list page. In the right-hand corner under the "Go to page . . ." box, you'll find an important bit of information in tiny text.

This indicates the date and time that this category was last updated. When items are listed on eBay, they do not always immediately appear in their categories. Instead, they are sometimes held aside until the eBay system updates that particular category, at which time all items in the "holding pen" are added. This process, called indexing, occurs once every five to ten minutes (or longer for certain items and categories).

On the left-hand side of the page you will find other tools for sorting and filtering the contents of a category. Many categories now have what is called a Finder, which provides a precision filtering tool using item attributes specific to the category. For example, the Rugs Finder section contains selectable attributes for age, shape, size, style, and background color. In addition, there is a box for entering search keywords.

The next section is called Categories. You can view a list of the subcategories one level down. For Rugs, Carpets, they are Small (1×2–4), Medium (4×2–9×6), Large (9×7–9×12), Larger than 9×12, Runners, and Other.

Below this, the Search Options section contains some limiting factors for your search. These are "Items listed with PayPal," "Buy It Now items," "Gift items," and "Completed listings." Next is a "Listings" checkbox with a drop-down box containing filter options for "Ending within," "Ending in more than," and "Started within." Under this drop-down box is another with various times from "1 hour" up to "7 days."

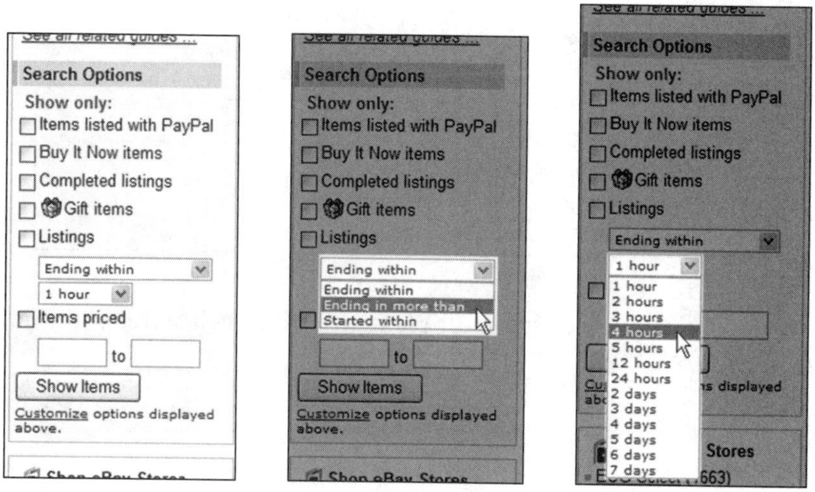

Note the small link for "Customize options displayed above." This link lets you alert the options appearing for Search Options. For example, click the link, select the option "Multiple item listings," and click the little blue arrow that points to the right.

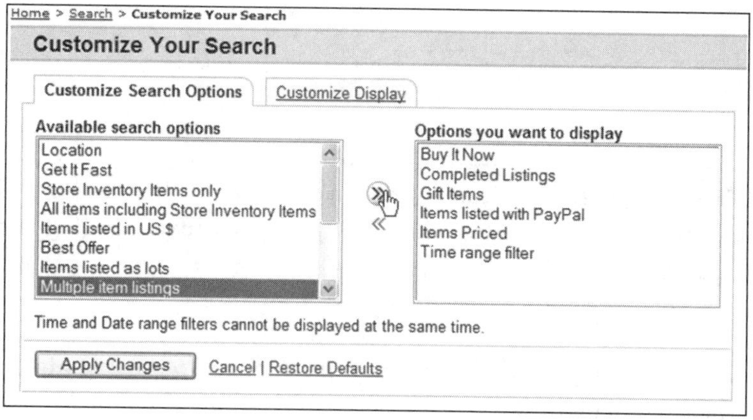

Now the option "Multiple item listings" appears in the right-hand window. Click the "Apply changes" button.

Home > Search > Customize Your Search

Customize Your Search

| Customize Search Options | Customize Display |

Available search options
- Location
- Get It Fast
- Store Inventory Items only
- All items including Store Inventory Items
- Items listed in US $
- Best Offer
- Items listed as lots
- Items from specific seller

Options you want to display
- Buy It Now
- Completed Listings
- Gift Items
- Items listed with PayPal
- Items Priced
- Time range filter
- Multiple item listings

Time and Date range filters cannot be displayed at the same time.

Apply Changes | Cancel | Restore Defaults

Now the option for viewing multiple item listings is inserted into the Search Options section.

Search Options

Show only:
- ☐ Items listed with PayPal
- ☐ Buy It Now items
- ☐ Completed listings
- ☐ 🌐 Gift items
- ☐ Multiple item listings
  - At least ▾ [   ]
- ☐ Listings
  - Ending within ▾
  - 1 hour ▾
- ☐ Items priced
  - [   ] to [   ]

Show Items

Customize options displayed above.

GRIFF TIP! Look for the "customize" links on many other eBay pages to customize just about any feature to suit your particular shopping and selling needs.

For now, let's move back up to the top of the page, to the actual item titles as shown in the category itself.

Directly under the bar containing the last update information is a bar labeled Featured Items.

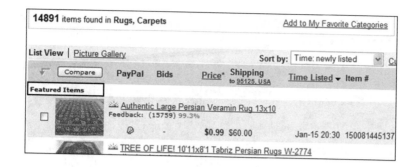

Featured Items

When the sellers of these items listed them to eBay, they selected a special option, Featured Plus. It costs the seller $19.95 to have an item appear as a Featured Plus. The benefit of Featured Plus is that these items will always appear on the top of page one of their category as well as within the category pages themselves.

The Featured Items section usually fits on the first page of the category, but for the more populated categories, it can extend two or three pages into the list of category pages. At the end of the Featured Items, the All Items section begins. Note: An item that appears in the Featured Items section of a category will also appear in the All Items section.

Each time eBay updates a category, items that were listed after the previous update are added to the top of both the Featured and All Items sections in chronological order according to the actual time that the seller submitted them. Items are added to the top of each list and are scrolled down and onto the next page as new items are added after them. Think of it as a tall stack of plates with new plates constantly added to the top of the stack.

You can probably see why sellers who list their items so that they appear in the Featured Items section are at an advantage over those who do not. Those items are always on the first or second page of every category for current view, and on eBay, where there are sometimes hundreds of item pages, it pays to be on the top of the stack!

On the left-hand side of the category list, you should see Gallery thumbnail images for those items where the seller opted to employ a Gallery picture.

Featured Items

Authentic Large Persian Veramin Rug 13x10
Feedback: (15759) 99.3%
$0.99 $60.00   Jan-15 20:30 150081445137

TREE OF LIFE! 10'11x8'1 Tabriz Persian Rugs W-2774
Feedback: (2157) 99.5%
$0.99 See description   Jan-15 20:30 120075938091

ECG MOST BEAUTIFUL 8x12 LEGACY COLLECTION RUG
Feedback: (13016) 99.1%
$9.99 $189.00   Jan-15 20:20 130069594220

Rare Vegetable Afghan Chobi Large Rug 9x8
Feedback: (15759) 99.3%
$0.99 $60.00   Jan-15 20:18 150081443131

QRUG 7'x10' PERSIAN RUGS SENSATIONAL TABRIZ RUG 17216
Feedback: (2722) 99.7%
$1.00 $95.00   Jan-15 20:12 290072712670

QRUG 4'7"x 10'2" UNIQUE AZARBAIJAN RUGS TRIBAL RUG 1749
Feedback: (2722) 99.7%
$1.00 $95.00   Jan-15 20:02 290072709968

12 9X9 1 RM-SZ KAFAS TABRIZ 1960s 120KPSI RUG NR D-1064
Feedback: (7450) 99.5%
$0.99 $340.00 Buy It Now $120.00   Jan-15 19:55 160074383042

REMARKABLE! 12'3x8'3 Najafabad Persian Rugs W-3366

Gallery pictures allow browsers to scan through the category items more efficiently. It's also an excellent way for sellers to promote their items. A title may be descriptive and enticing, but as we all know, a picture is worth a thousand title keywords.

Not all the items in the category list will have Gallery thumbnails. For those items where the seller did not opt for a Gallery image but supplied photos, there will be a camera icon.

ECG 30% OFF YOUR SHIP FEE .. 3x5 LEGACY COLLECTION RUG
Feedback: (4293) 99.4%
$0.99 $62.30   Jan-15 11:09 13006942

4x6 Oriental Pakistani Wool Rug
Orig. price $1699.00 Beige & Blue gray w/Black backg
Feedback: (2) 100%
$650.00 Not specified   Jan-15 11:08 2800709

RUNNER 3'6 X 9'1 PERSIAN CARPET HAMEDAN RUG - 6800
Feedback: (2241) 99.9%

If there is no Gallery thumbnail and no green camera icon to the left of an item title, then the seller may not have provided a picture for the item. This is not always the case. The only way to tell for sure is to click the item title to open the item description page.

To the right of the Gallery thumbnail or the camera icon is the item title as provided by the seller.

You may have noticed that there are many different styles of composition for titles. Some sellers use all caps, some use long strings of punctuation to create eye-catching designs, others use words of enticement such as "L@@K," "Must See," or the ever-popular "Best on eBay." (In Section Two of this book, we describe the pros and cons of different title composition styles and provide tips for creating the most effective item titles.)

Note: The small "pp" icon indicates that the seller accepts PayPal for payments, and the "shield" icon means the seller provides PayPal Buyer Protection.

The next column, Price, shows the current price of the item as of the last category index update.

The next column, Bids, indicates the number of bids received as of the last category index update. A Buy It Now icon indicates the seller listed the item with a Buy It Now format. If someone bids on the item (and the reserve, if any, has been met), the icon will disappear and the number of bids will show in the space.

The final column, Time Left, displays the absolute closing time for the item in Pacific Standard Time.

If you find an item that interests you, you can click either the Gallery image or the item title to open up the Item Description Page.

The Product Finder

eBay recently enhanced the ability to locate specific items with a new tool called Finder. With Finder, you can filter the items in the category using an expanded range of item attributes. Currently, this feature extends to most eBay categories.

In the Art, Sculpture, Carvings category, the box Sculpture Finder is on the left-hand side.

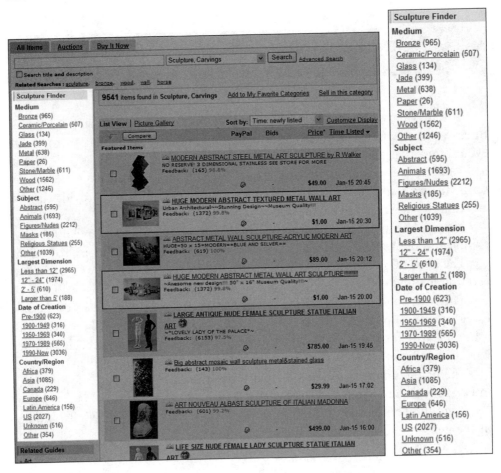

This box contains a long list of attributes, such as Medium, Subject, Largest Dimension, Date of Creation, and Country/Region.

Use any of these links in any combination to target only those items in which you are interested. For example, if you were seeking nineteenth-century bronze, you could spend a few hours browsing the more than nine thousand items currently listed in the Art > Sculpture, Carvings category or simply click the link for "Bronze" under the Sculpture Finder.

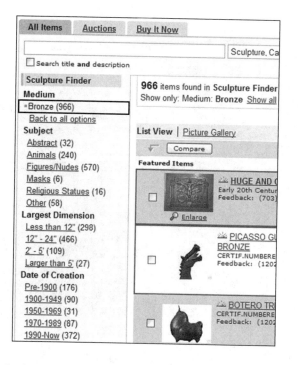

And then click the link "Pre-1900" under Date of Creation.

Results: From more than 9,000 items down to 176 items, all of which are for nineteenth-century or earlier bronze sculptures.

Below the Finder list is the same Search Options section we saw in Antiques > Rugs, Carpets. Above the Finder list you'll always find a text entry box for keyword searches. You can combine the Finder links, keyword search, and Search Options to focus your browsing and searching on only those items that interest you most.

BROWSING BY EBAY STORES

eBay Stores are a way for sellers to offer their customers both auction and fixed-price merchandise on eBay through an online storefront. To browse, search, and buy at the eBay Stores home page, go to the eBay home page and click the link at the top of the left-hand column marked "eBay Stores" (under Specialty Sites).

This will take you to the eBay Stores home page:

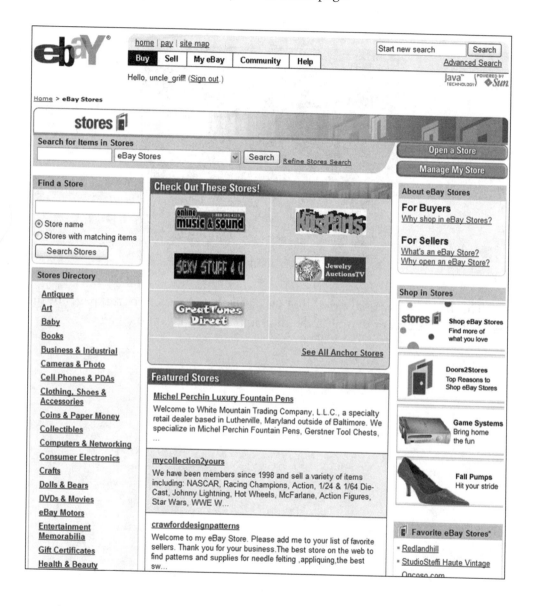

The eBay Stores home page looks similar to the eBay home page except that, instead of a Categories box, there is a box for Stores Directory sorted by the same category list as for the eBay main home page. The eBay Stores browsing experience is entirely different from the main eBay site. The focus is on individual eBay Stores as opposed to items. For example, we'll start with a top-level category, Antiques.

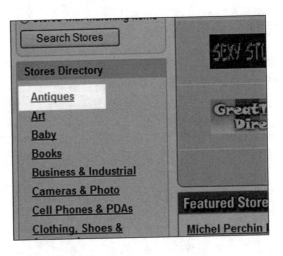

This brings us to a page that looks a bit like the Antiques portal page for the main eBay site, except that no individual items are listed on the page.

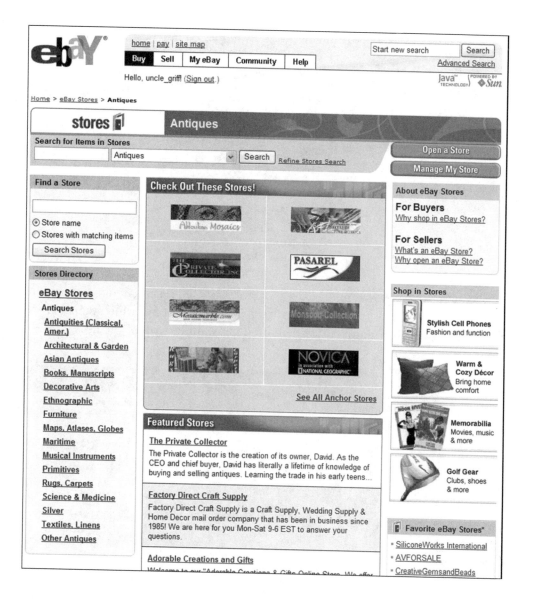

Choose a subcategory on the left, for example, Architectural & Garden.

Now the page shows individual eBay Stores, including a matching item count for each. Note that eBay Stores are ordered by number of matching items in each store, with those having the most matching items on the top of the list.

You can either click down another level or select an individual eBay Store from the list. Let's drill down one more level to the subcategory Chandeliers, Fixtures, Sconces.

This brings us to a page of eBay Stores.

stores | **All Stores in Chandeliers, Fixtures, Sconces**

Search for Items in Stores

[ ] Chandeliers, Fixtures, Sconces ▾ [Search] Refine Stores Search

▸ Stores Help for Buyers
▸ Stores Help for Sellers

Find a Store

[ ]

◉ Store name
○ Stores with matching items
[Search Stores]

Stores Directory

eBay Stores

Antiques

Architectural & Garden

Ceiling Tins

Chandeliers, Fixtures, Sconces

Doors

Finials

Fireplaces, Mantles

Garden

Hardware

Signs

Stained Glass

Tiles

Weathervanes, Lightning Rods

Windows, Sashes, Locks

Other

Sort by: Number of Items ▾

divinnecollection — 80 items in Chandeliers, Fixtures, Sconces
Antiques, Fine Art, Collectibles & More!

Virginia Antiques — 75 items in Chandeliers, Fixtures, Sconces
Style Furniture, Ornaments in Bronze, Marble or Alabaster, Chandeliers, Garnitures, Artistic Mirrors, porcelains, sevres, petit bronzes, Artistic and Antique Iron Balconies and Doors. Etc.

Mxkhk collectibles — 72 items in Chandeliers, Fixtures, Sconces
Welcome to my eBay Store. Please add me to your list of favorite sellers. Thank you for your business.

J F PEGAN COMPANY — 71 items in Chandeliers, Fixtures, Sconces
SELLING BRASS CHANDELIERS, SCONCES, SHADES, NEWEL POST LIGHTING. RESTORATION OF ANTIQUE LIGHTING OVER 30 YEARS. BUILD CUSTOM VICTORIAN LIGHTING. WE ARE A UL LISTED SHOP. ALL LIGHTING MEETS UL CODES.

europeanlighting — 66 items in Chandeliers, Fixtures, Sconces
We specialize in European Antiques: Furniture, Chandeliers and Decorative items. Art Deco and Nouveau, French, French Country, Chippendale, English, Victorian are the styles we like to work with. We a...

LUZHARRY — 48 items in Chandeliers, Fixtures, Sconces
WELLCOME TO LUZHARRY ANTIQUES. WE SELL FURNITURE, ILUMINATION, PAINTS, BUST AND MORE, MORE....... PLEASE CHECK MY LIST. THANKS SO MUCH.

frenchcellartoattic — 35 items in Chandeliers, Fixtures, Sconces
Hello,you'll find in my shop a multitude of old objects,in good condition for decoration,installation of your home,even to supplement your collection.All these items are not current,some are rare,but ...

CAMMY'S ANTIQUES — 30 items in Chandeliers, Fixtures, Sconces
Victorian Antiques is an store that has been offering antique furniture, porcelains, bronzes, collectibles and chandeliers for more than 10 years in the Miami area. The store address is 5423 NW 74 A...

Mlmk92 collectibles — 26 items in Chandeliers, Fixtures, Sconces
Please add me to your list of favourite sellers and come again. I offer Prisms, Up to 22" Wide, Other, Other Figurines, Chandeliers, Fixtures, Sconces, and Other Glass.

Lamp Doctor Chandeliers and Sconces — 25 items in Chandeliers, Fixtures, Sconces
Welcome to the Lamp Doctor. We have 100s of Vintage and Antique Chandeliers, Sconces and Lamps. We also feature our original Custom Designed one of a kind theme Chandeliers, Sconces and Lamps that y...

Each one has at least one item in the selected category. Let's visit one of these eBay Stores. Cammy's Antiques looks intriguing:

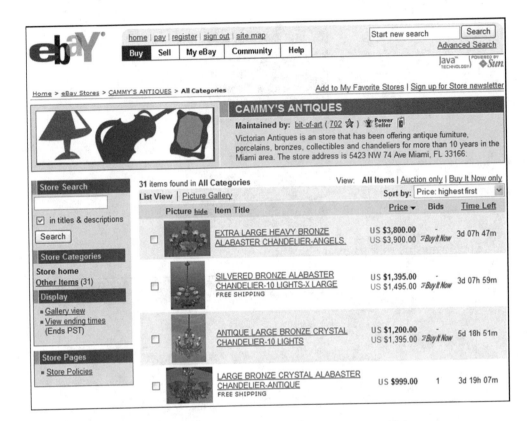

Another way to browse eBay Stores containing items matching a specific category (for example, Antiques > Architectural & Garden > Chandeliers, Fixtures, Sconces) is to navigate to the first page of that category. Then, look for the random selection of a few matching eBay Stores as well as the Shop eBay Stores link in the More on eBay box for that category.

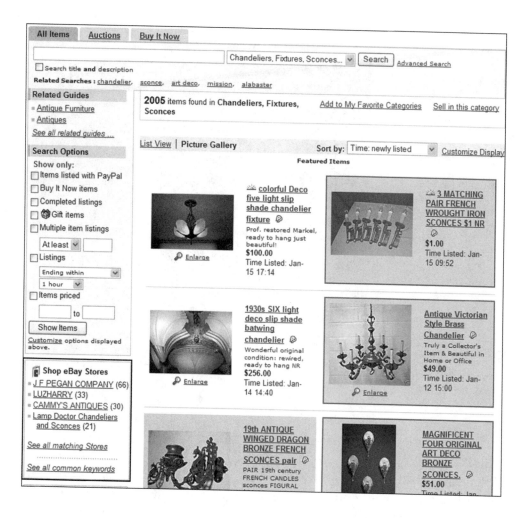

You can also get to an individual eBay Store by clicking on the red Stores icon next to a seller's User ID or by clicking the link "Visit my eBay Store!" found in that seller's eBay listings. (Only those sellers who have set up an eBay Store will display the Stores icon.)

Browsing is one-half of the eBay-shopping picture. When it comes to serious treasure hunting, most eBay shoppers rely on Search.

Searching eBay

Although casually browsing eBay Categories and eBay Stores can be a fun and rewarding way to hunt down treasure on eBay, it's not the most efficient option, in that it takes time and effort to scan through so many items. However, if you have a specific type of item in mind, an efficient and popular method for locating those items is Search.

Given that there are several million items on eBay at any given moment, tailoring and fine-tuning a search can help you locate the items you seek faster and more effectively. To hone your search to perfection, use the collection of search tools found on the Advanced Search page. To get there, click the "Advanced search" link on the upper right-hand corner of almost every eBay page.

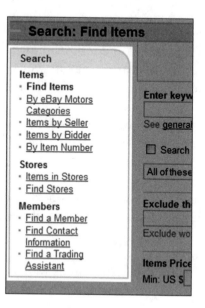

This will take you to the Search: Find Items page.

There are ten options for searching eBay:

Find Items (by keyword or item number)
By eBay Motors Categories*
Items by Seller
Items by Bidder
By Item Number
Items in Stores
Find Stores
Find a Member
Find Contact Information
Find Trading Assistant

Let's start with the single most popular way for searching eBay: Title Keyword Search.

SEARCHING BY TITLE—TITLE SEARCH

Title Search searches for keyword matches in the titles created by sellers for their items. To use Title Search, you type one or more keywords into any keyword search box. (The keywords used should relate to the type of item for which you are searching.)

The system then searches all listed item titles (within a single category or all of eBay, depending on your choice) and returns those that match your search.

Title searches can be as simple as typing one word and as complex as a long list of words and special commands. Let's explore the default search view for Search: Find Items.

Besides the text entry box, the Search: Find Items page provides six other filters to help you tailor or restrict the returned results of your Title Search.

In This Category

This feature limits the selected search to only one top-level category, an effective way to reduce large numbers of items to a targeted few.

Search Title and Description

Searches the contents of all item descriptions as well as titles. This is a great tool for increasing the number of returned results in cases where certain keywords

---

*eBay Motors is a separate eBay site for vehicles and vehicle accessories.

may not appear in the title (such as a model number or name), but it can also dramatically increase the returned results, sometimes by tens of thousands.

Completed Listings Only

This filter is a popular and valuable tool for viewing matching items that have closed within the last twenty-one days. If you are a seller, you will want to start using this tool for market research.

There is also a drop-down box for four keyword options: All of These Words, Any of These Words, Exact Phrase, and Exact Match Only.

Continuing, you can sort and filter by price range using Items Prices, by including or excluding sellers using From Sellers, by location, by currency, and by quantity (Multiple Item Listings). You can also filter for specific item attributes including Buy It Now items, items listed with PayPal as a payment options, free shipping, Get It Fast items, gift items, Giving Works items, items where the seller has provided the Best Offer feature, Classified Ads, Store Inventory only, and by ending and starting times by the hour. You can also filter by the number of bids.

Finally, you can sort the results using Sort By, View Results, and Results per Page to change the display and layout for returned results.

Sort By

Select an option here to sort the returned list of items by one of the five following options: "Time: ending soonest," "Time: newly listed," "Price: lowest first," "Price: highest first," and "Distance: nearest first."

NOTE: The "Distance: nearest first" option replaces the old "Search by region" feature, but don't despair: This is an improvement. Items in the sorted list will show those nearest to you first. The sort is based on the distance in miles between your zip code and the zip code of the seller.

View Results

There are three possible choices: All Items (displays all items, Gallery and non-Gallery alike), Picture Gallery (displays only those items for which the seller has added a Gallery image), and Show Item Numbers (displays the item number in a column to the left of item title).

Results per Page

Select from twenty-five, fifty, one hundred, or two hundred results per page.

We will use some of these options in a later example. For now, let's focus on the nuances of and tricks for creating effective Title Searches.

A Simple Title Search

Let's say you are looking for certain types of Beatles-related items. One way to find all the Beatles items at eBay is to type in the word *beatles* in the Title Search text entry box and then click the Search button.

This Title Search will return a list of all items that have the word *beatles* in their title. At the time of this writing, there were 19,296 matching items on eBay.

This page is called a Search Results page.

On the left-hand side of the page is the box Matching Categories, which, if you click the appropriate "More . . ." link, will show all of the matching subcategories for that particular main category. For searches that return a high volume of results, the Matching Categories feature can help narrow the range of your title keyword search to specific types of items. For example, you may be looking to add to your collection of Beatles movie memorabilia and not be interested in perusing Beatles recordings. In this case, the matching category link for Movie Memorabilia reduces the number of items you would otherwise need to scan from an overwhelming 19,296 down to a manageable 91.

If the matching category you seek doesn't appear in the Matching Categories box, try clicking the link "More . . ." under any of the top-level matching categories. For example, click the link "More . . ." under Entertainment Memorabilia to expand the section with other matching subcategories.

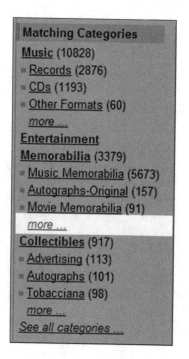

Now we view all of the matching subcategories for Entertainment Memorabilia.

The Matching Categories box is a handy tool for most Title Searches. But when you are looking for something specific, you can use some simple Title Search tips to focus the scope of your searches down to a few, or even just one item.

Tailoring a Simple Title Search

Many of these 19,296 Beatles-related items may not be on your treasure hunt list. For example, say you are looking for only old vinyl Beatles albums, not CDs or CD-ROMS or songbooks or videos. You can tailor your search by going back to the Search page and in the "Exclude these words" box, type in words such as *CD* and *CD-ROM*. Type each word with a space between them.

This reduces the number of items to 17,058 items—

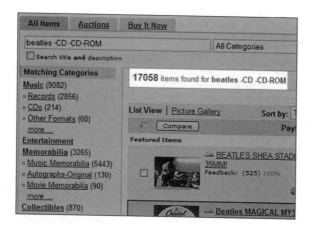

—still too many items to browse quickly. Let's add *book* and *poster* to the exclusion list.

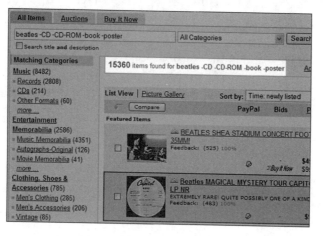

This trims the number of returned results to 15,360.

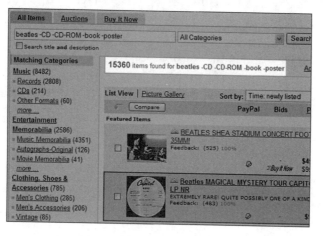

We show fewer items, but still too many to browse efficiently. We need to narrow this search down even more.

Let's add some other words to include, instead of exclude. We know we are looking for Beatles albums. What other words besides *album* would a seller use to describe such an item? *LP* and *vinyl* come to mind. But how do we add them?

Go back to the Search page. We'll keep our excluded words: *CD, CD-ROM, book,* and *poster,* and we'll expand our search words to the following: *beatles (lp,vinyl,album).*

Search: Find Items

Search

Favorite Searches: Screens & P

Items
- **Find Items**
- By eBay Motors Categories
- Items by Seller
- Items by Bidder
- By Item Number

Enter keyword or item number

beatles (lp,vinyl,album)

In this category

All Categories

See general search tips and advanced search commands.

☐ Search title **and** description   ☐ Completed listings or

All of these words ⌄

Stores
- Items in Stores
- Find Stores

Exclude these words

CD CD-ROM book poster

Exclude words from your search

Members
- Find a Member
- Find Contact Information
- Find a Trading Assistant

Items Priced

Min: US $ Max: US $

This is a more advanced search method. The words in parentheses form an "OR search." This search looks for all items that have *beatles* and *lp* OR *beatles* and *vinyl* OR *beatles* and *album*. Note the syntax:

word [space] (word[comma]word[comma]word)

There are no spaces between the words and commas inside the parentheses.

The results for this more detailed Title Search show 2,917 matching items.

This is a much easier list to scroll through. Still, we could continue to tweak this search by adding keywords to the OR list or the excluded list and reduce the results to an even more manageable number.

Once you have tailored a Title Search to your liking, you can save it on your My eBay Favorites page by looking on the top of the first page of returned results for the link "Add to Favorites."

Effective Title Search Tips from eBay

- Try as many related keyword words as possible.
  What keywords would you use to describe the item if you were selling it?
- **Use more than one specific keyword to target your search.**
  As we have seen above, *beatles poster* will return fewer and more targeted listings than a search for *beatles*.

- **Use conjunctions and articles (*and, or, the, a*) carefully.**
  Use *and, or, the,* and *a* only if you're searching for items containing these words—for example, *Tommy James and the Shondells* or *Truth or Dare* or *A Beautiful Mind*. If the number of returned matches is too low, try the search minus the conjunction or article.
- **Use punctuation only when required.**
  For example, you'll be successful if you search for *Elvis T-shirt* (correct punctuation with hyphen) or *Elvis tee shirt* (correct wording without hyphen). But don't try *Elvis: T-shirt* (unnecessary colon) or *Elvis-tee-shirt* (incorrect hyphens).
- **Use an asterisk to perform a "wildcard" search that includes plural forms of nouns and alternative endings.**
  If searching for diamond rings doesn't return enough matches, find more items with little overlap by entering *diamond ring**.
  Using the asterisk, you can also search for items with multiple endings. For example: *Beatles man** would return items such as *Beatles manager, Beatles mania, Beatles Nowhere Man*, and so on.
- **Increase your results by selecting the "Search titles and descriptions" option.**
  Search always looks in the title of the items for sale to find the keywords that you specify. You can find many more items by searching both the title and the description for each item. Just click on the option "Search titles and descriptions" under the search box.
- **Search for exact phrases using quotation marks (" ").**
  Typing *"Statue of Liberty"* or *"Gone with the Wind"* inside quotes will find items with those exact words in sequence. Without the quotation marks, you could wind up with many other listings containing the words *statue* or *liberty*.
- **Use the minus sign (–) to narrow your search.**
  For example, *antique –lamp* tells the search engine to include the word *antique* but not *lamp*. Remember there's no space after the sign (e.g., *–card, –teddy*).
- **Sort your results by starting date, ending date, or price.**
  After you see the results of your search, you can use the sort menu to rank these items by starting date, ending date, or bid price. The drop-down sort menu is right above your search results.
- **For the closest matches, specify a date, color, or brand.**
  For example, to find a particular Barbie item, don't just type *Barbie* in the

search box. If you are looking for a Barbie dress made in the 1960s, enter *Barbie dress 196**. If you want only red dresses, type *Barbie red dress*. The trick is to be specific and use a narrowly defined search!

SEARCH COMMAND CHART

The following advanced search commands will work for any eBay Title Search:

To Search For	Use the Command	Example
One word **AND** another	Use space between words	**baseball autograph** Returns items with the words *baseball* **and** *autograph* in the title
One word **OR** another	(word 1,word 2) *Attention: No spaces after the comma!*	**(baseball,autograph)** Returns all items with the words *baseball* **or** *autograph* in the title
EXACTLY these words	"word 1 word 2"	**"baseball autograph"** Returns items with **exactly** the words *baseball* and *autograph,* in that specific order, separated by a space, in the title
One word **BUT NOT** another	– (minus symbol) *Attention: No spaces after the minus sign!*	**baseball –autograph** Returns items containing the word *baseball* and will **exclude** all items containing the word *autograph* in the title
One word **BUT NOT SEVERAL** others	–(word 1,word 2,word 3) *Attention: No spaces after the minus sign or the comma!*	**baseball –(autograph,card, star)** Returns items containing word *baseball* and will **exclude all** items containing the words *autograph, card,* and *star* in the title
Any words starting with a **SPECIFIC SEQUENCE OF LETTERS**	* (asterisk symbol)	**base*** Returns items with **words starting** with *base,* such as *baseball* card, *baseball* cap, and *iron bases*

SEARCH COMMAND CHART *(continued)*

To Search For	Use the Command	Example
Words **OUT OF A GROUP**	@1 word 1 word 2 word 3	**@1 baseball autograph card** Returns all items containing **two out of the three words** specified. This example will return items containing the words *baseball* and *autograph*, *baseball* and *card*, or *autograph* and *card* in the title. You can try searching for three words out of four by using @2 in the beginning of the command.
One word **ALONG WITH AN ADVANCED SEARCH**	+ (plus symbol) *Attention: No spaces after the plus sign!*	**@1 baseball autograph card +star** Returns items containing two out of the three words specified **plus** the word *star* in the title.

You can also use any of these commands to search item descriptions by clicking on the option to "Search titles and descriptions" under the search box.

TITLE SEARCHING TIPS (SMART SEARCH)

Misspellings

Most sellers take great pains to ensure that their title keywords are spelled correctly. Then there are those sellers for whom spelling has always been a challenge. These sellers often spell keywords incorrectly. This can decrease the potential for a high price for that item since the misspelling will prevent the item from appearing in most Title Search results—bad news for the seller, but good news for the crafty eBay treasure hunter (that's you!).

An effective way to take advantage of these unfortunate spelling errors is to regularly run Title Searches using the most common misspellings of the appropriate keywords—for example, singular versus plural.

Sellers may list many types of items as plural or singular. As shown above in "Effective Title Search Tips from eBay," the use of the singular root of a word along with the wildcard asterisk in place of the *s* or *es* for the plural will return both singular and plural forms of a specific keyword.

Creating a Custom-Tailored Title Search—
Another Example Using Item Location

Let's explore how to custom-tailor a title search to find only those items that are located near me.

Let's say I was looking to purchase a good used grand piano (preferably from a local seller here in the Bay Area of San Jose, California). I start by going to the Advanced Search page and I enter the words *grand* and *piano* in the Search Title box. Then I scroll down toward the bottom of the page, check the "Items near me" box, and select an acceptable distance from my zip code (twenty-five miles—I am not willing to travel too far from home).

Note that my zip code was automatically filled in. Once you sign in to eBay, the system automatically inserts the zip code of your registration address directly into the box provided.

After I click the "Search" button, the eBay search engine returns the following results:

Home > All Categories > Search Results for 'grand piano'

| All Items | Auctions | Buy It Now | | Sign in to see your customized search options |

grand piano | All Categories | Search | Advanced Search
☐ Search title **and** description

Matching Categories
Musical Instruments (437)
· Keyboard, Piano (427)
· Sheet Music, Song Books (6)
· Other Instruments (2)
  more ...
Collectibles (86)
· Decorative Collectibles (47)
· Holiday, Seasonal (6)
· Clocks (5)
  more ...
Jewelry & Watches (68)
· Charms & Charm Bracelets (37)
· Vintage, Antique (9)
· Jewelry Boxes & Supplies (5)
  more ...
See all categories ...

Search Options
Show only:
☐ Items listed with PayPal
☐ Buy It Now items
☐ Gift items
☐ Items listed as lots
☐ Completed listings
☐ Listings
  Starting today
☐ Items priced
  to
Show Items
Customize options displayed above.

743 items found for **grand piano**   · Add to Favorites

List View | Picture Gallery   Sort by: Time: ending soonest   Customize Display

Compare	Item Title	PayPal	Price	Bids	Time Left ▲
Featured Items					
☐	VERY RARE ANTIQUE 1867-1880 VIENNA GRAND PIANO by F. BLUMEL of VIENNA (PRIZE MEDAL, LONDON 1862)		$7,999.97 $8,499.98 *Buy It Now*	-	2h 42m
Optimize your selling success! Find out how to promote your items					
☐	HEY LOOKIE HERE~Black Baby Grand Piano w/ Bench		$9.99	2	2m
☐	1911 Steinway Miniature Grand Piano Vintage Ad		$6.99	-	2m
☐	Doll Furniture Brown Wood Grand Piano		$0.99	-	13m
☐	L@@K NOW! Pink Baby Grand Piano w/Bench!! W@W!!		$9.99 $24.95 *Buy It Now*	-	28m
☐	GREAT 1912 Steinway "ORPHEUS' LEGIONS" GRAND PIANO AD		$2.50	1	39m
☐	Miniature Desk Clock MINI BABY GRAND STYLE PIANO Black		$9.90	-	42m
☐	1920 AD Steinway Grand Piano New York Play Piano		$36.00	14	43m

In the San Jose area at the time I ran this search, 743 items had the words *grand* and *piano*. Some of the items are actual pianos, but a few are not; for example, the clock in the shape of a grand piano. I can filter out all the items that are not musical instruments by clicking the link to the left for "Keyboard, Piano" under Matching Categories. The "(427)" next to the link gives the number of items within that category that contain the words *grand* and *piano* in their title.

Saving a Search with My eBay

Instead of running this search manually every day, I can save it in my My eBay Favorites page and elect for the eBay e-mail system to alert me when a seller within a twenty-five-mile radius of my zip code lists an item matching my title search criteria. To do so, I click the link "Add to Favorites" (found in the upper right-hand side of the page).

This takes us to a page for setting the options for the saved search:

We can make this a new search or replace an existing search in the drop-down list. Let's give this search a new name, "grand piano," and we'll check the box for "E-mail me daily for . . ." selecting a duration from the drop-down list. Then, with a click of the "Save search" button, this new search will be inserted into my My eBay on the My Favorite Searches page in alphabetical order.

For the next 180 days, eBay will automatically send me an e-mail alert (once a day) when new items matching my search criteria are added to the site.

NOTE: You can save up to one hundred separate Favorite Searches in "My eBay" and you can check up to six Favorite Searches checked for e-mail alerts.

There are other ways of searching using the eBay Search page. Some of them may come in handy for you in the future.

Advanced Searching

Besides the "Exclude the words" and "Items near me" options, the advanced search option page provides several other advanced filters for Title Search. For keyword searches, the drop-down box returns three options:

- "All these words" (returns listings with all the provided keywords in their title in any order)
- "Any of these words" (returns listings with at least one of the provided keywords)
- "Exact phrase" (only returns listings with all of the keywords in the exact order provided)
- "Exact match only"

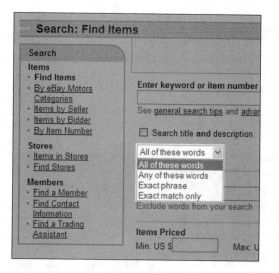

"Items Priced" lets you filter results by a price range.

"From Sellers" lets you include or exclude up to ten seller IDs.

As we saw earlier, you can also use the Items Near Me feature in Location to locate items near you based on the number of miles from you and your zip or postal code. In addition to search based on locations in miles from a zip code, you can also search based on the location in miles from a popular city.

Location also lets you select one of three options:

- Item on eBay.com
- Items located in a specific country (based on seller location)
- Items available to a specific country (based on the shipping preferences selected by the seller when listing the item)

Use the Currency search option to select a specific currency from the drop-down list. By selecting the default, "Any currency," your search will cover all eBay global sites including the United States. If you select a currency from the drop-down box, your search will be limited to the eBay country site for that currency.

Multiple Item Listings helps you pinpoint multiple quantities of an item by number as well as those items listed as lots.

What is a "lot"? A lot is a group of similar or identical items that are for sale together to one buyer (a case of batteries, three dresses, a CD collection, a pallet of shoes, etc.).

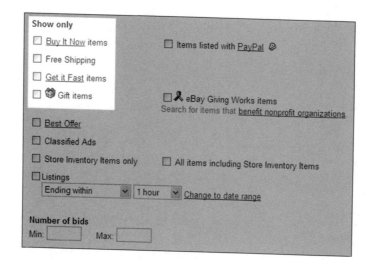

Show Only filters return item results by format (Buy It Now or Auction), payment method ("Items listed with PayPal"), free shipping (for items where the seller has indicated "Free shipping"), Get It Fast (for items where the seller is offering expedited shipping), and gift items (items for which the seller will provide or offer extra services such as gift wrapping, gift card, and expedited shipping directly to the gift recipient).

In addition, a new filter was recently added for the eBay Giving Works, which will limit the results to only those items benefiting nonprofit organizations.

You can also filter your search to include only those items where the seller is offering the Best Offer* feature, items listed in the Classified Ad format (like real estate or services), Store inventory items only, listing end times, or number of minimum and maximum bids.

Show only

☐ Buy It Now items   ☐ Items listed with PayPal
☐ Free Shipping
☐ Get it Fast items
☐ Gift items   ☐ eBay Giving Works items
                            Search for items that benefit nonprofit organizations

☐ Best Offer
☐ Classified Ads
☐ Store Inventory Items only   ☐ All items including Store Inventory Items
☐ Listings
   Ending within ▾   1 hour ▾   Change to date range

Number of bids
Min: [____]   Max: [____]

---

*Sellers may, at their discretion, add a Best Offer option to their Fixed Price or Buy It Now listings. A buyer can submit their best offer for any item displaying the "Best offer" button. The seller can accept the offer, reject it, or supply a counteroffer.)

By eBay Motor Categories

Use this search to locate items in eBay Motors.

Search: By eBay Motors Categories

Customize search options

Search

Items
- Find Items
- By eBay Motors Categories
- Items by Seller
- Items by Bidder
- By Item Number

Stores
- Items in Stores
- Find Stores

Members
- Find a Member
- Find Contact Information
- Find a Trading Assistant

Favorite Searches: grand piano Go

This feature is currently limited to eBay Motors categories. More categories may be added in the future.

What are you looking for?
Cars & Trucks
Motorcycles
Parts & Accessories
Powersports

Vehicle make
Any

Vehicle model
Any

Vehicle year
From: To:

Transmission type
Any

Enter keyword or item number

☐ Search title and description   ☐ Completed listings only

Items near me
☐ Items within 500 miles of
ZIP or Postal Code 95116 or Select a popular city...

Sort by
Time: ending soonest

View results
All items

Results per page
50

Search   Clear search

Items by Seller

To search for items listed by a specific seller, click the link "Items by Seller."

Search: Items by Seller

Search

Items
- Find Items
- By eBay Motors Categories
- **Items by Seller**
- Items by Bidder
- By Item Number

Stores
- Items in Stores
- Find Stores

Members
- Find a Member
- Find Contact Information
- Find a Trading Assistant

Enter seller's User ID

uncle_griff

Find items offered by a particular seller.

☐ Include completed listings   Last 30 days ▾

☐ Include bidders' and buyers' email addresses
(Only available if you are the seller of the listed items.)

☑ Show close and exact User ID matches

Sort by   Results per page
Time: ending soonest ▾   50 ▾

Search

The options for an "Items by Seller" search are:

Include completed listings. Selecting one of the options here will limit the results to closed listings from a specific period from "Last Day" to "Last 30 Days."

Include bidder's e-mail addresses. This option is restricted to a seller searching on her own User ID for a list of her listings. This is a useful tool for garnering e-mail addresses for the high bidders of each closed listing in order to send e-mail notices or invoices.

Results per page. If you have a slow dial-up Internet connection, set this option to fifty or lower, since anything higher may take a longer time to display, especially if the seller has hundreds of items listed. If, however, you have a high-speed connection through DSL, cable, or some other high-speed or broadband connection, you may want to select a higher number of items displayed per page. Choose the number per page from the drop-down box.

Items by Bidder

Just as you can search items by seller, you can also search for items by bidder.

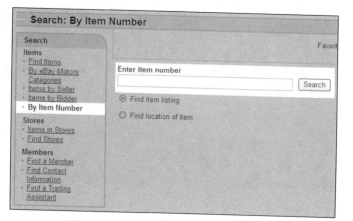

You have the option of including completed listings (last thirty days) by any bidder or for high bidders only, and for the number of results displayed on one page. Note the "Results per page" option of "All items on one page."

Searching by Item Number

If you know an item's number, you can reach it quickly by typing it into the same keyword text box used for typing in keywords. You can also click the "By Item Number" link in the Search box and enter the item number.

Click the "Search" button to go directly to that item page.

Items in Stores

This search is identical to the Find Items search with one added filter: "Items in Stores."

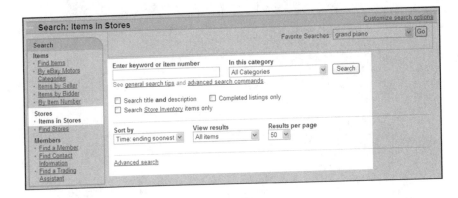

NOTE: The items that are specifically listed in eBay Stores are not included in a regular Find Items search. Use this Title Search to find store items.

As more and more eBay shoppers spend more and more time shopping eBay Stores for great items at good value, they are relying more and more on this option.

Find Stores

This is a versatile tool for using keywords or a store name to look for stores with matching items or store name and descriptions.

Members

The Members section provides three options for finding other members.

Find a Member

To locate another member, enter their User ID (or if you know it, their e-mail address). This will take you to either their feedback profile or, if the User ID or e-mail address does not belong to a registered user, a page that will alert you of such.

Find Contact Information

This search will return the name, city, zip code, and phone number of another member, but only if you and the other member are the buyer and seller (or seller and buyer) in a recent or current transaction.

Enter the User ID of the member and then the item number of the transaction.

In the interest of fairness and full disclosure, whenever a member requests another member's contact information, both parties automatically receive the contact information of the other member.

Find a Trading Assistant

Trading Assistants are eBay sellers who sell for others on consignment. If you have something you want to sell on eBay but you don't have the time, experience, or inclination, you may want to find an eBay Trading Assistant in your area who can sell the item for you.

This covers the options for Advanced Search. If none of these search options returns results, you may want to use the eBay Want It Now feature to tell sellers what it is you seek so they can list matching items on eBay.

Want It Now

What if you know what you want but cannot find it on eBay, even after searching entire categories? You can use a recently introduced tool called Want It Now.

With Want It Now, you can alert all sellers on eBay about the exact type of item or items for which you are searching. Go to the Want It Now page by clicking the link on the home page under the Category section:

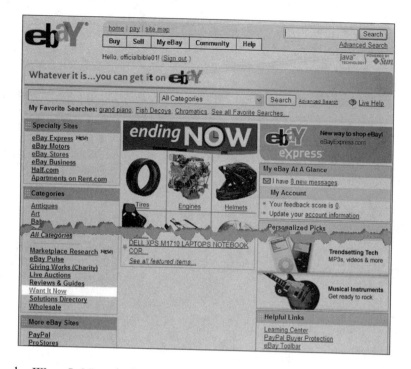

On the Want It Now hub page, click the button "Post To Want It Now."

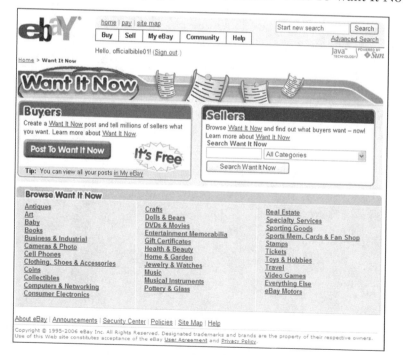

Enter in a title and description for the item you want.

eBay®

home | pay | site map

| Buy | Sell | My eBay | Community | Help |

Start new search   Search

Advanced Search

Java™ TECHNOLOGY / ◆Sun POWERED BY

Hello, officialbible01! (Sign out.)

Home > Buy > Want It Now > Create a Post

Help

Want It Now: Create a Post

Tell millions of sellers what you're looking for and get responses emailed to you. It's **free**. Learn more about Want It Now.

I am searching for

Dodge Aspen or Plymouth Volare Station Wagon

Tip: Be specific. Think of words sellers might use to search for your post.
11 characters left.

Category

eBay Motors Vehicles ▾

Choose the best category to help sellers find your item.
If you prefer, you may specify a category number instead.

Describe it in more detail

Perfect condition only.
No rust or damage
1976 - 1980
Slant Six
Station Wagon only

Tip: Be as detailed as possible; specify brand, condition, color, size, price range, etc. See examples.
408 characters left.

Important posting tips

eBay Motors Vehicles

For better results, include the following in your post:

- Condition
- Year
- Distinguishing features
- Model/part number
- Type of vehicle
- Make and model
- Body style and type
- Package or series

Picture (optional)

[   ] Browse...

Preview picture

Click the "Post To Want It Now" button and your Want It Now post is confirmed with an actual number!

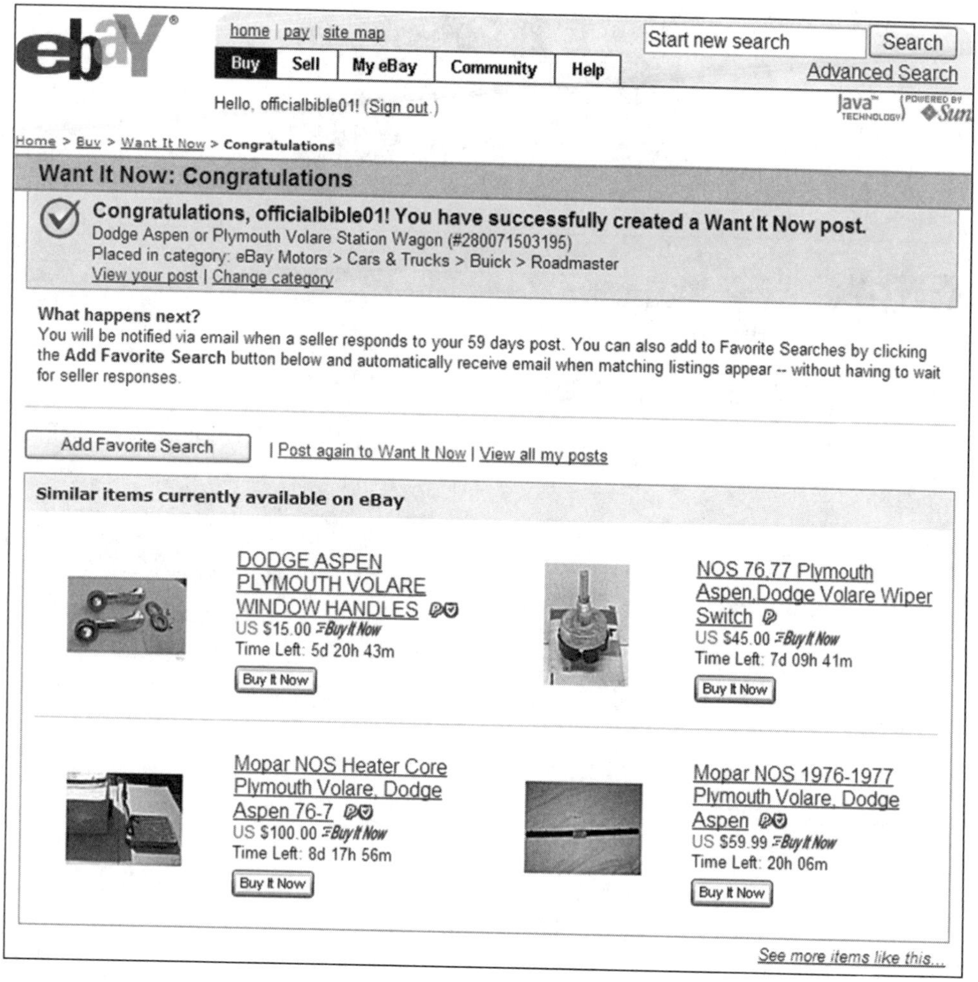

Click "View Your Post" to view it.

Want It Now: Congratulations

✓ **Congratulations, officialbible**
Dodge Aspen or Plymouth Volare Sta
Placed in category: eBay Motors > C
View your post | Change category

---

eBay®   home | pay | site map   Start new search | Search |
                                                            Advanced Search
[Buy | Sell | My eBay | Community | Help]

         Hello, officialbible01! (Sign out.)   Java™ (POWERED BY
                                                      TECHNOLOGY ◆Sun

Home > Buy > Want It Now > eBay Motors > Cars & Trucks > Buick > Roadmaster

| **Dodge Aspen or Plymouth Volare Station Wagon** | Post number: 280071503195 |

You are signed in

Edit this post
Delete this post

Responses:	0 responses	Time left:	**59 days 22 hours**	**Buyer information**
	[Respond >]	Date placed:	Jan-16-07 22:28:04 PST	Feedback Score: 0
				Member since Nov-27-06 in United States
				Ask a question about this post
		Location:	San Jose , CA United States	

Description

Perfect condition only.
No rust or damage
Upholstery must be in better than good condition
Any mileage considered
1976 - 1980
Slant Six only
Station Wagon only

Responses

There are no responses to this post.

Ready to respond with a listing?

You can sell an item like this one or provide the item number of an existing listing on eBay. Just click the **Respond** button. Learn more about Want It Now.

[Respond >]

The post will remain on the site for thirty days. Others can see your location, feedback score, and your "Member since" status. If a seller has an item listed on eBay that matches your want, he clicks the respond button and fills in the information.

Home > Buy > Want It Now > eBay Motors > Cars & Trucks > Buick > Roadmaster

Dodge Aspen or Plymouth Volare Station Wagon

Post number: 280071503195

Responses:	0 responses				

Respond >

Time left:	59 days 22 hours	**Buyer information**
Date placed:	Jan-16-07 22:28:04 PST	Feedback Score: 0
		Member since Nov-27-06 in United States
Location:	San Jose , CA United States	Ask a question about this post

Description

Perfect condition only.
No rust or damage
Upholstery must be in better than good condition
Any mileage considered
1976 - 1980
Slant Six only
Station Wagon only

---

ebaY®

home | pay | site map

| Buy | Sell | My eBay | Community | Help |

Hello, uncle_griff! (Sign out)

Start new search   Search

Advanced Search

Java™ TECHNOLOGY ◆Sun

Home > Buy > Want It Now > Respond

Want It Now: Respond

Help

Dodge Aspen or Plymouth Volare Station Wagon

Please note: The Want It Now post you are responding to is not a legally binding contract. There is no guarantee that the buyer will purchase your item. Learn more about Want It Now.

Haven't listed your item yet?	or	**Is the item already listed on eBay?**

1. Click the **Sell Your Item** button below.
2. List the item as you normally would.
3. Your item will be automatically added as a response to this post and an email will be sent to the buyer.

Sell Your Item >

Enter the item number of an item that is already listed for sale on eBay.

Item number

Don't know the item number? View the items you're selling in a new window.

Respond To Post >

The seller can either list his matching item right away or provide the item number of a matching item from his current eBay listings.

Sellers can view lists of Want It Now items by category from the same Want It Now hub page.

Your wanted post is now available for all sellers to view, and if they list a matching item, they can send you an e-mail alerting you of the listing. One note: The seller never sees your e-mail address or User ID. You, of course, can view the item and the seller's User ID (but not her e-mail address). This provides a solid wall of security to help avoid spam and unsolicited offers to purchase outside of eBay.

Using these search tips, filters and tools, you can hunt for eBay treasure with the precision of a shark! Pam Withers, an avid eBay buyer, sent me the following story about finding a long-lost item on eBay:

> When I was about five, I received a wooden apple as a gift. No big deal . . . but the apple contained a little wooden tea set. It was adorable . . . and I lost it! I had looked for many years (I am now fifty-four) to find one like it, to no avail. Then, one day, I asked about this little wooden apple tea set on eBay and was amazed to get a response. The funny part of this story is that my last name is Withers and so was the seller's. However, the seller thought that I was his daughter, who lived in the same town, and was just trying to play games! Imagine his (and my) surprise after returning e-mails a couple times when we got to the bottom of the whole thing! I still laugh when I think about his response to my first e-mail to him after learning that he had what I wanted. Thinking I was his daughter, he simply mailed back an e-mail that said, "Why don't you come over and look at it?" After he received my response to that e-mail, he e-mailed me again, explaining how he had been thinking I was his daughter. He was very embarrassed! . . . Call it luck or coincidence . . . he had the wooden apple tea set and I bought it. By the way, even though we have the same last name, we are not related. Ain't life amazing?

Now that you know, like Pam, how to browse and search for your heart's desire, it's time to learn how, once you have found it, to bid for or buy it!

4

Shopping on eBay—
Buy It!

Now that you know how to search and browse eBay like an expert, you are ready to start shopping!

Most hard-core Internet users will agree—online shopping, and in particular shopping at eBay, is the most fun anyone can have on a computer. The exquisite thrill of hunting for, bidding on, and winning your first eBay purchase never really fades, even after many years of eBay buying! I started buying on eBay back in 1996 and have never stopped enjoying it, and I have a house overflowing with eBay-bought treasure to prove it.

You discover a priceless treasure you cannot live without. Your bidding finger is sweaty with anticipation. You gotta have it. You just can't wait to get a bid in.

Stop right there! You should never just rush in and bid or buy. To ensure that your eBay buying experience is safe and satisfying, you must always do a quick bit of homework before you bid or buy.

eBay shopper Sharon Maracci had a bit of shock when she learned her eBay purchase was thousands of miles away.

I wanted to buy a discontinued Fisher-Price toddler bed for my niece. I had bid on several on eBay but was always outbid at the last minute. I couldn't afford to bid too much because I knew shipping would be very high.

Finally I was the high bidder for the bed by going over what I could afford, only to find out that the bed was all the way in New York. When I wrote the seller about my concern over shipping, she wrote back, "I actually am selling the bed because I'm moving. I just got a job offer from Cisco in Silicon Valley. If that's anywhere near you, I'll throw the bed in the moving van and you can get it when I arrive." I said sure.

Two weeks later, I got a call. The seller had been given temporary housing by Cisco in an apartment complex less than a mile from my house in Campbell. Now my niece is sleeping in that bed that came to her all the way from New York shipped courtesy of Cisco.

(And I have a really cute picture of my niece in the bed!)

Sharon lucked out this time, as the seller of the bed was more than happy to help resolve her shipping problem (eBay sellers can be very accommodating), but the lesson of the story is to always ask a seller about shipping details before you submit a bid or commit to an outright purchase. This is just one of the important items on our eBay Safe Trading Checklist, which we will outline in detail later in this chapter.

First, let's shop for something specific. My friend's birthday is coming up and I would like to buy him a new, brand-name 4.0 megapixel digital camera. I want to pay for it with PayPal. My budget cap is $400. I don't want to bid for one, so I want to search for Buy It Now listings only.

Let's start on the eBay home page in the Cameras & Photo category.

Then, I click the link "Digital Cameras."

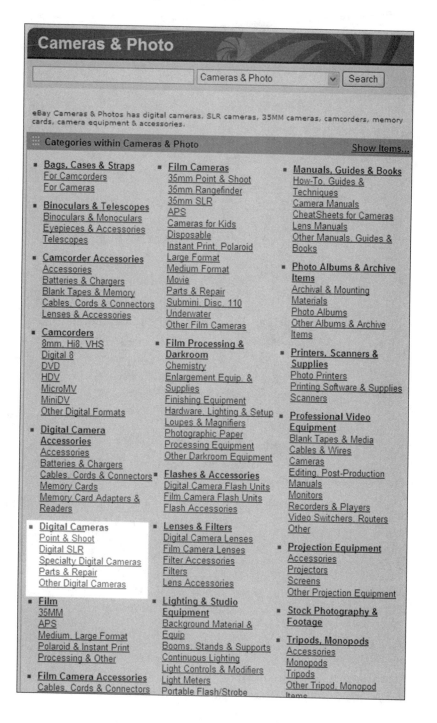

This gives us all 31,266 items currently listed in that category.

Let's filter out all the Auction-only items by clicking the "Buy It Now" tab on the top of the results page.

Let's continue to filter the results using our search criteria with the Digital Cameras Finder. I don't really have a camera type in mind, so I'll leave that set to the default, "Any." Same with "Brand" and "Optical Zoom," but I do know that the camera should be at least 4.0 megapixels and I only want to view new cameras, so I select those options and click "Show Items."

This leaves 393 items to browse . . . but we are not done yet. Scroll down to the Search Options box and check "Items listed with PayPal" and enter our price range, $0 to $400. Then click the "Show Items" button.

We have filtered the results down to only those items that meet our specific search criteria. Using eBay's Compare Items feature, we can select the best examples, compare them side-by-side in an easy-to-read column format, and pick the best one. To display the Compare Item check boxes, click the link "Customize Display" . . .

. . . and select the option "Show comparison check boxes," then click "Apply Changes."

Now you see a row of check boxes to the left of each item's Gallery image.

These check boxes allow us to mark and save items in which we are interested so that we can line them up and compare them.

I browse through the two pages of items and select four cameras by checking their boxes. Each one may be a good candidate for consideration. Then I scroll down to the bottom of the page and click the "Compare" button.

This lines up all my selected listings so that I can more easily compare for item features, prices, shipping options, and individual sellers (based on their feedback numbers and percentage of positive comments).

Compare Items

Watch All   Remove All   Sort by: Order Selected: recent first ▼

Item	Remove Item	Remove Item	Remove Item	Remove Item
	+ 1GB ~NEW~ NIKON COOLPIX L4 4MP DIGITAL CAMERA +3 BONUS +1GB Buy It Now Watch this Item	Sony Cyber-shot DSC-S40 Digital Camera & DPP-FP30 NEW Buy It Now Make Offer Watch this Item	Canon PowerShot A520 4.0 Megapixel Brand New In Box Buy It Now Make Offer Watch this Item	PANASONIC LEICA DMC- LC 43 4.0 MEGAPIXEL 3X ZOOM HIGH Q Bid Now! Buy It Now Watch this Item
Time Left	2 days 9 hours	2 days 23 hours	5 days 5 hours	6 days 2 hours
Bids	Purchases			0 bids
Seller	emilyandlily (192102 ⭐) 99.6% Positive ⭐Power Seller	miamilakestrade (520 ⭐) 99.8% Positive	superdrew99 (187 ⭐) 98.4% Positive	charles a one (25 ⭐) 100% Positive
Price	US $124.85 ⊐Buy It Now	US $145.00 ⊐Buy It Now or Best Offer	US $139.99 ⊐Buy It Now or Best Offer	US $169.95 US $169.95 ⊐Buy It Now
Shipping to 95125, USA	US $19.99 UPS Ground (Plus optional insurance) 🏷 Shipping discounts available for multiple purchases.	US $21.87 UPS Ground	US $19.99 US Postal Service First Class Mail	US $25.95 UPS Standard United States
Ships From	United States	United States	United States	Canada
Payment Methods	PayPal Money order/Cashiers check	PayPal	PayPal	PayPal Money order/Cashiers check
PayPal Buyer Protection	Yes	Yes	Yes	No
Digital Cameras				
Digital Camera Type	Point & Shoot	Point & Shoot	Point & Shoot	
Digital Camera Brand	Nikon	Sony	Canon	
Product Line	Nikon Coolpix	Sony Cyber-Shot	Canon PowerShot	
Model	L4	DSC-S40, DSC-S40 with DPP-FP30 Digital Photo Printer	A520	
Resolution	4	4.1	4	
Manufacturer Part Number	25546, COOLPIXL4	DSCS40/DPP	9715A001, 9715A001AA, 9715A001BA, 9715A005, 9715A016, 9715A043	
Bundled Kits	Camera Bag, Extra Battery, Extra Memory	Camera Bag	--	
Optical Zoom	3x	3x	4x	
Digital Zoom	4x	2x	3.6x	
Manufacturer Warranty	Yes	--	Yes	
Flash Type	Built-in flash	Built-in flash	Built-in flash	
Memory Card Format	SD Memory Card	Integrated, Memory Stick	MultiMediaCard	
Battery Type	2 x AA alkaline battery (included)	2 x AA alkaline battery	2 x AA alkaline battery (included)	
Condition	New, Never Opened	New, Never Opened	New, Never Opened	
Return Policy				
Item must be returned within		7 Days		
Return Policy Details		Returns accepted if the item is defective or DOA.		
Refund will be given as		Money Back		
Return Policy				
Item must be returned within				7 Days
Return Policy Details				Refund or Exchange within 7 Days after delivery. S&H is non-refundable. Buyer is responsible for return shipping and insurance cost. Buyer needs to contact us within 7 days at www.info@charlsgiftstore.com for RMA# (Return Merchandise Authorization Number) before sending item(s) back Thanks Charles

Refund will be given as				Money Back
Digital Cameras				
Digital Camera Type				Point & Shoot
Digital Camera Brand				Panasonic
Resolution				4
Bundled Kits				Camera Bag, Lens Cleaning Kit, Memory Reader
Optical Zoom				3x
Manufacturer Warranty				Yes
Condition				New, Never Opened
	Remove Item	Remove Item	Remove Item	Remove Item

Watch All   Remove All

After comparing prices, shipping, packages, and sellers, I decide on this camera:

Compare Items

Watch All   Remove All

	Remove Item	Remo
Item	+ 1GB ~NEW~ NIKON COOLPIX L4 4MP DIGITAL CAMERA +3 BONUS +1GB Buy It Now Watch this Item	Son S40 Bu
Time Left	2 days 9 hours	2 days
Bids	Purchases	
Seller	emilyandlily (192102) 99.6% Positive Power Seller	miami (520 me
Price	US $124.85 =BuyItNow	US $1
Shipping to 95125, USA	US $19.99 UPS Ground (Plus optional insurance) Shipping discounts available for multiple purchases.	US $2 UPS
Ships From	United States	United
Payment Methods	PayPal Money order/Cashiers check	PayPal
PayPal Buyer Protection	Yes	Yes

I like that the shipping cost is less than $20 and that the seller is including a 1 gigabyte SD memory card. If I click on the title, it takes me directly to the item page:

If you're like me, you're impatient. You want to click that "Buy It Now" button right now! But you shouldn't ever rush into a purchase. We need to inspect the merchandise and the seller's terms of service a bit more closely first.

Before You Bid or Buy—a Safe Trading Checklist

We still need to learn a few things about the listing and the seller before we actually commit to bidding on or buying this camera. Enter the Safe Trading Checklist:

✔ Check the seller's Feedback.
✔ Read the Item Description page thoroughly.

- Is there a reserve?
- Is there a Buy It Now option?
- How many items are offered?
- How much time is left?

✔ Examine the photos.

✔ Read and understand the seller's TOS (Terms of Service).
  - What types of payment does the seller accept?
  - Does the seller offer escrow?
  - Does the seller offer a return or refund policy?
  - Does the seller ship internationally?
  - Does the seller have special requirements?
  - Does the seller have specific time limits for contact and receiving payment?

Eventually, this simple checklist should become second nature, but till then, keep it handy whenever you are shopping on eBay. Let's apply the checklist to our digital camera listing.

✔ CHECK THE SELLER'S FEEDBACK

Start off by scanning the box Meet the Seller:

This box tells us a lot about the seller. She has a feedback score of 192,122. That's 192,122 unique positive comments received from other eBay members since she started on eBay, minus any and all unique negative comments (more on feedback scoring later). Her positive feedback rating is 99.6 percent, which is extremely good. She registered on eBay on February 10, 2003. All together, these feedback statistics are reassuring, but we can (and should) go deeper by reading the seller's complete Feedback Profile.

To read a seller's Feedback Profile, click either the number in parentheses next to the seller's User ID or the link "Read feedback comments."

Make this a habit. Before you do anything, before you read through the item description or start figuring how much you are willing to spend, and for heaven's sake, before you bid or buy, always check the seller's Feedback Profile first.

⬅ Back to your last item   Home > Community > Feedback Forum > Member Profile

Member Profile: emilyandlily (192122 ⭐) ⚡ Power Seller 🔲

Feedback Score:	192122
Positive Feedback:	99.6%

Members who left a positive:	192854
Members who left a negative:	743
All positive feedback received:	212804

Learn about what these numbers mean.

Recent Ratings:

		Past Month	Past 6 Months	Past 12 Months
⊕	positive	11342	59088	102060
◎	neutral	228	1276	2156
⊖	negative	18	65	96

Bid Retractions (Past 6 months): 0

Member since: Feb-10-03
Location: United States
- ID History
- Items for Sale
- Visit my Store
- Add to Favorite Sellers
- View My World page
- View my Reviews & Guides

Contact Member

Feedback Received | From Buyers | From Sellers | Left for Others

221195 feedback received by emilyandlily (3150 ratings mutually withdrawn)   Page 1 of 8848

Comment	From	Date / Time	Item #
⊕ Received item was good. Like camera should have said camera was refurbished.	Buyer virnafaye (3)	Jan-18-07 13:29	180070224986
⊕ thank you! great camera but having trouble with the dock charger any ideas?	Buyer mohses1 (1)	Jan-18-07 13:28	180071491747
⊕ very good seller, and rapid shipment.	Buyer dsxiao (13 ⭐)	Jan-18-07 13:24	180072132283
⊕ Item as Described, Fast Shipping, All Good.	Buyer coreseller (168 ⭐)	Jan-18-07 13:23	180074278124
⊕ Thanks, just as advertised. Would do business again.	Buyer lolaburg (147 ⭐)	Jan-18-07 13:23	180071675633
⊕ Great Camera! Great Price! Fast Shipping! Very Pleased! Thank You!!!	Buyer minimaggied (86 ⭐)	Jan-18-07 13:22	180073022720
⊕ Great camera, fast delivery! Would love to do business again!	Buyer xainy86 (8)	Jan-18-07 13:19	180073461352
⊕ As described. Shipped fast. Fast e-mail communication.	Buyer gargantulakon (200 ⭐)	Jan-18-07 13:18	180072742072
⊕ Great Product, fast shippment 100% Recomended.	Buyer hupriti (31 ⭐)	Jan-18-07 13:18	180071045628
⊕ excellent service - recommend - delighted with product	Buyer knocknagoney (80 ⭐)	Jan-18-07 13:16	180072711470
⊕ WOW!!!! What an awesome camera. Great Service. Takes alot to make me WOW!!! A+++	Buyer leadfootdave (91 ⭐)	Jan-18-07 13:16	180073152904
⊕ thank you for your services - recommended :)	Buyer peanutswithchocolate	Jan-18-07 13:12	180053719013

This seller has excellent feedback. Note: Most high-volume sellers receive a small percentage of negative feedback. It's important to take the negatives in context and as a percentage of the seller's total. This seller has a .04 percent negative feedback score. That's less than 1 percent negative to positive—an excellent ratio indeed!

The shooting star next to the feedback number is red, which indicates that this seller has a feedback score of 100,000 or higher. There are different colors and types of stars for different levels of feedback. A change of star status is a major milestone for every eBay member, buyer and seller alike.

Yellow star = 10 to 49 points
Blue star = 50 to 99 points
Turquoise star = 100 to 499 points
Purple star = 500 to 999 points
Red star = 1,000 to 4,999 points
Green star = 5,000 to 9,999 points
Yellow shooting star = 10,000 to 24,999 points
Turquoise shooting star = 25,000 to 49,999 points
Purple shooting star = 50,000 to 99,999 points
Red shooting star = 100,000 or higher

In addition to feedback, you should view the seller's About Me page if she has created one. Many (but, sad to say, not all) sellers have an About Me page. (All sellers should!) If a member has created an About Me page, a little Me icon will appear to the right of his feedback number:

africadirect (12099 ☆) Power Seller me Top 5,000 Reviewer

Just click the icon to view that seller's About Me page.

You can learn a lot about sellers by what they tell you on their About Me page. Some sellers use their About Me page to advertise their standard payment, shipping, packing, and return policies. Other sellers use their About Me page to talk about their business. Member africadirect tells us about traveling in Africa looking for merchandise to sell on eBay:

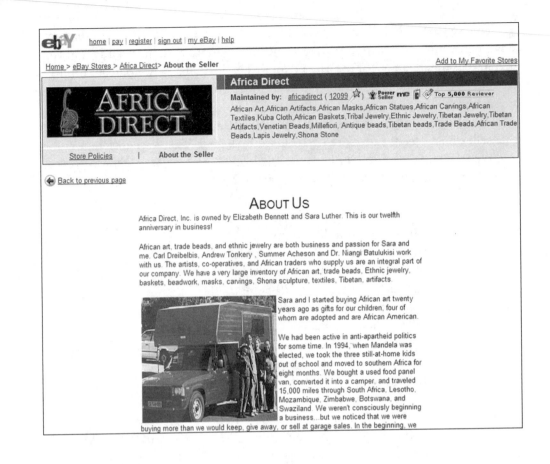

✔ **READ THE ITEM DESCRIPTION PAGE THOROUGHLY**

Start at the top. For auction format listings, look for the amount shown as the value for "Starting bid" or "Current bid." The starting bid shows the amount needed to start the bidding. The first bidder must enter this amount or more to start the auction. Once a bid has been submitted, the indication changes to "Current bid." It changes each time a bidder submits a bid (with only one exception—a bidder cannot raise his own bid by rebidding). Any bid amount you are considering as your bid—for an item that has already received one or more bids—must be greater than the amount shown for the current bid.

More about bidding later.

Is There a Reserve?

Our seller is not specifying a reserve for our item of interest, but many sellers will place a reserve price on their item. The optional reserve price is the amount below which the item will not be sold. The reserve price is always private—only the seller knows the reserve price for his or her listing.

You can always tell if a listing has a reserve price by the indication next to the current bid amount, which will state "Reserve not met." Here is one from a different listing:

This item's reserve has not yet been met. If the item were to close at this point, there would be no sale—that is, the seller is not obliged to sell the item and the high bidder has no claim on the item.

Two Important Features of Reserve Price Listings

1. If, in a reserve listing, the bidder bids an amount lower than the reserve, the amount for the current bid will increase accordingly, but the reserve indication will remain "Reserve not met."
2. If a bidder should bid an amount equal to or greater than the reserve amount, the amount for the current bid will rise, and the indication next to the amount will change to "Reserve met."

Q. Griff, why would a seller use a reserve? Why doesn't the seller just start the bidding at the reserve amount?

A. Because in most cases where the starting bid amount is equal to or near the market value of the item, few people will actually bid. It's all about psychology.

For example, a seller has a recognizable collectible that she will not consider selling for less than $100, and the item has a high-end book or market value of $125. The seller offers the collectible for bid at eBay without a reserve, but with a starting bid of $100. Potential buyers for the item will be lukewarm at best about bidding on the item since there is so little room for play. Sure, the item is

$25 lower than high market, but the smaller the margin for a possible bargain, the less likely any bidder is to jump in and bid.

If, however, the same seller offers the collectible item with a starting bid of $1 and a reserve of $100, potential buyers are more likely to bid because the possibility of a bargain is much greater; that is, at least the appearance of a possible bargain is greater. Remember, no one but the seller knows the reserve amount. At a starting bid of $1, someone is more inclined to start the bidding.

Eventually, a second bidder will enter the fray, and then something very interesting happens that I call "ownership delusion." Once a person has the high bid on an item, emotionally they immediately begin to consider the item "theirs"— which is truly a delusion since the seller is the actual owner of the item until the auction ends.

The strength of this "ownership delusion" is directly proportional to the bidder's desire to own the item, and this desire increases dramatically once a new bidder outbids a current bidder. The previous high bidder irrationally feels as though he or she has been robbed. The first and strongest instinct of those who believe they have been robbed is to retrieve the item, in this case by rebidding until they are once again the high bidder.

This often starts a back-and-forth of "It's mine!" "No, it's mine!" "Excuse me, I believe this is my item you are attempting to win." "Yours? *Au contraire*, the item is most definitely mine!" "What? Who do you think you are?" With both parties bidding and rebidding, in the heat of battle the reserve price is met and is even surpassed, with one person happily winning the item—sometimes for much more than she would have dreamed of paying if the same item were offered to her for direct sale.

The auction becomes much more than just a fun shopping format. It becomes a life-and-death struggle between the champion and the vanquished, and nobody wants to be the vanquished.

Actually, the real champion in a case like this is the seller, who is more than pleased to watch two bidders fight for the honor of overpaying for an item.

Let's get back to the checklist.

Is There a Buy It Now Option?

Some listings will have two ways for a bidder to win the item. The old standard way is to bid for it and hope for the best. A second format was introduced in 1999 that allows a potential bidder to skip the bidding and purchase the item directly for a price specified by the seller. This format at eBay is called Buy It Now.

If the seller has provided potential buyers with the Buy It Now option, a Buy It Now button will display under the Place Bid button. Next to the button will be the Buy It Now price:

In this example, the seller has provided a Buy It Now price of $249. The Buy It Now option will immediately disappear if a buyer places any bid less than the stated Buy It Now price, in this example, $249. (A bid of $249 or higher will close the auction with a final price of $249.)

If a buyer opts to pay a Buy It Now price, the listing will immediately close and show the following:

If a seller has opted to have a Buy It Now price and a reserve price for the listing, the text will state:

Current bid:	US $0.01	Place Bid >
	Reserve not met	
⇌Buy It Now price:	US $770.00	Buy It Now >
End time:	Jan-25-07 07:22:13 PST (6 days 15 hours)	
Shipping costs:	US $20.00 UPS Ground Service to United States	
Ships to:	United States	
Item location:	Baltimore, MD, United States	
History:	1 bid	

In this instance, the Buy It Now option will remain in place, even if bidding starts, as long as the bidding is below the seller's reserve price.

In some cases, the Buy It Now price might be equal to or lower than the maximum bid amount you are willing to pay for the item. In that case, it might be smart to simply Buy It Now!

How Many Items Is the Seller Offering in This Listing?

If the seller is offering more than one of the item, a Quantity field will show the number of items available. If there is no indication of quantity, then the seller is offering only one lot. Note that "one lot" can mean one piece or a lot of two or more pieces all sold together.

⇌Buy It Now price:	US $124.85	Buy It Now >
End time:	Jan-20-07 22:27:29 PST (2 days 7 hours)	
Shipping costs:	US $19.99 (discount available) UPS Ground Service to United States (more services)	
Ships to:	United States, Canada	
Item location:	Fast Ship!, United States	
Quantity:	5 available	
History:	Purchases	
You can also:	Watch this item	
	Get alerts via Text message or IM Sell one like this	

If a quantity is displayed, the format is no longer the standard eBay proxy auction format but is instead either a Multiple Item Listing (aka Dutch Auction) or a straight, no-auction-format-at-all Fixed Price Listing.

The procedures for each auction format are different. We discuss them in detail later in this chapter.

When Does the Listing End?

You can determine when the item closes by looking for the End Time field. Under End Time, you will find the actual closing date and time and, in parentheses, the time left in days and hours.

You can also view the starting date and time of the listing by clicking the "Show" link in the Listing and Payment Details field.

This will show the exact date and time (Pacific Standard Time) the listing went "live."

Just under the End Time field, the Shipping Costs field displays the cost of shipping the item to your location.

NOTE: If the seller has provided more than one option for shipping, the most expensive shipping option will appear in this field. To determine if the seller has included less expensive shipping options, scroll down to the bottom of the listing page to the Shipping, Payment Details and Return Policy section.

The Ships To field lets buyers know the countries to which the seller will ship.

The Item Location field shows where the item is located.

The History field shows the actual number of bids placed on this item. It does not necessarily show the actual number of bidders, since a bidder may bid more than once. If there has been at least one bid, the number will display as a link.

The High Bidder field displays the bidder number of the current high bidder.

Current bid:	US $440.00 [Place Bid >]
End time:	Jan-20-07 15:11:11 PST (1 day 23 hours)
Shipping costs:	US $20.00 US Postal Service Priority Mail® Service to United States
Ships to:	United States
Item location:	Plano, Texas, United States
History:	6 bids
High bidder:	Bidder 3
You can also:	[Watch this item] Get alerts via Text message, IM or Cell phone Sell one like this

Not ready to make a bid or to Buy It Now? Click the "Watch this item" button to put the item on your Watch list in My eBay.

Current bid:	US $440.00 [Place Bid >]
End time:	Jan-20-07 15:11:11 PST (1 day 23 hours)
Shipping costs:	US $20.00 US Postal Service Priority Mail® Service to United States
Ships to:	United States
Item location:	Plano, Texas, United States
History:	6 bids
High bidder:	Bidder 3
You can also:	[Watch this item] Get alerts via Text message, IM or Cell phone Sell one like this

Click the appropriate links if you would like to receive an alert by text message, instant message, or cell phone:

Current bid:	**US $440.00** [Place Bid >]
End time:	**Jan-20-07 15:11:11 PST** (1 day 23 hours)
Shipping costs:	**US $20.00** US Postal Service Priority Mail® Service to <u>United States</u>
Ships to:	United States
Item location:	Plano, Texas, United States
History:	<u>6 bids</u>
High bidder:	<u>Bidder 3</u>
You can also:	[Watch this item]
	Get alerts via <u>Text message</u>, <u>IM</u> or <u>Cell phone</u>
	<u>Sell one like this</u>

Next, we read through the Meet the Seller box, which provides critical seller statistics such as User ID, seller status, Feedback (score and percentage), if the seller accepts PayPal and, if she does, what type of PayPal Buyer Protection the seller provides to buyers (more just ahead).

<u>Shoot</u> > <u>6.0 to 6.9 Megapixels</u> > <u>Other</u>

+1GB   Item number: 180076105690

<u>Watch this item</u> in My eBay | <u>Email to a friend</u>

Meet the seller

Seller: <u>emilyandlily</u> (<u>192167</u> 🌟) 🏆 Power Seller

Feedback: **99.6% Positive**

Member: since Feb-10-03 in United States

- <u>Read feedback comments</u>
- <u>Ask seller a question</u>
- <u>Add to Favorite Sellers</u>
- View seller's other items: <u>Store</u> | <u>List</u>
- Visit seller's Store:
  <u>Emilyandlily Store</u>

Buy safely

1. **Check the seller's reputation**
   Score: 192167 | 99.6% Positive
   <u>Read feedback comments</u>

2. **Check how you're protected**
   PayPal This item is covered up to $2,000 <u>See eligibility</u>

Click the seller's User ID to reach his or her My World page:

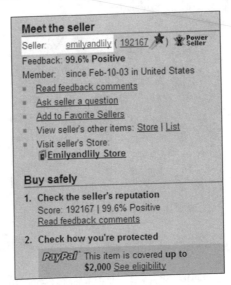

(My World is a relatively new feature on eBay. You automatically get an eBay My World page when you become an eBay member. A My World page gives members of the eBay community ways to create customizable, personal pages that feature content they create themselves.)

Directly under the seller's User ID are three links. The first link, "Read feedback comments," will take you to the seller's feedback page. The "Ask seller a question" link allows for quick and safe correspondence between you and the seller. Click this link to open a My Messages e-mail form.

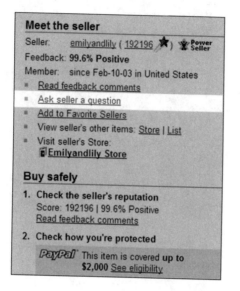

The last bit of information in the Meet the Seller box indicates if the seller accepts PayPal and if so, if the seller qualifies to provide you buyer protection up to $2,000.

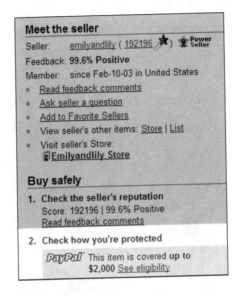

There are two levels of PayPal Buyer Protection. If the Buy Safely box shows the above, then you are covered for up to $2,000. If the box shows the following, you are covered by PayPal for up to $200:

If the box contains no indication of PayPal, the buyer is not providing PayPal as a payment option.

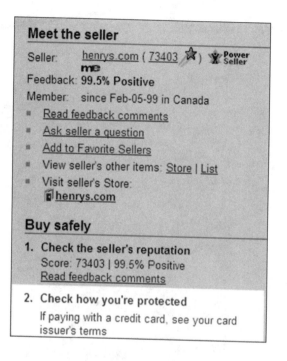

NOTE: Neither eBay nor PayPal offers protection for transactions that are not made through PayPal. If you pay a seller with a check, money order, or bank transfer, that payment is not covered by eBay or PayPal protection. If you pay a seller with a credit card through the seller's own credit card processing, your credit card issuer may provide you with some level of buyer protection. Contact them for details.

That covers the top section of the Item Description page. Let's read the actual (seller-supplied) description. Here is the seller's description for the item on which we plan on submitting a bid.

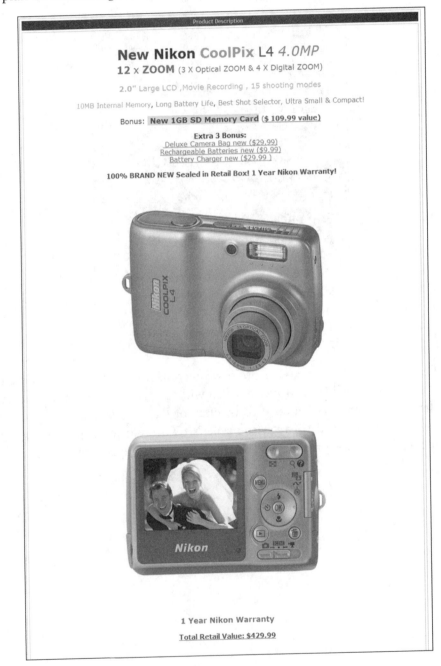

Product Description

New Nikon CoolPix L4 *4.0MP*
12 x ZOOM (3 X Optical ZOOM & 4 X Digital ZOOM)

2.0" Large LCD ,Movie Recording , 15 shooting modes

10MB Internal Memory, Long Battery Life, Best Shot Selector, Ultra Small & Compact!

Bonus: New 1GB SD Memory Card ($ 109.99 value)

Extra 3 Bonus:
Deluxe Camera Bag new ($29.99)
Rechargeable Batteries new ($9.99)
Battery Charger new ($29.99)

100% BRAND NEW Sealed in Retail Box! 1 Year Nikon Warranty!

1 Year Nikon Warranty

Total Retail Value: $429.99

From the Manufacturer

The Nikon Coolpix L4 combines an array of high-quality components including a 3x Zoom-Nikkor lens and a bright 2.0-inch LCD screen with in-camera image-improvement features, housed in lightweight, compact, yet elegantly finished bodies.

It boasts a powerful 3x Zoom-Nikkor lenses with a focal range equivalent to that of a 38-114mm (35mm equivalent), providing the freedom to zoom in for tight personal portraits or out to capture expansive outdoor scenes.

The CCD delivers higher performance within tighter dimensions, greatly adding to the camera's compact form and portability while offering generous effective megapixel value of 4.0 for the Coolpix L4, ensuring the refined image clarity that users have come to expect from other members of the Coolpix family.

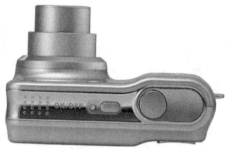

The camera also features a bright, easy-to-view 2.0-inch LCD that's now even easier to operate with new icons and function selections as well as a new color scheme that is easier on the eye.

Specific design aspects of the Coolpix L4 make it streamlined and comfortable to hold, with a smooth, elegant finish that suggests a much higher level of sophistication. The curved grip contributes both to the camera's design elegance and its shooting stability.

The strikingly compact dimensions and light camera weight make the L4 ideal for taking anywhere you may go, reinforced by the convenience of AA-size battery compatibility. One of the most widely available battery sizes in the world--in alkaline, lithium, rechargeable, or other forms--AA compatibility allows near-ubiquitous use anywhere in the world.

In common with the entire current Coolpix digital camera range, this latest addition features a number of Nikon-inspired capabilities that give the user the power to automatically improve recorded images in-camera. Available in playback mode, for example, the D-Lighting function selects and creates a copy of images with excessive backlight or insufficient flash illumination, adding light and detail wherever needed while keeping other areas as they were.

Nikon's Face-priority AF function automatically detects and focuses in on people's faces, regardless of where they are in the frame, ensuring superb crisp-focus portraits. The In-Camera Red-Eye Fix function analyzes each image, automatically finding and then correcting the accidental red-eye that sometimes occurs in flash photography, for more natural-looking portraits.

A choice of 15 different Scene modes--four with Scene assist--makes the challenge of achieving desired results in a wide range of everyday situations that much simpler. By choosing the Scene mode best suited to the subject at hand, the Coolpix L2, L3 or L4 automatically selects the ideal settings for exactly the picture you had in mind, whether indoor party or outdoor nighttime fireworks display. Scene assist displays useful framing guides in the monitor, helping you compose shots for optimal results.

The Coolpix L4 is also compatible with widely available SD memory cards. The provision of 10 MB of internal memory allows the user to keep shooting when no additional memory is available, as well as easily moving images from one SD card to another.

The Coolpix L4 digital camera also offers movie-shooting capability in three sizes: TV movie size (640) for viewing on TV or computers; convenient Small size (320); and Smaller size (160) for extended recording or Internet usage.

With the Coolpix L4, ease of use and convenience are still priorities, even when the shooting is over. Printing is kept simple, with PictBridge capability enabling connection to a compatible printer without the need of a computer and USB connectivity eases data transfer to computers and other peripherals.

Completing the picture is the complimentary PictureProject accessory software, which greatly simplifies the importing, editing, and organizing of images. It even offers compatibility with a range of plug-ins that allows functions to be extended on demand.

Nikon Coolpix L4 feature highlights:

High performance from a small CCD
Utilizing space-efficient design parameters that help facilitate the compact size of the Coolpix L2/L3/L4, the 1/2.5-inch CCD adds the advantage of outstandingly high performance. Boasting effective pixel values of 4 million, the CCD enables the capture of crisp-focus images that retain their high quality even when significantly enlarged.

3x zoom capability
The remarkably compact dimensions of the Coolpix L-line cameras belie the incorporation of powerful 38-114mm Zoom-Nikkor lenses (35mm equivalent), ensuring the freedom of a 3x zoom. This precision lens allows zooming in for tightly composed portraits or zooming way out for expansively wide views, providing greater compositional independence than the average digital camera. Macro mode allows shooting from as close as 4 centimeters.

Simple-to-use features improve images in-camera
A range of unique Nikon functions enables the photographer to actually improve images in-camera. Available in playback mode, the D-Lighting function selects and creates a copy of images with excessive backlight or insufficient flash illumination, adding light and detail wherever needed while keeping other areas as they were. The Face-priority AF function automatically detects and then focuses in on people's faces, regardless of where they are in the frame, ensuring superb crisp-focus portraits. The In-Camera Red-Eye Fix function analyzes each image, automatically finding and then correcting any accidental red-eye, which sometimes occurs in flash photography, to produce more natural-looking portraits.

AA-size battery compatibility
Despite its compact dimensions, the Coolpix L4 is compatible with AA-size batteries, one of the most widely available battery sizes in the world. The power to shoot approximately 250 shots when using alkaline batteries greatly augments its compact convenience.

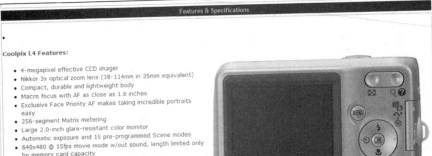

Features & Specifications

Coolpix L4 Features:

- 4-megapixel effective CCD imager
- Nikkor 3x optical zoom lens (38-114mm in 35mm equivalent)
- Compact, durable and lightweight body
- Macro focus with AF as close as 1.6 inches
- Exclusive Face Priority AF makes taking incredible portraits easy
- 256-segment Matrix metering
- Large 2.0-inch glare-resistant color monitor
- Automatic exposure and 15 pre-programmed Scene modes
- 640x480 @ 15fps movie mode w/out sound, length limited only by memory card capacity
- Built-in flash with auto, fill, slow sync, and red-eye reduction
- Nikon's D-Lighting automatically brightens dark images in playback mode
- In-Camera Red-Eye Fix™ automatically fixes most instances of red-eye in the camera
- 10MB internal memory and SD memory card slot
- USB connectivity, PictBridge direct-print compliant
- Powered by two standard AA type batteries

Coolpix L4 Specifications

Effective pixels:	4.0 million
CCD:	1/2.5-inch high-density CCD (4.23 million total pixels)
Image modes:	4M* High (2272), 4M Normal (2272), 2M (1600), PC (1024), TV (640)
Lens:	3x Zoom-Nikkor; 6.3-18.9mm (35mm format equivalent to approx. 38-114mm); f/2.8-4.9; 7 elements in 6 groups; Digital zoom: up to 4x
Focus system:	Contrast gradient TTL
Focus range (approx.):	Normal: 30cm (1 ft.) to infinity Macro: 4cm (1.6 in.) to infinity
LCD monitor:	2.0-inch type, 115,000-dot TFT LCD monitor with brightness adjustment
Storage media:	Internal memory (approx. 10MB), SD memory card
Shooting modes:	Auto, 4 modes with Scene assist (Portrait, Landscape, Sports, Night Portrait), 11 Scene modes (Party/Indoor, Beach/Snow, Sunset, Dusk/Dawn, Night Landscape, Close Up, Museum, Fireworks Show, Copy, Back Light, Panorama Assist), BSS (Best Shot Selector), Color options, Blur Warning, Date Imprint, Self-timer (10 sec.)
Movie: Without sound:	TV movie (640) at 15fps, Small size (320) at 15fps, Smaller size (160) at 15fps
Capture modes:	1) Single 2) Multi-shot 16 3) Sports (3-shots) 4) Sports composite (16 shots)
Number of frames (w/internal memory):	4M High: approx. 3, 4M NORMAL approx. 7, 2M Normal approx. 15
Built-in flash:	Range: Approx. 0.4-3.0m/16 in. - 9 ft. 10 in. (W), 0.4-1.7m/1 ft. 4 in. - 5 ft. 7 in. (T) Flash modes: Auto, Auto with Red-eye Reduction (In-Camera Red-eye Fix), Flash Cancel, Anytime Flash and Slow sync.
Interface:	USB, Video output
Supported languages:	German, English, Spanish, French, Italian, Dutch, Russian, Swedish, Japanese, Simplified Chinese, Traditional Chinese, Korean, selectable in menu display
Power requirements:	Rechargeable Ni-MH Battery EN-MH1 x 2, AA-size battery (LR6 alkaline, ZR6 oxynide, or lithium) x 2, AC Adapter EH-65A (optional)
Battery life (approx.):	250 shots with alkaline, 600 shots with lithium, or 450 shots with EN-MH1 (based on CIPA standard)
Dimensions (WxHxD):	Approx. 86.5 x 60.5 x 34.5mm (3.4 x 2.4 x 1.4 in.) excluding projections
Weight (approx.):	115g (4.1 oz.) without battery and SD memory card
Supplied accessories*:	Disposable AA Alkaline battery x 2, USB Cable UC-E6, Video Cable EG-CP11(L4), Strap, PictureProject CD-ROM
Optional accessories:	Battery Charger MH-71, Rechargeable Ni-MH Battery EN-MH1 (EN-MH1-B2), AC Adapter EH-65A * Supplied accessories may differ by country or area.
PictureProject System Requirements	OS Macintosh: Mac® OS X version 10.1.5 or later (version 10.2.8 or later required for Burn Disc option) / Windows: Windows® XP Home Edition/Professional, Windows® 2000 Professional, Windows® Me, Windows® 98SE pre-installed models RAM Macintosh: 64MB or more recommended/ Windows: 64MB or more recommended (128MB with Pictmotion option) Hard disk 60MB required for installation Display 800 x 600 or more with 16-bit color (full color recommended) Others CD-ROM drive required for installation Only built-in USB ports are supported

Specifications are as represented by the manufacturer

The description of the actual item accurately describes the item and, along with the picture the seller provided, provides a sufficient accounting of the item's condition.

✔ EXAMINE THE ITEM PICTURES

This seller has provided several good photos of both the item and the extras:

This seller has provided clear, sharp, well-lit photos of the camera. If the item you are viewing has less-than-perfect photos, e-mail the seller and ask him or her for some better shots (and please do mention this book as an excellent guide for taking perfect eBay item pictures. Thank you).

This seller's pictures are clear, focused, and show the item in various aspects.

Are There Views of the Item That You Would Like to See?

Most sellers will provide photos of all aspects of an item. Sometimes they don't. For example, I might like to see a top view of this camera.

If there is a view that you need to see before you make your bid, again, e-mail the seller and ask for a photo of that particular view. I once found a beautiful chest of drawers on eBay. The seller provided excellent pictures of the chest including the back, underside, top, and bottom. However, I needed to see a photo of the drawer sides, specifically the method used to join the sides of the drawer to the drawer front, to determine if the chest was handmade or machine-made. I e-mailed the seller asking if he could send a photo of the drawer sides, and he happily agreed. The photos proved that the chest was indeed handmade, and I bid accordingly. In the end, I didn't win the chest. I was sniped (eBay lingo for being outbid in the final minutes)!

✔ READ AND UNDERSTAND THE SELLER'S TOS (TERMS OF SERVICE).

This seller has provided a comprehensive set of shipping and handling terms.

Shipping Information

- Will ship to United States and Canada only.
- US Continent lower 48 states: $19.99.
- Hawaii and Alaska: $22.
- PO Box address: $22.
- $3 Insurance fee.
- Canada: $48 (no PO BOX, please) Canadian buyer is responsible for customs tax.
- Shipped within 48 hours after the confirmed payment.
- No APO/FPO address, please. No local pick up.

Payment Information

PayPal VERIFIED / VISA MasterCard Discover	• Pay with your credit cards • Paypal e-check normally takes 5 business days to clear.
Money order / Cashier's check	Ship in 2 business days after we receive the payment.
Important Notes:	• No personal/business check • For payment by money order or cashier's check, buyer must include item number, user ID, and print shipping address in the mail. And please email me for money order payment details.

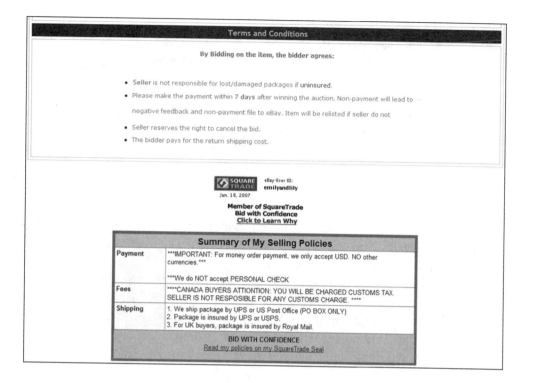

What Type of Payment Does the Seller Accept?

Our camera seller accepts PayPal, money orders, and cashier's checks, all of which are acceptable on eBay. In fact, there are five possible payment options that sellers may accept (at their discretion):

> PayPal
> Credit cards
> Wire transfer/electronic check
> Money orders (domestic and international)
> Checks (personal and cashier's or bank)

Sellers are usually clear about which of the above they accept. The first place to look for a seller's payment options is in the top section of the listing page, as shown above. But there should also be some indication inside the item description.

If the seller has not provided details about accepted payment methods, remember to ask for details before you bid! (Use the Ask the Seller a Question e-mail feature as described above.)

Let's explore the five acceptable payment options in detail.

PayPal

Our seller accepts PayPal, a practice that more and more sellers are now adopting. PayPal is the quickest and easiest way to pay safely for eBay purchases.

> **GRIFF TIP!** If you don't have a PayPal account, you should open one now. Opening a PayPal account is quick and easy! Go to *www.paypal.com* and follow the instructions.

Credit Cards

Most eBay sellers accept credit cards for payment through PayPal (more on PayPal in the next chapter). They may also provide credit card payment options through their own, non-PayPal merchant account.

Using PayPal is the quickest and safest way to pay for an eBay item. If the seller is not offering the PayPal option but does offer to accept credit cards through their own merchant account, check with your credit card issuer before you bid and obtain details regarding the buyer protection your card issuer provides. Lean toward those items where you can pay with PayPal.

Electronic Check

Most online payment services, such as PayPal, will provide secure electronic bank transfer as a buyer payment option. Some online payment services will back up wire transfers and electronic checks for their full amount. Check the payment service's terms before using. PayPal is an excellent option.

Money Orders

Over time, fewer and fewer eBay sellers are accepting money orders for payment. Again, don't assume. If the seller doesn't state his terms, ask first before bidding.

Paying with a money order is not as quick as with a credit card, nor does a money order offer the buyer the same protection as a credit card. In fact, money orders offer very little protection. Stick with PayPal.

Checks

Along with money orders, it seems fewer and fewer sellers are willing to accept a check as payment for an eBay item. Still, there are some sellers who, for whatever reason, prefer to do business with checks (go figure). Sellers who accept checks usually specify a waiting period of three or more days in their item description before they will ship the item. This is to allow ample time for the check to clear their account.

Checks are not nearly as secure as PayPal and are not covered by PayPal Buyer Protection. Oh, did I mention PayPal already?

About Paying in Cash
Don't.

Please read the following very carefully!

Sending cash for payment is not advised. In fact, eBay policy prohibits sellers from providing it as a payment option in their listings (except for completing transactions face-to-face, but even this is not recommended). To view the entire Accepted Payments Policy, click the "Help" link on the top of any eBay page and then click through the links for Help Topics > Rules and Policies > Rules for Sellers > Accepted Payment Policy.

Here is a section of the policy that outlines what is and isn't acceptable as payment methods for eBay transactions:

Permitted on eBay.com: Sellers may offer to accept PayPal, credit cards including MasterCard/Visa /Amex/Discover, debit cards and bank electronic payments online for eBay purchases. Sellers may also offer to accept bank-to-bank transfers, often known as bank wire transfers or bank cash transfers. Sellers may accept COD (cash on delivery) or cash for in-person transactions. Sellers may offer to accept personal checks, money orders, cashier's checks, certified checks, and other negotiable instruments.

Not permitted on eBay.com: Sellers may not solicit buyers to mail cash. Sellers may not ask buyers to send cash through instant cash transfer services (non-bank, point-to-point cash transfers) such as Western Union or MoneyGram. Sellers may not solicit payment through "topping off" of a seller's pre-paid credit or debit card. Finally, sellers may not request payment through online payment methods not specifically permitted in this policy.

eBay does allow sellers to state cash as a payment option, but only for COD and in-person transactions. However, whenever you pay cash for an item in person, make sure the seller hands you a detailed and signed receipt at the time of the transfer of goods and money. If you are purchasing a vehicle, demand the seller provide a legal and clear title along with the receipt and ask for a license or passport (to check the face with the name on the title) before you hand over the cash.

One portion of the above bears repeating in big bold letters:

ALERT: NEVER SEND PAYMENT FOR AN EBAY TRANSACTION THROUGH A CASH TRANSFER SERVICE SUCH AS WESTERN UNION OR MONEYGRAM!

As stated above, eBay policy prohibits sellers from offering these services as payment options. Any solicitations stating either of the above as the only payment options, no matter what the reason given by the seller, should be viewed with suspicion and should not be completed. Instead, report the incident to eBay by clicking the Security Center link on the bottom of any eBay page. Cash transfer services are only intended as a method of sending cash to a trusted friend or relative. They should never be used for completing an online transaction.

Does the Seller Offer Online Escrow?

Online escrow through a trusted third-party, *www.escrow.com*, provides transaction protection for both the buyer and seller. It is an excellent solution for new sellers with little or no feedback history upon which to base an assessment of that seller's honesty. In addition, many buyers of big-ticket items are more comfortable bidding or buying if the seller provides online escrow as an option.

If a seller offers escrow, you will find the indication at the top of the item page and sometimes within the seller's item description.

NOTE: eBay recommends only one online escrow service: *www.escrow.com*. Do not agree to use any other escrow service!

First, the buyer and seller agree to the terms of the escrow transaction. This may include a number of days for the buyer to inspect the item, shipping information, and who pays the escrow fee.

Then the buyer sends payment to escrow.com, which verifies and processes the payment. Once the payment has been verified (cleared), escrow.com authorizes the seller to ship the merchandise to the buyer.

Once the buyer receives the item, he has the previously agreed-upon number of days to inspect and accept the item. Once he informs escrow.com that he accepts the item, escrow.com pays the seller.

Online escrow can offer great peace of mind for certain types of eBay transactions. If you are looking at possibly buying a big-ticket item such as an expensive car, a piece of jewelry, or a work of art and the seller for the item has little or no feedback, you may want to ask her if she would consider using online escrow should you be the high bidder or buyer when the listing closes. Always ask the seller about using escrow *before* you bid!

Of course, many newer eBay sellers, realizing that their lack of a feedback history at eBay may give pause to otherwise eager potential bidders or buyers, will offer the escrow option in their listing description, but note that eBay sellers are not required to accept escrow. It is a seller choice. If a seller does not offer it explicitly, contact the seller to inquire about escrow as a payment option before you bid.

Sellers who offer escrow services will have various terms for sharing or not sharing the costs of using an online escrow service. Again, make sure you understand who is bearing what costs for using escrow before you bid!

Our seller does not indicate escrow as an option. Not surprising. The seller has extremely good feedback and a long history with eBay and is providing the option to pay with PayPal, which provides the buyer with up to $2,000 in coverage should something go awry with the transaction.

Does the Seller Provide a Return or Refund Policy?

Most anyone who sells online realizes that a buyer cannot know if she is truly happy with an item until that item is actually in her hands. No one wants to be stuck with an item she doesn't like.

Most, but not all, sellers understand this and will offer a reasonable return and refund policy. Make sure to check for a seller's return policy before you bid. If the seller has not provided a return policy, send him an e-mail inquiry.

The best return policy is one that offers you your full money back for any reason whatsoever, no questions asked, no return fees. The worst return policy is none at all. A seller will usually indicate "no returns" by stating that the item is sold "as is." Bid if you must on such an item, but always remember: Caveat emptor (Latin for "Buyer beware"). You bid at your own risk!

The majority of sellers offer something in between. Some sellers will accept returns but will charge you a fee for doing so. Others restrict returns to a specific time, such as three days upon receipt. Make sure you fully understand the seller's return policy before you submit your bid.

Our seller is selling the camera with a one-year warranty and is shipping the item insured. That should cover most situations, but never assume! If you require further information about a possible return or refund, you must first e-mail her with the question and wait for her response before actually buying or bidding. I have done ample research about the camera, the seller, and the current price and feel confident that the camera is brand-new. I also double-checked with the manufacturer, and the camera is indeed under warrany.

Does the Seller Ship Internationally?

Although the eBay community of buyers and sellers extends around the globe, some eBay sellers (mostly based on the U.S. site) will not ship items outside of the United States. These sellers will usually state this fact clearly within their terms. Our seller states right off that he will only ship to the United States and Canada.

If you are an eBay buyer based outside of the United States, make sure that the item's seller is agreeable to shipping internationally before you bid.

Another option for non-U.S. buyers is to establish a contact within the United States (a friend or family member) who will accept delivery of eBay items on your behalf.

Does the Seller Have Special Requirements for Buyers?

For example, some sellers prohibit bidding by eBay members who have a certain number of negative comments in their feedback profile or hidden feedback. (Members who are exclusively buyers or who are not selling at the moment can opt to hide all their feedback comments. Their feedback number will still display. Not recommended.)

Sellers are free to employ this type of restriction based on feedback.

Does the Seller Have Specific Time Limits for Contact and for Receiving Payments?

eBay sellers are usually quite specific about how long they will wait for contact and payment from you, the buyer. Read these specifications before you bid!

STILL HAVE QUESTIONS? ASK THE SELLER!

If you go through the checklist and you still have questions about the item or the seller's terms, ask the seller before you bid.

GRIFF TIP! While I was with eBay Customer Support, I learned the three biggest mistakes a bidder can make:

1. Not reading a seller's feedback profile before bidding
2. Not reading carefully the seller's item description before bidding
3. Not asking the seller for details left out of the description (assuming)

We showed you how to avoid mistake number 1 in the section before this one. Let's dive into how to avoid mistakes number 2 and 3.

The seller supplies all of the text found between the Description bar and the Payment Options/Payment Instructions bars. You simply must make a habit of carefully and thoroughly reading everything the seller has provided in the way of a description, payment options, shipping and handling charges, return policies, any bidder restrictions, and so on.

If you have questions or concerns about the item or the seller's policies, you must e-mail the seller for a clarification before you bid. Hold off bidding on or buying an item until the seller has answered your questions to your satisfaction. You can always place the item in your My eBay Watch list for access later once the seller has answered your questions and concerns to your satisfaction.

ONLINE PAYMENTS—THE SAFEST WAY TO BUY ON EBAY

The best way to ensure your security as an eBay buyer is to give preference to items for which the seller accepts online payments through PayPal or some other similar, trusted payment service.

During the first few years of Internet commerce, many folks had reservations about using their credit cards online. They feared that enterprising thieves would break into an online transmission to hijack the credit card information for their own use.

Today, most e-commerce Web sites employ a special form of data transmission for sensitive data such as credit card numbers. This special form is called Secure Socket Layer or SSL. SSL uses an extremely secure type of data encryption that makes it virtually impossible for anyone to break into an SSL transmission of data.

Without getting extremely technical about how SSL works, all you need to know about any e-commerce Web site's security is that it provides SSL for you. How do you tell if a Web site is using SSL?

First, check the Web site's own text, especially on the page or pages where you are asked to enter your credit card information. If it is using SSL, it will state the fact clearly on this page for your peace of mind.

Second, check your Web browser's status bar (the little bar along the bottom of the Web browser) and address window (where the current Web page's URL or address is displayed). If the page you are viewing is employing SSL technology, a little yellow padlock will show on the far right-hand side of the browser status bar.

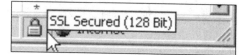

Another way to determine if the page you are viewing is using SSL technology is to look at the URL or address for the page. The URL for the page can be found in the little window on the top of your Web browser marked Address or Location. URLs usually start with "http://www . . ." The URL for a SSL page will start with "https:// . . ."

That's the Safe Trading Checklist! I know it seems like a lot of information and steps to keep in mind, and the first few times you bid on or purchase an item on eBay, you will want to keep at least the top-level Checklist items in mind. However, after you have bid on or bought a few items on eBay, the Checklist will become second nature, I promise.

We've Found It . . . We've Checked It Out . . . Let's Buy it!

We've gone through our Safe Trading Checklist and are now ready to commit. As we have seen, we have two options. We can bid for an item or buy it outright with Buy It Now. Exciting, isn't it?

Since I will purchase the camera with Buy It Now, let's put the listing aside for now on my Watch List and cover the basics of bidding on eBay first.

(The seller is offering five of these cameras, so chances are extremely good there will still be at least one available by the time we return to the watched listing.)

BIDDING

Two auction formats are in use at eBay: the Proxy format and the Multiple Item Listing (also known as the Dutch Auction).

eBay's Proxy Bidding System

The majority of items listed on eBay in an auction format (as opposed to those listed exclusively with the fixed price Buy It Now format) are using the default eBay Proxy Bidding system.

The Proxy Bidding system is not at all complicated. To begin, let's use a real-life auction example to illustrate the concept of proxy bidding in the off-line world.

What Are Friends For (If Not to Act as Proxies)?

You and I are old friends who have met at an off-line auction. Some dear old richer–than–King Tut grandma has passed away, and her loving family, unable to agree on how to split up her worldly goods, has decided to call in a local auctioneer to sell it all—money being easier to split than worldly goods. (Too bad none of the heirs uses eBay or bought this book—they could have sold it all online!)

There's a wonderful old Oriental rug at the auction that you desperately want for your living room, but the auctioneer isn't putting it up for bid until noon, and you have to leave at eleven forty-five to meet a client fifteen minutes away. (By the way, you're a real estate agent.)

Oh, what to do? You can't leave your client hanging, but you simply must have this rug!

Thinking quickly, you lean over and ask in a whisper if I might be willing to bid for you in your absence.

"Why, dear old friend, of course I would! How much are you willing to spend?" I whisper back.

You look around quickly to see if anyone is listening. People are. You think fast.

"I will write it down so no one hears it."

You rummage in your bag for a slip of paper and pen, find them, and, using your thigh as a desk, scribble a figure. You then hand the slip of paper to me. I read, *Bid $1,000 and not a single penny more. Destroy this immediately!*

I silently mouth, "No problem. Consider it done!"

I have just agreed to act as your proxy; that is, I will bid for you in your absence.

At noon, the auctioneer puts up the rug as promised. He asks for an opening bid of $100. Someone else starts the bidding. The auctioneer accepts the bid of $100 and asks for a bid of $125—$25 being his choice of increment. I, your best friend and proxy, spring into action. I raise my hand and enter the fray with a bid of $125.

Thus it begins. The auctioneer calls out for a bid of $150, and sure enough, another bidder bids. I rebid $175. The bidder bids again, $200. I rebid $250. And so on it goes back and forth between us as we battle it out to see who will pay the most. Suddenly, the bidding stalls out at $550. The other bidder has reached her limit! The auctioneer roars, "I have five hundred fifty. Do I hear six hundred? Six hundred? Going, going . . . gone! Sold to the handsome man in the back row for five hundred fifty dollars!"

You, my dear old friend, arrive back at the auction at twelve-thirty, and I rush up to meet you to share the good news.

"I got it for five hundred fifty dollars!"

You are deliriously happy. You have sold a house and I, your dear old friend, have successfully acted as your proxy and nabbed you the prize you sought. You bear-hug me with joy. You were willing to pay $1,000, but your plucky proxy got it for you for only $550. (I don't charge a percentage. After all, we are dear old friends.)

Bidding at eBay is nearly identical to our example above, except instead of me acting as your proxy, eBay does.

Let's use a real eBay listing to illustrate the process, step by step. Here is an interesting Oriental rug I found on eBay. The starting bid is only 99¢. There are no bids.

We've read the Title and Description sections, viewed the pictures, and made sure we understand the seller's terms of service. Now we have to settle on the maximum price we are willing to pay.

After due consideration, I decide we are willing to pay up to $25 and not a penny more.

I could bid the 99¢ starting bid amount and then check every few minutes to see if a new bidder has joined the auction so I can outbid him or her, or I could simply submit a proxy bid, much like you did at the real live estate auction, but instead of me acting as your proxy, the eBay system will do so. You only need to decide on a maximum amount you will pay for the item (just like in the live auction), and once you have, you then submit it as a bid. The eBay system will act as I did for you at the live auction by rebidding every time someone outbids you, up to the exact amount you submit as your bid (your proxy bid). If no one bids over the amount of your proxy, you win the item for the current high bid. If someone bids more than your proxy, you lose, or better put, don't have to shell out any dough.

I scroll down to the bottom of the Item Description page to the section Ready to Bid? I type my absolute maximum bid amount, $25, in the box "Your maximum bid."

Ready to bid?	
Rare Vegetable Afghan Chobi Rug 8x6	
Item title:	Rare Vegetable Afghan Chobi Rug 8x6
Starting bid:	US $0.99
Your maximum bid:	US $ [25] (Enter US $0.99 **or more**)
	[Place Bid >] You will confirm in the next step.
eBay automatically bids on your behalf **up to** your maximum bid. Learn about bidding.	

Then I click the "Place bid" button to go to the Review and Confirm Bid page.

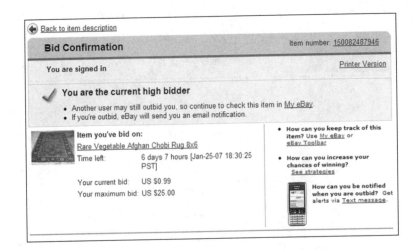

Reviewing this information, we see not only my maximum bid but also shipping and handling (if provided by the seller), as well as sales tax of 7 percent for all buyers located in Florida (the seller's home state).

Since there are no previous bidders, we know what the current bid will be once I submit my bid of $25. It will be 99¢. And indeed, the next screen shows my Bid Confirmation:

| Rare Vegetable Afghan Chobi Rug 8x6 | Item number: 150082487946 |

You are signed in

This item is being tracked in My eBay | Email to a friend | Printer Version

✓ You are the current high bidder

Important: Another user may still outbid you, so check this item again in My eBay before it ends.

Time left:	6 days 7 hours
Current bid:	US $0.99
Your maximum bid:	US $25.00

How do you keep track of this item? Use My eBay

How does bidding work? See example

How can you be notified when you are outbid? Get alerts via Text message or IM

Current bid:	US $0.99 [Place Bid >]
End time:	Jan-25-07 18:30:25 PST (6 days 7 hours)
Shipping costs:	US $50.00 UPS Ground Service to United States
Ships to:	United States
Item location:	Not Specified, United States
History:	1 bid
High bidder:	uncle_griff (1270 ★) me

View larger picture

This item is being tracked in My eBay

You can also: Get alerts via Text message, IM or Cell phone
Sell one like this

Meet the seller

Seller:	pakobelrugs (15786 ★) Power Seller
Feedback:	99.3% Positive
Member:	since Jun-04-02 in United States

- Read feedback comments
- Ask seller a question
- Add to Favorite Sellers
- View seller's other items

Buy safely

1. Check the seller's reputation
   Score: 15786 | 99.3% Positive
   Read feedback comments

2. Check how you're protected
   PayPal This item is covered up to $2,000 See eligibility
   Returns: Seller accepts returns. 3 Days Money Back

The current bid shows as 99¢. Why not my maximum of $25? Since I am the first bidder, there are no bids beneath my bid to boost it up toward or to the maximum amount, $25. In addition, I cannot bid against myself and raise the current bid. Thus even though I submit a bid of $25, the current bid will show me as the high bidder with a current bid of 99¢.

What if there had been bids made previous to mine? If this is the case, then the displayed current bid amount is what the current high bid would be once I actually submit my bid (and if the current high bid for the item is the maximum proxy bid amount submitted by the current high bidder). This point is important. The actual outcome of your bid is not known in the Review and Confirm Bid page—it can only be known once you have committed to your bid by actually submitting it. Let's look at another example using another rug from the same seller—one that already has two bids and the current bid is $1.29.

Rare Vegetable Afghan Chobi Rug 9x6   Item number: 150081783147

You are signed in   Watch this item in My eBay | Email to a friend

Current bid:	US $1.29 [Place Bid >]
End time:	Jan-23-07 17:30:31 PST (4 days 6 hours)
Shipping costs:	US $50.00 UPS Ground Service to United States
Ships to:	United States
Item location:	Not Specified, United States
History:	2 bids
High bidder:	wildcatmira (185 ☆)

You can also: [Watch this item]
Get alerts via Text message, IM or Cell phone
Sell one like this

Meet the seller
Seller: pakobelrugs (15786 ☆) ⚡ Power Seller
Feedback: **99.3% Positive**
Member: since Jun-04-02 in United States
» Read feedback comments
» Ask seller a question
» Add to Favorite Sellers
» **View seller's other items**

Buy safely
1. **Check the seller's reputation**
Score: 15786 | 99.3% Positive
Read feedback comments
2. **Check how you're protected**
PayPal This item is covered up to $2,000 See eligibility
Returns: Seller accepts returns. 3 Days Money Back

View larger picture

I am willing to pay $103. I submit that as my bid.

Ready to bid?
Rare Vegetable Afghan Chobi Rug 9x6

Item title: Rare Vegetable Afghan Chobi Rug 9x6

Current bid: US $1.29

Your maximum bid: US $ [103] (Enter US $1.54 **or more**)

[Place Bid >] You will confirm in the next step.

eBay automatically bids on your behalf **up to** your maximum bid.
Learn about bidding.

The Review and Confirm Bid screen:

ebaY ®

Review and Confirm Bid

Hello uncle_griff! (Not you?)

Item you're bidding on:
Rare Vegetable Afghan Chobi Rug 9x6
Current bid: US $1.29
Your maximum bid: US $103.00
Shipping and handling:US $50.00 -- UPS Ground.
Shipping insurance: US $5.00(Optional)
Payment methods: PayPal, Personal check, Money order/Cashiers check, Visa/MasterCard, American Express, Other - See Payment Instructions.

By clicking on the button below, you commit to buy this item from the seller if you're the winning bidder.

[Confirm Bid]

You are agreeing to a contract -- You will enter into a legally binding contract to purchase the item from the seller if you're the winning bidder. You are responsible for reading the full item listing, including the seller's instructions and accepted payment methods. Seller assumes all responsibility for listing this item.

And the final Bid Confirmation:

Congratulations to me. I am the current high bidder at $46.70. What does this tell me about the previous high bidder? Her actual maximum bid, held by proxy on eBay, was one increment below the current bid of $46.70. The increment amount is $1 when the current high bid is between $25 and $99. Therefore, the previous bidder's maximum bid was $45.50. (A bidder can bid any amount over one increment above the current bid. Many bidders, myself included, like to bid in odd bid amounts—for example, $178.56. As long as the amount is at least one increment over the current bid, the bid is acceptable.)

What do you want to bet she rebids and outbids my maximum bid of $103? We will check back later.

BID INCREMENTS

Bid increments—the minimum amount needed for a bit to be accepted—are pre-set and are determined by the amount of the current high bid. Here is a table showing the bid increments used by eBay Proxy Bidding:

Current Price	Bid Increment
$ 0.01 - $ 0.99	$ 0.05
$ 1.00 - $ 4.99	$ 0.25
$ 5.00 - $ 24.99	$ 0.50
$ 25.00 - $ 99.99	$ 1.00
$ 100.00 - $ 249.99	$ 2.50
$ 250.00 - $ 499.99	$ 5.00
$ 500.00 - $ 999.99	$ 10.00
$ 1000.00 - $ 2499.99	$ 25.00
$ 2500.00 - $ 4999.99	$ 50.00
$ 5000.00 and up	$ 100.00

NOTE: A bidder may be outbid by less than a full increment. This would happen if the winning bidder's maximum bid beat the second-highest maximum by an amount less than the full increment.

A bid increment will go higher than the standard increment in two situations:

- To meet the reserve amount
- To beat a competing bidder's high bid

If you were bidding against another bidder's maximum bid, your bid would have to meet the other bidder's maximum bid plus one cent to become the current high bidder on the item.

Sometimes the auction page for an item will show that there are two bids, yet there is only one bidder. This happens when a member places more than one bid to increase their maximum bid amount. For example, if you are the first bidder on an item and you place a second bid to increase your maximum bid amount, the item page would show the current high bid at the opening bid amount, but would show that two bids have been placed on this item.

Tie Bids

In cases where a tie bid is submitted, the current high bid is given to the tie bidder who bid first. That is, if you submit a maximum bid equal to the current (hidden) maximum bid for an item, the current high bid will jump up to the current bidder's maximum bid amount and the earlier bidder will show as the current high bidder.

Bidding and Reserves

If one or more bidders bid amounts less than seller's hidden reserve, the bidding proceeds as any other proxy auction (with the indication next to the current price stating "Reserve not met").

Once a bidder submits a bid equal to or greater than the seller's hidden reserve, the current high bid jumps up to the reserve amount. From there, the bidding again proceeds as a regular proxy bidding auction (with the indication next to the current price changing to "Reserve met").

PROXY BIDDING STRATEGIES

Always give serious consideration to the absolute maximum you are willing to pay for an item. In this case, you decide that you would not pay a penny more than $1,000. This means that should you be outbid for $1,000.01 (rare but possible), you will not whine at losing out for a penny. If you can picture yourself at the auction's closing and you are spitting and kicking at being outbid for one cent, and you can also picture yourself saying, "Darn it! I would have paid $1,000.02!" then you are telling yourself a big fat lie when you say your maximum is $1,000, because your real maximum is at least $1000.02.

The solution? Settle on an absolute maximum and stick to it. Think, "If someone outbids my maximum by even a penny, then I will breathe a sigh of relief at not having to shell out more than my maximum." So much for deciding exactly how much to bid; now, you need to decide when to bid it.

Bid Early—Bid High

As a bidding strategy and tool, the eBay Proxy Bidding system works like a charm. You simply determine a maximum amount you are willing to pay for an item, bid that amount, and walk away. The Proxy Bidding system will execute your bid and protect your high-bidder position by outbidding all new bids using the lowest increment possible until and if someone bids an amount higher than your proxy bid. This offers you the convenience of submitting your absolute maximum bid early in a listing's run rather than having to revisit the listing over and over to rebid every time you are outbid. Early proxy bidding provides not only convenience but also, more important, peace of mind. eBay will act as your trusty proxy, freeing up your time to hunt for other eBay treasure.

Sniping

There is, however, another popular bidding strategy known in eBay parlance as sniping—that is, waiting until the last moments of an auction-format listing and then submitting a maximum bid mere minutes or even seconds before the listing closes. It's a heart-pounding, sweat-inducing roller-coaster ride and definitely not for the faint of heart or weak of wallet.

Does sniping work? Sometimes, but all potential snipers should consider the possible risks. If you tend to get caught up in the frenzy of last-minute bidding to the extent that you suffer a momentary lapse of common sense and end up insanely bidding much more than you would have under more relaxed circumstances, then sniping may not be for you. Remember, regardless of when you bid, the rules of the auction format still apply—he who bids highest wins. Someone equally as caught up as you might snipe an insane bid amount just a few pennies short of your insane bid amount, in which case you will be the proud winning—albeit overpaying—bidder.

Also, your success at sniping depends to some extent on the speed of your Internet connection: The slower your Internet connection, the less likely your chances of success.

What about these sniping software and sniping services I see advertised? What are they? Do they provide an advantage? Sniping software or a sniping service snipes your bids for you. You enter the item number, the time you want your bid submitted, and the amount of your bid. The software or service supposedly does the rest. The only possible advantages that sniping software or sniping services provide are that they allow a sniper to be somewhere else at the end of the auction (such as in bed asleep), and if it is a service, it may have a high-speed Internet connection faster than yours.

NOTE: As of this writing, eBay neither prohibits nor condones the use of sniping software or services. Use them at your own risk.

That being said, if you decide to snipe, the next section explains how to do it.

A Popular Manual Sniping Method

Bring up the item for which you intend to snipe. Oh, boy! Look what I found! An auction listing for a pair of Hummels!

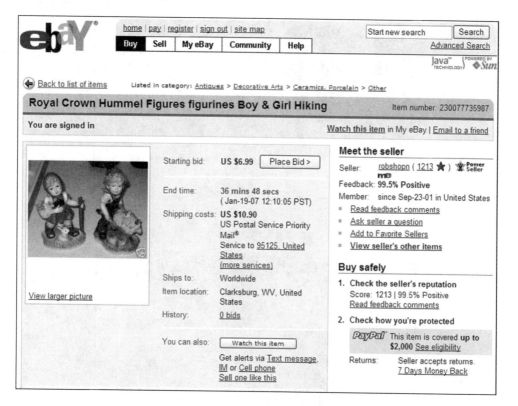

Aren't they just irresistibly adorable? I simply have to snipe them! (Don't get the wrong idea. I don't collect Hummels to keep and to cherish. I buy them as therapy. Truth is, whenever I am having a bad day, smashing a Hummel to bits with a big hammer calms my nerves. And before you real Hummel collectors have a fit, keep in mind that by reducing the population of cute ceramic figurines, I am actually increasing the value of your collection. You're welcome.)

The next step is to determine a safe but effective snipe time. If your Internet connection is superfast, you can usually get away with waiting until the last few seconds to snipe. If instead your connection is slow, you may have to snipe sooner rather than later. To make a more accurate determination of the time it might take over your connection, visit any listing set to close in the next hour. Note the end time.

Royal Crown Hummel Figures figurines Boy & Girl Hiking

You are signed in

Starting bid:	US $6.99 [Place Bid >]
End time:	33 mins 33 secs (Jan-19-07 12:10:05 PST)
Shipping costs:	US $10.90 US Postal Service Priority Mail® Service to 95125, United States (more services)
Ships to:	Worldwide
Item location:	Clarksburg, WV, United States
History:	0 bids

View larger picture

Refresh the window and note the new end time.

Royal Crown Hummel Figures figurines Boy & Girl Hiking

You are signed in

Starting bid:	US $6.99 [Place Bid >]
End time:	33 mins 32 secs (Jan-19-07 12:10:05 PST)
Shipping costs:	US $10.90 US Postal Service Priority Mail® Service to 95125, United States (more services)
Ships to:	Worldwide
Item location:	Clarksburg, WV, United States
History:	0 bids

View larger picture

The difference in seconds is the minimum amount of time you should wait before the auction closes to submit your snipe bid. In the example above, this would be one second. Thus, my snipe bid should be submitted no later than "End time— 1 secs," but to be safe, I might want to leave myself three or four seconds more. Thus, I will submit my snipe bid at "End time—5 secs."

Determine a snipe bid amount. Snipers tend to use high snipe bid amounts as an offensive move against other snipers. Although chances are good that you, as a sniper, won't actually have to pay your high snipe amount should you win the item, it is possible you might get stuck if someone snipes you with a bid just under yours.

Open a Web browser window and navigate to the item you wish to snipe. Do this five minutes or more before a listing is set to close.

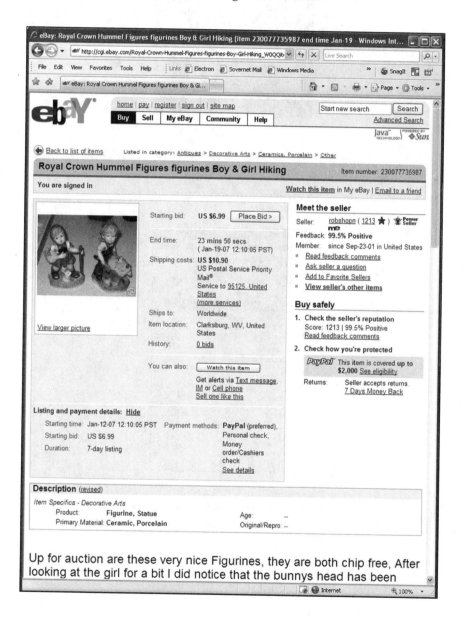

Once the item is displayed, open another copy of the window with the item by simultaneously pressing the Ctrl and N keys on your Windows computer keyboard.

Substitute the Apple or Command key for the Ctrl key if you use a Mac. (You can also open a copy of the window by clicking "File, New, Window" or "File, New Window" on the Web browser's menu command bar.)

Now you have two windows open, preferably to the same item page. If not, navigate to the item so that the two windows look like this:

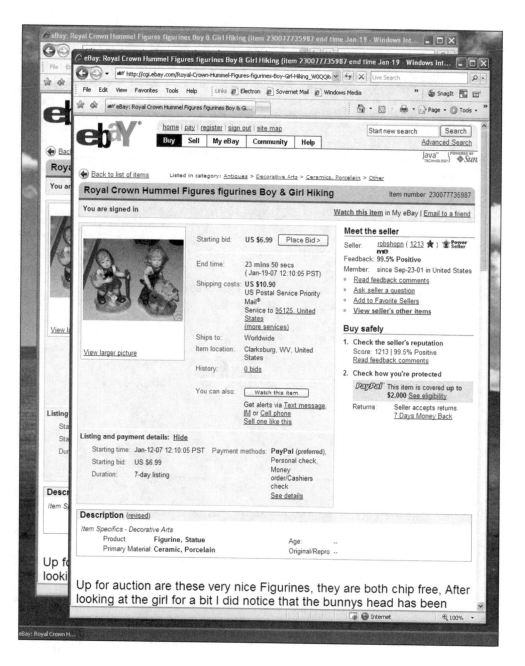

Click the "Place bid" button.

In this window, enter a bid amount in the "Your maximum bid" text box and click the "Continue" button to reach:

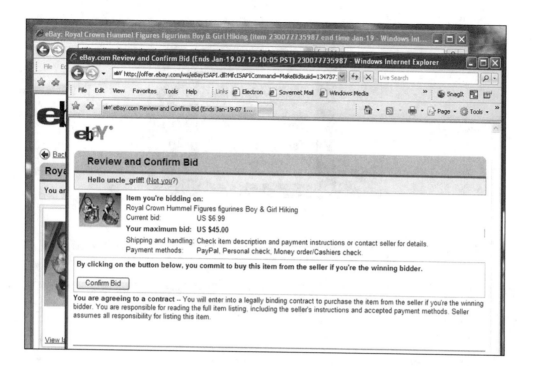

Leave this window open on the Review and Confirm Bid page with the "Confirm bid" button showing.

Arrange the two Web browser windows side by side. You can drag the windows and resize them with your mouse. Another quick way to do this if your operating system is any version of Windows is to open both windows. (Make sure any and all other programs or applications are closed or else they will tile as well.) Then, right-click anywhere on the Windows task bar. Select "Tile windows horizontally."

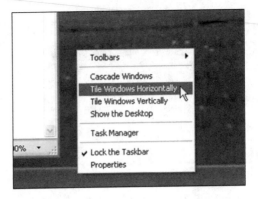

This will display the two open browser windows side by side like so:

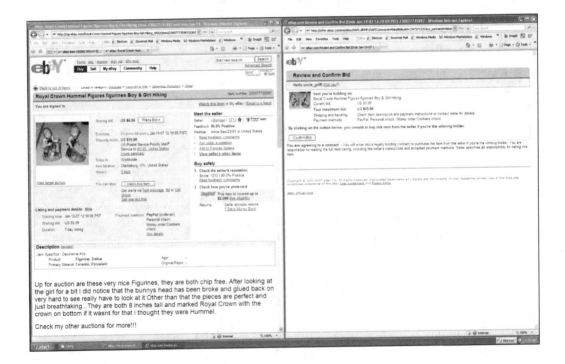

Make sure the second window is opened to the Review and Confirm Bid page and that it shows the "Confirm bid" button clearly. Use the first window to watch the time wind down by refreshing the page at regular intervals. Click the browser's "Refresh" or "Reload" button to refresh the page:

When the End Time reaches 15 minutes (left), a special "Refresh" button will appear to the right and slightly above the "Place bid" button.

Click this "Refresh" button to show the latest time left.

When the time left shown in the first window is close to or at your predetermined snipe time, quickly move your mouse to the second window and click the "Confirm bid" button.

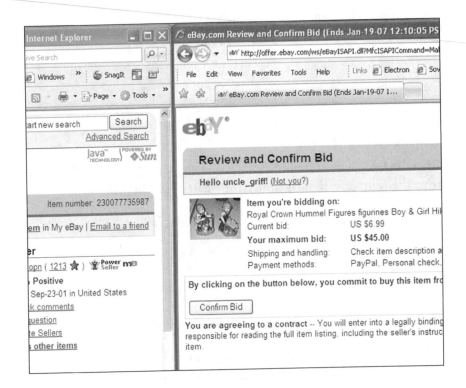

When window one shows five seconds or less left, it's time to snipe! Click that "Confirm bid" button! Let's hope that when it refreshes, we see the following screen:

Hooray! I am now the proud owner of yet another set of "smashingly" cute ceramic figurines!

eBay member Bill Cawlfield told me an amazing tale of sniping from a most unusual location:

Well, I had to have this one radio, about three years ago. The item was going to end while I was flying. This was long before sniper programs. So, not thinking about having someone else snipe for me, I decided to snipe from a plane on the way from Denver to L.A. The connection was just awful in those days, maybe 7,600 baud. I finally loaded the item page, turned off all graphics, and counted down the seconds, not daring to hit "Refresh" because that would tie up the reload too long.

I hit "Confirm bid" and then refreshed, which took another couple of minutes . . . I won! It proves that speed does not count, only the size. Sniping from thirty-five thousand feet—a new meaning of the mile-high club.

MULTIPLE ITEM BIDDING—HOW IT WORKS

Whereas the Proxy Bidding format is used for listings with one single lot up for sale, the Multiple Item Listing format is used for selling multiple identical items in one listing.

Multiple Item bidding does not work like Proxy Bidding. When you bid in a Multiple Item Listing, you specify the number of items you're interested in and the price you're willing to pay. All winning bidders will pay the same price: the lowest successful bid.

For Multiple Item Listings, you cannot enter a maximum bid. The amount of your bid is the price you pay (if yours is the winning bid). For example, if there are ten items available and an opening bid of $4, and there is one bidder who bids $20 for ten items, that bidder pays $20 for each item.

Much of the time, all buyers pay the starting price in Multiple Item Listings. However, if there are more bids than items, the items will go to the earliest successful bids.

To beat another bid, you must place a higher total bid per item than other bids, regardless of how many items you are bidding on. Reducing this total bid value in subsequent bids is not permitted.

For example, for a listing with ten available items and two bidders:

- Bidder A bid for three items at $5 each.
- Bidder B bid for eight items at $6 each.

In this case, the lowest successful bid is $5. So the outcome of this listing is:

- Bidder B wins eight items at $5 each.
- Bidder A wins two items at $5 each.

Winning bidders have the right to refuse partial quantities. This means that if you win some but not all of the quantity you bid for, you don't have to buy any of them. In the above example, Bidder A bid on three items but won only two of them. Bidder A can refuse to complete the purchase, as she didn't win the quantity she bid on.

Successful bids are displayed when you click on the "See winning bidders list" link. The complete bidding history (including any unsuccessful bids) is displayed when you click on "Bidders list."

Most Multiple Item Listings are for vast quantities of a single item, for example, mounted insects. In the example shown below, the seller was offering ten bottles of Fierce Cologne by Abercrombie and Fitch.

We can see how many of these sold by clicking "Bidders list."

home	pay	site map	
Buy	Sell	My eBay	Community	Help

Start new search   Search
Advanced Search

Hello, uncle_griff! (Sign out)

Java™ TECHNOLOGY ◆Sun POWERED BY

← Back to item description

Bid History

Item number: 230079178384

Email to a friend | **Watch this item** in My eBay

Item title: 1.7fl oz. Fierce Cologne from Abercrombie and Fitch
Quantity: 0 available
Currently: US $48.00
Time left: Auction has ended

Only actual bids (not automatic bids generated up to a bidder's maximum) are shown. Automatic bids may be placed days or hours before a listing ends. Learn more about bidding.

Bidder	Bid amount	Quantity wanted	Quantity winning	Date of bid
	US $48.00	1	1	Jan-20-07 17:12:44 PST
	US $48.00**	10	9	Jan-20-07 16:39:21 PST
	US $31.00	1	0	Jan-20-07 14:05:50 PST
	US $30.00	5	0	Jan-20-07 12:44:24 PST
	US $28.51	1	0	Jan-19-07 22:23:53 PST
	US $27.00	1	0	Jan-20-07 05:23:59 PST
	US $27.00	1	0	Jan-20-07 10:02:46 PST
	US $26.01	1	0	Jan-20-07 11:54:26 PST
	US $26.00	1	0	Jan-20-07 12:27:51 PST
	US $24.87	1	0	Jan-20-07 06:51:32 PST
	US $22.00	1	0	Jan-18-07 20:26:52 PST
	US $20.00	1	0	Jan-19-07 16:49:08 PST
	US $17.00	1	0	Jan-19-07 08:06:38 PST
	US $15.00	2	0	Jan-18-07 08:00:30 PST
	US $15.00	2	0	Jan-18-07 12:12:58 PST
	US $5.00	2	0	Jan-18-07 18:35:08 PST
	US $4.00	1	0	Jan-17-07 17:03:46 PST
	US $3.00	4	0	Jan-18-07 09:42:43 PST
	US $2.00	2	0	Jan-17-07 17:50:08 PST
	US $2.00	1	0	Jan-18-07 10:09:58 PST
	US $1.00	1	0	Jan-17-07 17:58:51 PST
	US $1.00	10	0	Jan-17-07 21:44:17 PST
	US $0.99	2	0	Jan-17-07 08:22:20 PST

** Bidder has been outbid on some items. Learn more about how winning bids are determined for multiple item auctions.
You can retract your bid under certain circumstances only.

There were twenty-three individual eBay bidders chasing ten bottles of cologne—an ideal situation for the seller! They started at 99¢ and ended up selling for $48 each to the two bidders shown in the highlighted box at the top of the list. One bidder actually ended up with nine bottles. I suppose that might be considered a lifetime supply.

Points to Keep in Mind About Multiple Item Listing Bidding

Multiple Item Listing bid amounts are not kept secret during the auction. The amount you bid is the amount that shows in the bidding history immediately after you bid.

Your Bid Value is calculated as the amount of your bid times the quantity of items for which you have bid. For example, the Bid Value for a listing in which you bid $30 for two items is $60. A rebid by a Multiple Item Listing bidder must have a Bid Value greater than his or her previous bid. Thus, if I bid for two items at $30 apiece, my bid value is $60. If I rebid in this auction, my Bid Value cannot be equal to or lower than $60. Thus, I could not bid $31 for one item. This automatic restriction is intended to prevent one bidder from tying up all the items in a Multiple Item Listing and then rebidding for a lower quantity at the last moment of the auction.

The Bid History for a Multiple Item Listing shows everyone who has bid, successful or not. The Winning Bidders List shows the current successful bidders for the item.

Regardless of their actual bid amounts, the winning bidders in a Multiple Item Listing all pay the same final price (known as the lowest successful bid) times the quantity they each bid for. The lowest successful bid is the amount bid by the last bidder on the Winning Bidders List. In our example above, everyone shown on the list of winning Multiple Item Listing bidders would pay the lowest successful bid, in this case $15.

BUY IT NOW—HOW IT WORKS

For all their fun and excitement, auctions are not for everyone or for every buying situation. Sometimes, a seller may want to move an item fast or a buyer may want to purchase an item immediately instead of waiting for three or more days for an auction to close.

To meet both needs, eBay instituted a fixed-price format called Buy It Now.

Buy It Now is fairly simple. All items that offer the option will have a Buy It Now icon next to their title in both Category and Title Search list results.

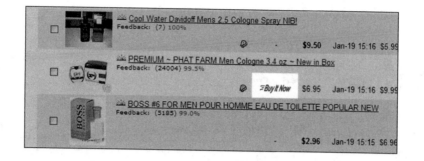

There are two types of Buy It Now listings: those with an auction-format option and those without (otherwise known as Fixed Price). When you open a Buy It Now item's description page, you will find either type. Those that are straight fixed-price with no auction component will look something like this:

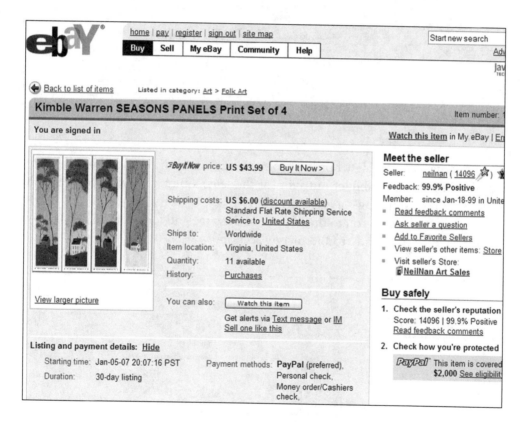

Those with an auction component look like this listing:

I can always use a new bottle of cologne but I don't want to bid on this item. I am willing to simply buy it outright for the seller's Buy It Now price of $19.90 (plus $7.90 for shipping—a great deal!).

To Buy It Now, I scroll to the bottom of the page and look for the Buy It Now section next to the Ready to Bid or Buy section.

Click the button, review the details, and click the "Review and commit to buy" button . . .

. . . and it's mine. No bidding, no wondering if you will win it.

To complete the transaction, click the "Pay Now" button.

Buy It Now—Immediate Payment

Sellers may opt to include a special component to their Buy It Now listings, called Immediate Payment Required. Our seller has, in fact, included this option.

To win a Buy It Now item when the Immediate Payment Required option is displayed, you must pay for the item using PayPal as soon as possible. The item will not close until you do so, which means that until you complete the transaction through PayPal, someone else can come along and Buy It Now right from under you.

Why use this immediate payment feature? Some sellers have been inconvenienced by the new or confused buyer who clicks the Buy It Now button without understanding how Buy It Now works. When the buyer discovers that clicking the button effectively ends the listing and obliges him to purchase, he backs out.

The Immediate Payment Required option prevents this type of confusion from ending a Buy It Now listing until the buyer pays for the item.

Whether you bid on an item and won it or bought it outright using Buy It Now, the next step is to pay for it. We cover how to pay for an item in the next chapter.

For now, it's time to go back and purchase the digital camera we discussed earlier using Buy It Now.

Now that I've bought the camera, I will immediately pay for it . . . in the next chapter, after we pay for our bottle of cologne.

5

Shopping at eBay—Pay for It!

Congratulations! You've bought your first item on eBay. Get out your pocketbook—it's time to complete the transaction. But first, I want to share a story sent to me that illustrates the generosity and kindness typical of eBay members.

eBay seller Terry Wagner lives in New Jersey with her husband and three little girls. Terry lost her Internet-based job a few years ago. At the same time, she learned that she had a rare blood disorder that makes her feel constantly fatigued, with daily dizzy spells, leg and hand cramps, and pounding headaches.

By 2001, Terry was in constant pain. Her disability insurance had been cut off. Her dad was fighting bladder cancer and her mom was recovering from heart surgery. Then came the terrible events of September 11. Terry had previously worked at the World Trade Center, and she lost many old friends in the attacks.

"I knew people who never came home. I cried for days and days and still cry when I think about it."

Christmas 2001 looked bleak at best. Terry was hunting for affordable gifts at eBay when she came across a beautiful but expensive quilt—a perfect gift for her mother. Terry e-mailed the seller to ask if she had any less expensive quilts. The seller wrote back and told Terry that she did indeed and would be happy to hold one for her.

"After a few weeks, I had to write her back and explain that I still couldn't afford the less-expensive quilt and was so sorry for leaving her hanging."

Two days later, Terry received an e-mail with the subject line "Ho, ho, ho! We want to send you the quilt!" The seller had told her husband about Terry and, as the seller explained to Terry, "He took money out of his pocket and said, 'Send her the quilt!'"

The seller insisted Terry send her address so she could send the quilt to her in time to give to her mom for Christmas.

"She sent not only the quilt for my mom, but a small gift for me and a small gift for my thirteen-year-old daughter, who had written her to thank her for making us all so happy!"

Terry and the generous seller correspond regularly and have exchanged family photos as well.

"I just can't get over the kindness. This is not the first person that I have met via eBay who has turned out to show what true human spirit is all about! Life continues to be a struggle. I'm in pain every day, but my friends on eBay keep me smiling."

Completing the Transaction

Many sellers offer detailed instructions on how to complete a transaction for their item by including payment options and shipping and handling amounts in their item descriptions. In fact, some sellers will actually provide a link to an auction management service—or even better, a "Pay now" button right on the closed listing page—where you can immediately view an invoice for the item and select a payment method. Let's go back and pay for the two items we won in the previous chapter. Here's that closed item page for the cologne. The first step is to click the "Pay now" button:

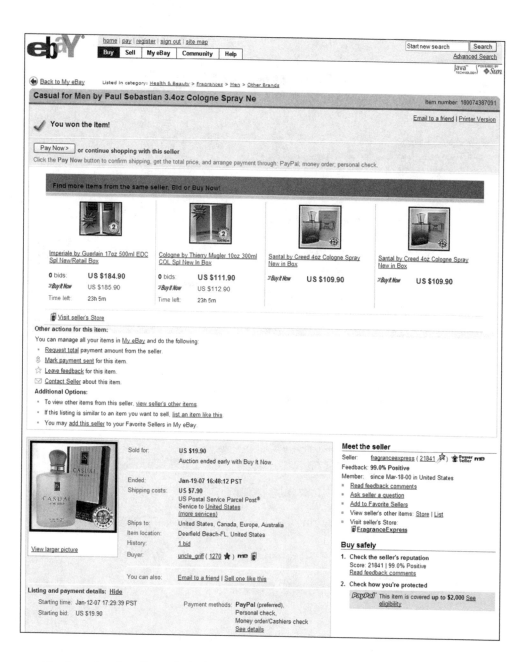

Review the details and click "Continue to PayPal."

eb**Y**®

Review Your PayPal Purchases From Multiple Sellers

Help

You are paying for **1 item** from **1 PayPal seller** totaling US **$27.80**

Prefer to pay sellers individually? Pay one seller at a time.

Review shipping address

Sellers should ship to: Jim Griffith
eBay Inc
2145 Hamilton Ave
San Jose, CA 95125
United States
Change shipping address

Review payment details - Multiple seller purchase

Seller: fragranceexpress (21841 ☆) 🏆 Power Seller 📗

Remove this seller's items

Select	Item Title	Qty.	Price	Subtotal
☑	Casual for Men by Paul Sebastian 3.4oz Cologne Spray Ne (180074387091)	1	US $19.90	US $19.90

Payment Instructions
AFTER THE AUCTION YOU WILL RECEIVE AN INVOICE EMAIL. WE ACCEPT
PAYPAL CREDIT CARDS CHECKS/MONEY ORDERS WESTERN & UNION.
SHIPPING: US Domestic $7.90 FOR THE FIRST ITEM AND $2.90 FOR EACH
ADDITIONAL ITEM. Canada:$11.90 FIRST ITEM AND $3.90 EACH ADDITIONAL
ITEM. International $14.90 FOR THE FIRST ITEM AND $4.90 FOR EACH
ADDITIONAL ITEM. OUR PAYMENT ADDRESS IS P.O. Box 970240 - Coconut
Creek - FL 33097. QUESTIONS? CALL: 1-800-FRAGRANCE (372-4726)

Shipping and handling via US Postal Service Parcel Post: US $7.90

Shipping insurance:(Optional US $1.30) Add

Seller discounts (-) or charges (+): Add

Seller Total: US $27.80
recalculate

☐ I will enter an eBay gift certificate or coupon on PayPal.
Questions about the total? Request total from seller

Seller: antiqueaday (3110 ★) 🏆 Power Seller 📗

▷ You have removed this seller's items from this payment. You will need to pay for these items later.
To pay for these items now, Add these items back.

Seller: emilyandlily (192650 ★) 🏆 Power Seller 📗

▷ You have removed this seller's items from this payment. You will need to pay for these items later.
To pay for these items now, Add these items back.

Seller: old14753 (1733 ★) 🏆 Power Seller 📗

▷ You have removed this seller's items from this payment. You will need to pay for these items later.
To pay for these items now, Add these items back.

Grand Total (recalculate): US $27.80

Confirm payment method

PayPal
MasterCard VISA AMEX DISCOVER eCHECK

Pay with PayPal and your purchase is
covered **up to $2,000** See eligibility

Continue to PayPal >

On the next screen, you have two choices.

PayPal
an eb**Y** company

Complete Your eBay Payment

Shop without sharing your financial information. When you pay with PayPal, your credit/debit card and bank account numbers are never seen by the seller or merchant. Your financial information stays safe. Plus, you're protected 100% against unauthorized payments sent from your account.

Log In

If you've already saved your information with PayPal, login here.

Email Address: [_____]
(e.g. name@domain.com)

PayPal Password: [•••••••••]

[Log In]

Problems logging in?
Forgot your email?
Forgot your password?

New to PayPal?

You have chosen to pay with your credit card or debit card. PayPal is the secure card processor for your seller, **fragranceexpress**. Learn more about PayPal

MasterCard VISA DISCOVER AMEX eCHECK

Country: [United States   ▼]

[Sign Up]

Item(s) to purchase

Item #	Item Title	Qty
180074387091	Casual for Men by Paul Sebastian 3.4oz Cologne Spray Ne	1

If you are already signed up for PayPal, simply type in your PayPal log-in (your e-mail address) and password and click "Log in."

If you haven't yet opened up a PayPal account, well, what are you waiting for? Click the link "Sign up and pay with PayPal."

Review the payment details:

PayPal
an eb**Y** company

Log Out

Complete Your Payment

Secure Transaction

Click **Pay** to confirm the details below and complete your payment. Learn more about PayPal policies and your payment-source rights and remedies.

Shipping Address: eBay Inc
2145 Hamilton Ave
San Jose, CA 95125
United States

Edit address

				Pay

Item Details

Item #	Item Title	Qty	Price	Subtotal
180074387091	Casual for Men by Paul Sebastian 3.4oz Cologne Spray Ne	1	$19.90 USD	$19.90 USD
			US Shipping & Handling via USPS Parcel Post (includes any seller handling fees) :	$7.90 USD
Add Instructions to Seller (optional)			US Insurance (optional) :	--
			Total:	**$27.80 USD**
			Edit payment details	

Click "Pay" . . .

PayPal
an eb**Y** company

Log Out

Payment Complete

Secure Transaction

Your payment of **$27.80 USD** to the seller **fragranceexpress** is complete. You will receive an email receipt for this transaction shortly. [View Printable Receipt]

PayPal
Privacy is built in.

Shop Without Sharing Your Financial Information
When you pay with PayPal, your credit card and bank numbers are never seen by the seller or merchant. Your financial information stays safe. Plus, you're protected 100% against unauthorized payments sent from your account.

PayPal. Privacy is built in. Learn more

View My PayPal Account

Return to eBay

. . . and you are done! You can also print out a receipt by clicking the link on this page.

This seller offered PayPal, and so the payment process was incredibly easy and took literally less than a minute to complete. If you follow the suggestions for shopping on eBay provided in previous chapters, you can limit your searches to only those sellers that offer PayPal. However, you will also come across items that you really want but which include little or no information from the seller on how to complete the transaction.

If you did your homework by either reading the item description carefully or e-mailing the seller before you bid on or bought the item, you should at least have a good idea of the following:

> The amount due for shipping/handling
> The types of payment the seller accepts

Here are some examples of eBay sellers' shipping and payment terms taken from actual eBay listings:

HIGH BIDDER pays $29.99 UPS shipping cost within the continental USA. Alaska & Hawaii $10.00 more. No International orders, please. No APO/FPO Addresses. Cashier's Checks, Money Order, or use your credit card with either PayPal, BidPay.Com. NY State Residents must add 8.25% Sales Tax to final total.

SHIPPING INFO: All of our prints are professionally packed and double wrapped for safe delivery. Shipping/packing charges are $6.50 for Insured UPS (Priority Mail for Box holders, APO/FPO addresses or upon request). I will ship ANY NUMBER of Gallery quality prints together for that price!

(International orders are sent via DHL Worldwide. International shipping costs are: Canada - $16.00, all other International - $24.00). (Please allow 2-4 days for order processing).

I'm always happy to combine multiple items to save on shipping! Buyer to pay actual shipping charges. I never charge a handling fee!

CUSTOMER POLICY

- 100% Satisfaction Guaranteed. If you are not satisfied with your purchase, please return the item within 5 days in the same condition you have received and we will refund your money less S/H.
- You may return any unopened merchandise in its mint condition within 7 days of receiving your order. You will be charged a 20 % restocking fee and Shipping and Handling fee is not refundable.
- You may, at your own expense, return item within 5 days upon received shipment.
- If you receive wrong item by our simply mistake, we do sincerely apologize and please return item with original package material condition , replacement will ship out within 3 business days upon received shipment
- If you purchased insurance and receive an item that's damage; contact us immediately; Exchange for damage or defective product within 3 business days upon received shipment;
- **Damage or Defective items will not be replaced if there are signs of use or tampering**

Payment Policy
Personal Check: Will hold 7 to 10 days until check clears.
Money Order/Cashiers Checks: Will process right away.
PayPal: Our PayPal ID: saleinstore@yahoo.com We reserve rights to refuse any non-confirmed address payments.

Sales Tax
6% In State of Florida and 0 % out of State where sales tax is charged.

Shipping

- We ship USA ONLY!!!
- We are not responsible for any charges or any matters incurred with Customs of International Shipments.
- Shipping/handling: $7.75 and each additional $3.50 You can add insurance $1.50. It is optional.
- If you make the payment through PayPal we will ship to the address provided by PayPal. (if the shipment address is not updated in PayPal and you get the shipment in your old address, we are not responsible for returning or lost items.)

Summary of My Selling Policies

Payment	1) We accept payment via Paypal (preferred) , Money Order, Bid Pay, Cashier's check and/or Personal Check (please allow 10 business days for checks to clear). 2) We prefer payment via paypal. 3) Payment is due within 7 days of the end of auction. If payment is not received, a non-paying bidder alert will be issued.
Fees	1) Pennsylvania residents add 6% sales tax. Philadelphia residents 7% sales tax.
Shipping	1) Domestic Shipping, handling and insurance fees are fixed and stated in each auction. 2) We gladly ship anywhere in the world. International customers should e-mail for specific shipping costs to your country, and you are responsible for any tariffs or duties applicable for your country. We will Not devalue your purchase to reduce your duty, so Please do not ask. 3) We ship USPS Priority or USPS Parcel Post. 4) Shipping fees include insurance and delivery confirmation. Tracking numbers provided upon request. 5) We may offer Shipping discounts for multiple purchases boxed together.
Delivery	1) Items are usually shipped within 3-4 business days after payment is received, larger or very fragile items may take longer. 2) We will e-mail shipping confirmation. 3) We ship two days a week. 4) International Buyers: Your shipping and insurance fees will vary from the fees quoted in this auction. Please let us know how you wish your item to be shipped before you pay, so we can calculate your fees accordingly. 5) International Buyers: There might be a delay of up to one week in our shipment of your item, as we only get to the Post Office once weekly.
Refunds & Returns	1) ALL of our auctions are Guaranteed. In the unlikely event we mistakenly misrepresented an item, we offer a Full Refund of the Bid Price. Just email us within FOUR days of delivery. Bidders are still responsible for ALL shipping, handling and insurance costs, including ALL return shipping costs. 2) Please understand that all information pertaining to age, condition, origin, etc. are approximations. Unless specified, all items are used, second-hand, or antique. We do not sell on approval. If you are unsure of any information provided or require additional information, please email us Prior to Bidding. We are human, list many used and antique items, and may sometimes make mistakes pertaining to condition, age, authenticity, etc. These are just honest mistakes or oversights, not attempts to defraud. Please allow us an opportunity to recify an error before leaving neutral or negative feedback. Failure to do so may result in reciprocal feedback. If you make a mistake, we will afford you this same common courtesy. 3) Please inform us before returning an item. Returns will Not be accepted without prior notification AND approval via e-mail. 4) If an item arrives damaged due to shipping, please notify us within 4 days. Your package is insured and we will give you instructions for filing an insurance claim.
Contact Me	1) The best way to contact us is via e-mail at ~ ~~~~~~~ ~~~ ~~ ~~~ ~~~ 2) We will ususally respond within 24 hours. 3) If you try to contact us over the weekend or holiday we will respond by the next business day. Our offices are closed on weekends and holidays. 4) On weekdays you can also call us at 215 2 3 4131 from 10:30 am to 5:00 pm Eastern Standard Time. Please do not hesitate to call or email us during or after any auction.

BID WITH CONFIDENCE
Read my policies on my SquareTrade Seal

By contrast, here is an example of a listing where the seller hasn't included any shipping or payment terms.

Description (revised)

very neat primitive wicker piece looks like a haywood wakefield piece i didn't see a mark saw a very simalar piece priced at 800.00 has alot of old pealy paint and nice 40s green paint.has barley twist legs and a bottom shelf sits alittle off kilter as do the legs adds carature to the piece.low starting bid no resurve.

If you were interested in purchasing this item, you would have to e-mail the seller for more information. This seller would do his potential customers—and himself—a great service by putting some shipping and payment information into the description.

CONTACT THE SELLER

Usually, once an eBay listing has closed, the seller will send an e-mail to the winning bidder or buyer with exact payment instructions. However, there is no set protocol or rule stating who should e-mail whom first. As a bidder, instead of waiting for the seller to contact you, you should always e-mail the seller immediately after the listing has closed. If the seller hasn't included an actual price for shipping or hasn't provided the eBay Shipping Calculator in his item description, provide your shipping address in the e-mail and your preferred method of payment so the seller can calculate shipping and respond with an amount.

ASK THE SELLER A QUESTION

As we mentioned in the previous chapter, whenever you have a question or doubt about an item, e-mail the seller. Use the "Ask seller a question" link on the Item Description page.

The Ask Seller a Question form looks like this:

My Messages: Ask a Question

[i] Making a Best Offer? Submit your Best Offer price to the seller directly.

Ask a question

To:	**fredstuf**
From:	uncle_griff
Item:	Wrought Iron and Wicker End Table or Plant Stand (230097813161)
Subject:	Select a question about this item ▼

Enter your question here

976 characters left. No HTML.
Note: The seller may include your question in the item description.

eBay will send your message to fredstuf's My Messages Inbox and email address.

☐ Hide my email address from fredstuf.
☐ Send a copy to my email address.

[Send] Cancel

Fill in your message and click the "Submit question" button. Your message will be e-mailed to the seller with a blind carbon copy sent to your own e-mail address for your records.

Remember, the key to successful eBay trading is effective communication. You can never be too comprehensive or detailed in your message. Provide the seller with all the information he or she will need to provide you with a detailed and complete answer.

PAYMENT OPTIONS

As noted in the last chapter, all eBay sellers may offer at least one of the following five allowable payment methods:

Online payment services (PayPal, etc.)
Credit cards (through the seller's own merchant account)
Electronic (wire) transfers
Money orders
Checks

Online Payment Services

Before 1998, any eBay seller who wished to accept credit card payments had to apply and pay for a special merchant account. Now, with online payment services anyone can accept credit cards without the expense or hassle of setting up a merchant account at a bank.

The most popular online payment service with eBay buyers and sellers is PayPal. In fact, PayPal has been the eBay member online payment service of choice since 1999, long before PayPal became a part of the eBay team!

GRIFF TIP! Although PayPal is by far the online payment method of choice, there are other online payment services which are allowed on eBay. To view the current list of which are and which are not allowed, visit the Accepted Payments Policy page.

Click "Help" on the top of any eBay page and follow the links for Help Topics > Rules and Policies > Rules for Sellers > Accepted Payment Policy.

PayPal

Opening a PayPal account is easy. Just go to *www.paypal.com* and click the link "Sign Up."

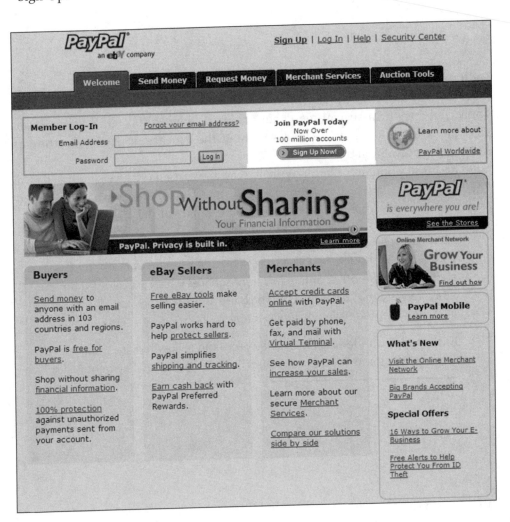

Follow the easy instructions from there.

Make it a habit in your search for treasure at eBay to give preference to those items where the seller accepts PayPal for payment. Using PayPal to buy on eBay affords you the highest possible level of security. It's also the quickest way to pay for an item. That means it's not only the safest way to pay for the item but also the fastest way to get your item shipped to you, since most sellers will ship an item the same day payment is received.

Credit Cards

Many sellers have established their own merchant accounts for accepting credit cards. Although paying with a credit card through such an account is usually safe and secure, always ask the seller if he or she can provide you with a secure method of transmitting your credit details (a secure server link).

Did you know you can also use a credit card to pay a seller through PayPal?

Bank-to-Bank Wire Transfers

A bank wire transfer involves the transfer of funds from one bank to another. Bank wire transfers are not to be confused with point-to-point cash wire transfers (i.e., Western Union, MoneyGram, etc.), which are not allowed as a payment method on eBay.

Bank-to-bank wire transfers, though not commonly used on eBay.com as a payment option, are popular in certain categories such as eBay Motors. However, they are not generally backed up by the issuing or receiving banks and so entail some risk.

Use PayPal instead.

Money Orders

Although paying with money orders is very old-fashioned, a few eBay sellers accept them either as one of a selection of payment options or, in some cases, as the only payment method!

When paying with a money order, make it a habit to write the item number and the seller's eBay User ID in the memo section of the money order, and make sure to keep your money order receipt in a safe place in case you need it later.

Money orders are not as reliable, quick, or safe as paying with PayPal.

Checks

As a payment method, checks are less popular than they were in the early days of eBay. It's easy to see why as more and more eBay sellers are accepting PayPal. Still, some sellers will accept only checks or money orders.

If you pay using a check, make sure to keep a record of the check in your checking account register. Although not as secure or fast as paying with a credit card, a canceled check could be sufficient evidence of your having paid for an item.

As with a money order, make sure you put the item number and seller's User ID in the check's memo field.

GRIFF TIP! Checks, money orders . . . you have to write them out with a pen, buy a stamp and find an envelope, mail them out to the seller, wait for them to arrive, and wait for them to clear. When you think about it, checks and money orders are really so last century. You might as well invest in a powdered wig and a quill pen. Maybe you could even make your own ink and paper!

That's why for convenience and security, I only shop with sellers who offer PayPal. You should too!

Cash?

Fuggedaboudit. Never send cash through the mail. Should something go wrong (the seller doesn't receive the cash or you don't receive your item), you will have no record of payment and, consequently, no avenue of redress.

Cash as payment is appropriate only if you plan to pay for and pick up the item yourself—for example, if you bought something at eBay from a seller in your area. When paying with cash, make sure you obtain a detailed and signed receipt. If the item is a vehicle, don't hand over the cash until the seller has provided adequate proof of identity and a legal, clear title.

The "Pay Now" Button

As we have seen above with our two purchases, many eBay sellers will provide their buyers with the ease and speed of the "Pay now" button. This button facilitates the last steps of an eBay transaction by collecting all of the payment and shipping information and options into one central place.

Look for the "Pay now" button on the closed listing page as well as in any end-of-listing e-mails you receive.

GRIFF TIP! Since each seller will have different payment options, shipping totals, and so on, always follow the individual seller's instructions as stated in the item description Terms of Service to request a total or to pay for the item.

236

Managing Bids and Purchases with My eBay

The My eBay All Buying page—there is simply no better tool for tracking your current bids and completed auctions within the last thirty days. You can read more about My eBay in Section One, chapter 2.

COMPILING AND ARCHIVING LISTINGS IN WHICH YOU ARE THE WINNER

It's smart to save a copy of all your winning bids at eBay (and it's good practice for later, when you start saving listings where you are the seller). You never know when you might need the copy. For example, if you sell the item later, you may need some documentation to show how much you paid for it. A copy of your payment receipt plus a printout of the Item Description page should be more than adequate proof of price and date of sale.

This simple archive consists of copies of each Item Description page in which you were the buyer. To make a print record, navigate to an Item Description page, let it load completely (look for "Done" on the status bar on the bottom of the browser window), then look for the "Printer version" link on the bottom of the listing page under the "Other Options" section.

This creates a summary version of the item page containing only the important item and transaction details.

Printer Version: All | Summary

ebaY

Listed in category: Cameras & Photo > Digital Cameras > Point & Shoot > 6.0 to 6.9 Megapixels > Other

~NEW~ NIKON COOLPIX L4 4MP DIGITAL CAMERA +3 BONUS +1GB

Item number: 180076105690

BONUS:* * 1GB CARD +BATTERIES +CHARGER + ** DELUXE CASE

✓ You committed to buy (Click 'Pay Now' to complete your purchase)   As of Jan-19-07 21:11:20 PST
(The seller has sent you an invoice.)

Buy It Now price:	US $124.85
Shipping cost:	US $19.99 UPS Ground Service to United States
Ships to:	United States, Canada
Item location:	Fast Ship!, United States
Quantity:	4 available
End time:	Jan-20-07 22:27:29 PST (1 day 1 hour)
History:	Purchases
Seller:	emilyandlily (192697) ★ Power Seller
Store:	Emilyandlily Store
Feedback:	192697 (99.6% positive)
Member:	since Feb-10-03 in United States

Make no payments for 3 months
and pay no interest if paid in 3 months on your first purchase over $50 with the PayPal Plus Credit Card. Plus, earn rewards on every purchase you make! Get the PayPal Plus Credit Card and use anywhere MasterCard is accepted.
See details | Apply now

Print the printer version of the item page by selecting "File, Print . . ." on your Web browser's command bar.

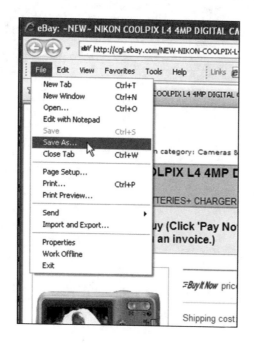

It helps to have a color printer.

You can save a soft or computer copy of any item page by clicking the "File, Save As . . ." command on your Web browser's menu command bar.

If you are using Windows, when you save the file, in the "Save as type" box choose "Web Page, complete (*htm,*html)" and note where you save it. (We are saving ours in the My Documents folder.)

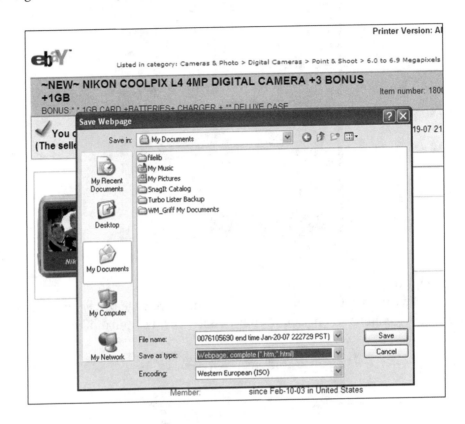

If you are using a Mac computer, depending on which Web browser you are using, choose "File" and then "Save As . . ." and select "Web Archive" as format (for Internet Explorer).

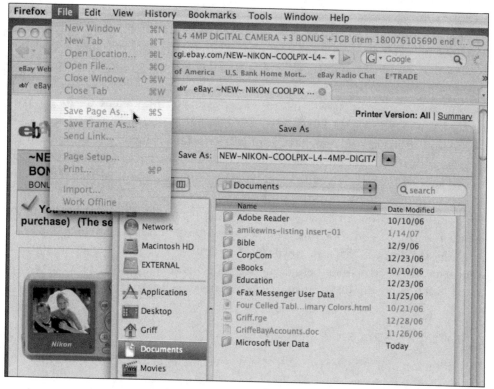

In either case, with Windows or Mac, you may also want to give the saved file a name that will make it easier to locate in the future. You can type in a new name in the "Save As . . ." box.

GRIFF TIP! Some sellers have limited Web server space for their pictures. Soon after one of their listings ends, they tend to delete old picture files from their Web server to free up space for pictures of new listings. Consequently, it is not uncommon to visit a completed listing and find the images are all missing and in their place are little boxes with red X's. Therefore, if you wish to archive a closed listing as hard or soft copy and you want to include the pictures of that item, you should do so as soon as possible after the item closes, before the seller has deleted the picture files.

Unpacking Your Item

You've contacted the seller and paid for the item, and the seller has shipped the item to you.

Finally, the package arrives and you are giddy with delight. In fact, waiting for the UPS, FedEx, or USPS deliveryman to drop off your treasure is no small part of the appeal of regularly shopping on eBay. Your first impulse is to rip the package open.

But wait. If the item is fragile or expensive, you may want to go get your camera and maybe a friend or family member before you open the package.

As you open the package, have your friend or family member photograph the process with a minimum of three shots: one shot of the package before you open it, one shot of the package when you have just finished opening it, and one shot of you lifting the item out of the package.

Even better, use your video camera if you have one. Either way, you want to create a record of your opening the package and inspecting the item.

Why the record? Why, for insurance, of course! If, for whatever reason, the item was damaged, either before or during transit, the photos or video could prove invaluable when submitting a claim with the carrier service.

E-MAIL THE SELLER . . . AGAIN!

As a common courtesy, let the seller know that the package arrived and that you are pleased with the item.

If you are not pleased, or if the item arrived damaged or never arrived, let him know, but make sure to do so in a friendly, non-accusing manner. Any good eBay seller will usually bend over backward to assist with insurance claims or missing packages.

LEAVE FEEDBACK

Based on your experience with the seller, leave appropriate feedback to let the rest of the eBay world know. You can leave feedback by clicking the "Feedback" link in My eBay > My Account or the appropriate link on the closed-item page.

6

Other Bidding and Buying Options and Considerations

In the previous chapters, we've covered almost every aspect of bidding, buying, and paying for goods offered by eBay sellers. Well, almost everything. In addition to the basics (in which you are now considered competent!) there are other aspects of eBay about which you need to know.

eBay Express

In 2006, eBay introduced a radically new way for buyers to shop, called eBay Express. You can reach eBay Express from the links on the eBay home page:

eBay Express isn't a separate eBay site; Express provides a "view" of existing items on eBay that meet certain eligibility criteria.

The inventory of items on eBay Express consists mainly of brand-new, brand-name, and hard-to-find products across a wide range of categories. Everything on eBay Express is offered at a fixed price by top eBay sellers. eBay Express items can be placed in a Shopping Cart so you can buy from multiple eBay Express merchants and, when ready, pay for everything—including shipping—in a single, secure payment using PayPal or your credit card.

Best of all, every single eBay Express transaction is fully covered by free Buyer Protection for the amount of the transaction (with conditions stated on the eBay Express pages).

You can peruse a category and filter it down to very specific items. For example, I am always looking for brand-new, short sleeve, button-down shirts, size 2X.

I started buying on eBay Express in the summer of 2006, and though the experience is quite different from the traditional, familiar auction format I know and love on eBay.com, I have discovered that eBay Express is an extremely effective, satisfying, and, quite frankly, fun way to find and buy specific types of items such as electronic devices, computers, clothing, and accessories. I strongly urge anyone who buys on eBay to explore eBay Express. You will not be disappointed!

Half.com

Half.com is a separate site from eBay.com. Many eBay sellers also offer items on Half. Half was designed specifically for music, movies, books, video games, and certain types of electronic devices. If you are searching for any of the above, try eBay, of course, but don't forget to search Half.com as well.

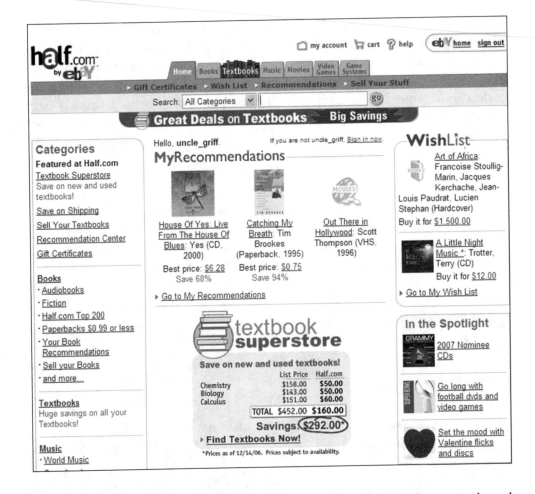

The appeal of buying on Half.com is that one can find both new and used hard-to-find or out-of-print books, CDs, and DVDs at extraordinarily low prices.

I practice what I preach. Most of the music CDs and books in my personal library came from sellers on Half.com!

Buying Big Stuff at eBay

When most folks think of eBay, they tend to think of things that can fit in a cardboard box: toys, collectibles, clothing, pottery, small pieces of furniture, and the like. Although many of the items for sale on eBay are indeed small enough to ship through the regular post, more and more eBay sellers are putting up big items for bid and sale. These items need special buyer consideration.

EBAY MOTORS—CARS, TRUCKS, BOATS, AND SO ON

eBay is the perfect place to buy a car. Car sellers range from the individual owner to used, new, and classic car dealerships.

All things automotive have their own special area on eBay, called eBay Motors. This includes cars, trucks, motorcycles, boats, ATVs, campers, snowmobiles, buses, and aircraft. Also for sale on the eBay Motors site are accessories for all of the above as well as manuals, collectibles, tools, parts, and apparel.

You can get to eBay Motors from the home page:

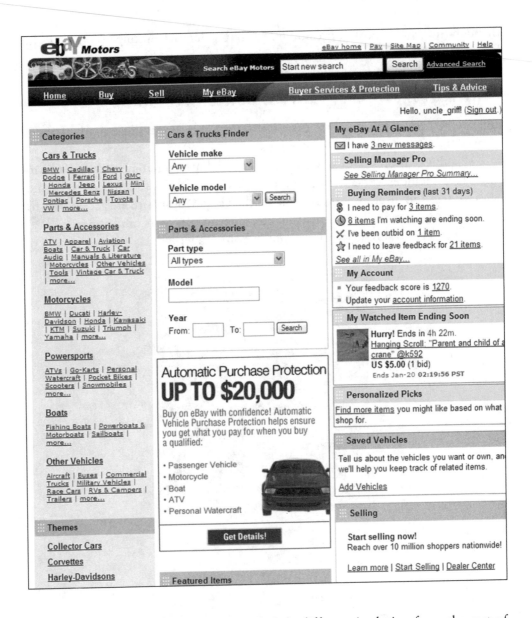

Although the eBay Motors site is slightly different in design from the rest of eBay, the basic layout of the site is identical. Categories are on the left-hand side of the page and include every aspect of all things automotive, nautical, and aero-nautical.

Searching, bidding, and paying for items at eBay Motors is done just as on the rest of eBay, with a few special considerations.

Some eBay Motors sellers have special payment terms, such as a percentage deposit immediately at the end of the listing. As always, make sure that you read the seller's terms carefully and that you fully understand and accept them before you bid. When in doubt, contact the seller for information and clarification.

If you are buying a car, boat, or any other similarly heavy item at eBay Motors, you will probably be more involved in the shipping aspect of the item than you might be for nonautomotive items. Unless the big item is near your location, you will have to arrange and pay for shipping. If the item you are interested in will need to be shipped, you should determine a close estimate of the shipping costs before you bid.

Most eBay Motors sellers provide, within the item descriptions, links to various third-party auto shippers who can help you, before you bid, to figure shipping costs from the car's current location to your location.

If you are considering a purchase of a vehicle on eBay Motors there is one place you should definitely visit: On the eBay Motors page, click the tab for the Buyer Services & Protection hub page.

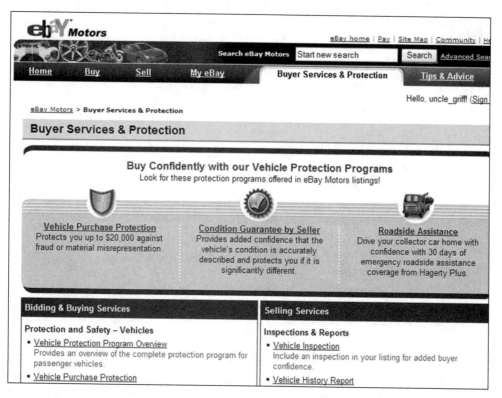

Although you should at least peruse all of the links on the Buyer Services & Protection page, pay special attention to the link "Vehicle Protection Program Overview."

ebY **Motors**

eBay home | Pay | Site Map | Community |

Search eBay Motors Start new search Search Advanced S

| Home | Buy | Sell | My eBay | Buyer Services & Protection | Tips & Advice |

Hello, uncle_griff! (Si

eBay Motors > Buyer Services & Protection > Vehicle Purchase Protection

Vehicle Purchase Protection

Choose a Topic

Overview
Purchase Protection
Eligibility
How to File a
Reimbursement
Request

Overview

Buy with confidence on eBay Motors!
The Vehicle Purchase Protection program helps protect your vehicle purchase against fraud and material misrepresentation. This program is provided by eBay Motors for FREE on all eligible transactions complet the eBay Motors site. There's no sign-up, opt-in, or registration necessary. Your vehicle purchase is prote for up to $20,000 or the vehicle purchase price, whichever is lower. The following table provides a summar vehicles types eligible and the protection offered for each.

Vehicle Type	Maximum Reimbursement[1]	Fraud[2]	Material Misrepresentation[3]	Per Reimbursement Processing Fee[4]	Minim Dama Requirer (if applic
Car or Truck	$20,000	✔	✔	$100	$1,50
Motorcycle	$20,000	✔	✔	$100	$1,50
ATV	$20,000	✔	✔	$100	$1,00
Go-Kart	$20,000	✔	✔	$100	$1,00
Scooter or Moped	$20,000	✔	✔	$100	$1,00
Personal Watercraft	$20,000	✔	✔	$100	$1,00
Snowmobile	$20,000	✔	✔	$100	$1,00
Boat	$20,000	✔	✔	$100	$1,50
Bus	$20,000	✔	✔	$100	$1,50
Commercial Truck	$20,000	✔	✔	$100	$1,50
RV or Camper	$20,000	✔	✔	$100	$1,50
Race Car	$20,000	✔	n/a	$100	n/a
Trailer (non-RV)	$20,000	✔	✔	$100	$1,00

Finally, check out the Tips & Advice link. There you will find an excellent How to Buy tutorial for purchasing vehicles on eBay Motors. All of the information you need for effective car searching and purchasing on eBay Motors can be found under this page.

REAL ESTATE

eBay might not jump to mind when you are hunting for a new home or property, but as of this writing there are thousands of listings in the eBay Real Estate category, ranging from residential homes to businesses.

Also as of this writing, all items in the eBay Real Estate category are non-binding. The real estate listings look and feel just like other eBay listings in the auction format, and anyone may submit a bid, but the owner is not obliged to sell to the high bidder.

In addition, sellers in the Real Estate category can also list in a special format called Ad Format, which again is not binding but can be an effective way for a home buyer and seller to find each other. In Ad Format listings, there is no bidding. Buyer and seller contact each other directly and discuss a possible transaction, one-on-one.

When considering buying or bidding on real estate at eBay . . .

- Obtain as much information as possible before you bid. If the house or property is listed by an individual, e-mail the seller for more pictures, et cetera.
- Whenever possible, arrange to view the property before bidding.
- For more information, visit the Real Estate page. From the eBay home page, look for and click the links for "Real Estate."

This will take you to the Real Estate home page.

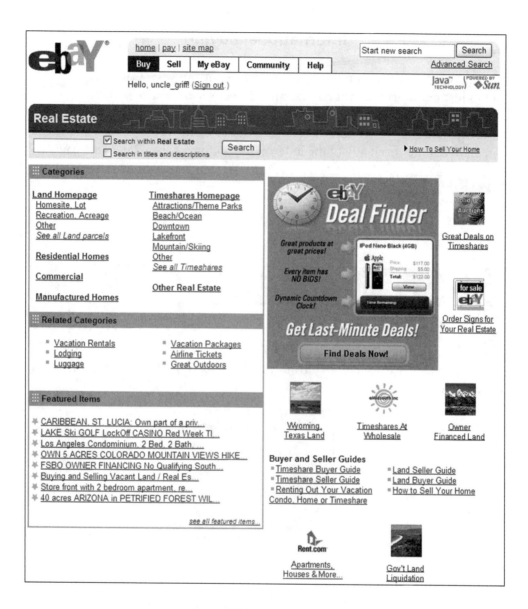

From here you can view homes, land, commercial property, and time-shares. Give special attention to the Buyer and Seller Guides.

International Buying

eBay may have started out as a small hobby site in San Jose, California, in 1995, but in just ten short years, it has expanded to cover the entire planet!

As of this writing, more than fifty countries are represented on eBay on thirty-three separate eBay International sites. You can navigate directly to any of the eBay International sites from any of the links on the bottom of the eBay home page.

Or you can select a country from the drop-down box on the left just above the list of country links.

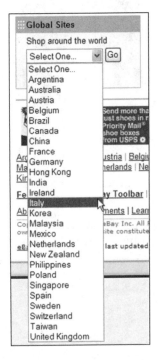

Although instantly recognizable by the eBay logo and colors, each international eBay site has its own distinct look, feel, and language.

Although *www.ebay.com* may have been the first and, for a while, the most popular of all the eBay sites, eBay's international sites are growing at an astounding clip. As eBay continues to expand around the world, folks from other countries are searching both their own eBay sites and the U.S. eBay site.

Any registered eBay member can search for and bid on items listed on any of the eBay International sites. The only requirement is some ability to read and understand the description and terms for the item. For example, loads of fabulous items are listed on the eBay Italia site:

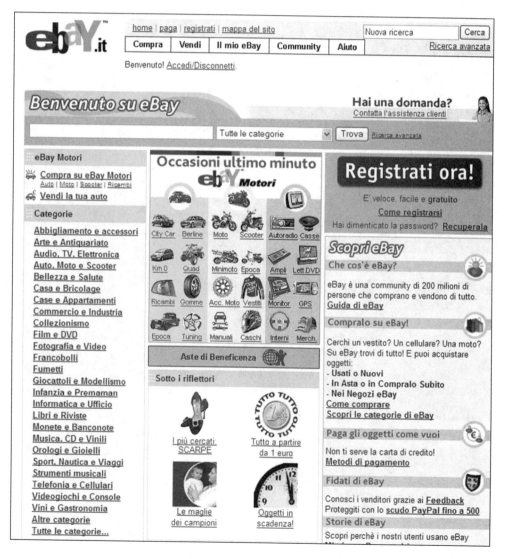

If you have some grasp of Italian and the seller is not averse to shipping the item to your location, then by all means, *compralo su eBay Italia* (buy it on eBay Italy)!

SEARCHING INTERNATIONAL EBAY SITES

In addition to shopping on various international eBay sites, you can also include selected international sites in your eBay keyword searches by selecting the appropriate option under the Location area on the fully expanded Search page. Click the "Advanced Search" link on the top of any eBay page, and scroll down to the section for Location:

There are three options. The default is to search all items listed on the U.S. site (eBay.com) only. You can change this to "Worldwide."

The second option will limit the returned results to only one selected eBay site. Click on the "Items located in" button and pick the appropriate country from the drop-down list. Note: Even though you have limited your search to a specific country, make sure to read a seller's descriptions carefully to make sure she will ship to your country.

The third option will show all items that are available to you. Check the button "Items available to," then select your country location from the drop-down list.

This will limit the search results to all listings where the sellers are willing to ship to your country.

Finally, you can also search for items listed in a specific currency by selecting a currency from the drop-down list.

MORE ON CURRENCY

When you are shopping on an eBay International site, the items listed will show bid amounts in the currency of that country. If you are going to shop on the eBay global sites (and I encourage you to do so), it helps to have a basic understanding of how eBay displays the conversion rate between various currencies.

On eBay, you can see the current bid price of an international item in your currency by looking on the top of the Item Description page next to the seller-specified currency:

Plate: Wedgwood Rococo 6inch New Wedgewood

You are signed in

Starting bid:	GBP 4.99 [Place Bid >]
	(Approximately US $9.84)
End time:	Jan-26-07 21:24:38 PST
	(6 days 22 hours)
Ships to:	Worldwide
Item location:	Bull In A China Shop - Online, United Kingdom
History:	0 bids
You can also:	[Watch this item]

View larger picture

Get alerts via Text message or IM
Sell one like this

This seller is located in the United Kingdom but has made his items available to U.S. shoppers. The price shown will be in the seller's currency first, with a conversion to the shopper's currency in parentheses.

NOTE: This feature displays the price in both your currency and the seller's currency only when you have accessed the item through the eBay U.S. Advanced Search box, or if the seller has listed the item on the U.S. site (but is registered on an international site), or if the seller has made his item available to U.S. buyers.

You can also get a more accurate conversion amount by using one of the several online currency-conversion sites, such as *www.xe.com*.

Keep in mind that should you win an item listed on an international site, you are obligated to pay the seller the final bid amount in the currency of the seller's country. The closest estimate of the final bid price is shown in red in parentheses next to the high bid. Use this figure when writing a check, making a wire transfer, or using your credit card.

PayPal will make the conversion for you automatically with no extra input on your end. If the seller accepts PayPal, this is one more reason to pay with your PayPal account.

Credit card issuers will convert currency automatically from dollars into the foreign currency of the international eBay seller. You only need to know the correct amount in dollars for the final bid price.

For wire transfers handled directly by your bank, your bank will convert the currencies for you. Again, you need only let them know the amount in dollars. (There are usually bank charges for sending a wire transfer. Ask your bank.) As for international money orders or checks, you will have to find out from the seller how to make out the amounts so they are properly converted.

INTERNATIONAL PAYMENT OPTIONS

If the seller accepts online credit card payments, pay using your credit card. Most international sellers now have access to some type of online payment service. PayPal, for example, is now available to sellers in many countries around the world.

If you have a preferred method of paying and the seller doesn't offer that method in their item description, suggest it via e-mail to the seller, before you bid! Otherwise, understand that you are obligated to use one of the payment methods specified by the seller in his auction description.

An international money order is a workable alternative for those listings where the seller cannot offer an online credit card payment option. Note that in a limited number of foreign countries, USPS international money orders are accepted. Check with the USPS site for more information (*www.usps.com*).

Remember to include any and all shipping costs and any additional fees/taxes with your payment.

SHIPPING COSTS AND METHODS

International shipping costs are dependent on one or more of the following factors:

- The weight and dimensions of the packaged item
- The method of shipment (ground, next day air, etc.) and the carrier (UPS, international post, FedEx, etc.)
- Seller location
- Buyer location

In addition to shipping costs, buyers are usually responsible for any additional costs such as duties, taxes, and customs clearance fees. When in doubt, ask the seller before bidding or purchasing.

> **GRIFF TIP!** Never ask a seller to fudge a customs form. A customs form must accurately describe what is in the box and its value. Asking a seller to lie about either not only is unethical but could result in your item being held up and even confiscated at customs!

To calculate costs for UPS-shipped items, visit the UPS Quick Cost Calculator at *www.servicecenter.ups.com/ebay/ebay.html#qcost*.

FedEx also has a rate calculator page, at *www.fedex.com/us*.

TAXES

In most instances, as a U.S. buyer purchasing from an international seller, you will not be liable for taxes. If you are unsure, e-mail the seller and ask about any applicable sales or VAT taxes before you bid.

OTHER LANGUAGES

It's overstating the obvious, but if you are interested in bidding on or buying an item from a French-speaking seller on the eBay France site, it would probably be a good idea to have some fluency in French.

If you don't, you may want to e-mail the seller first, in English, asking politely for a description in English.

There are Web sites that can help you translate text or an entire Web page from one language to another. My favorite is Babel Fish, at *http://babelfish .altavista.com/*

> **GRIFF TIP!** Translation Web sites can be helpful in getting the gist of information from an item description, but they tend to translate word for word with no regard for idioms and colloquialisms. This can result in translated sentences that do not make sense or, worse, mean something other than what they appear to mean.

CUSTOMS

The duty rate for many items typically bought online is zero; however, you should never assume this is the case.

All goods brought into another country must clear that country's customs. In some cases, a customs duty may apply. If so, the recipient of the item is liable for the duty.

The sender is responsible for filling out a customs form for the item before the item is shipped. Again, not all items incur a customs duty. It can depend on the country, the value of the item, the type of item, and the type of delivery. For example, it is much less complicated to send an item via international post as opposed to a courier service (private shipping company). There is no duty for most items valued at less than $200 sent via international post. In any case, make sure that the seller provides you with a receipt on his letterhead for customs, indicating the age and the value of the item. The value can usually be the price the buyer pays the seller. Depending on the item, you may need to make an export declaration or acquire an export license.

The U.S. Customs Web site has a page devoted to Internet transactions: *www.cbp.gov/xp/cgov/import/infrequent_importer_info/internet_purchases.xml*.

Buying Locally

Another way to buy things is to do so locally. eBay provides a simple search tool that lists only items by sellers in your metropolitan area. The tool is based on zip code. You enter your zip code and select a distance radius from that zip code. You can find the option on the Advanced Search page.

Items near me

☐ Items within 200 ▾ miles of

ZIP or Postal Code 95125 or Select a popular city... ▾

You can also sort any category or search result list to show the items nearest you first.

Regional trading comes in handy for such items as:

- Hard-to-ship items such as cars, appliances, and furniture
- Fragile or breakable items including glassware, computers, and chandeliers
- Items of local interest such as tickets and real estate

eBay Guidelines, Rules, and Help for Buyers

eBay Buyer Guidelines and Rules

All members of the eBay Community have a responsibility to ensure that their buying, selling, and chatting on the site are conducted within the eBay rules and policies. During my time with eBay Customer Support, the lion's share of the buyer mistakes and subsequent difficulties I witnessed were due primarily to ignorance of these rules and policies.

You can avoid difficulties of this sort by reading through the eBay rules and guidelines. Included in this chapter are the most basic topics regarding bidding and buying rules and guidelines. Everything in this chapter can also be found on the eBay site Help.

You can reach these pages from the eBay Navigation Bar via the box "Help." Then click "Help topics" and scroll down to "eBay policies."

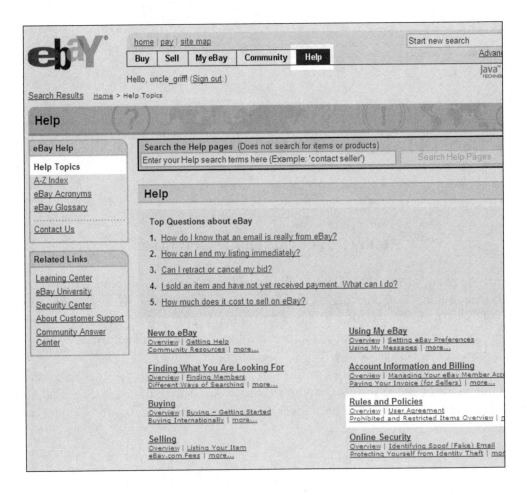

Click the link "Rules for buyers."

From there, follow the various links for each buyer rule or policy.

eBay®

home | pay | site map

| Buy | Sell | My eBay | Community | Help |

Start new search

Advanc

Java™ TECHNOL

Hello, uncle_griff! (Sign out.)

Search Results   Home > Help Topics > Rules and Policies > Rules for Buyers

Help

eBay Help

Help Topics
A-Z Index
eBay Acronyms
eBay Glossary

Contact Us

Related Links

Learning Center
eBay University
Security Center
About Customer Support
Community Answer Center

Search Results

Search the Help pages (Does not search for items or products)

Enter your Help search terms here (Example: 'contact seller')

Search Help Pages

Rules for Buyers

Rules for Buyers Overview

Invalid Bid Retraction Policy

Unwelcome and Malicious Buying Policy

Unpaid Item Policy

Non-binding Bid Policy

The rules are fairly simple and straightforward. The most important rules for any buyer to keep in mind:

- Every winning bid or purchase is binding.*
- Buyers should pay for their eBay purchases quickly.

Here's a Buyer Trust and Safety Checklist.

GRIFF TIP! You can never have too many checklists!

---

*Except for Real Estate auction format listings and Ad Format listings.

A BUYER TRUST AND SAFETY CHECKLIST

Much of the grief and frustration in the world is traceable to someone, somewhere, who makes a few innocent assumptions and then forges ahead, only to find himself unexpectedly enmeshed in chaos and confusion—realizing too late that his initial assumptions were, in fact, false.

This holds true for eBay members as well. Whenever shopping on eBay, never assume! A fully informed eBay shopper is a happy eBay buyer. This means asking questions, doing research, and informing yourself of the eBay rules regarding bidding and buying.

Here is a basic checklist for the responsible eBay Buyer:

Ask First

If a seller isn't clear in her listing about the condition of an item or her payment and shipping terms, ask her before you bid.

Research

If you are unsure about an item's value, condition, or authenticity, ask or research before you bid. For the actual condition or authenticity of an item, always ask the seller first. For value, use the eBay chat boards or search the Internet to do some price comparison. Browse the various eBay topic-specific chat boards to seek out experts in a field and ask them about a particular item.

Check Feedback and Leave Feedback

Although I have mentioned it many times throughout the preceding chapters, it bears repeating—always check a seller's Feedback, even before you read his item description or look at the item pictures! And don't just rely on the Feedback number. Page through the list of comments left for that seller to best determine what type of seller he is.

No rule states that you must leave Feedback for sellers. However, the giving and receiving of Feedback is a lot like the sport of log rolling—both parties must cooperate for it to work.

To establish your own sterling Feedback history, you will often have to take the initiative and leave positive Feedback first.

Keep Your eBay Password to Yourself

Never grant access to your eBay account to anyone except maybe your spouse, and only if you trust him or her unconditionally. Avoid granting password access to your children. No matter what the circumstances may be in your defense, you are responsible for any and all activity conducted using your eBay User ID, and you, as the account holder, will be held responsible if your account is employed for nefarious or illegal activity on eBay.

Use a Secure Method of Payment

Look for those listings in which the seller accepts payment with a credit or debit card or provides a bank-to-bank wire transfer or electronic check option through PayPal and give these listings preference. Many good, honest sellers do not accept credit cards, so if you simply must have their item, make sure their feedback is acceptable to you and read up on their return policy. If a seller doesn't have a refund policy on her item page, e-mail her to ask about it before you bid.

And of course, no matter what the circumstances, *never pay for anything online using cash or Western Union!*

Avoid Questionable or Prohibited Activity

Some specific bidding activities are prohibited on eBay. It is your responsibility to know what these prohibited activities are and to avoid employing them. For example, although you may retract a bid for special circumstance, you cannot chronically retract bids as a way of shopping on eBay. You can find a comprehensive list of questionable and prohibited activity by clicking on the "Help" link on the eBay Navigation Bar and clicking the links "eBay Policies" and "Rules for buyers" (as described earlier).

EBAY RULES FOR BUYERS

The following are the more common buyer infractions and how to avoid them.

- **Transaction interference.** Defined as e-mailing buyers in an open or ended transaction to warn them away from a seller or item. If you have had an unsatisfactory experience with a seller, you can let the rest of the eBay Community know by leaving appropriate feedback.
- **Contacting a seller and offering to purchase the listed item outside of eBay.** Although not a major offense in the scheme of things, it is definitely not in keeping with the spirit of eBay.
- **Bid retraction.** You can, as a bidder, retract your bid for any eBay auction that has not yet ended. The link for retracting a bid can be found by entering the words "retract a bid" in the Search Help box on the eBay Help page:

ebaY
home | pay | site map
Buy | Sell | My eBay | Community | Help

Start new search | Search
Advanced Search

Hello, uncle_griff (Sign out)

Java™ (POWERED BY) ◆Sun
TECHNOLOGY

My eBay Home > Help > Search

Help

eBay Help

Help Topics
A-Z Index
eBay Acronyms
eBay Glossary

Contact Us

Related Links

Learning Center
eBay University
Security Center
About Customer Support
Community Answer
Center

Search Help

retract a bid

Search Help | tips

39 help topics were found for "retract a bid":

Can I retract or cancel my bid ?
A bid may be retracted (cancelled) by the buyer in some cases if the retraction meets the requirements of our Bid Ret...

Retracting a Bid
...Retracting a Bid When you are the winning......on eBay. Remember that all bids on eBay are binding, except......bid...

Changing Maximum Bid
...Changing Maximum Bid In most cases you, as......bid you will need to retract your original bid first and......

Invalid Bid Retraction
...Invalid Bid Retraction A bid is a binding contract. Except under......the reserve price and then retracts his bid ...

These are just a few. There are more policies to be found on the eBay site.

It's OK to retract a bid if . . .

- You accidentally enter a wrong bid amount. For instance, you bid $99.50 instead of $9.95. (If this occurs, you will need to quickly reenter the correct bid amount.)
- The description of an item you have bid on has changed significantly.
- You cannot reach the seller. This means that you have tried calling the seller and his or her phone number doesn't work, or you have tried e-mailing a message to the seller and it comes back undeliverable.

It's not OK to retract a bid if . . .

- You change your mind about the item.
- You decide you can't really afford it.
- You bid a little higher than you promised yourself you'd go.

- You bid only to uncover the seller's reserve amount or the current high bidder's maximum bid. (This is a serious offense that could result in the suspension of your eBay registration.)
- You found another item you like better or that has a better price.

Special Retraction Rules

If you place a bid before the last twelve-hour period of the auction:

- You can retract the bid with more than twelve hours left before the listing ends. When you do this, all your previous bids will also be eliminated. You will have to bid again if you canceled the previous bid due to an incorrect bid amount.
- You cannot retract the bid during the last twelve hours of the listing unless the seller agrees. You will have to contact the seller via e-mail and request she cancel your bid.

If you place a bid during the last twelve-hour period of the auction:

- You may only retract a bid within one hour after placing it.
- When you retract a bid within the last twelve hours of the listing, you will eliminate only the most recent bid you placed. Bids you placed prior to the last twelve hours will not be retracted.

Your total number of bid retractions in the past six months is displayed in your Feedback Profile on the top of the page in the ID Card section:

eBay will thoroughly investigate bid retractions, and abuse of this feature may result in the suspension of your eBay account.

Unwelcome Buyers

No one wants to be unwelcome or unwanted. However, sometimes a seller may state terms for who may bid or purchase, and those terms may exclude you. Unwelcome buyer activity is defined as bidding or buying in violation of the terms set forth by the seller in the listing description. Some examples:

- Seller states he ships to "home country" only and the buyer is outside the stated shipping area.
- Seller states she will not accept bids from members who have negative feedback.
- Bidder rebids after the seller has canceled his bid and requested he not bid on or purchase her items. (Sellers have every right to reject bids from certain bidders for whatever reason they choose. A bidder who has been asked not to bid must comply with that seller's wishes.)
- Bidder uses a second eBay registration to bid on an item after his first registration has been blocked by a seller.

Shill Bidding

Shill bidding occurs when a seller uses a second User ID to artificially raise the bid amount for his item. Shill bidding is strictly prohibited and can result in permanent suspension from eBay. Even the appearance of shill bidding can result in suspension; thus family members and individuals living together, working together, or sharing a computer must refrain from bidding on each other's items, even if the intention is to actually purchase said items.

Unpaid Items (UPIs)

When a buyer bids on and wins or buys an item at eBay and subsequently does not pay the seller for that item, the transaction becomes what is known in eBay parlance as an Unpaid Item, or UPI for short. (At eBay, we used to call them nonpaying buyers. Before that, they were called deadbeat bidders. Some sellers still use that term. We don't.)

A bid is binding at eBay. Winning the bid and then not following through with the transaction is against eBay rules.

When a buyer does not pay for his item, the seller can file an Unpaid Item report with eBay. In filing, the seller will be prompted to select a reason for the request. If the reason selected is "Buyer backed out," an Unpaid Item alert will be made against your account.

Buyers with one or more UPIs run the risk of scathing negative feedback. In addition, upon receipt of a third UPI alert, that bidder is suspended from eBay.

AVOID BIDDING ON QUESTIONABLE ITEMS

During your quest for treasure at eBay, you may stumble upon an item that is not allowed on eBay. There are many types of items that sellers may not list on eBay. Some of these prohibited items are no-brainers—controlled substances, nuclear weapons, counterfeit items—but others are not so obvious.

Did you know that the sale of bear parts is not allowed at eBay? Bear rugs, paws, heads, organs, and so on can be sold legally everywhere in the United States save for one state, California. Since the black bear is the California state animal, it is illegal in California to trade bear parts. eBay is headquartered in California, and thus is subject to the state prohibition against the sale of bear parts.

There is a list of prohibited items on the eBay Web site at *http://pages.ebay .com/help/policies/items-ov.html*.

Navigate to this page by clicking the "Help" link on the eBay Navigation Bar, then click the "Selling" topic, and finally the link for "What items may not be sold on eBay?"

Feedback Offenses

eBay hopes that all members will only leave negative feedback as a last resort in a dispute where no resolution is possible. The worst possible step a buyer can take is to leave negative feedback without first attempting to work out the dispute directly with the seller. Please read this next Griff Tip carefully and make it your mantra:

GRIFF TIP! Never leave negative feedback for another member until you have exhausted all other modes of communication, including e-mail and a phone call if necessary! Negative feedback should always be employed only as a last resort when all other attempts at a resolution have failed.

If you are not happy with the item, contact the seller and let him know *before you leave negative feedback*! Most eBay sellers will work with you to reach a solution that is satisfactory to all. Your duty is to at least give that seller a chance to make it right. So it's always best to try to work out a solution with the seller first. If you and the seller are unable to reach a solution agreeable to both parties, then consider dispute resolution through a third party such as SquareTrade (*www.squaretrade.com*), which I will cover later in this chapter.

- It bears repeating: *Leave negative feedback only as a last resort.*
- Never use profanity or vulgar language in your feedback comments or responses to others. Not only does vulgar language reflect badly on you, it could be grounds for the removal of the feedback, which would defeat the entire reason for leaving it in the first place.
- Never include any part of another user's contact information in a feedback comment or response. This includes names! This is another criterion for feedback removal, and besides, it's not fair to violate anyone's privacy.
- Never post a Web or e-mail link in a feedback comment or response. Doing so could result in the removal of the comment by eBay.

In fact, my advice to all who are considering leaving a scathing feedback comment: Never say anything in public (including in feedback) that you would be embarrassed for your mother to hear or read. As I said earlier, what you say about a situation and how you say it speaks volumes about your own character. Choose your words wisely.

REPORTING QUESTIONABLE ACTIVITY OR ITEMS

eBay members can report questionable activity or items directly to eBay Trust & Safety (a special department of eBay Customer Support).

To do so:

1. Click the "Help" link on the eBay Navigation Bar.
2. Click the link "Contact Us."
3. Select the appropriate topics.
4. Follow the instructions from there to send your report.

Help　(?)　　　(?)　　　(!)

eBay Help

Help Topics
A-Z Index
eBay Acronyms
eBay Glossary

Contact Us

Related Links

Learning Center
Security Center
About Customer Support

Contact Us

① Select a Category　　2. Select a Subtopic　　3. Review Help and Email Us

Select the category that best matches your question or concern, and click the **Continue** button. Then pages to select the appropriate topics. If you have a PayPal question, please contact PayPal Custome

Note: Selecting the most appropriate topic will enable us to assist you more quickly and prevent delay

◉ **Listing Violations**
Report a listing violation or prohibited (banned) item

○ **Buying and Finding**
Ask about searching, bidding, paying for an item, or dispute resolution

○ **Account Security**
Report fake eBay emails, unauthorized account activity, or other safety concerns

○ **My Account, Registration, and Password**
Ask about My eBay or changing your contact information

○ **Selling and Managing Your Item**
Ask about photos, fees, tools, Stores, unpaid items, or problems with a buyer

○ **Suspension**
Ask about a suspended account, notices you've received from eBay, or sign-in problems

○ **Feedback**
Ask about eBay's Feedback system, or about feedback you've left or received

○ **View and Report Site Issues**
Examples include error messages, functionality that is not working, and pages that do not display. policy violations or specific issues with your eBay account.

Continue >

Within a matter of minutes of sending your report, you will receive an auto-acknowledgment e-mail from Customer Support to confirm the receipt of your e-mail report. Note: eBay Customer Support investigates each and every report sent in. However, it does not issue outcome reports back to the reporting member.

DISPUTE RESOLUTION

Most eBay sellers, especially the more successful sellers, know how important it is to put the needs of the customer first. Buying from these sellers is a dream. You can tell if a seller is a customer-first seller by checking her feedback and her item description.

Even so, you may someday find yourself in a dispute with a seller, and fault or blame may be impossible to assign. Don't get angry. Keep your mind focused on your goal: resolving the dispute as soon as possible and putting the transaction behind you. No other goal is worth pursuing! Any warlike behavior such as getting even, one-upmanship, or tit for tat is pointless and only contributes to the world's already vast pool of ill will. And it certainly won't get you a resolution. In the event of a dispute with a seller, stay calm and civil.

Even though you and I know that the customer is always right, some sellers are not convinced. It doesn't mean that they are bad sellers—just that they haven't quite gotten the picture yet. Help them. Never lose your temper. Keep your e-mails polite and not provocative. If you resist the temptation to start screaming in an e-mail, the seller will be more likely to listen to your complaint and your suggestions for resolution.

One of the options provided for impartial mediation is SquareTrade (*www .squaretrade.com*). SquareTrade is a third-party fee-based service that will assign a professional, qualified arbitrator to listen to both sides of the dispute before issuing the best remedy. In most instances, the SquareTrade arbitrator can assist in reaching a solution that is agreeable to both parties.

Many sellers sign up with SquareTrade as a matter of good business, thus agreeing to a certain standard of conduct on eBay. Sellers who sign up will display the SquareTrade icon in their item descriptions:

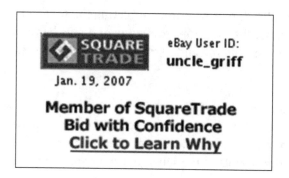

Resolving a Difficult Transaction

If you paid for an item but didn't receive it or if you paid for an item and received it but it is significantly different from the item description, follow these eight steps.

1. **Check the item listing** (within ten days after the listing ends). Review the seller's terms of sale (if available), item description, and shipping and payment terms. Have you allowed enough time for the seller to receive and confirm payment? Have you read the seller's shipping terms? There are many reasons why delivery may take longer than you expect. For example, shipping and customs for international transactions can take time. Additionally, international bank transfers can take up to fourteen days to complete.

    Media Mail shipments (containing items such as books, videotapes, DVDs, etc.) may take significantly longer than other shipping methods.

    Some items may be custom-made or assembled before shipping, which may cause delays.

2. **E-mail the seller** (within ten days after the listing ends). If you are still concerned, e-mail the seller with your questions. If you don't have the seller's e-mail address, you can request it from eBay or use the "Ask seller a question" link on the item listing page.

3. **Check your e-mail spam filters for messages from the seller** (within ten days after the listing ends). It's possible that the seller has tried to e-mail you but your spam filters are blocking her messages.

4. **Check your own contact information** (within ten days after the listing ends). It's possible that the seller has tried to e-mail you but your contact information is incorrect. Go to "My Account" in My eBay and click on "Personal Information." Make sure your e-mail address is correct.

5. **Call your seller** (anytime after completing the first four steps). Request the seller's contact information from eBay and give her a phone call. Many issues are just simple misunderstandings that can be resolved with a single phone call.

    ✔ Click the "Advanced search" link on the top of any eBay page.
    ✔ Click the option for "Find contact information" under the Members section in the Search box on the left-hand side of the page.
    ✔ Enter the User ID of the seller and the item number of your transaction.

    eBay will send you the phone number of the seller.

6. **Use eBay's Item Not Received or Significantly Not as Described process** (begin process no later than forty-five days after the listing ends). The majority of all transactions on eBay end successfully, but sometimes a problem can occur. The Item Not Received process is designed to help facilitate buyer and seller communication. To begin the process, go to the Security Center (a link is found at the bottom of every eBay page). Check the option for Item Not Received, click the "Report problem" button, and follow the instructions from there.

   If you paid for your item with PayPal, you will be linked to the PayPal Dispute Resolution Center in step 7 below. If you paid for the item using another payment method (check, money order, or a non-PayPal bank transfer or credit card funding), you will be directed through the eBay Item Not Received process. The Item Not Received process can help facilitate communication between you and the seller, but it is important to note that eBay purchases not paid for with PayPal are ineligible for protection or coverage.

7. **PayPal Resolution Center** (first forty-five days after the listing ends). If you paid with PayPal, the next step in the process is the PayPal Resolution Center, where you may open a dispute case. Your purchase may have enhanced protection for up to $2,000 coverage through PayPal Buyer Protection if the item description page shows the PayPal Buyer Protection shield under the Seller Information box. To reach the page directly, click the "Security Center" link on the bottom of the PayPal home page (*www.paypal.com*) and follow the instructions from there for PayPal Buyer Protection.

8. **Contact your credit card company** (first forty-five days after the listing ends). If you paid for your purchase through PayPal using a credit card, and if you and the seller are unable to reach a resolution through PayPal's Resolution Center, contact your credit card by calling the phone number on the back of the card. Credit card companies typically provide some level of identity and purchase protection whether you paid with your credit card through PayPal or directly to the seller. Contact your credit card company to learn more.

Spoof E-mail

Also known as "phishing e-mail." Nearly everyone with an e-mail account has received at least one. A spoof e-mail appears to be from a trusted company such as PayPal or eBay. They are usually formatted as an alert or warning that either your information needs updating or your registration or account has been flagged for some reason. A spoof e-mail often contains official company logos, text, links, and formatting. The "from" address and links appear to be from eBay. Overall, spoof e-mails often look official and legitimate. They aren't.

Some Spoof Examples
This is an example of an e-mail containing a form.

eBay or PayPal will never ask you to enter your User ID and password in an e-mail, nor would they ask you to click a link to a Web page containing entry fields for this information or other information such as your ATM PIN, security code, or social security number.

Some spoof e-mails are obvious by their bad syntax:

From:	www-data on behalf of ebay.com
To:	Griffith, Jim
Cc:	
Subject:	eBay unpaid individual part debate #320072987396 -- Answer required
Attachments:	

eBay unpaid individual part debate #320072987396 -- Answer required

Dear member,
eBay Mitgliedsterridawnn indicated that they already paid for individual part #320072987396

<u>Concerning the submitted details are the payment repeat.</u>

Respect,
eBay Internationala AG

Awkward sentence structure and misspellings are another giveaway.

Most spoof e-mails try to scare you into hasty action. Here is a fake suspension notice:

From: eBay Member <aw–confirm@ebay.com>
Reply-To: aw–confirm@ebay.com
Date: Sunday, January 14, 2007 3:30 PM
To: "Griffith, Jim" <griff@ebay.com>
Subject: FPA NOTICE: eBay Registration Suspension – Pending

eb̄aY

eBay sent you this message automatically.
Your registered name is included to help confirm this message originated from eBay. Learn more.

FPA NOTICE: eBay Registration Suspension - Pending

Dear member,

We regret to inform you that your eBay account has been suspended due to concerns we have for the safety and integrity of the eBay community.

As we state in the User Agreement, Section 8, we may immediately issue a warning, suspend, or terminate your membership and refuse to provide our services to you if we believe that your actions may cause legal liability for you, our users or us. We may also take these actions if you have breached the User Agreement or if we are unable to verify or authenticate any information you provide to us.

Please click bellow link to provide your informations to us :
http://www.ebay.com/ws2/eBayISAPI.dll?SignIn&co_partnerId=2&siteid=0&pageType=-1&pa1=&i1=-1&UsingSSL=1&bshowg if=0&favoritenav=1

Due to the suspension of this account, please note that you are prohibited from using eBay in any way. This includes the registering of a new account.

Please note that this suspension does not relieve you of your obligation to pay any fees you may currently owe to eBay.

Regards,

eBay Trust and Safety

This email appears in the language of the eBay site where you are registered.

Learn how you can protect yourself from spoof (fake) emails at:
http://pages.ebay.com/education/spooftutorial

See our Privacy Policy and User Agreement if you have questions about eBay's communication policies.
Privacy Policy: http://pages.ebay.com/help/policies/privacy-policy.html
User Agreement: http://pages.ebay.com/help/policies/user-agreement.html

Copyright © 2006 eBay, Inc. All Rights Reserved.
Designated trademarks and brands are the property of their respective owners.
eBay and the eBay logo are registered trademarks or trademarks of eBay, Inc.

http://www.enzoleonardi.it/software/eBayISAPI.dll?SignIn&co_partne...

This one looks a tad more official, but if you hover your mouse over the link, your e-mail application may display in the status bar on the e-mail window the actual Web address to which it leads. That site, *www.enzoleonardi.it*, is not an eBay domain.

Another ploy is to make a spoof seem like a question from another eBay member:

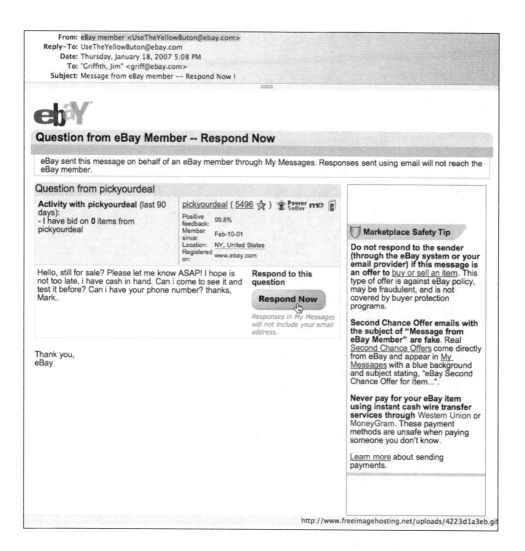

```
From:     eBay member <UseTheYellowButon@ebay.com>
Reply-To: UseTheYellowButon@ebay.com
Date:     Thursday, January 18, 2007 5:08 PM
To:       "Griffith, Jim" <griff@ebay.com>
Subject:  Message from eBay member -- Respond Now !
```

Question from eBay Member -- Respond Now

eBay sent this message on behalf of an eBay member through My Messages. Responses sent using email will not reach the eBay member.

Question from pickyourdeal

Activity with pickyourdeal (last 90 days):
- I have bid on **0** items from pickyourdeal

pickyourdeal (5496 ☆) 🏆 Power Seller me 📷

Positive feedback:	99.8%
Member since:	Feb-10-01
Location:	NY, United States
Registered on:	www.ebay.com

🛡 **Marketplace Safety Tip**

Do not respond to the sender (through the eBay system or your email provider) if this message is an offer to <u>buy or sell an item</u>. This type of offer is against eBay policy, may be fraudulent, and is not covered by buyer protection programs.

Hello, still for sale? Please let me know ASAP! I hope is not too late, i have cash in hand. Can i come to see it and test it before? Can i have your phone number? thanks, Mark..

Respond to this question

[**Respond Now**]

Responses in My Messages will not include your email address.

Second Chance Offer emails with the subject of "Message from eBay Member" are fake. Real <u>Second Chance Offers</u> come directly from eBay and appear in <u>My Messages</u> with a blue background and subject stating, "eBay Second Chance Offer for Item...".

Never pay for your eBay item using instant cash wire transfer services through Western Union or MoneyGram. These payment methods are unsafe when paying someone you don't know.

<u>Learn more</u> about sending payments.

Thank you,
eBay

http://www.freeimagehosting.net/uploads/4223d1a3eb.gif

I hovered my mouse over the "Respond now" button to reveal the Web page it links to, *www.freeimagehosting.net*, which is also not an eBay domain.

What should you do when you receive an e-mail that you suspect might be a spoof? First, never provide personal information (passwords, social security numbers, ATM PINs, etc.) when requested to so by instructions within an e-mail, no matter how convincing that e-mail might be. If you suspect that there may indeed be an issue or problem related to your registration or account, you should go directly to the site. Start by typing the site's address into the Address box in your Web browser. Then navigate to your account or registration page. On eBay, go to My eBay. On PayPal, go to My Account.

You can also verify any e-mail message by checking My Messages in My eBay. If the e-mail purporting to be from another member or eBay is not showing in your My Messages inbox, then it is not a legitimate member or eBay e-mail.

You can learn more about protecting yourself from spoof e-mails by visiting the eBay Security Center. The link for the Security Center is displayed on the bottom of all eBay Web pages—even the eBay Sign In page.

On the Security & Resolution Center page, follow the links "Spoof (fake) e-mail" and "eBay Marketplace safety."

ebaY®

home | pay | register | site map

| Buy | Sell | My eBay | Community | Help |

Start new search   Search
Advanced Search

Hello! Sign in or register.

Java™ TECHNOLOGY   POWERED BY ◆Sun

Home > Community > **Security & Resolution Center**

Security & Resolution Center

Have a problem? We can help.

○ **Item Not Received** - You didn't receive your item, or you received an item that was different than described.

○ **Unpaid Item** - You didn't receive payment for an item you sold on eBay.

○ **Spoof (fake) email** - You received a suspicious-looking email that appears to be from eBay or PayPal and you want eBay to take action.

◉ **Report another problem** - Get help with other eBay transaction problems or safety concerns.

[Report Problem]

::: eBay Marketplace Safety

Buying & Paying	**Selling**	**Rules & Policies**
Resources to help you have a safe buying experience on eBay.	Tips on how to become a trusted and successful eBay seller.	Guidelines that help make eBay a safe, well-lit marketplace.
Learn more.	Learn more.	Learn more.

::: Security & Resolution Center Tools

Item Not Received Process Item Not Received Process. Learn more about the process. Take the tour.

Security and Privacy Made Simpler
The "Security and Privacy -- Made Simpler" guide was developed through a partnership between the Better Business Bureau and Privacy & American Business and is co-sponsored by eBay and PayPal to assist business owners with security and privacy challenges that affect small and medium size businesses. Learn more.

AOL ◉

Secure your identity

Discover AOL® Firewall, phishing protection and Money Alerts.

click here to Learn More

🛡 Marketplace Safety Tip

Buy with confidence – look at your seller's feedback before placing a bid.

See all Marketplace Safety Tips

::: Trust & Safety Spotlight

eBay & Law Enforcement: Enforcing Laws that Protect Our Members

Police Blotter

Law Enforcement Only

::: Safety in the eBay Community

Trust & Safety Discussion Board

Get quick help from other members in the Answer Center.

Top 2 Discussions
▪ Protect Yourself from - Identity Theft
▪ Reports of a Counterfeit Cashier's Check Scheme

Latest Announcements
▪ Enhancements Made to Buyer Requirements

::: Safe Payment Reminder

Pay safely online by never using instant cash transfer services such as Western Union or MoneyGram International to pay for your eBay purchases.

Protecting yourself from spoof e-mail is easy. Do not respond to the e-mail, click any links contained inside the e-mail, or provide any personal information. Report the e-mail to eBay by forwarding it to *spoof@ebay.com* per the instructions on the eBay Security Center. Then delete the original e-mail.

In addition, you should download a free copy of the eBay Toolbar with Account Guard. The eBay Toolbar is a Web browser plug-in that not only alerts you when you are about to visit a spoofed eBay Web site but also makes shopping on eBay a lot simpler.

Download the eBay Toolbar by clicking the "Site Map" link on the top of any eBay page.

Then click the link for "eBay Toolbar" under Buying Resources.

Follow the instructions to dowload and install the eBay Toolbar into your Web browser.

How to Get Help on eBay

Although I have tried to make this book as comprehensive as possible—covering every imaginable aspect of eBay and more—it would be impossible to anticipate everything that could possibly happen on eBay. You may find yourself with an issue or question that this book does not address (heaven forfend!). The following pathways to eBay Help should address these rare instances.

EBAY HELP

As discussed in chapter 2, a mountain of information about all things eBay is on the eBay site itself. Most of it is pretty easy to find.

Click the "Help" link on the top of any eBay page. This will take you to the Help Hub.

From here, you can search Help in two ways:

- Navigating through Help topics
- Searching Help using keywords

If you need to send an e-mail to eBay Customer Support, click the "Contact us" link and follow the instructions from there.

LIVE HELP

In addition to the e-mail channel to Customer Support, you can also reach a support rep via our Live Help feature. Live Help lets you talk to a real, live support rep in a real-time instant-message chat session.

Click the link for "Live help" on the eBay home page.

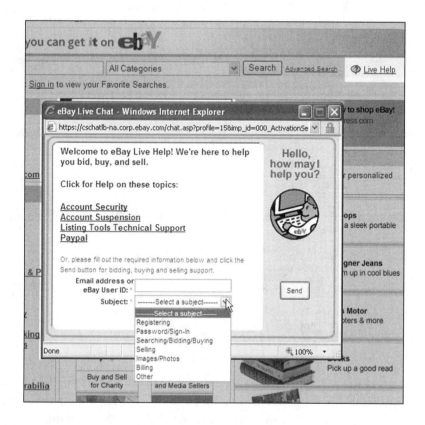

This will open a chat window. Enter your e-mail address or eBay User ID and select a topic from the drop-down list.

Wait while the window loads, and a rep will be with you shortly. eBay Help and eBay Live Help can provide answers to questions from the most basic to the most complex. However, eBay Help doesn't stop there. eBay provides other channels for learning, both on- and off-site. All of these channels are grouped together under the eBay Learning Center, the hub page for eBay Education.

EBAY EDUCATION

eBay is dedicated to helping new and experienced eBay members alike learn how to use the eBay site more effectively. To this end, many on- and off-line eBay educational initiatives are available to all eBay members.

You can reach the Learning Center at *http://pages.ebay.com/education*.

The Learning Center is your one-stop page for all things related to eBay Education, including on-site tours, tutorials, workshops, and seminars. In addition to the links to tours and tutorials, the left-hand sidebar has a link for eBay University.

eBay University

In June 2000, eBay started a program called eBay University. An eBay U seminar consists of a daylong series of one-hour classes or workshops on all aspects of buying and selling on eBay. The seminars are held in a different city approximately every two weeks throughout the year. Attendance at a single eBay U varies from about five hundred to fifteen hundred eager eBay members, both new and experienced.

The eBay University instructor roster is made up of eBay selling experts. Each instructor leads a specific seminar. Currently, I am the usual instructor for the "Basic Selling" portion of the seminar.

eBay University seminars are incredible learning experiences for both brand-new and seasoned eBay members.

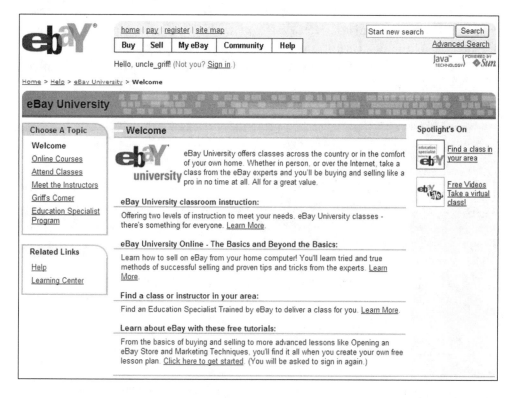

eBay University seminars provide an excellent opportunity for picking up a few tips, passing on your suggestions to eBay staff face-to-face, and meeting other eBay members (who are, without a doubt, the most enthusiastic and fun group of people I've ever had the pleasure of meeting).

If you are looking for eBay instruction and classes in a more traditional setting, check the eBay University schedule for a list of upcoming events at *www .ebay.com/university.*

If the eBay University schedule doesn't include your town, don't despair! In 2003, eBay University was expanded to include online seminars as well as on-site events. You can download the entire eBay U curriculum in streaming video or order the courses on CD-ROM. But wait! There's more!

eBay Education Specialist Program

In 2004, eBay launched the eBay Education Specialist program to help support the hundreds of individual instructors who either lead their own workshops or provide instruction to eager new eBay members across the country. If you are looking for a more immediate eBay class or if you require one-on-one coaching to help you get started selling on eBay, locate a specialist in your area through the eBay Education Specialist Directory. If you are currently teaching others how to use eBay, you might want to sign up to become an eBay Education Specialist.

The eBay Education Specialist Program page is reached by the sidebar link on the eBay University page.

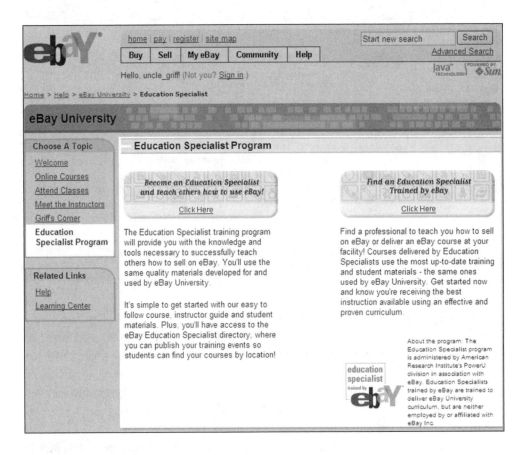

eBay Workshops

eBay hosts a series of regularly scheduled eBay Workshops on a wide variety of specific eBay topics, such as "International Trading" or "Repairing Antique Reed Organs." These workshops are presented in a moderated chat-board format with a guest "speaker" answering real-time questions from eBay members.

You can see the current schedule of chat workshops by visiting the Workshop section of the Community page.

eb**a**Y®

home | pay | register | site map

| Buy | Sell | My eBay | Community | Help |

Start new search   Search

Advanced Search

Hello, uncle_griff! (Not you? Sign in.)

Java™ TECHNOLOGY   POWERED BY ◆Sun

Home > Community

Community

View someone's member profile and more.

Enter a User ID   Find A Member

My eBay At A Glance

Sign in for a snapshot of your personalized information on this page.

Feedback

Feedback Forum
Learn about your trading partners, view their reputations, and express your opinions by leaving feedback on your transactions.

My World

Sign in to manage your My World.

My Watched Discussions

Sign in to view your watched discussions.

Connect

eBay MyWorld
Show everyone your special brand of eBayness.

My Groups

Sign in for access to your groups.

News

Announcements
Listing Template Design & Layout Clinic, Pricing of Freight, A Quick Start to Using Blackthorne Pro, and more (01/19/07)
Phone In Your Questions! Town Hall with Bill Cobb on Thursday, January 25 (01/19/07)
Updated: Category Updates Now Available (01/16/07)
See all Announcements... | See all System Announcements...

Calendar Events
- Next Town Hall - January 25th 4:00 PM PT
- Online Workshops — Learn More
- eBay University
- eBay Radio with Griff
- Community Events - Organized by eBay Members

The Chatter - eBay's official Community blog for interesting posts by and about our members and staff.

eBay Community Values

- We believe people are basically good.
- We believe everyone has something to contribute.
- We believe that an honest, open environment can bring out the best in people.
- We recognize and respect everyone as a unique individual.
- We encourage you to treat others the way you want to be treated.

Learn more about eBay Community Values...

Member Spotlight - Current Selections   Hall of Fame - 2006 Winners

See the About Me page for workshop events at *http://members.ebay.com/ aboutme/workshopevents.*

Workshop Calendar

Choose A Topic	Current Calendar
About	
Current Calendar	Friday 01/05 Member Workshop: How to Create a Selling Strategy & Why it's Important
Archives - 2006	Monday 01/08 Member Workshop: The Surprising Truth about Title Misspellings & Typos
Archives - 2005	Tuesday 01/09 Member Workshop: Time Management Skills for eBay Sellers
Archives - 2004	Wednesday 01/10 Member Workshop: 10 Tax Tips to Start 2007 Off Right
	Wednesday 01/10 Member Workshop: Upgrading to the New Turbo Lister
Related Links	Friday 01/12 eBay Workshop: Learn to use Blackthorne Pro
Workshop Discussion Board	Tuesday 01/16 Member Workshop: Power Up Your eBay Business!
	Wednesday 01/17 Member Workshop: Estimated Federal Income Taxes for the eBay Business Owner
Town Hall Events	Monday 01/22 Member Workshop: Listing Template Design & Layout Clinic
	Tuesday 01/23 Member Workshop: Multiple Modes And Pricing Of Freight
	Wednesday 01/24 Member Workshop: A Quick Start to Using Blackthorne Pro
	Friday 01/26 Member Workshop: Customer Satisfaction and Retention
	Tuesday 01/30 eBay Workshop: How much are your unwanted Christmas gifts worth?

If you have questions related to specific aspects of selling, you should check the Workshop schedule regularly.

If you are interested in hosting a workshop in your particular field, send an e-mail to *workshopevents@ebay.com*.

COMMUNITY DISCUSSION BOARDS

Chat boards played an important role in the formation and growth of eBay, and they continue to do so today. In fact, if there is one thing never lacking in the eBay Community, it's chat!

eBay started out with one chat board, called the AuctionWeb Bulletin Board. There, a new eBay member could learn from other eBay members about many topics, including how to list an item for sale, how to create and host digital pictures, how to pack an item correctly, and how to find the best deals on packing materials. On the AuctionWeb Bulletin Board, folks could meet and chat about almost anything.

Over time, this one board grew into two, then three, and then four. Today, there are over a hundred separate chat areas on eBay. Each is dedicated to a special topic or aspect of buying, selling, or collecting, and most contain hundreds of threaded discussions.

These discussion boards are often an excellent source of help and information provided by other expert eBay members themselves. I urge you to visit them by clicking on the "Community" link on the eBay Navigation Bar and selecting the link for either "Chat" or "Discussion boards."

Discussion Boards

eBay's discussion boards are a great place to find information on everything from art to travel. Browse the discussion boards below and see what you discover.

Community Help Boards

About Me Pages
Auction Listings
Bidding
Buyer Central: Professional Buying
Checkout
eBay Blogs Help NEW!
eBay Express NEW!
eBay My World NEW!
eBay Stores
eBay Wiki NEW!
Escrow/Insurance
Feedback
Half.com
International Trading
Live Auctions
Miscellaneous
My eBay
Packaging & Shipping
PayPal
Photos/HTML
Policies/User Agreement
Registration
Reviews & Guides NEW!
Search
Seller Central
Skype
Technical Issues
Trading Assistant
Trust & Safety (SafeHarbor)

eBay Tools Boards

eBay Board Usage Policy explanation
Accounting Assistant & Record Keeping
Blackthorne Basic/SA Basic
Blackthorne Pro/SA Pro
eBay Marketplace Research and Sales Reports
eBay Picture Services and Picture Manager
eBay Toolbar
File Exchange
Selling Manager
Selling Manager Pro
Turbo Lister

Category Specific Discussion Boards

Animals
Antiques
Art & Artists
Bears and Plush
Book Readers
Booksellers
Business & Industrial
Children's Clothing Boutique
Clothing, Shoes & Accessories
Coins & Paper Money
Collectibles
Comics
Computers, Networking & I.T
Cooks Nook
Country/Rural Style
Custom Made Items and Services NEW!
Decorative & Holiday
Disneyana
Dollhouses and Miniatures
Dolls
Dolls Artists and Limited Edition NEW!
eBay Motors
Handmade/Custom Clothing for Kids
Health & Beauty
Historical Memorabilia
Hobbies & Crafts
Home & Garden
Jewelry & Gemstones
Mid-Century/Modern
Motorcycle Boulevard
Movies & Memorabilia
Music & Musicians
Needle Arts & Vintage Textiles
Outdoor Sports
Photography
Pottery, Glass, & Porcelain
Products & Accessories for Infants NEW!
Science & Mystery
Scrapbooking
Shoes, Purses, and Fashion Accessories
Sports Cards, Memorabilia & Fan Shop
Toys & Hobbies
Victorian/Edwardian
Vintage
Vintage Clothing & Accessories
Watches, Clocks & Timepieces

The discussions can become pretty raucous at times, but it's all in good fun. Find a topic that interests you and either lurk (read the posts without participating) or get involved and ask a question, introduce yourself, or help answer questions. You will find instructions on how to use the chat forums—how to post, how to search, the rules of conduct, and so on—by clicking any of the links on the various chat pages.

eBay member Deanna Rittel has this to say about the eBay chat forums:

I truly enjoy the chat boards on eBay. I usually "hang out" at the Town Square but have been known to wander over to the others occasionally. I've learned more on them than I ever thought I would, and sometimes more than I ever needed to! In three days I had three different items that I needed to identify. In each case I literally had the item identified in less than five minutes. There are very knowledgeable and helpful people willing to help at the drop of a pin. Just last week, I posted on the Town Square that I was looking for a couple of specific state quarters for my two children who are collecting them. Everyone went through their change and located the ones I needed within minutes. We had been looking for them for weeks—a couple of months at least! One specific poster e-mailed me directly—he offered to send my children "mint uncirculated" coins every time they come out. He collects them also and told me he would love to make my children happy and complete their collection for them. These quarters only come out every few months and only five are issued each year. So these will take quite a few more years to complete. He said it was worth the money to make them happy. We have already received the quarters I had originally been looking for from some wonderful individuals on Town Square, and we also received the first shipment from the poster who is completing their collections. No one wanted to be reimbursed—I tried! My children are just absolutely thrilled, and to quote my six-year-old daughter, "Mom, have you ever met such a nice people? They aren't like those people who call you at work!" I work at an insurance company, if that tells you anything—I guess she really listens to my horror stories—LOL!

Finally, I would like to say that the eBay community is truly that—a community. There is always someone around on the boards to answer a question when you have one, make you laugh when you need to, offer a shoulder to cry on, and, of course, there is always a good dose of controversy when you need a good argument!

EBAY LIVE

In June 2001, eBay hosted its first live community conference in Anaheim, California. Over five thousand eBay members of all ages and occupations from across the continental United States attended the first eBay Live.

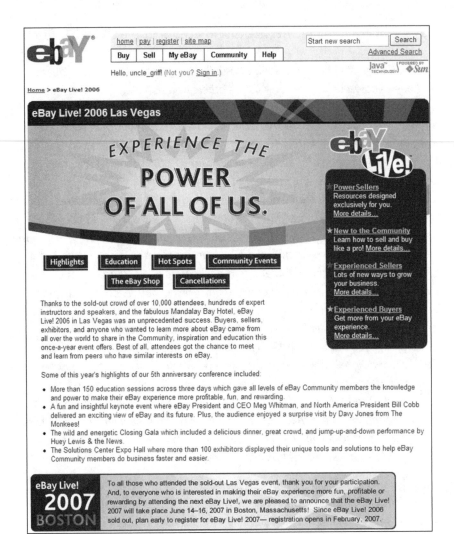

The three days of peace, love, and trading—featuring parties, workshops, seminars, roundtable discussions with eBay employees, vendor booths, guest speakers, special events, and panel discussions with eBay executive staff—was such a hit that we've made eBay Live an annual event. To date, eBay Live has been held in Orlando, New Orleans, San Jose, and Las Vegas. In 2007, we will be in Boston.

In addition, a special page is devoted to eBay Live at *http://pages.ebay.com/ ebaylive*.

So, you've reached the end of Section One. Take a deep breath. Section Two deals with the fine (and simple!) art of eBay selling.

Selling
the eBay Way!

"How do I get started selling on eBay?" This is definitely the question I hear most frequently. Selling on eBay is actually quite easy to grasp . . . once you have listed your first item. It's the first item that can overwhelm the new eBay seller into total paralysis. But don't panic—listing your first item on eBay will be a snap now that Griff is here to help guide you through the entire process, step-by-step. Not everyone has it so easy. Take Dave, for example.

In January 1996, business owner Dave Rayner suffered a serious back injury, costing him his business and livelihood. By March of that year, he and his wife were barely surviving off a combination of their diminishing savings and the meager wages she earned working at a grocery store twenty miles away from their home.

The night that Dave discovered eBay, he stumbled upon the eBay chat board and found eBay founder Pierre Omidyar chatting with others. Pierre personally welcomed Dave to eBay, and Dave noted Pierre's e-mail address.

When Dave needed to replace a malfunctioning computer mouse, he turned to eBay to find a quick replacement.

"I found an auction featuring PS 2 Mice with a starting bid of $1. Wow, that's a bargain, and it was a Dutch Auction to boot, so I bid for two mice at a top bid of a buck."

Dave watched the auction for a full day until the final seconds passed and the auction ended with him as a high bidder for two brand-new mice for $2. Or so he thought.

"I got an e-mail from the seller stating, 'CONGRATULATIONS! YOU'VE WON 2 LOTS of Mice for 400 DOLLARS!'"

Dave was dumbfounded. He discovered that he had misread the item description and was indeed the proud owner of two lots of two hundred mice at one dollar apiece, for a total of $400!

Dave went into a panic. His wife and he had only $600 left in their savings account.

"I knew my wife would go through the roof when I told her what I'd done. I e-mailed Pierre for help."

Within a day, Dave received a reply back from Pierre suggesting that Dave contact the seller to see if they might work out a solution. In the meantime, Dave had noticed an advertisement in a computer magazine for a company in Maine that was selling the very same type of computer mice that Dave had purchased at eBay.

"I called the company and asked if they'd be interested in buying four hundred mice. The guy on the other end said he would take them off my hands."

The gentleman offered to pay Dave $8 apiece for the mice, for a total of $3,200, which, after subtracting the initial $400 cost to the eBay seller, left Dave with a profit of $2,800!

Elated and relieved, Dave e-mailed Pierre to inform him of the tale's happy ending.

"Pierre told me if I could turn deals like that, I'd never have a problem selling on eBay. I started selling a week later after winning another mouse . . . you see, I sold all of that two-lot batch and forgot to keep one out for myself!"

Dave continued buying and selling at eBay for another year. In 1997, he started an image-hosting service called AuctionPix, which is today a profitable and popular image-hosting solution for thousands of other eBay sellers.

Dave has never looked back.

"I will always remember that day I opened the box to see four hundred mice staring back at me, knowing that not only had I turned a disaster into a profit but that I also had a chance to meet one of the nicest people in the online world— Pierre, founder of eBay!"

Selling Setup, Step-by-Step

If you have one thing you want to sell, you want to sell it quickly, and you don't have time to take a three-day course in eBay Selling 101, this section is for you.

Following the Steps

Selling your first item on eBay can be broken down into ten steps grouped into three sections:

Preparation
Step 1. Set up an eBay Seller's Account (one-time step) and PayPal account.
Step 2. Research your item.
Step 3. Photograph the item.
Step 4. Write the Item Description.
Step 5. Pack and weigh the item.

List the Item
Step 6. Sell your item.

After the Listing Ends
Step 7. Contact the buyer.
Step 8. Accept payment.
Step 9. Ship the item.
Step 10. Leave Feedback.

But first, here are the three most common questions asked by brand-new sellers:

How long will it take to list my first item?

If you use a digital camera to take a picture of your item for Step 3, and if you follow the next chapters carefully, the five preparation steps for listing your very first eBay item can take as little as forty-five minutes to one hour. Using a print-film camera will add from one to several hours to this time, depending on how quickly your local film developer does his job. The listing process moves much faster once you have listed a few items.

How long will it take to sell my first item?

Your first eBay item could sell on the first day you list it, if you provide the Buy It Now format as an option, or if you use the standard auction format and select the one-day duration. Otherwise, your item could take three, five, seven, or ten days to sell, depending on the duration you select.

How long will it take me to receive payment for my first item?

Receiving payment for your item after the sale can take as little as a few minutes if you use PayPal to accept credit card payments from your buyer, or it can take as long as a week or more for mailed checks or money orders.

In this chapter, I will start you on your way to eBay selling by first walking you through Step 1, setting up an eBay Seller's Account.

Setting Up an eBay Seller's Account

To sell something on eBay, you need to be a registered eBay user. If you are not yet registered, follow the instructions in Section One, chapter 1. Once you are registered, you are ready to set up an eBay Seller's Account. The process is fairly simple and quick.

To set up an eBay Seller's Account, you must provide eBay with credit card and bank account information, or you can utilize the ID Verify feature (provided to eBay by Verisign).

OPTION 1: SETTING UP A SELLER'S ACCOUNT WITH A CREDIT CARD AND BANK ACCOUNT INFORMATION

1. Click the "My eBay" link on the top of any eBay page.
2. Look on the left under "My account." Click the link labeled "Personal information."
3. Look for the "Checking account" row under Financial Information. Pan over to the right and click on the "Edit" link.

If this is your first time setting up a selling account for this eBay User ID, there will be no checking account information on file for you to edit. The system will then prompt you to set up a Seller's Account.

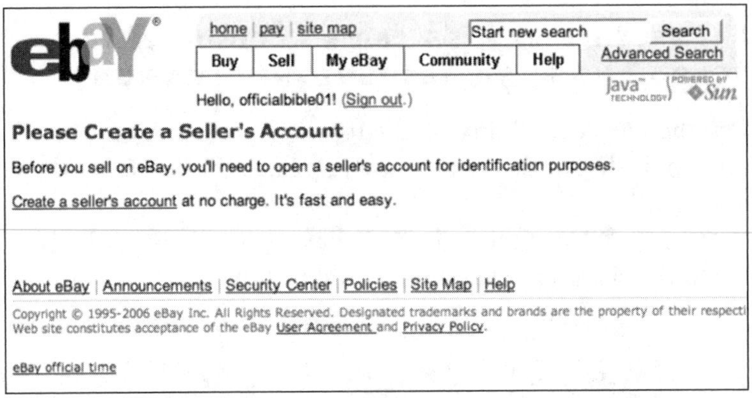

Click on the "Create a seller's account" link to reach the next screen.

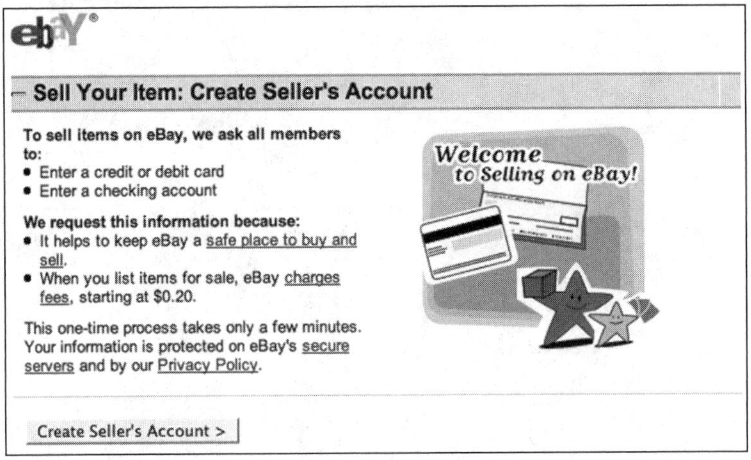

This screen describes what will be required during this process. You can pause here and go grab your credit card and bank account information (both must be registered in your name). Click any of the other links to learn more about specific components of a seller's account. For example, you can read up in advance on the fees you will be charged later for listing an item on eBay, and you can learn how eBay keeps your financial information absolutely secure.

When you have your checking and credit card information on hand, click the "Create Seller's Account" button. On the next page, you enter the requested credit card information.

eBaY ®

home | pay | site map

| Buy | Sell | My eBay | Community | Help |

Start new search   Search

Advanced Search

Hello, officialbible01! (Sign out.)

Java™ TECHNOLOGY   POWERED BY ◆Sun

Place Credit or Debit Card on File

Enter your personal or business credit or debit card information as it appears on your monthly statement. Your card will not be charged unless you authorize us to do so to pay selling fees.

Live help

Don't have a credit or debit card? Use ID Verify.

Credit or debit card

VISA

MasterCard   DISCOVER

AMEX

🔒 Information is protected on eBay's secure servers.

Expiration date

--Month-- ▼   --Year-- ▼

Card identification number

110110 [037]

3-digit number on the back of the card. For American Express, use the 4-digit number on the front. Learn more.

Continue >

Cardholder name

Address on your monthly statement

City

San Jose

State   **ZIP code**

CA ▼

Make sure that the address you supply matches the address you entered when you initially registered on eBay! Click "Continue" when you are ready to move on to the next page, where you will enter your bank account information:

Place Checking Account on File

Please place your checking account on file. This assures us of your identity and keeps eBay a safe place to buy and sell . Funds will not be deducted unless you authorize us to do so to pay selling fees.

Account holder (Personal or business)
James J Griffith

Bank name

US bank accounts only

Your Name
Your Street
Your City, State, zip   1000
                                                   Date

Pay to the
order of _____ $ _____
                                                   Dollars

Bank routing number   **Checking account number**
⑆_____⑆   1000   _____⑈
9 digits between the ⑆   Ignore   Approximately 10 digits usually
symbols   check   before the ⑈symbol
                          number

If you don't have these numbers, please call your bank for this information.

Note: The bank routing, checking account, and check numbers may appear in a different order on your check.

Continue >

When finished, click "Continue." Select which method you prefer for paying your eBay seller fees. I suggest "Bank account."

Select How to Pay Selling Fees

Please select how you want to pay selling fees. Fees are only charged when you list or sell items. If you owe fees, they are automatically charged each month. You can always check your balance and change how you pay selling fees in My eBay.

◉ **Checking account**
Bank: ▓▓▓▓▓▓▓
Routing number: 011▓▓▓▓▓
Checking account number:
XXXXXX1887

○ **Credit or debit card**
Card type: Visa
Card number: XXXX XXXX
XXXX 8306
Expiration date: ▓▓▓ ▓▓▓▓

Tip: If you select your checking account, you can avoid credit card interest rate charges.

Continue >

Click "Continue." If you followed my (and eBay's) advice and selected "Bank account," you will see the next page:

Authorize Checking Account

You have chosen to pay selling fees with your checking account. Before you can sell your item, please read and agree to the terms below.

Bank: TD BankNorth
Routing number: 011▓▓▓▓▓
Checking account number: XXXXXX1887

Direct Pay Authorization: If this payment method fails, eBay may charge the amount due to your credit card. By entering my User ID and password during the seller account creation process, I intend and consent to their use as an electronic signature, equivalent to my handwritten signature as provided under applicable federal and state law. This electronic signature shall only apply to these Terms and Conditions. By selecting, "With Checking Account" below, I

By clicking the **Authorize Checking Account** button, you agree to the terms above.

Authorize Checking Account >

Click the "Authorize checking account" button to complete the Seller's Account setup. You will be taken directly to the first step of the Sell Your Item process!

You could start listing your item right now, but let's hold off for a bit so you can learn the other preparation steps for listing on eBay.

TROUBLESHOOTING

If eBay is unable to verify the bank or credit card information you provided, it is most likely because eBay is unable to connect to your bank or credit card issuer for verification. The solutions are to:

1. Try another credit card and bank account.
2. Try again later (my least favorite).
3. Use ID Verify to verify your eBay Seller's Account information.

OPTION 2: SETTING UP AN EBAY SELLER'S ACCOUNT USING ID VERIFY

If your bank account information cannot be verified or if you would prefer not to provide a bank account or credit card to set up your seller's account, you can use ID Verify instead.

ID Verify is an identity verification service provided by Verisign. The process is quick, easy, and costs only $5.

GRIFF TIP! ID Verify requires you to enter financial and personal information that only you should know. This information is not kept on file and is checked only once for accuracy. You should have on hand all of your bank loan, car loan, mortgage, and credit card numbers so you don't have to go hunting for them in the middle of the process.

To verify your Seller's Account information using ID Verify, click the "Help" link on the top of any eBay web page. Enter "ID Verify" into the Search Help box and click the "Search Help" button.

Read up on ID Verify and then click the "ID Verify" link under the "To become ID Verified" section.

eBay®

home | pay | site map

Buy | Sell | My eBay | Community | **Help**

Start new search | Search

Advanced Search

Hello, officialbible01! (Sign out)

Java™ POWERED BY ◆Sun
TECHNOLOGY

My eBay   Home > Help Topics > Online Security > Account Security > About ID Verify

Help

eBay Help

Help Topics
A-Z Index
eBay Acronyms
eBay Glossary

Contact Us

Related Links

Learning Center
eBay University
Security Center

Search the Help pages (Does not search for items or products)

ID Verify

Search Help Pages   Tips

About ID Verify

ID Verify establishes an eBay member's proof of identity, helping both buyers and sellers trust each other. In the ID Verify process, a third-party company (Equifax in the U.S.) works with eBay to confirm members' identity by cross-checking their contact information using consumer and business databases.

The ID Verify icon 🥇 is displayed in a user's member profile and shows that they have successfully completed the ID Verification process.

Advantages of becoming ID Verified

- Wait 30 days after you become ID Verified to change your contact information. After the 30-day period, you can change your contact information. However, your ID Verify icon and status will be removed. To restore your ID Verify status you need to complete the verification process again, including the payment of the $5.00 application fee.

To become ID Verified:

1. Ensure that you have your appropriate credit information ready.
2. Go to the ID Verify page and then click the "Sign up now" link.
3. Read and accept the terms, including payment of a $5.00 application fee.
4. Review your eBay contact information and update if necessary on the Verify Account Information page.
5. Answer the verification questions to confirm your identity.

To reach the ID Verify page:

> **ebaY**®
>
> home | pay | site map   Start new search   Search
>
> Buy | Sell | My eBay | Community | Help | Advanced Search
>
> Hello, officialbible01! (Sign out.)   Java™ (POWERED BY ◆Sun)
>
> Home > Sell > Seller Central > Getting Started > ID Verify
>
> **ID Verify™**
>
> **ID Verify™**
>
> Establish your proof of identity with ID Verify - an easy way to gain others' trust as their trading partner. Signing up for ID Verify is quick and secure. After you're successfully verified, members will see an ID Verify icon 🌐 in your feedback profile. Learn more.
>
> **Fee:**
> Verification costs $5.00 and is valid until your name, address, or phone number change. This fee will be charged to your eBay account within 24 hours of your successful verification.
>
> **Note:** After successful verification, you will not be able to modify your contact information for 30 days.
>
> [Sign Up Now]

Follow the steps from there. The process takes only a few minutes, and once you have completed this simple and quick process, you will be ready to list items on eBay!

GRIFF TIP! ID Verify not only works as an alternative to setting up a Seller's Account with a credit card and a bank account but also removes bidding and listing restrictions based on Feedback scores. For example, using the Fixed Price format requires a seller to have a Feedback score of 30 or higher. With ID Verify, this restriction is removed. It also allows the seller with a Feedback score of 0 to 29 to set up an eBay Store. My advice? Set up your Seller's Account with both a credit card and a bank account as well as with ID Verify. You'll bypass pesky low-feedback restrictions and provide a greater sense of security for your potential buyers.

Congratulations! You have set up an eBay Seller's Account. Before we move on to the next step, I want to share another incredible eBay story sent to me by eBay member Heather Luce:

Several years ago I was working at a countywide newspaper as the editor. It was a fun job, but it wasn't anything I was terribly passionate about. On the side, I was doing my artwork and creating costumes for people to pose in as reference for my paintings. The costumes were primarily Renaissance in design, and my closets started to fill up. I began giving the costumes to friends and family, and after a while they told me, "No more!" Apparently their closets were starting to fill up too.

At that time, I had been to eBay a few times and had bought some small items. My experiences had all been pleasant, and on a whim I decided to try my hand at selling. I pulled out two of the costumes I had made but had never used for any of my paintings and listed them at $75 each, for seven-day listings. I still remember them: a milkmaid gown, "The Artiste," and a gold Italian Renaissance gown. Each gown sold for over $100 and I was instantly addicted. For four weeks I made new gowns and listed them while working full time at the newspaper. At the end of four weeks, I had made more money from the gowns I had sold on eBay than from my regular full-time job. I knew that I had found my passion, and two weeks later I quit my job and plunged full-time into the world of Renaissance costuming.

That was almost two years ago, and my business has grown by leaps and bounds. I now have a wonderful Web site and a customer base from all around the world. In fact, just today I sent a gown to Australia, and last week I was contacted by a woman from Germany who wants a new Renaissance gown. I've costumed actors for Renaissance fairs—even "Queen Elizabeth" (aka Ms. Flores)! I get e-mails all summer long from people claiming, "I saw one of your gowns at my Renaissance fair last weekend!"

In spite of the success of my business, it's been a huge struggle. During this time I was still going to college full time and I was also going through a divorce. There were times when I was worried that eBay wouldn't be enough and I would have to give up my dream job as a costume designer. But eBay has never failed me. My business has grown from a hobby to a full-time professional career and shows no signs of slowing down.

None of it would have been possible without eBay.

eBay allows average, everyday folks like me the opportunity to realize dreams. It puts us in touch with people from around the world for mere pennies. Nowhere else can you get as much advertising for your dollar—and be extremely successful in the process. eBay is a forum that allows people of all interests to shop in one convenient place. It allows for competitive pricing, and, most important to me, it allows sellers a chance to really get to know their customers.

I have made some of the most wonderful friendships through eBay. (I swear, I have the nicest customers in the world!)

Without eBay I would still be working at a job that was not my passion. Now I wake up every morning eager to get to work (which I can now do in my PJs!) and I spend all day and well into the night creating magnificent gowns—something I have always loved doing. The rewards come in the form of ecstatic e-mails (and sometimes boxes of chocolate through regular mail) from my customers. (Have I mentioned that I have the best customers in the world?)

Because of eBay I now work with a group of Renaissance-gown eBay sellers and we work to promote eBay as a whole and we share tips and tricks to provide our customers with the best service and quality garments possible. They are absolutely delightful to work with and we have all become good friends.

Opening a Premier- or Business-Level PayPal Account

NOTE: If you already have a PayPal Personal-level account and you plan on listing items on eBay, you must upgrade your PayPal Personal Level account to the Premier or Business level.

If you have not done so already, this is the time to open a PayPal account. You don't absolutely need a PayPal account to list on eBay, but since PayPal is the preferred method of online payment for eBay buyers, it only makes sense that you have one. In fact, not providing the option of PayPal to your buyers *will* put you at a serious disadvantage when competing against other sellers in your category.

Besides, if you are a new seller on eBay with little or no prior feedback history, providing the PayPal option to your buyers will give them more confidence in you as a seller.

Best of all, PayPal Premier and Business accounts offer the following premium services:

- All the core features of a Personal account
- Unlimited credit or debit card payment acceptance
- Subscriptions and recurring payments
- PayPal debit card
- Mass payment
- PayPal Shops
- Customizable transaction history logs
- Seven-day-a-week toll-free customer service
- Multiuser access
- Ability to do business under a corporate or group name

In summary, if you are an eBay seller hoping to start and run a business on eBay, you need a PayPal account.

Signing up for a new PayPal account is quick and easy. The complete steps for opening a PayPal account are described in the first section. Follow those steps and then return here. One tip: If you are setting up a new PayPal account, make sure to select the Premier or Business account level on the first screen of the Sign Up page.

If you already have a Personal-level account, take a moment and upgrade your account now to Premier or Business level. After you have logged into your PayPal account:

1. Click the "My account" tab and then click the "Upgrade account" link in the Enhance Account box.

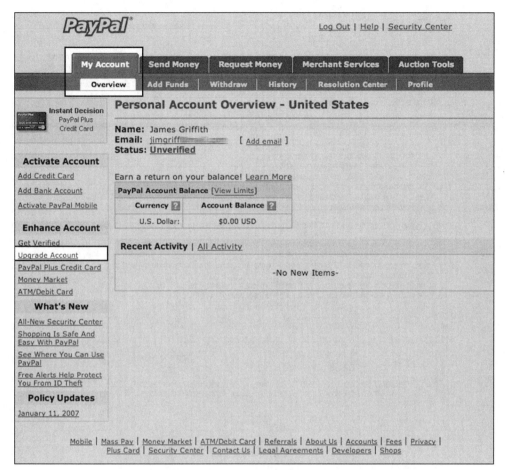

2. Read all the information and then click "Upgrade now."

PayPal®   Log Out | Help | Security Center

| My Account | Send Money | Request Money | Merchant Services | Auction Tools |

Upgrade Your Account

Premier accounts include all the benefits of a Personal account. You also have the ability to:

- Accept all payment types for low fees
- Set up your PayPal Shopping Cart
- Access exclusive, professional customer service seven days a week
- Be identified as a Premier account in your reputation pop-up box
- Be featured in PayPal Shops, where over 100 million PayPal customers can make instant purchases from your website!

Business accounts include **all the benefits of Premier accounts**. In addition, you can:

- Do business easily and affordably with our low-cost merchant account
- Operate under your business name
- Generate reports, financial statements and download settlement file
- Use eBay Tools
- Provide multiple employees with limited access to your account
- Get paid from buyers without PayPal accounts

Upgrade Now | Cancel

Mobile | Mass Pay | Money Market | ATM/Debit Card | Referrals | About Us | Accounts | Fees | Privacy | Plus Card | Security Center | Contact Us | Legal Agreements | Developers | Shops

VeriSign Secured
VERIFY ▶

About SSL Certificates

Copyright © 1999-2007 PayPal. All rights reserved.
Information about FDIC pass-through insurance

3. Choose a Business or Premier account and click "Continue."

PayPal®

Log Out | Help | Security Center

| My Account | Send Money | Request Money | Merchant Services | Auction Tools |

Choose a Name to Do Business Under

You're almost done upgrading your account!

Select from the types of PayPal accounts you need.

⦿ Premier account - do business under my name
◯ Business account - do business under my company or group's name

View the User Agreement.

Continue | Cancel |

Mobile | Mass Pay | Money Market | ATM/Debit Card | Referrals | About Us | Accounts | Fees | Privacy | Plus Card | Security Center | Contact Us | Legal Agreements | Developers | Shops

VeriSign Secured
VERIFY

About SSL Certificates

Copyright © 1999-2007 PayPal. All rights reserved.
Information about FDIC pass-through insurance

4. You have upgraded your PayPal Account!

Research Your Item

Many sellers skip this step. Don't! To ensure the best possible chances for your listing's success, you must first determine the current market value for the item on eBay, as well as determine and adopt the best possible listing practices of those who are already successfully selling on eBay.

First consideration: what to list?

Of course, it helps if you already know what you plan on selling. If so, then you are ready to start searching for similar items on eBay so you can compare and learn what works for that type of item and, more importantly, what doesn't.

Maybe you have no idea what to sell. In that case, select from your possessions something of little or no value to you—perhaps some thoughtful but unfortunate item gifted to you by a dear friend or relative. Don't let that treasure continue gathering dust in the back of the closet. Recycle it! eBay is the perfect "regifting" destination.

Whatever you select as your first eBay listing, try to make it something that is not too valuable, fragile, large, or heavy. Small, durable, and easy-to-pack items are best for a first-time listing. And except for choice collectibles or antiques, your first eBay item for sale should be something new, preferably in its original box.

Once you have settled on the your first item, it's time to research similar items . . . on eBay, of course!

COMPLETED LISTINGS SEARCH

eBay is not only an active and dynamic marketplace, it's also transparent; that is, anyone can view the market for any item or category. This transparency provides you with an excellent research tool called Completed Listings Search.

Using Completed Listings Search, any registered eBay member can, by keyword or category, search for any item that has closed in the last two weeks. Completed Listings Search lets you locate closed items that match yours so you can compare them by title, description, photos, starting and ending price, shipping and handling costs, payment options, number of bids, number of page hits, and so on. You can then adopt and tailor for your own use those listing practices that work (i.e., result in high final-bid amounts) and avoid like the plague those that don't (i.e., result in low or no bids).

NOTE: Use the best listing descriptions as examples to emulate in your own words and formatting, but never lift another seller's description and formatting to paste into yours!

At a local yard sale, I found a small, colorful pottery pitcher for only a quarter! The bottom is marked Honiton. It's small and easy to pack and ship. This little pitcher is an example of a perfect first item to list on eBay.

Start by clicking the "Advanced search" link on the top right-hand corner of any eBay page. In the box provided, enter the keyword or words that best describe your item. I have entered *honiton*. I then check the box "Completed listings only" and click "Search."

Sign in (if prompted). There are 224 matching closed items with *honiton* in their titles. Sort the results if appropriate. In this case, I notice there are books and lace items in the results. I am only interested in looking through pottery items, so I'll click the "Pottery & Glass" link on the left under Matching Categories.

This reduces the number of results to ninety-eight. Scroll through the list of completed listings.

That's better. In fact, there's a jug that is identical to mine (inside the outline)! We will look at that one, of course, and we will also pick a few other listings and compare them using this handy checklist:

Completed Listings Checklist

Title

Starting price

Description

Photos

Selling format

Number of bids

Payment options

Shipping/handling fees

Return/refund policy

Category

Hit counter

Title

Keywords are what eBay shoppers use to find items, so a good listing title should contain as many appropriate keywords as possible and few or no unsearchable words (such as "rare," "beautiful," "L@@K," etc.). Compare the following two titles and the number of bids received.

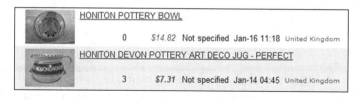

GRIFF TIP! If you are unfamiliar with the category or type of item you plan on listing—for example, a collectible such as a Honiton pitcher—the list of similar completed listings on eBay can provide clues. For example, my research has already taught me that my pitcher may be from the 1950s, might be called a Manaton vase, and was made in England! eBay isn't just a fun place to buy and sell; it's a veritable gold mine of information.

Starting Price

The starting price is the amount at which the bidding will begin. Check any listing on eBay that closes without a bid. Although other factors may be involved, the most common reason for an unsuccessful listing (i.e., no bids received) is that its starting price was too high.

Check the starting prices for those listings that have sold to determine what your starting price should be.

NOTE: A low starting price in conjunction with a reasonable reserve can provide the optimal solution: a starting price to entice bidders and a reserve to prevent your item from selling for lower than your lowest acceptable price.

Description

A good description will always include all item details (size, color, make, model, serial number, condition, age, etc.), as well as detailed shipping and handling costs and accepted payment methods (PayPal, checks, money orders). Also, the best descriptions on eBay always contain a detailed return and refund policy.

Then there are the one- or two-sentence descriptions, such as "Item in good condition. e-mail me with questions."

Which description do you imagine encourages the most bids and, consequently, the highest sales-to-listing ratio? Your research of completed-item descriptions may provide an answer.

Photos

Some listings include several sharp, well-lit, professional-looking digital photos. Other listings display one image, often poorly lit and focused. There are even listings with no photos. Study examples of photos for completed items. Think about how you can provide even better, more professional-looking photos.

Another important photo factor: Listings that have a Gallery image (the little thumbnail next to the item title) tend to receive more attention than those that don't. For example:

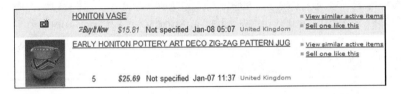

Selling Format

Although there is no hard-and-fast rule, some items are better served by the auction format (rare or valuable items), while others are usually best listed with a fixed-price format. By checking the successful listings that match your item, you can better determine which format might work best for you.

Number of Bids

The number of bids is a good indication of item desirability: the higher the bid number, the more this item was of interest to buyers. Low bid numbers? Check other factors such as starting price, photo, and description.

Payment Options

Most sellers provide more than one way for a buyer to pay for their item. The most popular online payment option is PayPal, and many buyers will shop only for items they can purchase with PayPal. Other sellers state they will accept money orders or checks only. Providing as many payment options as possible (and including PayPal) is definitely a best listing practice, but look at matching completed items for yourself to see if this holds true for your item. If you discover that many sellers of your type of item are not offering PayPal, maybe offering it will give you a competitive edge.

Shipping/Handling Fees

Your research will often show that, all other factors being equal, the seller that offers the clearest shipping and handling terms, the most reasonable shipping and handling fees, and more than one shipping option will usually win the most bidders (which often results in the highest final bid amounts). Later, we will see tools that you can provide your buyers so they can calculate accurate shipping costs before they bid or buy.

Return/Refund Policy

A reasonable and clear return and refund policy will go a long way toward instilling buyer confidence. Notice how listings with good return and refund policies often have a higher number of bids compared to those that don't. Find examples of return and refund polices that will work for you and adopt them.

Category

Although most eBay buyers find their items through a keyword search of titles (or titles and descriptions), many sellers limit their keyword descriptions to specific categories. Improperly categorizing an item often results in fewer buyers finding the item.

Also, some sellers can actually increase the potential of their listing by listing in two categories. Check your seller competition and see if they are listing their items in two categories.

Hit Counter

Sellers can add a free hit counter to the bottom of their listing description. The counter indicates the number of times the page has been viewed. An item with a high counter number and low or no bids indicates that something is amiss with one of the other checklist items.

In summary, research is crucial. You cannot expect to succeed in a marketplace unless you fully understand the workings of that marketplace, and that includes all possible listing practices, both good and bad. Adopt and emulate the good listing practices and avoid the bad. It's as simple as that! Finally, markets are not static. Make a habit of conducting regular searches of eBay completed listings.

GRIFF TIP! Never stop researching. Even if you should become an experienced and successful eBay seller, you will find the key to maintaining success is to stay on top of your competition, and the only way to do so is to check their listings, both current and completed.

Creating and Editing Digital Pictures of Your eBay Item

What Are Digital Pictures?

To define and explain what makes up a digital picture, we first need to define a film picture.

A film picture is a mechanical and chemical recording of visual information. It is created by focusing reflected light from an object or view onto a piece of film. The light changes the chemical layers that make up the film. When the exposed film is chemically developed, a reaction in the layers of chemicals on the film re-creates the initial visual information, but only as a negative of the original image. The negative is then converted into a print by a sort of reverse process of what happened in the camera. The image on the print picture is made up of microscopic bits of color so fine the eye cannot see them as separate dots but instead sees them as bands and areas of different color.

A digital picture is an electronic recording of light reflected off an object or scene that has been converted to, or created as, a digital computer file. In a digital image, the light from the camera lens (or from a scanned print) strikes a special recording device, which converts the light information into binary information (ones and zeros) and stores this information as a digital file either within the camera or on your computer.

Do I Need Digital Pictures of My eBay Item?

Do you want to sell your item? Then you will need a picture of your item. Items without pictures usually end up closing out with no bidders or buyers—a waste of time and insertion fees.

eBay buyers are a funny lot. They like to see what they are buying. Imagine that! As a seller, you must provide the best possible pictures of your wares if you want to generate any buyer interest. Your item pictures should be clear, focused, uncluttered, and as close a representation of your item as possible. In addition, they should be big enough to show all important details, but, since they will be digital files, small enough to download through the Internet and onto the item page as quickly as possible.

To the newbie, the whole concept of digital images can seem overwhelming. In reality, creating, editing, and uploading digital images is a snap if you approach the subject methodically, step-by-step. After you have finished your first digital picture, creating more will be a piece of cake, I promise.

There are three parts to quick and painless eBay picture mastery:

1. Taking the picture
2. Editing the picture
3. Uploading the picture to your listing

Parts 1 and 2 are described in great detail in this chapter. Part 3 is covered later in the book.

Read through this chapter carefully and you'll have a good image of your item ready for your first eBay listing in no time!

Taking the Picture—Selecting a Method

Before we set up the item to be photographed, we first need to consider which of the three basic options for creating digital pictures we will use. Depending on what equipment you have at your disposal, you could:

1. Take a picture of the item with a regular camera and have a local film developer convert your prints or negatives directly into digital files on a CD-ROM.
2. Take a picture of the item with a regular camera, have the film developed, and scan the prints into your computer using a flatbed scanner.
3. Take a picture of the item with a digital camera.

Which of the three options is right for you? Let's discuss their pros and cons.

FILM DEVELOPERS

If you don't have a digital camera or a flatbed scanner, use a regular film camera to take pictures of your item and take the exposed film to your local film developer—one that can create digital files of your images either on floppy disk or on CD-ROM. Most local film and camera stores, national chain pharmacies, and even some supermarkets now offer this service.

PRO: Film developers are ideal for the first-time or occasional seller. No shelling out for or mussing or fussing with a digital camera or scanner. If time and budget are concerns, and you don't have access to a digital camera, go with the film developer option.

CON: As a long-term option, buying and developing film will prove counterproductive. The money spent in just a few months on film and processing will pay for a good digital camera. Also, as part of developing—whether by machine or person—irreversible decisions will be made regarding the tone, brightness, and other aspects of your image files. Usually this is not an issue, but occasionally the resulting digital pictures may not be entirely to your liking.

FLATBED SCANNERS

Flatbed scanners create digital images of flat or nearly flat items. You can skip the camera steps altogether if you are selling flat items (comic books, trading cards, coins, stamps, ephemera, autographs, etc.). For flat stuff, scanning as opposed to photographing will provide you with the highest-quality image file possible.

Simply place your flat item directly on the flatbed scanner—no cameras or developers. Of course, you can also scan print photographs of your item.

PRO: The perfect tool for flat things. Otherwise . . .

CON: Same as for film developers if you are scanning photos of your items. You will still be paying for film and developing.

DIGITAL CAMERAS

Digital cameras work almost exactly like film cameras. They have a lens and a shutter and usually a flash, but instead of recording an image on film, the digital camera records it on a small chip containing millions of receptors. The chip and other hardware and software inside the camera then transfer the image into the ones and zeroes that make up a digital file, which will be stored on a small removable chip or disk inside the camera. The digital image can then be transferred to your computer by removing the chip or disk from the camera and inserting it directly into your computer or by connecting special cables from your digital camera to your computer. (Each make and model of digital camera has a slightly different way of transferring digital image files. Consult your camera's user manual or guide for more details.)

PRO: Easy to use. If you can shoot pics with a film camera, you can shoot pics with a digital camera. Most good digital cameras are point-and-shoot. There's no waiting for film to develop, and you have total control over the quality of your pictures. A digital camera can pay for itself in only a few months of regular eBay selling.

CON: The initial cost of a digital camera might be a burden to some new sellers. Still, good new and used digital cameras suitable for your eBay pictures are available starting as low as $50. Of course, check eBay first before you buy.

What to Look For in a Digital Camera

So many different brands, models, prices, and levels of quality are available in digital cameras that choosing one can be tough. What follows is my smart-shopping checklist for digital cameras.

Buy the Best You Can Afford

Although you don't need to buy a top-of-the line digital camera to take excellent images for eBay, it never pays to scrimp when purchasing an electronic gadget of any type. Buy the best your budget will allow.

2.0 Megapixels or Higher

Digital camera resolution is measured in megapixels. A pixel is the basic unit of programmable color in a computer image or in a digital camera, so the higher the number of megapixels, the higher the quality of the image. Today, most brand-name digital cameras start at a resolution of 2.0 megapixels. For creating images that are meant to be displayed on a Web page (such as an eBay item page), 2.0 megapixels is sufficient resolution.

Look for Brand Names

For example, Sony, Nikon, Olympus, Kodak, Canon, Fuji, HP, Leica, Epson, etc. If you've found a great deal and it's for a brand name you have never heard of before, it's probably best to avoid it.

Macro Is a Must

Look for cameras with "macro" capability (the ability to get your camera an inch away from an item without losing focus). Most new digital cameras have macro built in, but since macro is the digital camera feature that you will need when selling at eBay, ask before purchasing.

Zoom, Autofocus, and Autoexposure Come in Handy

Although not absolutely necessary, zoom, autofocus, and autoexposure can make your photography tasks easier. Luckily for you, nearly all recent digital camera makes and models have all three features built in.

Used Is OK

Buy new if possible, but don't rule out a used digital camera. You can find both new and used digital cameras at, oh, let's see . . . where might one find digital cameras . . . ?

Look for the Complete Package

If buying a used digital camera, look for deals where the seller provides the complete contents of the original package, including software, cables, and accessories. Owners who preserve all the original contents and packaging for a device such as a digital camera are usually the type of people who take excellent care of their belongings, including their digital cameras.

For more detailed information about digital camera features, price, and picture quality, try the Digital Photography Review Web site, *www.dpreview.com*. This excellent site contains hundreds of detailed professional and user reviews of all the most popular digital cameras. They can help you decide which model is right for your needs and budget.

For the record, I am currently using an older but trusty Sony DSC-F707 digital camera for all my eBay pictures and other fine photography projects.

Once you have decided which option works best for you, the next step is to set up the item and photograph it.

Taking the Picture—Setting Up the Item

SELECTING A SPACE

For one-time eBay sellers, any well-lit spot in your home or apartment will do just fine. Under certain conditions, you can also set up your shots outdoors.

The table for photographing your item should be about two feet deep by four feet wide by forty-two inches high. If you plan on selling only small items, you can scale these dimensions down accordingly except for the table height, which, to save you from bending over for long periods, should be no lower than thirty-six inches.

For our setup example, we will be photographing a small pottery pitcher. I have set up a table, some halogen work lights, and a digital camera on a tripod.

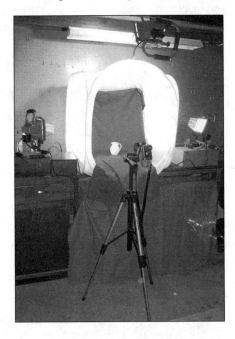

On the table, I placed a box to bring the height up to about forty inches. Then I draped a backdrop of dark blue cotton cloth over a piece of thin plywood, over the box, and down over the front of the table. (More on backdrops and lighting later.)

GRIFF TIP! If you intend to sell regularly on eBay, plan on setting aside a small studio space somewhere in your home or business location exclusively dedicated to taking digital pictures.

Your eBay photography studio can consist of nothing more than a movable table placed against a wall. The entire space needed should be two to four feet wide and eight feet tall. It will help with lighting if the walls surrounding your studio are painted white or at least a neutral color. Avoid spaces with walls or immovable objects painted a strong color, as they can "tint" the light reflected onto your item—usually an unwanted effect.

SETTING UP THE CAMERA

Whether you are using a film camera or a digital camera, the rules of picture taking are the same for both. If you have a tripod, use it. If not, find a sturdy, flat surface upon which you can rest the camera. In a pinch, try holding the camera steady and hope for the best.

Regular eBay sellers: Invest in a tripod. You can buy one new for about $20–$40, and you can find excellent new and used tripods . . . on eBay!

BACKDROPS

Many eBay sellers do not use backdrops for their item pictures. They instead simply plop the item on the nearest table or, in some cases, even in the baby's crib! This can often lead to interesting pictures.

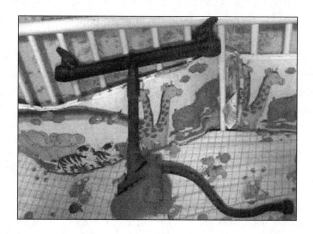

It's hard to tell just what is for sale in the following picture. Is it the dinette set or that thing on the table? The seller at least took the time to show the newspaper he plans to use for packing the thing.

You can avoid these sorts of embarrassing and unprofessional picture mistakes by using a solid-color backdrop to isolate and focus attention on your item.

A backdrop can be a wide piece of solid-colored paper, board, or cloth placed behind and under the item. As a rule, the backdrop's color should contrast with the color(s) and brightness of the item. For example, a pale item usually looks best on a dark background. A dark item usually looks best on a pale background.

Don't spend a fortune on backdrops. You can purchase fabric suitable for backdrops from any fabric store. Check the remnants bins for good deals. Look for matte-finished cotton or linen yardage in solid colors (no pattern), and purchase a selection of muted colors. For most purposes, you can get by with two to three yards of forty-five-inch-wide cloth.

You can also find incredible bargains for remnants . . . on eBay, of course! Search eBay using *cotton fabric*. Also search in eBay's Cameras & Photo category using *backdrop* to find good deals on professional backdrop cloth and paper rolls.

If you are photographing your item on the table against the wall, use push-pins to fasten the fabric or paper into place on the wall itself, or place a piece of poster board or thin plywood on the table against the wall and drape the backdrop over it (as in our example above). Make sure your backdrop covers both behind and underneath the item.

Here is another shot of my impromptu photo studio. I have two rolls of photography paper hung on the wall above the shooting area.

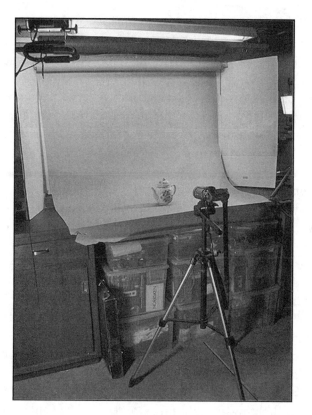

You may need to shoot large items in place. If so, try to isolate the object as best you can from its surroundings. If the item isn't too big, place a large sheet of paper or cloth behind it and follow the same rules below for lighting the object to its best advantage. Large bolts of scenic muslin work well. Again, try searching eBay's Cameras & Photo category.

LIGHTING YOUR ITEM

Inadequate lighting is a common digital picture mistake. How do you determine if your item is inadequately lit? A good rule of thumb is to rely on your camera. Aim the camera at the item. If the camera's built-in light meter or flash indicator shows that a flash is needed, then add more lighting, either artificial or natural.

Indoor—Direct Lighting

For most situations, your item should be lit from two or more directions. Three or more clip-on lamps with hundred-watt halogen floodlights will usually provide adequate illumination. Position the lights above and to the sides of the item. Make sure they are slightly in front of the item (avoid lighting from behind). Experiment with lighting positions. Move the lamps around to get the best positions and the right blending of light and shadows. Shadows are not always bad. For items with complex surfaces (carving, embroidery, etc.) a prominent shadow in one direction can help emphasize the surface texture. Still, for most items, you will want to "wash" the item to be photographed with light sources crossing each other from opposite directions.

Indoor—Indirect Lighting

Some items may not photograph as well in direct lighting. Examples might be glossy pottery or porcelain, glassware, shiny jewelry, or harsh white objects. In these cases, you may need to light the item indirectly with diffused or bounced light. There are a number of ways to accomplish this type of lighting. A quick and cheap way is to point the light sources away from the item and onto white or metallic sheets of poster board. You can even bounce strong light off a white ceiling. A more professional (and expensive) way is to use professional photography studio light boxes or reflective screens. These devices bounce and diffuse light off white or metallic material. The resulting diffused light illuminates the item without glare or harsh shadows.

NOTE: Reflected lighting usually takes more wattage than direct lighting to achieve the same level of illumination. Translation: Double or triple the number of lamps and hundred-watt bulbs when using reflected lighting. Without using a light meter, you can always take a test shot to see if your lighting is adequate.

GRIFF TIP! Check eBay for good lighting deals. I found two halogen work light trees for $35 each. Each tree has two 150-watt halogen lamps bolted to a solid, tripod-based, extendable pole. The combination of four 150-watt halogen lamps is more than adequate for most of my eBay photography needs. They provide excellent direct or diffused light when bounced off my studio's white ceiling or used with a translucent cloth light box.

ANOTHER GRIFF TIP! The light from halogen or tungsten incandescent lamps tends to be more hot (yellow or red) than cool (blue). This may distort the colors of your item. You can adjust for this by using your digital camera's white-balance feature if it has one. (Check your camera's manual.) Otherwise, you may need to use blue gels over your light sources or slightly blue reflective surfaces to counter the strong yellow light. Some sellers like to use full-spectrum light bulbs since they produce roughly the same neutral white light of sunlight. Verilux makes a good full-spectrum light bulb.

Outdoor—Direct and Indirect Lighting

Your indoor photography space should suffice for nearly all your eBay pictures, but in some instances you may find it necessary to take pictures outdoors.

When shooting outdoors, avoid placing the item in direct sunlight. Bright, harsh sunlight can wash out or distort colors and can also cast unwanted dark shadows. The north side of a house is usually a good spot for photographing your item outside, as northern light tends to be more even and less harsh, especially on a bright, sunny day. A slightly overcast day offers the ideal outdoor light for taking item pictures.

ANOTHER GRIFF TIP! When shooting your item outdoors, you should isolate the background with something solid. Of course you can and should experiment and try all types of compositions in your shots. If you are selling antique lawn furniture, it might look smashing against a hedge of privet but not so smashing against the family minivan. The only way to know for sure is to experiment. For those who are unsure of their design talents, a solid background will always do the trick as a first or last resort.

CAMERA SETTINGS

Resolution

Set or configure your digital camera to take medium- to high-resolution pictures. Resolution is usually described in pixels. The lowest resolution you should use is 640 by 480 pixels. For eBay pictures, you should not need anything higher than

1,024 by 768 pixels. At that resolution, the resulting image file will be large, but we will be reducing the size of the file in editing.

Some digital cameras come with "e-mail resolution." This setting is for taking small pictures suitable for sending as attachments to e-mail. Don't use this setting if it is lower than 640 by 480 pixels. As we will see in editing, you can always reduce the size of a digital picture, but you cannot increase the size without noticeable degradation of the image.

Autoexposure, Autofocus

Why make extra work for yourself? If your film or digital camera has autoexposure and/or autofocus, by all means use them.

Flash

Most cameras have a "flash off" setting. Make sure your digital camera flash is set to off. The intense light from a camera flash can wash out the colors of your item and can also obliterate details. If your film or digital camera indicates you need to use the camera's built-in flash to light the item properly, you should add more lamps and watts to your lighting scheme, as we discussed in the lighting section.

Macro

If you need to place your digital camera a few inches or less away from the item, make sure the camera's macro feature is enabled. Consult your digital camera's user manual for more information.

FRAMING THE ITEM IN THE CAMERA VIEWFINDER

We've draped a backdrop cloth down the wall and over the table. We have also set the lights, and the camera is set securely on its tripod. Finally, we have positioned the item on the table. Now it's time to frame the shot and take the picture.

First, this item is taller than it is wide, so I will shoot it in portrait mode. I do this by turning my camera ninety degrees clockwise, as shown here.

If your camera has a variable lens, set it to the widest angle. Position the camera and tripod in front of the item, usually no more than twenty-four inches away. (This varies with the size of the item you are photographing.) Adjust the height of the camera, using the tripod. Some items photograph best when shot straight on; others look better shot slightly from above. Try different angles and use the one that works best for your item. Our little pitcher looks best shot from slightly above, so I have raised the camera about a foot higher than the pitcher. While looking into the camera's viewfinder, move the camera away from or toward the item or, if your camera has zoom, zoom in or out until you have the item framed within the view window so that it nearly fills the frame.

SNAP THE SHOT

Everything is in place. The lighting looks good. The item fills the frame. It's time to take the picture. Here is what this first shot looks like.

Not bad. Remember, the pitcher is taller than it is wide, so I repositioned my camera to take the shot in portrait format. When the digital image is displayed, it shows in the default landscape format. That's why it appears on its side now. Later in editing, we will rotate the image clockwise ninety degrees.

Also, my digital camera's autoexposure was set so that the dark blue background actually appears almost black. I like it. We'll keep it.

GRIFF TIP! It's always best to get all your photography done in one session, so if you have two or more items to list at eBay, photograph them in succession.

I took two other shots of this pitcher; one of the other side and one of the underside to show the maker's mark. It always pays to show all aspects of your item, including flaws and imperfections!

We will use these pictures in our listing in the next chapter.

A LIST OF QUICK PICTURE-TAKING TIPS

Whether you use a digital camera or a film camera to take the picture, you should always follow a few simple picture-taking rules:

- If possible, avoid holding the camera to take the shot. Use a tripod or place the camera on a sturdy, flat surface. This will help guarantee the image is in focus. You can find good deals on inexpensive tripods on eBay, of course.
- Don't take a picture of the item sitting on your kitchen table where the rest of your fabulous 1970s-era kitchen will be in the picture (unless of course you are selling the kitchen). Isolate the item you are photographing by placing a solid-color cloth or paper backdrop behind it. As a general rule, if the item is light in color, use a darker background color. If the item is dark, use a lighter-colored background.
- Lighting—outdoors: Avoid photographing an item in direct sunlight. Bright sunlight can distort colors and cast dark shadows. If you must shoot outdoors on a sunny day, shoot the picture out of direct sunlight. A good spot is often the north side of a wall or building. An ideal time to shoot outdoors would be on a slightly overcast day.
- Lighting—indoors: Avoid using a flash to take a picture of your item. Just like direct sunlight, it can distort colors and cause white spots on shiny objects. Instead, light your item from three or more angles using any common household light sources such as table lamps with translucent shades, clip-on floodlights, or halogen work lights. (You can correct the yellow cast caused by incandescent lights by using your digital camera's "white balance" feature or later on during editing. Consult your digital camera manual for information on white balance.)
- If you are using a digital camera, make sure it is set at a pixel resolution of 640 by 480 or higher. (Again, your digital camera's manual will explain how to change your camera's resolution.)
- Whenever possible, aim your camera at the center of the item. Using zoom or by moving the camera closer or farther away, position the item image in the viewfinder so that it fills the frame with as little background showing as possible.
- In some instances, you may find it best to shoot the item from an angle above the item, but generally, you should position the item and the camera so that the camera is level with the item (the item and camera are roughly the same distance from the ground).

Although one image may suffice for your listing, take two or more photos to show a variety of aspects of the item: close-ups, the back of the item, and so on. If the item has a flaw, make sure to take a picture of it!

Once you have taken the pictures and have copies of them as digital image files, you will need to get them into your computer for editing and uploading. Transferring digital pictures from the digital camera to the computer depends on the make and model of the camera.

Most digital cameras store their images on a memory chip or card that can be popped out of the camera and into a chip or card reader or, in some cases, right into your computer if it has the appropriate slot.

Nearly every digital camera also provides an option for transferring digital picture files from the camera to a computer via a specially provided USB cable. Consult the user's manual that came with your digital camera for the methods for transferring your pictures.

SAVING YOUR DIGITAL IMAGE FILES

Before you move or copy your digital image files onto your computer, you should create a special folder on your computer where you can safely store them so they will be easy to find later.

Some cameras come with special software that will automatically set up special folders on your computer and transfer copies of the images into them. This feature can be useful in keeping your image files organized.

You can also create a special folder for your eBay images. For information on how to create a new folder on your computer, consult the Help section in your computer's operating system. For Windows, click "Start, Help." For Macs, click the "Help" link on the top of the desktop window.

Editing the Picture (Using Software)

Now that you've created digital images of your item and have moved them to your computer, you are no doubt itching to get them up on an eBay listing so you can start the sale of your item. Hold on, we aren't finished. We need to edit the image files first.

Many eBay sellers skip editing. Big mistake. It is highly unlikely that your image files are perfect right out of the camera. Many will need to be rotated. Some will need cropping. Almost all will need resizing. To rotate, crop, or resize an image file, you will need image editing software. You have options. You can pay for top-of-the-line image-editing software, such as:

Adobe Photoshop
Adobe Photoshop Elements
Corel Paint Shop Pro
Corel Photo-Paint

Or you can look for software that comes with your computer operating system or applications, for example:

iPhoto (Mac OS X)
Windows Photo Gallery (Vista)
Microsoft Picture Manager
Microsoft Photo Editor (Windows, older versions)

If you have recently purchased a new digital camera or scanner, it will have come packaged with a CD-ROM containing, among other things, a simple, bare-bones image-editing application. Slip the CD into your computer and look for the option for loading free software. Follow the instructions from there.

Finally, if all else fails, there is always the Internet. My favorite free image-editing software download is Irfanview, available for download at *www.irfanview.com*.

We'll use Irfanview for our image-editing software examples in this chapter. Irfanview sports a simple interface that resembles most other popular brands of image editing software.

If you are a Mac user, don't despair! The basic editing commands (Crop, Rotate, Resize) are available with any good image-editing software and can usually be found in roughly the same places on each application's menu command bar. This goes for Windows as well as Macintosh examples.

OPENING A DIGITAL PICTURE FILE

First, we need to find our digital picture files. I moved copies of the three digital picture files for my small pitcher from my camera to a folder called eBay Digital Pictures. The folder lives on my Windows desktop.

Once you know where the files are located on your computer, you can open them for editing. There are several ways to open these files for viewing or editing. One way in Windows (Classic View) is to click "Start," "Accessories," then "Windows Explorer."

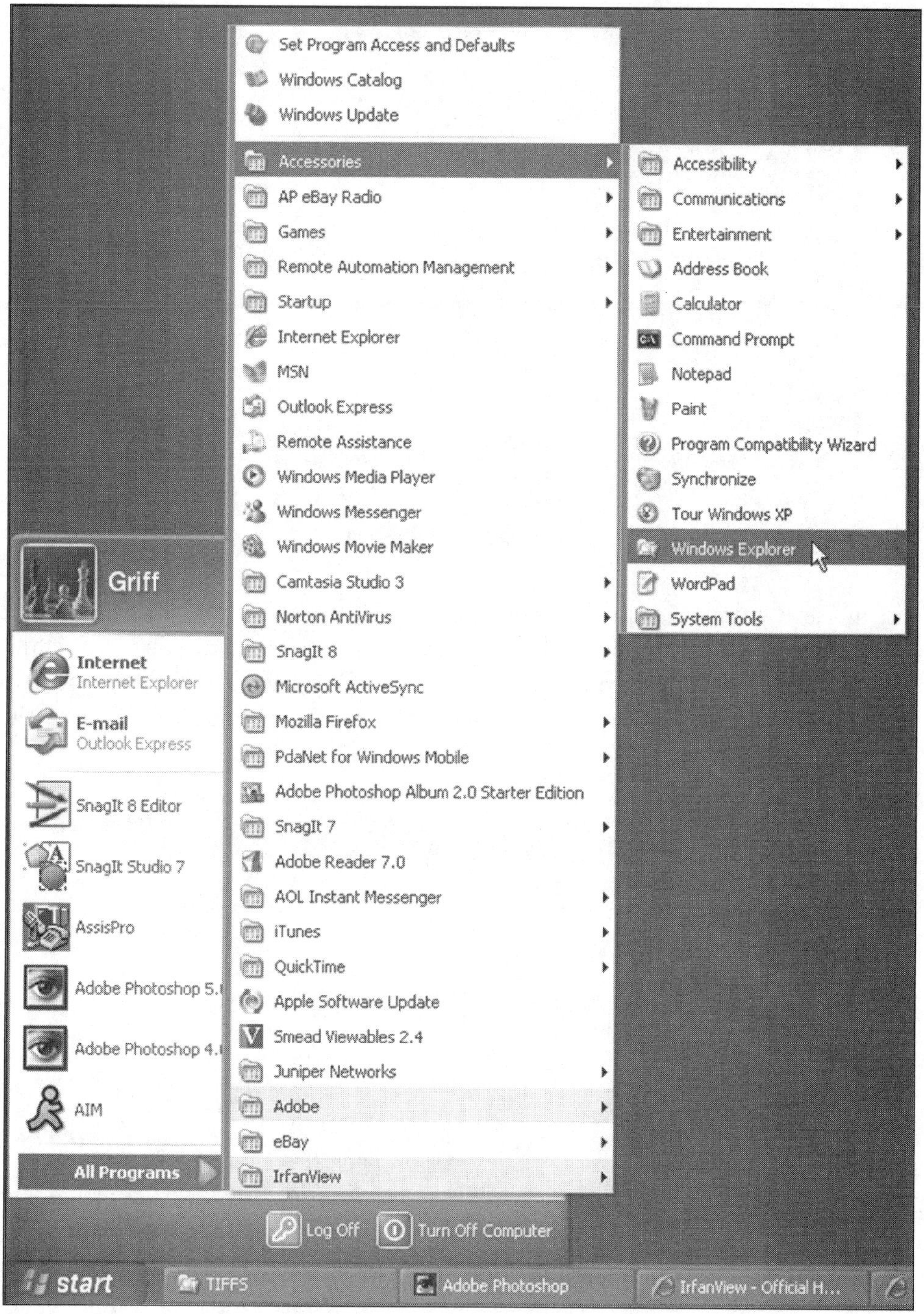
Set Program Access and Defaults
Windows Catalog
Windows Update
Accessories
AP eBay Radio
Games
Remote Automation Management
Startup
Internet Explorer
MSN
Outlook Express
Remote Assistance
Windows Media Player
Windows Messenger
Windows Movie Maker
Camtasia Studio 3
Norton AntiVirus
SnagIt 8
Microsoft ActiveSync
Mozilla Firefox
PdaNet for Windows Mobile
Adobe Photoshop Album 2.0 Starter Edition
SnagIt 7
Adobe Reader 7.0
AOL Instant Messenger
iTunes
QuickTime
Apple Software Update
Smead Viewables 2.4
Juniper Networks
Adobe
eBay
IrfanView
Accessibility
Communications
Entertainment
Address Book
Calculator
Command Prompt
Notepad
Paint
Program Compatibility Wizard
Synchronize
Tour Windows XP
Windows Explorer
WordPad
System Tools
Griff
Internet
Internet Explorer
E-mail
Outlook Express
SnagIt 8 Editor
SnagIt Studio 7
AssisPro
Adobe Photoshop 5.
Adobe Photoshop 4.
AIM
All Programs
Log Off
Turn Off Computer
start
TIFFS
Adobe Photoshop
IrfanView - Official H...

In the Windows Explorer window, navigate to your picture files, then select the file you wish to edit first by hovering your cursor over the file's name and clicking the right-hand mouse button. Select "Open With" from the pop-up menu and then "Choose Program" to select the appropriate application from the list of choices presented.

Another way to open files for editing would be to start Irfanview or any other image-editing application (by clicking on its shortcut either on your desktop or on the "Start, Programs" menu) and use the "File, Open . . ." command on the application's toolbar to bring up an Open dialog box.

IrfanView	_ □ ✕

File Edit Image Options View Help

Open...	O
Reopen	Shift+R
Open with external editor	Shift+E
Open as	▶
Thumbnails	T
Slideshow...	W
Batch Conversion/Rename...	B
Search files...	Ctrl+F
Rename File...	F2
Move File...	F7
Copy File...	F8
Delete File...	Del
Save	Ctrl+S
Save as...	S
Print...	Ctrl+P
Select TWAIN Source...	
Acquire/Batch scanning...	Ctrl+Shift+A
Copy Shop...	
MRUDs...	▶
Exit	Esc

P

No file loaded (use File->Open menu)

Still another way would be drag and drop each file from its folder into the Irfanview window.

Drag and Drop

This is an excellent time to illustrate a helpful computer feature that many people never use: drag and drop.

For Windows, start by placing the image-editing application window and the window containing the file you want to open next to each other on your computer screen in such a way that you can see the file you wish to open and the blank space inside the application window (in this example, Irfanview).

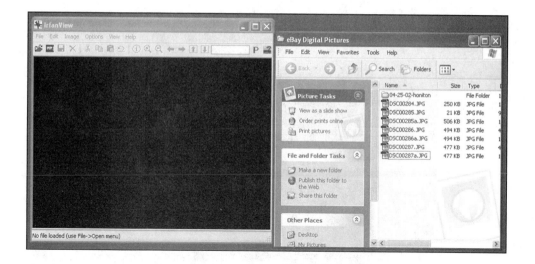

Place your cursor over the file name. Hold down the left-hand mouse button. While still holding down the left-hand mouse button, move your cursor over to the application window. You will notice that you are now "dragging" the file along with the cursor. Don't release the mouse button . . .

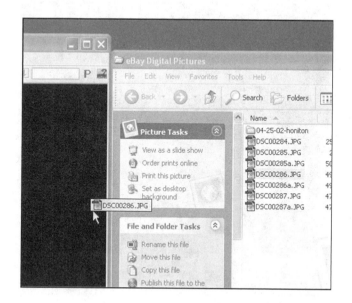

. . . until your cursor is completely over the application window. To "drop" the file, release the mouse button.

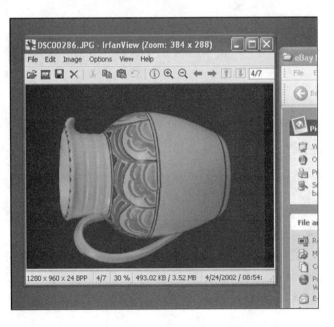

When you do release the mouse button, the file will "drop" into the application window and open.

Regardless of the method you use to open the file, the result is the same: We open our digital picture file in an image-editing application in order to perfect the picture for use on eBay.

Now that we've opened the digital picture file in a photo editor, let's start editing!

Editing Digital Pictures

ROTATE (AKA FLIP, SPIN, OR TRANSFORM)

Our jug picture was taken in portrait mode, that is, with the camera held at a right angle. The resulting picture shows the item on its side. For the picture to make sense when viewed on eBay, we need to rotate it ninety degrees clockwise.

All image-editing software has a command for rotating a digital picture. In Irfanview, the "Rotate . . ." command is found on the submenu under "Image."

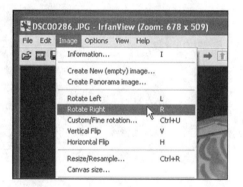

Our digital picture needs to rotate ninety degrees to the right.

Our digital picture is now right side up.

CROP

The next step is to crop all extraneous visual information from around the jug. Just before we snapped this picture, we framed the picture of the jug so that it nearly filled the frame of the digital viewfinder. Thus, there is little to crop. Still, nearly every digital picture can benefit from cropping. In our picture, there is just enough extra black border around the jug itself for us to crop.

We use the mouse to select an area on the digital picture by creating a box. To start, position your mouse cursor somewhere on the upper left-hand corner of the picture.

While holding down the mouse button, drag the cursor diagonally down toward the right-hand side of the picture.

Once you have reached the other corner, release the mouse button. You will see something like the following:

You can change the dimensions of the box by dragging the sides with your mouse cursor. Note: Not all image-editing software allows for repositioning of the crop lines. For those applications, you will have to press the "Cancel" key and redraw the box till it's perfect.

When you have arranged the sides of the box to your liking, click "Edit" on the menu command bar and select "Crop . . ."

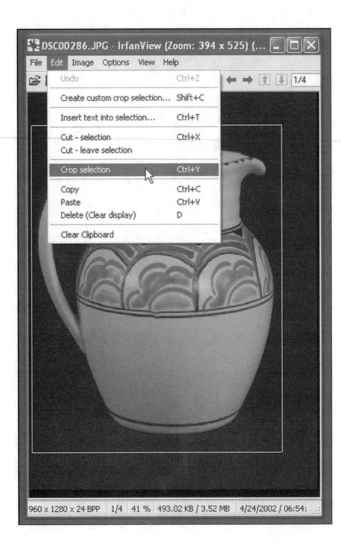

This will crop out everything outside of the white box.

The cropped digital picture!

RESIZE

If the picture doesn't look too big, why are we resizing?

Irfanview has automatically "zoomed out" on the view so that we can see the entire image within the application window without scrolling back and forth. At the moment, we are viewing the digital picture at 25 percent of its actual size.

Remember, millions of items are for sale at eBay. If your digital picture files are so big that they take forever to download onto an eBay shopper's computer, that shopper might just give up waiting and browse away from your listing in search of other similar items. Also, we are going to use a feature called eBay Picture Services. For our pictures to work with this service, they have to be within a certain range of height/width pixel dimensions, and that can be accomplished only by resizing.

Let's reset the display option so we can see just how big the digital picture actually is. Click "View" and then "Display options." The current display setting is "Fit image to window." Let's change it to "Do not fit to anything."

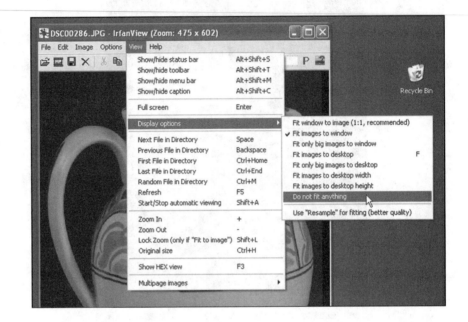

I've reduced the window, but you can clearly see that this digital picture is enormous.

In full-screen view, only the very top of the jug is viewable. Remember, the larger the image size, the longer it will take to appear on a bidder's screen. If you were to load this digital picture on your eBay listing, it would take forever to download over a dial-up connection. In addition, a viewer would have to scroll back and forth and up and down to view the item (and never in its entirety).

Let's resize the picture.

Click on "Image" and then "Resize . . ." on the menu command bar.

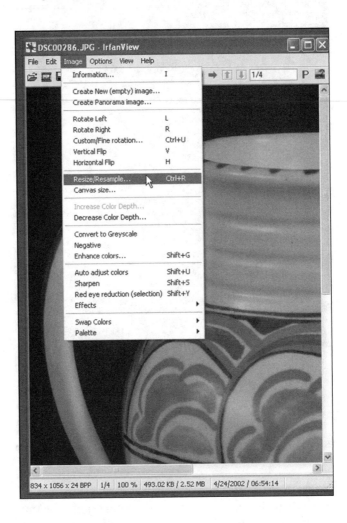

Any command that is followed by ellipsis points will bring up a dialog box:

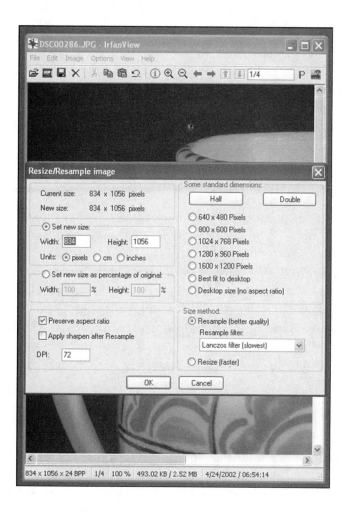

Make sure that "Pixels" is selected for the "Units" option.

When creating digital pictures for viewing over the Web, the standard measurement is always pixels.

Our jug picture is 834 pixels by 1,056 pixels. Remember, you should think of a pixel as that dot of light on your computer monitor. Pixel density varies from monitor to monitor, so pixels do not relate in any absolute way to inches or centimeters. However, the number of pixels for height and width of a digital picture is extremely important.

GRIFF'S PIXEL GUIDELINES

After much experimentation, and with the changes to eBay Picture Services since the first edition of *The Official eBay Bible*, I have adjusted the old pixel guidelines to the following.

If you keep your digital pictures between a minimum of 330 pixels high and 440 pixels wide and a maximum of 600 pixels high by 800 pixels wide, your digital pictures will always be large enough to show the complete item in detail (provided you have followed all of the previous steps for digital pictures), yet small enough to download quickly for those bidders with slow dial-up connections. In addition, they will be the optimum size for eBay Picture Services.

NOTE: If you plan on using the SuperSize option for eBay Picture Services, your images will work best if they are as close to (but preferably no bigger than) 600 pixels tall by 800 pixels wide as possible. We'll learn more about eBay Picture Services later when we list the item.

When faced with higher-than-acceptable pixel dimensions for height and width, always select the larger of the two and reduce it to within the range suggested above. The largest dimension of our image is the height, 1,056 pixels. Let's reduce it to 600.

Notice that you don't have to change the other dimension; it changes automatically, and in ratio, to 474 pixels. All good image-editing software is configured to keep the ratio between height and width constant. When you change one dimension, the other will change to keep the correct proportion.

Changing the height from 1,056 pixels to 600 pixels automatically reduces the width to 474. This is well within the parameters of Griff's Pixel Guidelines. Click "OK" to accept this new size.

Here is the resized digital picture of our jug.

It's a perfectly proportioned picture, if I do say so myself.
Let's save a copy of this priceless work of art.

Saving and Archiving Your eBay Digital Pictures

Once we have edited our digital picture to perfection, we must save it to our computer.

I'm a digital pack rat. Pictures, e-mails, text files . . . I archive most everything sent to me or created on my computer. Unless an image is unusable, I archive all of my pictures. Why? Given the low cost of storage on CD-ROM or an extra backup hard drive, it seems foolish to delete perfectly good pictures. Besides, as the mantra of all pack rats goes, you never know when you might need them!

You may not be as obsessively concerned about saving your images as I am, but you should keep copies of your eBay item pictures for at least three months after your eBay listing ends. And if you are going to save copies of your picture files, you might as well start out right, with a system!

First things first. We need to save our magnificently edited digital picture. With the edited digital picture open in your image-editing application, choose "File" and "Save as . . ."

In the resulting Save As dialog box, select a folder on your hard drive for your edited eBay picture. I have created a main folder called eBay Pictures inside the folder for My Pictures. I give the new file a file name of "honiton-01" and I change the "Save as type" from Windows Bitmap (BMP) to JPG.

Nearly every good image-editing application will prompt you, before saving a JPG file, to select a JPEG quality factor. For example, in Photoshop, you are automatically asked to select a quality level between 1 and 10 when you click the "Save" button. The Irfanview "JPG/GIF save options" dialog box displays a slider that you can move left to right to change the JPEG quality factor.

Why would you want to change from high quality to lower quality? The higher the quality value for a JPEG digital file, the bigger the file is in kilobytes and the longer it takes to download. You want pictures that snap as quickly as possible into your item description.

When creating digital images for eBay items, lowering the image-quality factor will have little or no discernible effect on the final digital picture. As a rule, I usually reduce the image quality factor to a point midway between the lowest and highest qualities (which I have done for this picture). Let's save it to view the change, if any.

We have perfected the image for eBay and there is virtually no change at all in our image's quality. In fact, it looks better than ever. But what if there had been a noticeable and consequently unacceptable change in the image's quality? Would we be stuck with it? Not at all! You still have the original image saved on your hard drive. (Remember, we saved the edited version as a brand-new file.) You can simply start the editing process again with the original digital file.

Taking good pictures is a skill that anyone with an eye can acquire. Hundreds of good books on basic photography are available on- and off-line. I urge you to explore the basics of photography. The knowledge and skill will help you create better and better eBay images.

You've now got your perfect pictures captured, edited, named, and saved—ready to go on your eBay listing. Our next task is to compose a good item description worthy of our excellent photo and to put the two together in our first eBay listing.

3

Writing a Description and Packing the Item

To review, we have activated our eBay Seller's Account, we've located an item to sell and researched similar items using the Completed Listings page, and we've taken and edited digital pictures of the item.

Before listing our item on eBay, we still have two more steps to complete:

- Writing an item description
- Packing (and weighing) the item

But first, let's hear from an artist who "self-represented" herself to success on eBay.

Traditionally, only those lucky enough to have the support of a great agent, gallery owner, or patron could count on any semblance of a sustainable career as an artist. Often, an artist's success is limited by the twin evil realities of geography and the unavoidable curse of obscurity. Starving is never romantic. Artists usually pick up a second line of work—a "day gig"—to make ends meet. Trouble is, balancing a day gig and one's art often takes so much energy that both suffer.

However, as artist Keri Lyn Shosted discovered, starving as an artist is not inevitable. eBay can offer an artist instant access to a vast potential customer base from around the globe.

"I went from begging galleries to give my work a shot to selling full time—for over three years now on eBay, with a large following of customers and about fifteen shops around the country carrying my line of dog art prints. Not to mention over a

hundred commissioned paintings, all brought to me through the magic of eBay. I even now have a greeting-card company in Canada publishing my work. . . . How did they find me? eBay!"

Hundreds of artists and craftsmen have leveraged eBay as a platform for finding eager customers for their work.

"I know that eBay has made what was once impossible a reality for many other eBay members as well, especially artists. By cutting out the middleman-hundred-percent-markup of a gallery, buyers are now able to search thousands of artists and buy direct."

With dedication and planning, anyone can make a go at eBay selling, even artists!

The next step is to create the text for our item description.

A Simple and Thorough Description

Every item for sale at eBay should have a clear, concise, and comprehensive item description. You could simply type in your description extemporaneously in the box on the Sell Your Item form, but I want you to get into the habit of always typing your description into a text editor before you start the listing. For Windows computers, use Notepad. For Mac, use TextEdit.

NOTE TO MAC USERS: We will use Windows to illustrate our examples. Macintosh users should follow the instructions step-by-step. The only difference for Mac users will be the name of the text editor and the steps necessary to open the text editor and Web browser. Everything else in this chapter is identical for Windows and for Mac users.

OPENING A TEXT EDITOR

PC users: To start, we open a blank Notepad file. Notepad can be started from the Windows Start menu at "Programs > Accessories > Notepad."

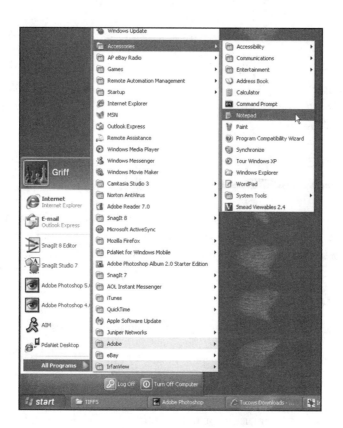

(Mac users: Look in your Applications folder for a program called TextEdit.)
This will open an untitled Notepad (or TextEdit) window.

For the remainder of this chapter, you will type everything into your Notepad (or, for Mac, TextEdit) window. (Please do not use Word, WordPad, or, some other word-processing application. This exercise will work perfectly only if you use a plain text editor.)

Now, let's start writing our description. Every good item description should contain the following:

1. A detailed description of the item
2. Your terms of service for payment, shipping, and returns

We are going to use eBay Picture Services for our pictures, so we don't need to include them in our item description. (We cover other image-hosting options in Section Two, chapter 7, "Advanced Image Hosting Solutions.")

A DETAILED DESCRIPTION

Your item description should include the following item attributes, as appropriate:

Name of the item
Age
Dimensions
Place of origin or manufacture
Condition (including flaws and imperfections)

Here's what I wrote about our pottery pitcher:

```
Untitled - Notepad                                    _ □ ×
File  Edit  Format  View  Help  eFax
Honiton Exton Small Pitcher

I was culling treasure from the china closet and found this
Honiton pitcher, 4 1/2 inches tall, circa 1950's. White clay.
Exton shape. Pitcher is in excellent condition; no cracks,
breaks, chips or stains. Embossed mark on bottom: "Honiton
Potteries Exton England" with a black hand painted "t."

A Brief History of Honiton Pottery: Hontiton pottery was (and
is) located in the town of Honiton in Devon, England. The
pottery was started by Foster and Hunt at the turn of the
19th/210th century. It was purchased by Charles Collard
shortly after WWI. In 1947, Collard sold the pottery to Norman
Hull and Harry Barratt who ran it until 1961 when it was sold
to Paul Redvers. All production ceased in 1997 and the pottery
was shuttered. The premises were recently reopended as pottery
and craft shop.

Payment:

PayPal (preferred)

Money Orders

Checks

Shipping: I will ship this item anywhere to anyone.
International bidders and buyers welcome. Please enter your
zip code in the box provided below this description. This will
provide you up to three shipping options and costs from which
you may select one.

Return Policy: If you win or purchase this item from me
through this listing and upon receiving it, are not 100%
satisfied, you may return it to me within 14 days from the
close of the listing, for a full refund of the winning bid
plus shipping. |
```

Honiton Exton Small Pitcher

I was culling treasure from the china closet and found this Honiton pitcher, 4½ inches tall, circa 1950s. White clay. Exton shape. Pitcher is in excellent condition; no cracks, breaks, chips or stains. Embossed mark on bottom: "Honiton Potteries Exton England" with a black hand-painted "t."

In a short paragraph, I included the history of the pottery. This type of information can help spark interest in new collectors:

A Brief History of Honiton Pottery: Honiton pottery was (and is) located in the town of Honiton in Devon, England. The pottery was started by Foster and Hunt at the turn of the 19th/20th century. It was purchased by Charles Collard shortly after WWI. In 1947, Collard sold the pottery to Norman Hull and Harry Barratt, who ran it until 1961, when it was sold to Paul Redvers. All production ceased in 1997 and the pottery was shuttered. The premises were recently reopened as a pottery and craft shop.

Next I typed in my payment, shipping, and return policies and fees:

Payment:

PayPal (preferred)

Money Orders

Checks

Shipping: I will ship this item anywhere to anyone. International bidders and buyers welcome. Please enter your zip code in the box provided below this description. This will provide you up to three shipping options and costs from which you may select one.

Return Policy: If you win or purchase this item from me through this listing and upon receiving it are not 100% satisfied, you may return it to me within 14 days from the close of the listing, for a full refund of the winning bid plus shipping.

It pays to be as detailed as possible regarding a buyer's obligations. Buyers don't like surprises. Make sure you provide as clear a picture as possible regarding acceptable payment options, shipping fees, and any other special Terms of Service (TOS).

Later, we will copy and paste this description into the Item Description text entry box on the eBay Sell Your Item form.

NOTE: Also later, we will format the description text using a simple and elegant eBay tool called the Description Editor, which is built into the eBay Sell Your Item form. We could also format the item description manually using basic HTML commands. Although I much prefer the simple method, for those who are more adventurous, advanced HTML tips can be found in chapter 6, "HTML for eBay Sellers."

It's always wise to save your finished item description text as a file on your computer's hard drive. That way, you always have a copy ready to edit and then copy and paste into the eBay Sell Your Item Web form.

Select "File" and then "Save As . . ." from the Notepad toolbar.

1. In the "Save in" box, choose a location on your hard drive for the new file. We will use the desktop.
2. In the box "File name," type in a name (we'll type *itemtext.txt*).
3. Click "Save."

Packing—Do It Right!

Now that we've written and saved our item description for later access, the next step is to pack the item. Why pack the item now? Shouldn't we pack it after the item sells?

During the Sell Your Item process, you will have the opportunity to add the eBay Shipping Calculator to your item listing so potential buyers can view the shipping fee to their zip or postal code before they bid or buy. To add the Shipping Calculator, you will need to enter the weight of the item plus the box and shipping materials, and maybe the dimensions of the package, into the Calculated Shipping box. Besides, it is much safer to store a listed item in a properly packed box as opposed to on an open shelf or tabletop where it could be damaged.

You could be the most accommodating, customer-oriented seller in the world, but it's all for naught if you pack the item inadequately. No one wants to receive an item that has been damaged in transit. If you take pains to pack your items properly, you will avoid the hassles of having to fill out insurance forms and, more importantly, of having to placate an unhappy buyer with a refund. It takes just about as much work to pack an item properly as it does to pack it poorly, so you might as well do it right.

eBay seller Melissa Hornyak provided a great tip on shipping clothing:

EBAY MEMBER TIP! When shipping articles of clothing (mostly what I sell), put the item in a plastic bag and tape it before placing it into the box/envelope/whatever. This protects the item from rain, in case the package ends up sitting on someone's front porch for a while. This saves many a ruined item and shows buyers that you are willing to do a little bit extra to make sure that their purchases arrive in the promised condition.

PICTURE IT WHILE PACKING IT

If the item you are packing is extremely fragile or valuable, you may want to take digital or film pictures of the item as you pack it. Whenever I have sold a rare or breakable item, I take two digital pictures of it: one of it sitting just outside the box into which I am about to pack it, and one showing the item sitting in the box before sealing it.

Documenting the packing of the item with pictures could prove to be wise insurance. On the remote chance that the item is damaged in transit, you will have a record of the item's condition just prior to your sealing the package. Plus, even under the best of circumstances, it can be extremely difficult to win a claim of damage in transit from any of the major carriers. Armed with evidence of a properly wrapped and packed parcel, you stand a slightly better chance of collecting an insurance claim for any item damaged in transit by a carrier.

I do know of one seller who actually videotapes the packing of extremely valuable or breakable items from start to final sealing. Again, although this precaution is not necessary, especially for sturdy or less expensive items, you can never overdo documenting and packing the item. Better safe than sorry.

MATERIALS—OVERDO IT (A LITTLE)

When packing, you should always err on the side of caution. Give the item just a bit more protection than it may actually need for making the trip safe and sound. For breakables such as pottery and glass, always double-box (see below). For all items, use a box that is at least 25 percent bigger in all dimensions than the item you are packing. For items that could be damaged by moisture, seal them in plastic before sending. Bendable items such as old LPs, photographs, autographs, ephemera, and so on should always be packed sandwiched between stiff boards.

PACKING MATERIALS

Styrofoam packing peanuts are probably the most commonly used packing material for eBay items. They are extremely lightweight and so don't noticeably increase the weight of the package, they are reusable, and they work for any size box.

Biodegradable packing peanuts are growing in popularity among eBay sellers. They are usually made of air-puffed corn or potato starch. When wet, they disintegrate harmlessly into the environment. Biodegradable peanuts may be "green" and are thus a commendable choice for protecting the environment, but they do not offer the same level of protection as Styrofoam. Bio peanuts tend to compress and deform under pressure. If you use them, use a slightly larger box and more bio peanuts than you would for Styrofoam peanuts.

Shredded paper is an inexpensive and abundant packing material, but it is not recommended as a primary packing material since by volume, paper weighs more than Styrofoam and is prone to compression. However, for those items that are not superfragile, shredded paper can be a cost-effective secondary packing material if used correctly. (By the way, we are talking about thin strips of shredded newspaper. Never use balled-up or scrunched-up sheets of newspaper.) If you do a lot of packing and you have access to enough paper (newspaper, old printouts, etc.), you may want to invest in a small paper shredder to make your own shredded paper.

Bubble wrap should be used to protect all individual items before placing them in their packing box. Even when packing in peanuts, the extra layer of bubble wrap helps protect the item from damage. The combination of peanuts or shredded paper and sufficient bubble wrap will help guarantee your item arrives at its destination safe and sound.

Use the right-size bubble wrap for the right job. The rule of thumb for size: the more fragile the item, the bigger the size of the bubble. Wrap the item with the bubbles facing in against the item. If you are using the proper-size bubble wrap for the item, wrapping around the item twice will suffice. Finally, use just enough tape to hold the bubble wrap together; one or two small tabs of tape should be enough. Don't bind the bubble-wrapped item like a mummy! Pulling, tearing, and unwrapping excessively taped items can be extremely painful and frustrating for those of us with arthritis. Thank you.

eBay seller Leah has some excellent points about packing in general and is happy to share them with you:

> "Don't be stingy with bubble wrap.
>
> "When packing a box, shake it. If you hear things moving around, you need to add more packing materials.
>
> "Make sure the box is folded properly (i.e., the two small ends of the box go in the inside, not the outside) and taped securely.
>
> "Don't write the 'to' address on top of the packing tape. The party the package is being sent to will be lucky to actually receive the package. (The tape could separate and only a small portion of the address will be left.)"

I have to admit—I never thought of that last one. Thanks, Leah!

BOXES AND CONTAINERS

The lion's share of all eBay items are shipped in plain corrugated boxes. You can buy these from a packaging supplier, from your local post office, from moving companies, and from eBay sellers! You can also pick them up for free from many supermarkets. (For obvious hygiene concerns, avoid using boxes from Dumpsters or those that were initially used to store perishables.)

Regardless of the source, the primary concerns when selecting a box for shipping are condition, size, and strength. The golden rule of packing is to avoid having any part of your item touching the sides of the packing container. This means that the box you select for your item should be about 25 percent bigger in all three dimensions than the item you are packing—height, width, and length (including the bubble wrap, if used). A 25 percent difference in size will usually leave adequate room for packing material to fill around the sides, top, and bottom of the item.

WHERE TO GET PACKING SUPPLIES

Here's a suggestion from eBay seller Michael Ford (heritageharborcollectibles) about how to get free shipping supplies from the USPS Web site (to be used only if you are using USPS Priority Mail or Express Mail).

EBAY MEMBER TIP! On the USPS Web site (*www.usps.com*), sellers can order any size box, from video size to large boxes designed to hold tons of books . . . sturdy and reliable, delivered fast, and absolutely free. This also includes Priority Mail labels, mailing labels, various customs forms, protective mailers, envelopes—nearly anything and everything you need to ship an item using USPS Priority Mail or Express Mail. It's so easy! Everything you desire will be mailed directly to you for free!

You'll never have to worry again about asking people for boxes or running to the store to grab a package of labels! Of course, you can only use these boxes and forms for the service they are designed for, in most cases Priority Mail or Express Mail.

You will save time and money by always looking for ways to reduce shipping costs. There is no need to spend $3 on a pack of labels or $5 on a roll of tape that'll be gone after you wrap up a few boxes. Be smart.

You're selling items on eBay to make money; don't let your bottom line get swallowed up by the costs of mailing supplies. Locate good sources of bulk mailing supplies both online (on eBay, of course!) and in your neighborhood. For example, take advantage of any low-price or dollar stores in your area.

Excellent advice, Mike. Thanks!

eBay is an excellent source of great deals for all types of packing materials. In fact, a handful of eBay sellers have made a full-time business of selling packing materials exclusively. Check out the Shipping and Packing Supplies categories under the main category Everything Else on the eBay home page.

DOUBLE-BOXING

You should double-box extremely fragile items including glass, pottery, thin metal, or items constructed of delicate materials such as paper or papier-mâché. In fact, some sellers double-box everything they ship. It helps provide maximum protection against damage or breakage in transit.

Wrap the item in a layer of bubble wrap.

Select a first (inner) box that is at least 25 percent bigger than the item and a second (outer) box that is at least 25 percent bigger than the first box.

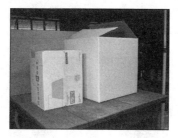

Add a layer of packing material (foam or peanuts) to the bottom of the first box. Place the item inside the box.

Fill the spaces between the wrapped item and the box walls with packing material. The item should not touch the box walls at any point. Here is my first box filled to the top.

Lightly seal the first box with a single strip of packing tape. You may need to reopen the box before shipping.

Add a layer of packing material to the bottom of the second box and place the first box inside the second box.

Use packing material to fill in the space between the boxes. Note that there should be at least three inches of space between the two boxes.

Add a layer of packing material to cover the top of the inner box.

Seal the outer box with a small piece of tape (in case you need to open the box before shipping the item to the buyer). Write the name or a description of the item on a sticky note and stick it on the box (for easy identification later). Now it's time to weigh the box.

Place the box on a postal scale. On the sticky note, jot down the weight in pounds and ounces. You will need the weight when you list the item. Our item weighs 2.25 pounds.

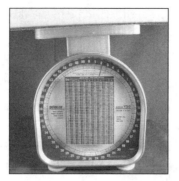

For now, store the boxed item in a safe place. Later, after the item has sold, you'll place a shipping invoice or receipt in the box, seal the box more securely, print out and slap on a prepaid shipping label, and ship the box to the buyer.

PACKING IN A SMOKING HOUSEHOLD

Nothing is quite as nasty as opening a box and having your nose assaulted with the smell of stale cigarette smoke. Secondhand tobacco smoke permeates everything it contacts. The smoker is usually unable to smell this residual odor, but it is painfully apparent to the nonsmoker. Once an item has been "smoked," it is almost impossible to eliminate the smell unless the item is safely washable. For most art and antiques, this is usually not the case.

If you or someone else in your household smokes, store your items and packing materials either in a sealed smoke-free room or in a separate building.

Or maybe it's finally time for the patch!

USED PACKING MATERIALS

Saving and reusing packing materials is not only a thrifty habit, it's a "green" duty. By reusing materials, you help extend their usefulness. This is extremely important for materials that may not be easily reclaimable, such as Styrofoam peanuts.

Keep your packing materials clean. If you save packing materials for reuse, store them in a dry, smoke-free environment.

Boxes can usually be used at least twice, if not three or four times, depending on how well they have weathered previous shipping. Always check used corrugated cardboard boxes for fold fatigue before reusing. If the sides of the used box feel soft or floppy, it may be at the end of its safe usefulness. Cover up any old shipping labels. Don't tear them off. Doing so usually results in some of the outer skin of the box coming off as well, which can weaken the structural integrity of the container.

As long as they are kept clean and dry, packing peanuts have an indefinite shelf life. Use your judgment. If the peanuts are starting to look funky to you, then they will probably look funky to your buyers. When a batch of peanuts reach the end of their usefulness, you should take them to your local recycling center for proper disposal.

Shredded paper is best used once (if at all) and then discarded. Paper excelsior is biodegradable and can always be sent to your local recycling center or placed in your compost pile.

Bubble wrap is endlessly reusable as long as it's clean and as long as the bubbles are intact. Do not use bubble wrap if even only a few of its bubbles have popped. It will be just your luck that the place where the bubbles are popped is where your item will be damaged in transit. It happens.

Let's summarize: We've photographed the item, typed and saved a description, packed the item, and weighed it in its box. We have noted the weight for inclusion in our description and for use with the eBay Shipping Calculator.

Now we can go to eBay and start the Sell Your Item process!

The eBay Sell Your Item Form

The eBay Sell Your Item form (aka "SYI form" and "Sell form") has been at the heart of eBay since day one back in 1995. The very first version was extremely basic: text entry boxes for typing a title, description, item quantity, and starting bid, and a drop-down box for selecting a listing duration. That was it. In order to format the text, you had to know at least basic HTML tags. If you wanted to include a digital photo, the only option was to have space on a separate image hosting service and to know the HTML tags for embedding the image into the description.

Over time, the SYI form has evolved to meet the changing needs of eBay sellers. Today's SYI form is still easy to use and contains a smorgasbord of excellent features and tools for each aspect of listing. eBay sellers no longer need to possess HTML and image hosting expertise. The SYI form has it all built in for you!

NOTE: The Sell Your Item form, like all features on eBay, is subject to changes in layout and design. Although what I show here for screen-shot examples may look slightly different when you list your item, the core functionality of the five steps will remain the same. They are:

Select a category
Title and description
Pictures and details
Payment and shipping
Review and submit

So let's begin. Click the "Sell" link on the eBay Navigation Bar to reach the first part of the SYI form (sign in if necessary).

The first step is to select a category.

SELECTING A CATEGORY

There are over 50,000 categories on eBay. You have to choose one, ideally, the one that is most appropriate. Don't panic! Selecting the right category for your item is actually a snap. There are three possible options.

Let eBay Suggest a Category

The What Are You Selling? feature provides you with a text entry box. If you are not sure what category would be best suited to your item, let eBay suggest one for you. Enter words that describe what it is you are selling and eBay will provide you with a list of suggested categories based on matching items on the site. First I enter *honiton* and click the "Sell it" button.

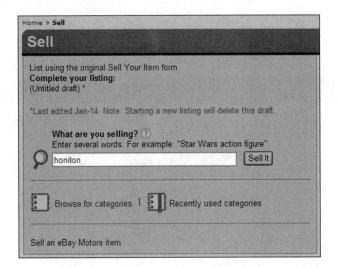

I am presented with a list of appropriate categories.

Sell: Select a Category

Help buyers find your listing.
- Select the category that best describes your item.
- Reach more buyers by selecting two categories. (additional fees apply)

(?)
Help

| Browse for categories | Search for categories | Recently used categories |

honiton [Search]

Categories	% item match
☐ Antiques > Textiles, Linens > Lace, Crochet, Doilies > Other	19%
☐ Collectibles > Postcards & Paper > Postcards > Non-US Countries, Town Views > UK > Devon	19%
☐ Pottery & Glass > Pottery & China > Art Pottery > Other	9%
☐ Collectibles > Housewares & Kitchenware > Kitchenware > Egg Cups	7%
☐ Pottery & Glass > Pottery & China > Art Pottery > British Art	7%
☐ Collectibles > Vintage Sewing > Tools, Scissors, Measures	4%
☐ Crafts > Lacemaking, Tatting > Other Lacemaking, Tatting	4%
☐ Antiques > Decorative Arts > Ceramics, Porcelain > Other	1%

[Save and Continue >]

eBay will search every current listing title for those containing the keywords we provided and then rank the returned items by category with the highest percentage of matches per category on the top of the list. This doesn't necessarily mean that the first category will be the right category for your item every time, but the odds are excellent that one of the three highest-rated categories will probably be worth considering as a good category for your item.

It appears the most appropriate category for our item might be Pottery & China > Art Pottery > British Art. If we want to select this category, we check the box next to the category and click the "Save and continue" button.

Browse and Select

I can also click "Browse for categories" to locate an appropriate category for my item.

When you browse for categories, you are presented with the following category selector:

Start from the left and select appropriate categories until you reach the end of the category hierarchy.

Sell: Select a Category

Help buyers find your listing.
- Select the category that best describes your item.
- Reach more buyers by selecting two categories. (additional fees apply)

(?) Help

Browse for categories | Search for categories | Recently used categories

Crafts >	Glass >	Art Pottery >	Abingdon
Dolls & Bears >	Pottery & China >	China, Dinnerware >	American Art
DVDs & Movies >		Wholesale Lots	Asian
Entertainment Memorabilia >			Aynsley
Gift Certificates			Bennington
Health & Beauty >			Blue Mountain
Home & Garden >			British Art
Jewelry & Watches >			Brush/Brush-McCoy
Music >			Buffalo
Musical Instruments >			Camark
Pottery & Glass >			Catalina
Real Estate >			Colorado Pottery
Specialty Services >			Coors Pottery

(✓) You have finished selecting a category. Click the **Save and Continue** button below.

Category number: 1043

Categories you have selected
- Pottery & Glass > Pottery & China > Art Pottery > British Art | See sample listings | Remove
- Add a second category (additional fees apply)

[Save and Continue >]

GRIFF TIP! Note that you can also add a second category if there is one that is appropriate. Listing one item in two categories can, on average, boost bids by 18 percent and final sale price by 17 percent. It's like having your item in two places at once—more buyers are likely to find it, and your chances of success increase.

NOTE: Listing in two categories doubles most of the listing fees. For example, suppose you sell your item in an auction-style listing and set a starting price of 99¢. If you list your item in two categories, the Insertion Fee would be 60¢ (twice the usual fee of 30¢). If you use the Bold feature to make your item title appear in bold text, this upgrade would cost $2 (twice the usual fee of $1). We review all of these fees in depth in Chapter 3.

Recently Used Categories

If you have listed on eBay before now, you can select a category from your previously used categories.

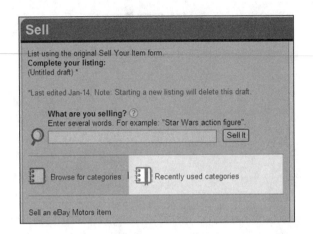

Whatever category selection method you employ, once you click the "Save and Continue" button, you are taken to the top of the Sell Your Item form.

SETTING THE SHOW/HIDE OPTIONS

Before we continue, we need to customize the Sell Your Item form to show all the tools and features we will need for this listing. Click the "Show/Hide options" icon on the right side of the page.

This brings up a special Options box where you can, at any time, change your default options that display on the SYI form.

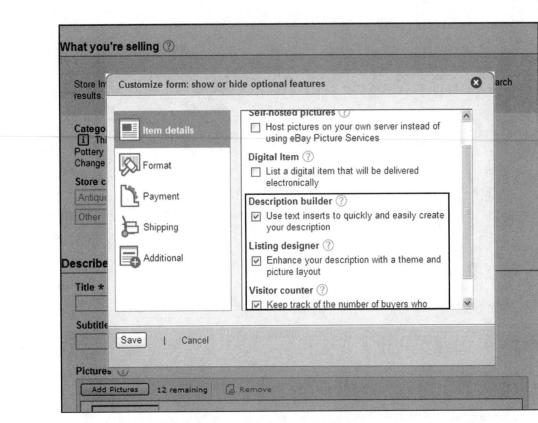

Make sure the "Item detail" icon is highlighted in the left-hand column and check the following: Description Builder, Listing Designer, and Visitor Counter (the Visitor Counter will display a unique-hit odometer on your listing page to show you how many unique visitors have opened your listing to view it).

Next highlight "Format" in the left-hand column and check the boxes for "Donate prcentage of sale" and "Scheduled start." (You may not need them for your first listing, but it's good to know what each one looks like in case you do need them in the future.)

Highlight "Payment" and check the boxes for "Immediate payment" and whatever "Additional payment methods" you offer. (For your listings, that might be "Money order / cashier's check" and "Personal check.")

Highlight "Shipping" and select the "3 domestic and 3 international services" option from the drop down box.

Finally (almost done . . . we only have to set these options once) highlight "Additional" and check the options for "Buyer requirements" and "Return policy." Later, if you need to start charging sales tax or providing more detailed checkout instructions, you can return to this feature and select these options at any time.

"Sales tax?" you ask. "But Griff, I am not a business (yet). I am only selling one insignificant item! Do I have to charge sales tax?"

You might. Your state may require you to collect a sales tax from any buyer who resides in your state. If so, you can select your state from the drop-down box and enter the appropriate percentage for your state. This amount will be added to the total of any bidder who is located in your state. There's more on sales tax and other business-related questions in chapter 5.

To save all of your options, click the "Save" button. This will take you back to the SYI form with all your selected options in place.

GRIFF TIP! You can always return to and change the Show/Hide options to suit your current selling needs.

WHAT YOU'RE SELLING

In this section, if you have an eBay Store, you can assign an eBay Store category to your item. We examine eBay Stores in depth later in the book, so we'll skip over this section for now.

DESCRIBE YOUR ITEM

Title

Next, we type our item's title into the Title box. Your title should be composed entirely of keywords that relate directly to your item. Here's our title: *Honiton Collard Poole Devon Pitcher Jug Creamer Exton*

Describe your item ⑦

Title * ⑦

| Honiton Collard Poole Devon Pitcher Jug Creamer Exton | 2 characters remaining |

Subtitle ($0.02) ⑦

It may not sound elegant, but elegant syntax is not our goal when it comes to creating an item title. Remember that most shoppers on eBay use keywords to search titles for those items in which they are interested. I did some research in Completed Listings and discovered that past items similar to mine did best when they contained words such as *jug, creamer,* and *pitcher,* and all words relating to the place of manufacture, such as *Devon, Collard,* and *Poole. Exton* is the design of the piece.

Some Item Title Tips

1. Avoid using punctuation or symbols in your titles. They will not help buyers find your item, and they take up valuable character space.
2. In cases where a noun in your title could be plural or singular, type the singular and plural forms if there is enough room.
3. Avoid editorial adjectives such as *rare*, *wonderful*, *stupendous*, *gorgeous*, and the like. No one wakes up in the morning thinking, "Say, I think I will search eBay for all the rare items up for bid or sale." Don't believe me? Go search on the word *rare*. I did and found more than 414,000 items.

That being the case, the Subtitle feature might be a better place for using such words. In fact, in your optional subtitle, you can expound on your wondrous and rare item to help market it.

4. Usually, articles or prepositions are superfluous in an eBay item title. Use them only if they are absolutely necessary or if there is enough space after you have exhausted all the possible keywords relating directly to your item.

Subtitle

The subtitle provides the opportunity to offer preview information about your item to prospective buyers. Describe interesting details and facts about your item such as age, origin, or previous ownership. Promote the extras you offer, such as free shipping or discounts on shipping of combined items. I will opt for the Subtitle feature. Here is the text of my subtitle:

Subtitle is a perfect tool for special promotions such as free shipping. It could be the extra enticement needed to compel a shopper into clicking my item title. Think of it as getting the customer into the door of your shop. (Later, I will add a Buy It Now price, which will include my initial cost, plus shipping and 10 percent.)

One other subtitle plus: The text of a subtitle is included in any search that included title and description.

Next, we add our pictures.

Adding Pictures

Adding pictures used to be a real challenge back in the early days of eBay. Today, it's a snap with eBay's built-in Picture Services feature. With eBay Picture Services, all you need to do to add up to twelve photos of your item is to find each photo on your computer and click it twice. Couldn't be simpler! (For those who prefer the challenge of hosting and embedding their own images, stay tuned for chapter 7, "Advanced Image Hosting Solutions," where we will go over the finer points of hosting your own images.)

NOTE: Those with a Windows computer using Internet Explorer will see two eBay Picture Services options: Basic and Enhanced. Mac users will only see one: Basic. The Basic version of eBay Picture Services will suit our purposes just fine, but for clarity, we will look at both versions.

eBay Picture Services—Basic

Remember, we have copies of our edited digital pictures ready to go on our computer's hard drive. To begin, click on the Add Pictures button.

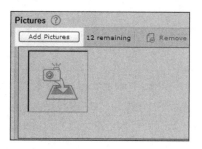

This will bring up the Basic box. (If not, click the "Basic" tab on the top of the window.)

Note that you can add up to twelve images using eBay Picture Services. The first image is always free. Subsequent images are 15¢ each.

From here we click the "Browse . . ." button for each picture we want to add.

We have three images to display. We click the first "Browse . . ." button to open a file window. We then navigate to the image files for the item. Mine are in a subfolder called eBay Pictures.

We select our first photo by double-clicking the file name or file photo thumbnail if displayed. This inserts the path for the photo file into the box on the Basic window.

Repeat the above steps for each photo.

GRIFF TIP! Does it matter which image is first? Yes. The image in the first position will appear as your Gallery image should you opt for Gallery. The Gallery image is the thumbnail that appears next to your item's title in the category and search result lists. Consequently, make sure your first image is one that will look enticing when resized down to a small thumbnail.

When all the photos have been selected, the next step is to select any of the available options in the Basic window: Picture Pack, SuperSize Pictures, or Picture Show (all explained in detail later in the section). We will have three photos and I always opt in for Gallery and SuperSize. That comes to 30¢ plus 35¢ for Gallery and 75¢ for SuperSize, or $1.45 in total. However, with Picture Pack, I pay only $1.00 for all of these features, saving me 45¢.

Picture Pack ($1.00 for up to 6 pictures or $1.50 for 7 to 12 pictures)
☑ Get Gallery, Supersize, Picture Show and additional pictures for maximum exposure.

Supersize Pictures ($0.75)
☐ Display extra large pictures

Picture Show (free)
☐ Multiple pictures will appear in a slideshow player at top of the item page

[Upload Pictures] | Cancel

Click the "Upload Pictures" button. This will return you to the SYI form displaying the three photos selected.

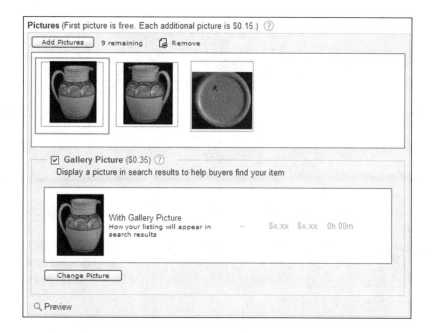

eBay Picture Services—Enhanced

If you have a Windows computer using Internet Explorer, you have access to the Enhanced version of eBay Picture Services, which provides additional features for selecting and editing images. To begin, click the "Add pictures" button.

Click on the "Enhanced" link at the top of the window.

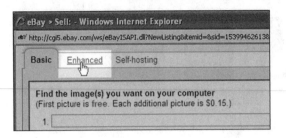

You may be prompted with a yellow highlighted alert bar across the top of the window or a dialog box asking something like, "If you trust the Web site and the add-on and want to install it, click here." You do want to install it (and of course you can definitely trust the eBay Picture Services control to be safe and secure!). Before the ActiveX control installs, you are prompted with the following Internet Explorer alert box:

You may be prompted with a yellow highlighted alert bar across the top of the window or a dialog box asking something like, "If you trust the Web site and the add-on and want to install it, click here." You do want to install it (and of course you can definitely trust the eBay Picture Services control to be safe and secure!). Before the ActiveX control installs, you are prompted with the following Internet Explorer alert box:

Again, this ActiveX control is perfectly safe. Click the "Install" button to install it as a browser add-on. This is the only time you will be prompted to install the control from this computer. (If you use another computer that has never had the control installed, you will be prompted to install it in order to use Enhanced eBay Picture Services.)

Once the ActiveX control is installed, the Enhanced window will change to the following view:

To add a photo, click the "Add pictures" button in box 1.

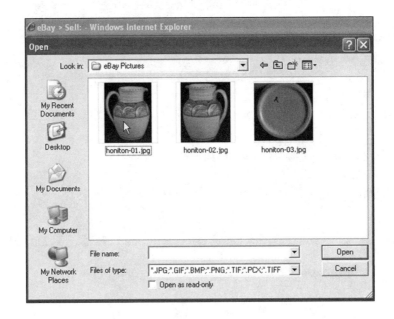

In the Open window, navigate to the photo files and double-click on the photo you want for your first image.

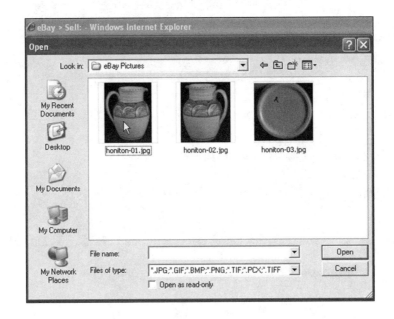

This will add that picture to the first eBay Picture Services box in the Enhanced window.

Following the same steps, add the other photos.

In the chapter on digital photography, we learned how to edit an image for eBay using third-party software. The Enhanced version of eBay Picture Services includes a simple editing feature as well. I'll add a fourth, unedited image of our pitcher to better show how the edit feature works.

eBay Picture Services Edit Features

Once the image we wish to edit is displayed in the main eBay Picture Services window, we can edit it using the command buttons displayed for "Rotate," "Crop," and "Autofix." (Autofix adjusts the contrast and brightness of the image based on what eBay Picture Services thinks works best.)

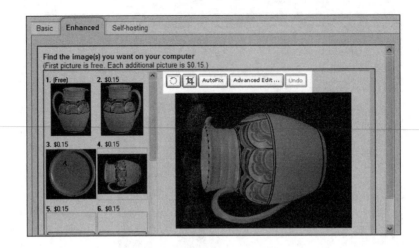

Click on "Advanced edit" for more control over the editing features.

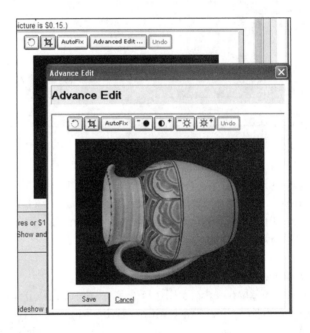

The Advanced Edit window has five command buttons: "Rotate," "Crop" (move the corner nodes to adjust a "keep" area), "Decrease/increase contrast," "Decrease/increase brightness," and "Undo."

Let's click the "Increase contrast" button and the "Increase brightness" button three times each:

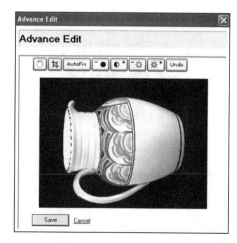

Oops. Too much! Let's click "Undo" and then click the "Rotate" button three times to display the jug upright.

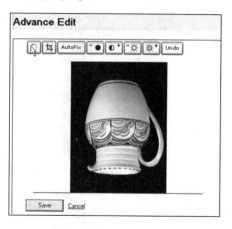

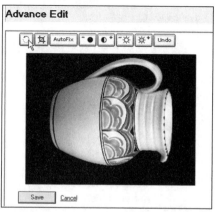

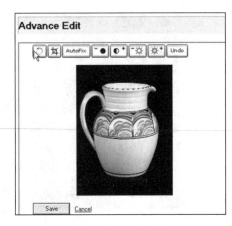

Now let's crop the image. Click the "Crop" button to display the crop nodes.

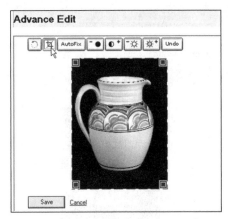

Drag the nodes to create a box around the item. Once you have it just where you want it and you have finished editing, click the "Save" button.

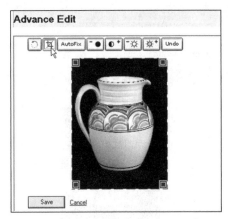

"But Griff," I hear you say, "if eBay Picture Services lets me rotate and crop, why did we spend time learning how to edit using separate software?"

Good question. Notice that eBay Picture Services does not supply the resize command. That's one good reason. There's another. I want all eBay sellers to be as educated as possible about all areas of listing. An educated seller is usually a more effective, more successful seller.

NOTE: These digital pictures haven't yet been uploaded to eBay! They have only been selected. Once we click the "Upload Pictures" button on the bottom of this window, uploading will begin. But first, we have more information to fill in on this page.

Picture Options

As we learned earlier, there are three options for how your pictures are displayed:

1. SuperSize
2. Picture Show
3. Picture Pack

Let's take a closer look at each of the options.

SuperSize

The SuperSize option allows you to upload images of about 600 pixels tall by 800 pixels wide. The images will initially be displayed as thumbnails with a viewer window of about 500 by 500 pixels. The viewer (your potential buyer) then has the option of enlarging the image to its original size.

NOTE: SuperSize cannot enlarge an image to pixel dimensions greater than those of the original image as uploaded. If you upload an image that is 330 by 440 pixels, SuperSize will not display the image any larger than that.

Picture Show

This option can be added to SuperSize or used alone. It adds a slide-show viewer window at the top of your listing page. Viewers can watch the show progress automatically, or they can use the buttons below the images to stop the show on any slide of their choice or move manually back and forward through the images.

GRIFF TIP! If you only have one image to show, don't opt for Picture Show or Picture Pack.

Picture Pack

The first eBay Picture Services photo is free. Additional photos (up to twelve in total) are 15¢ each, the SuperSize feature is 75¢ per listing, and Gallery images (thumbnails) are 35¢ each. You can save money by using Picture Pack, a discounted bundled-feature option that provides free images, Gallery thumbnails, and SuperSize all for one price. The discounted price for up to six images is $1. From seven up to twelve images, the fee is $1.50, for a savings of up to $1.40.

Let's take advantage of this discount and select Picture Pack. Once we click Upload Pictures, an Upload box will display.

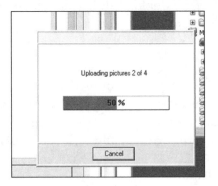

Here are the four pictures uploaded to eBay.

That's all we need to do! eBay will insert the images along with thumbnails into our description page.

Description

eBay provides a robust Description Editor tool that works for all platforms and Web browsers. There are two views of the Description tool: Standard and HTML. The Standard view is for typing or pasting unformatted text, which the seller can then "dress up" with special editing tools. The HTML window view is for typing or pasting HTML formatted text or prebuilt templates. Here is the HTML view:

The HTML window has two simple tools: Spell Check and Inserts (more on Inserts later). If you have a description that has been preformatted with HTML, you copy and paste that text into this window. Most new sellers (and millions of experienced sellers) rely on the easier-to-use Standard window.

The Standard view has Spell Check, Inserts, and a selection of text-formatting tools as well. These tools let you change the color, typeface, and size of your text. It also provides alignment tools for blocks of text and a tool for creating bulleted or numbered lists.

We've already created our description text in a text file. The easiest and quickest way to add it to our listing is to copy and paste it into the Standard window (for formatting plain text using the Description Editor toolbar) or the HTML window (for text that you have already formatted with HTML) of the Description box on the Sell Your Item form. We do this by using the Copy and Paste features that come built into Windows or Mac operating systems.

If you already know how to cut, copy, and paste, skip ahead to the next step. If not, take a moment to read the following instructions. Knowing how to manipulate text on a computer will save you a lot of time in the future. And time is money.

Cut, Copy, and Paste

I'm always amazed to find out just how many otherwise computer-savvy folks have no idea how to use the three basic text editing commands:

Cut
Copy
Paste

Cut, Copy, and Paste are the ultimate time-saving tools for moving text from one place to another or creating copies of long pages of text. If you sell on eBay, make no mistake: You will need them. If they are new to you, you will wonder how you lived without them.

These three commands can be executed in three different ways.

Copy, Cut, and Paste Using the Main Menu Bar

The first and most common place to find the commands is under the Edit menu bar command for any Windows (or Mac) application. Here is an example of where the Edit menu commands are usually found in Notepad's Edit menu command.

Let's say we want to copy some text from Notepad and paste it into the Item Description box on the eBay Sell Your Item page. First, we highlight some or all of the text in Notepad by clicking the cursor on one side of the text and dragging the cursor across the text while holding down the left mouse button.

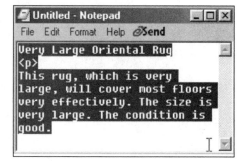

You can also easily select all the text in the file by clicking "Edit," and then "Select All." Let's select all of the text with our mouse. Then we click "Edit" on the Notepad menu bar and select "Copy" from the drop-down menu.

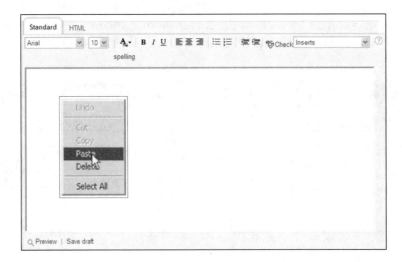

This command will copy all of the selected text into a built-in Windows or Mac applet called Clipboard. Anything copied to the Windows Clipboard can be pasted into the same or another application. Until some new text is selected and copied to the Clipboard, this text will be available for pasting into any other application any number of times. Now we can paste the contents of the Clipboard (the entire text of the Notepad file) into another application, namely, the Sell Your Item page's text entry box Item Description.

Copy, Cut, and Paste Using Pop-up Menus
In the example below, I clicked my cursor so it is blinking inside the Description Editor box. I then clicked the right-hand button on my mouse and selected "Paste" from the resulting pop-up menu box.

This will cause the text copied from Notepad to be pasted into the Item Description box.

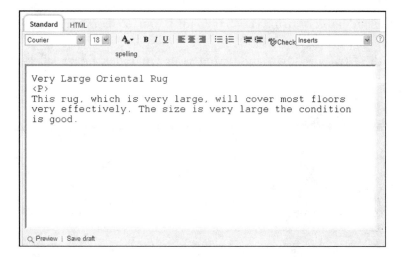

The "Cut" command is similar to the "Copy" command with one difference—the "Copy" command leaves the original text untouched and copies it to the Windows Clipboard. The "Cut" command cuts, or removes, the original text and copies it to the Windows Clipboard. The "Cut" command comes in handy when you want to actually move text from one place to another.

Cut, Copy, and Paste Using Keystrokes

Keystrokes are the most efficient way of accessing the basic text-editing commands. In the old, old, old days of DOS (before Windows—yes, there was a time before Windows), way before everyone used a pointer device such as a mouse, anyone who did a lot of text editing or word processing relied upon these keystroke combinations. There were no other options!

It takes a little practice to get used to them, but once you are comfortable using keystrokes for text editing, you won't ever want to use anything else! Any tip or trick that keeps you from moving your hand over to the mouse and back a hundred times a day not only saves time but also will help prevent repetitive-motion pain or injury.

To copy using keystrokes, first select the text you want to copy by placing your mouse cursor to the left of the text. Next, hold down the right mouse button and drag the cursor to the right (and down if you need to copy more than one line of text), as in previous illustrations.

Once your selected text is highlighted, press and hold down the Ctrl key on your keyboard (Mac users: substitute the Apple key—otherwise known as the Command key—for Ctrl). Note: Use your little finger on your left hand. Do not get into the bad habit of using two hands for keystroke combinations—it will defeat the whole purpose!

Keep the Ctrl key down and, using your left index finger, click the C key once.

This will copy the text to the Windows Clipboard.

Next, select the application and location where you wish the text to be copied. (Usually, this means clicking the mouse cursor into a box or blank page so that it is blinking in just the place you want the text to appear.) Now, using the keyboard, once again hold down the Ctrl key, and this time, click the V key once.

This keystroke combination (Ctrl + V) pastes the text into the application where the mouse cursor is currently active.

A third common text-editing keystroke combination is Ctrl + X for cut.

The following combinations work for most Windows applications, but not all!

Ctrl + A for Select All
Ctrl + N for New Window
Ctrl + S for Save

Try them all and see how much more efficient and quick they are when compared to selecting commands from a menu!

Now we're ready to go back to the Notepad file (or Mac TextEdit/Simple Text file) containing our item description. Click on the "Edit" and "Select All" commands on the text file's menu command bar.

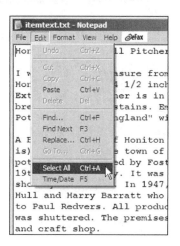

This will highlight all of the text in the file. Once it is highlighted, click on "Edit" and "Copy" on the text file's menu command bar, as we did in the earlier exercise.

Go back to the Internet Explorer window showing the eBay Sell Your Item form. Click your mouse cursor anywhere inside the box marked Item Description. With the mouse cursor blinking in the box, click your mouse's right-hand button and select "Paste."

This will paste a copy of the entire item description text into the Item Description box.

NOTE: You could type your item description directly into the Item Description box on the Sell Your Item form. However, I suggest that you always type your description in a separate file before you begin the listing. It is easier to proof your description in the bigger Notepad window, and if the text in the Item Description box is erased for some reason (it does happen), you won't have to retype it over—you would only need to copy and paste it from the Notepad file.

Formatting Your Description with the Description Editor

Use the Description Editor toolbar to format your text with different colors, font sizes, alignments, typefaces, bulleted lists, and other standard formatting.

For example, to change the size of a section of text, highlight the selected text with your mouse.

Then select the new text size from the Size drop-down box. We'll select 18 point.

The new, larger text appears in the window.

Another Description Editor feature lets you create bulleted lists. First, make sure that the items you wish to bullet are separated by double line breaks. Then highlight them and click one of the two bullet option buttons. One will create a numbered list. The other will create a bulleted list. Let's create a bulleted list for our Terms of Service.

Use your mouse to highlight all of the text to be included in the bulleted list.

Description * (?)

Standard | HTML

Arial | 18 | **A** | **B** *I* U | ☰ ☲ ☲ | ☷ ☷ | ☷ ☷ | ABC Check | Inserts | (?)

spelling

Devon, England. The pottery was started by Foster and Hunt at the turn of the 19th/210th century. It was purchased by Charles Collard shortly after WWI. In 1947, Collard sold the pottery to Norman Hull and Harry Barratt who ran it until 1961 when it was sold to Paul Redvers. All production ceased in 1997 and the pottery was shuttered. The premises were recently reopened as pottery and craft shop.

Payment Terms: I accept and prefer payment through PayPal. I also accept personal checks (items shipped immediately after check has cleared) or money orders.

Shipping: I will ship this item anywhere to anyone. International bidders and buyers welcome. Please enter your zip code in the box provided below this description. This will provide you up to three shipping options and costs from which you may select one.

Return Policy: If you win or purchase this item from me through this listing and upon receiving it are not 100% satisfied, you may return it to me within 14 days from the close of the listing for a full refund of the winning bid plus shipping.

🔍 Preview | Save draft

Click the "Bulleted list" button on the Description toolbar.

The selected text is reformatted with bullets.

I urge you to explore and experiment with all of the Description Editor features. Your listing will look much more professional if it is not just plain, unformatted text. However, don't go overboard! It's always best to err on the side of caution by using less rather than more formatting.

Using Inserts

The Inserts tool is one of the best features of the Description Editor, but it seems to be the one that is most often overlooked. The inserts feature provides for two prebuilt inserts:

> Seller's Other Items
> Add to Favorite Sellers List

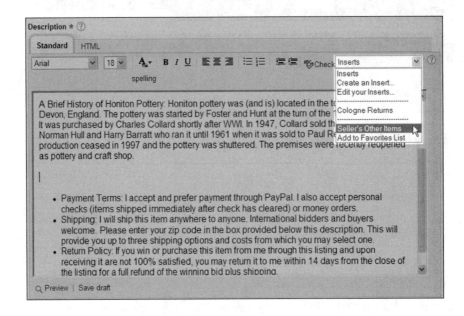

If you select one or both of these inserts, the corresponding text links will appear in your description at the point where you left your mouse cursor:

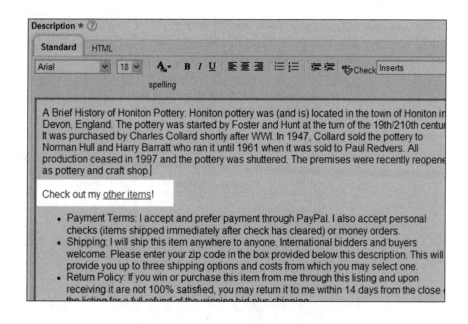

But the best part of the Inserts feature is that you can create your own text inserts, name them, and have them ready to use at your discretion. For example, you could create different Terms of Service to use for different products. You then create an insert for each and copy and paste the text into the custom insert.

Normally, my return policy is very generous, especially for items I list from my own collection of antiques and collectibles. However, when I sell new cologne or perfume, my return policy is slightly restrictive. So I'd like to create a custom insert for a special refund policy to use for my cologne and perfume listings. From the Inserts drop-down box, select "Create Insert."

In the pop-up box, name your insert and type or copy and paste your text into the Enter Your Text or HTML box. (Note: you can also use HTML-formatted text in a custom insert.)

Click the "Save" button. Your newly created insert is now included on the list of available inserts.

Think of the possibilities. You could actually create entire listing templates, fully formatted with HTML, to use for all your future listings!

Our description is not superfancy, but it is clean, professional, and, most important, readable. Readability is the single most important aspect of an item text description layout. Later, in Section Two, chapter 6, "HTML for eBay Sellers," we will learn how to dress up the description with other HTML tags.

Listing Designer

Although our listing description with its current layout and formatting looks good as is, we can also add a professional-looking graphic border around the entire image by selecting one of the more than one hundred designs available through the Listing Designer feature.

You can preview any of these designs by highlighting it, then selecting the Preview Listing link. I am partial to the template named Blue Bricks.

You can also change the layout of your eBay Picture Services photos by selecting a layout from the drop-down box.

The feature costs a dime. I believe it adds great deal of color and interest to your item description, and it's definitely cheaper than trying to design and use a border of your own or paying a Web designer to make one for you.

Visitor Counter
See how many potential buyers have viewed your listing by adding a free visitor counter to your listing page. Let's select the retro computer style.

HOW YOU'RE SELLING

Selecting a Selling Format
In this step, you will select a selling format based on how you want to sell your item. Depending on your seller and feedback status, you will see one, two, or three option tabs on the top of the Selling format window:

> Online Auction
> Fixed Price
> eBay Store Format

Every new seller will see the Online Auction option tab. You need a feedback score of 10+ (or you need to have completed the ID Verify process) in order to display the Fixed Price option tab. We have two available format options: the standard Online Auction format and, since we completed the ID Verify process, the Fixed Price format.

```
How you're selling

Get ideas about pricing by searching completed listings.

Selling format  ⑦

┌──────────────────┬──────────────┐
│  Online Auction  │  Fixed Price │
└──────────────────┴──────────────┘

   Starting price * ⑦    Reserve price ( fee varies ) ⑦
   $ [_____]          $ [_____]

   Buy It Now price ( fee varies ) ⑦
   $ [_____]

   Quantity * ⑦
   [1____]  items

   Duration ⑦
   [7 days  ▾]

   Private listing ⑦
   ☐ Allow buyers to remain anonymous to other eBay users
```

The eBay Store option tab will appear only if you have set up an eBay Store (more on eBay Stores later).

SELLING FORMAT: ONLINE AUCTION

Starting Price

A starting price is mandatory. It is the amount needed to start the bidding. What should your starting price be? It depends on the market value for the item, of course. Keep in mind the two basic tenets of any auction format:

1. Low starting prices tend to attract potential bidders.
2. High starting prices tend to discourage bidding.

It's that simple. In my experience at eBay, the most common reason for no bids is a starting price that is too high. Many sellers enter a starting price that is approximately equal to the current market value of the item, but this is a mistake. In an auction-format marketplace, bidders expect to set the final price. If a seller doesn't allow enough room for bidders to play, they simply will not enter the bidding.

Your research prior to listing should have given you some sense of the current market value for your item on eBay. Of course, your starting price should take this market research into consideration, but regardless of the market value,

431

always remember that the lower your starting price, the better the chances that two or more buyers will submit a bid.

The amount of your starting price will determine the insertion fee charged to your Seller's Account. Here is the schedule of insertion fees:

Insertion Fees	
Starting or Reserve Price	Insertion Fee
$0.01 - $0.99	$0.20
$1.00 - $9.99	$0.40
$10.00 - $24.99	$0.60
$25.00 - $49.99	$1.20
$50.00 - $199.99	$2.40
$200.00 - $499.99	$3.60
$500.00 or more	$4.80

I am entering a starting price of 99¢, which will incur an insertion fee of 20¢.

Selling format ⑦

Online Auction   Fixed Price

Starting price * ⑦   **Reserve price** (fee varies) ⑦
$ 99 $

Buy It Now price (fee varies) ⑦
$

Quantity * ⑦
1   items

Duration ⑦
7 days ▾

Private listing ⑦
☐ Allow buyers to remain anonymous to other eBay users

If I need some insurance that my item won't sell for less than a certain amount, I could always opt for a reserve price.

Reserve Price

The reserve price is an optional tool you as the seller can use to protect your investment. Your reserve amount can be any amount above the starting price. The reserve will be hidden from the public. Buyers will know that you have added a reserve by the text indication of Reserve Not Met next to the Current Bid. If someone bids an amount equal to or greater than your reserve, the indication next to the Current Bid will change to Reserve Met.

If you add a reserve to your listing, you will be charged a fee. If your item sells—that is, if someone bids an amount equal to or greater than the reserve— the fee will be refunded. Here is the reserve fee schedule:

Reserve Price	Fee
$0.01 – $49.99	$1.00
$50.00 – $199.99	$2.00
$200.00 and up	1% of Reserve Price (up to $50)

I almost never use a reserve price, and this example will be no exception. Thus I will leave this box empty.

Buy It Now

The Buy It Now feature is also optional. If you opt for a Buy It Now price, set it at the lowest amount you are willing to take for the item. The first buyer who's willing to pay your price gets your item. To set a Buy It Now price, you need to meet at least one of these requirements:

- Achieve a feedback score of at least 10
- Verify your contact information (using ID Verify)
- If you have a PayPal account, achieve a feedback score of 5 and accept PayPal as a payment method

If a buyer is willing to meet your Buy It Now price before the first bid comes in, your item will sell immediately to that buyer, and your item listing will be considered complete.

If a bid comes in first, the Buy It Now option disappears. In that case, the item listing will proceed normally. If you have also set a minimum price, or reserve price, the Buy It Now feature will disappear after the first bid that is at least as high as the reserve price.

I am setting a Buy It Now price of $14.

Quantity and Duration

I have a quantity of one item, so I type *1* in the appropriate box.

NOTE: Typing any other number will default your listing to a Multiple Item Listing. The quantity number should reflect the lot. If you have six wineglasses to sell as a set, then the quantity should be 1, not 6.

The duration choices are one, three, five, seven, and ten days. I have selected a seven-day duration.

I've been asked thousands of times in the last nine years what the best duration is for ensuring a successful sale. There is no one right answer. In fact, there are as many strategies for durations (and for ending times and days of the week) as there are sellers on eBay. First, your market research may yield some clues. Check the listings that received the most bids and sold for the highest amounts and determine if they share some pattern in their times, days, and durations. Second, experiment with as many as you can to see what works best for your items.

Private Listing

Checking this box will hide the User IDs of all your bidders from the rest of the world. It will not hide them from you (if you are signed in as the seller of the item, you will be able to view the bidder list with User IDs showing).

A seller may employ this feature for numerous reasons. Some sellers do not want other sellers, off and on eBay, to contact their bidders with offers to sell them their own items. Other sellers use this feature to help protect the User IDs from scammers who contact the bidders on the list and attempt to send them bogus Second Chance Offers.

Historically, Pierre Omidyar created the feature on eBay at the request of sellers in the Mature Audience category as a way of "brown-bagging" the identities of the bidders on their wares. Of course, Uncle Griff has no comment.

SELLING FORMAT: FIXED PRICE

To sell your item in the Fixed Price format, click the "Fixed Price" tab on the top of the Selling Format box.

The Fixed Price format differs from the Online Auction format in one obvious way: there is no starting bid, only a fixed price that the potential buyer can either pay or not.

A Fixed Price format listing will appear as a Buy It Now listing to a buyer.

Just as for the Online Auction format, we must indicate a Buy It Now price, quantity, and duration. In addition, there is a recently introduced option called Best Offer.

With Best Offer, you can allow buyers to send you their best offers for your consideration. Once a buyer makes a Best Offer, you can choose one of the following:

- Accept the Best Offer and close the listing.
- Decline the Best Offer and tell the buyer why the offer was rejected.
- Allow the offer to expire on its own in 48 hours (the offer will also expire when the listing ends).
- Respond with a counteroffer.

If we check the box for Best Offer, other suboptions will appear:

The suboptions allow you to review and respond to every offer you receive, or you can opt to automatically decline any offer below a price that you set.

I somtimes add a Best Offer option to my Fixed Price listings, and I usually do not set an amount for automatic decline. I get a kick out of seeing both the tempting and the downright ridiculous offers I often receive. By the way, I never get angry or upset over a lowball offer. As the saying goes, "If you don't ask, you don't get—a stingy buyer just might catch me on a good day, and I just might respond to her outrageously low offer with a reasonable counteroffer that she just might accept. Or I might even just accept her original offer. It happens. We all have merchandise that on any given bad day we might just want to dump.

To learn more about Best Offer, click the "Help" link on the top of any eBay page, then click the "A–Z index" link. From there, click the "B" link and then "Best Offer: overview."

ONLINE AUCTION VERSUS FIXED PRICE

Deciding when to use the Online Auction format and when to use Fixed Price isn't always cut and dried, but there is a general rule of thumb that seems to work for most eBay sellers: The rarer or more hotly sought after your item is, the better served you may be by listing it in the Online Auction format. If, however, your item's appeal is primarily the value you can present by way of a good price, then the Fixed Price format is probably the right choice.

For example, antiques, art, collectibles, the latest iPod or gaming console, a wad of gum chewed and spit out by an uncouth celebrity (whose mama should have taught her better manners) . . . all these items are usually listed in the Online Auction format.

On the other hand, commodity items such as digital cameras, housewares, clothing, shoes, accessories, and jewelry, where the value is in the asking price as compared to prices for similar items in other markets, are usually best listed as Fixed Price.

Scheduled Start

Leave this box blank if you want to have your listing go live once it is submitted. The listing will be immediately time-stamped with the start time and will end one, three, five, seven, or ten days later on the hour, minute, and second indicated as the start time.

A scheduled start also allows you to schedule a listing by date and time up to three weeks in the future. To schedule a time for your listing, click the "Date" and "Time" boxes and select a start date and time.

After you have finished and submitted the listing, it will appear in the Pending Items section of My eBay, All Selling.

- You can schedule a maximum of three thousand listings, up to three weeks in advance of the time you wish them to start.
- A fee will apply for each listing you schedule to start at a later time.
- Fees charged are applicable at the actual start time, not when the listings are submitted using the Sell Your Item form, so you will incur no fees if you delete a pending listing from your pending queue.

Donate a Percentage of Sale

From the very first days of eBay, generous sellers have utilized the site as a way of raising funds for the charities of their choice. From before and during 9/11 up to Hurricane Katrina relief efforts, eBay members have always come through for their fellow man, especially when the need is greatest.

Today, there is a special tool on eBay for this purpose. It is called the Giving Works. The "Donate" section on the SYI is the seller tool for using the Giving Works. The process is simple: A seller who wants to donate some or all of the proceeds of his listing to a worthy cause selects a listed nonprofit group from the extensive list of charities registered with MissionFish (the company that runs the Giving Works tool). He then selects a percentage of the proceeds of the sale—from 10 to 100 percent—to donate to the charity.

I always try to have at least one of my active listings set up to donate 100 percent of the funds to one of the several charities that I like to support. I urge you to consider giving a bit as well—maybe not right now, but remember where you saw this feature so you can access it quickly in the future.

Payment Methods You Accept

This portion of the Sell Your Item form is where you integrate your PayPal account into your listing. PayPal is the preferred payment method for sellers and buyers on eBay.

Type your PayPal e-mail address into the box provided.

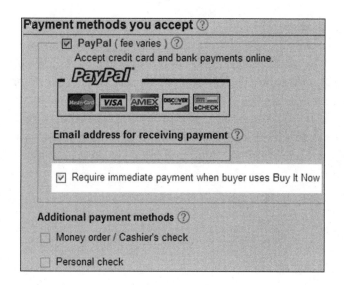

Payment methods you accept ⓘ

☑ PayPal (fee varies) ⓘ
Accept credit card and bank payments online.

PayPal®

[MasterCard] [VISA] [AMEX] [DISCOVER] [eCHECK]

Email address for receiving payment ⓘ
[   ]

☐ Require immediate payment when buyer uses Buy It Now

Additional payment methods ⓘ
☐ Money order / Cashier's check
☐ Personal check

As I mentioned earlier, we are providing a Buy It Now price. I recommend that any seller providing the Buy It Now option for buyers should consider requiring immediate payment for all Buy It Now purchases. Here's why: Later on, we will talk about buyers who bid or buy and then fail to pay for the item. The incidence of these Unpaid Items (as eBay calls them) is fairly low, but you can help reduce the possibility that your listing will end up as an Unpaid Item by checking this box.

Now, if someone clicks the "Buy It Now" button, she will be clicked through to her PayPal account and instructed to pay for the item in order to close it out. Until the buyer actually sends payment to you via PayPal, the item remains open to other buyers.

NOTE: If you employ the Immediate Payment Required option, the options for check and money order are grayed out. However, on a dual-format Auction / Buy It Now listing with Immediate Payment Required where a buyer wins by submitting a bid, as opposed to using Buy It Now, the seller can still accept a check or money order from her.

I use this feature for all of my Buy It Now and Fixed Price listings. There is one disadvantage to employing this option: If you provide discounts for combined purchases, you will have to issue the discount as a refund after the buyer pays for all their items.

Additional Payment Methods

Sellers may accept payment via money order, cashier's check, or personal check.

NOTE: Sellers may not request payment via cash transfer services such as Western Union or MoneyGram. Sellers also may not offer to accept payment in cash (except for items that are exchanged in person, for example, picking up a big appliance or car).

Shipping Calculator

Remember earlier when we packed and then weighed our item and you wondered to yourself, "Why are we packing the item now? We haven't even listed it yet!"

Well, here's why—the eBay Shipping Calculator! This excellent tool is one of my favorite parts of the Sell Your Item format. It will save you time—and, we hope, money as well. Let's explore all of the options and features.

First, if you are joining us from outside this chapter, you may need to change your SYI Show/Hide options. Follow the earlier instructions for showing all shipping options on page 395.

Here is the default view that all new eBay sellers will see:

If you click the drop-down box, you will see four options:

Flat: Same cost to all buyers
Calculated: Cost varies by item location
Freight: Large items over 150 pounds
No shipping: Local pickup only

With the Flat option, you are presented with drop-down boxes for selecting available providers and services and a box for entering the flat amounts.

With the Calculated option, you are presented with boxes for entering the weight (and dimensions if necessary).

When should a seller use flat rates and when should a seller use calculated rates? Shipping option strategies vary from seller to seller: Here's mine. I use the Flat option for any item weighing less than a pound or that fits in an envelope. I use Calculated for all other shipping up to 150 pounds. I use the Freight option for items weighing over 150 pounds. I never opt for Local Pickup Only.

GRIFF TIP! Never assume that you cannot ship heavy or large items. You can! And it isn't that difficult to do. Only use Local Pickup Only as a last resort—for example, an otherwise unremarkable old sofa or other piece of furniture, or a used appliance.

I see many new eBay sellers who, fearing that shipping a heavy or big item is beyond their capabilities, go right for Local Pickup Only. By doing so, they are cutting out millions of potential buyers who would be more than willing to pay for the extra shipping and, if necessary, crating.

Here are the other two options in full-screen view with all their text entry boxes. Freight: Large items over 150 lbs.

Shipping ⑦

Domestic shipping ⑦
[Freight: Large items over 150 lbs. ▼]

Commodity type ⑦
[Machinery (used) ▼]

Pickup location ⑦   Pickup details
[Residence ▼]   ☐ Driver must go inside building for pickup
                            ☐ I need assistance to pack or crate my item and will provide dimensions

Weight ⑦ Dimensions ⑦   Class (NMFC) ⑦
[0] lbs. [   ] in. X [   ] in. X [   ] in.   [-- ▼]

Domestic options ⑦
• Handling cost: US $0.00
Change

No shipping: Local pickup only

Shipping ⑦

Domestic shipping ⑦
[No shipping: Local pickup only ▼]

Item is available for local pickup only.

Item location ⑦
San Jose, CA, 95116, United States
Change location

This is fairly straightforward. You can select one, two, or three shipping services and costs for domestic buyers and up to one, two, or three shipping services for international buyers. You can also offer separate shipping options for domestic and international buyers. For example, you can offer calculated rates for domestic buyers and flat rates for international buyers, or vice versa. (You cannot offer both options—Flat and Calculated—to one buyer location.)

If you choose to provide only one shipping service option for domestic and one for international, the buyer will only be presented with that single option by default. If you select two or more services, the buyer will have the option at checkout time to select the shipping service (and cost) she prefers. You will be alerted by invoice and within My eBay as to which service your buyer selected.

I am all for choice. Choice is good. Buyers often like the opportunity to select from a menu of choices, especially for shipping. Offer as many shipping option choices to your buyer as you can.

Here are the choices for domestic shipping:

Domestic shipping (?)

Calculated: Cost varies by buyer location

Package (?)

Package (or thick envelope)

☐ Irregular package

Weight (?)

2+ to 3 lbs

Services (?) ▣ Research rates

-

-
US Postal Service Priority Mail (2 to 3 working days)
US Postal Service Express Mail (1 working day)
US Postal Service Parcel Post (2 to 9 working days)
US Postal Service Media Mail (2 to 9 working days)
US Postal Service First Class Mail (2 to 5 working days)
UPS Ground (1 to 6 working days)
UPS 3 Day Select (1 to 3 working days)
UPS 2nd Day Air (1 to 2 working days)
UPS Next Day Air Saver (1 working day)
UPS Next Day Air (1 working day)

Here are the available services you can offer an international buyer:

Pay close attention to the Ship To boxes in the International shipping section. The drop-down options are:

- Worldwide
- Choose custom location
- Canada

Now you can begin to see the range of options and combinations you can provide your buyers. For example, you could offer three Calculated options for your domestic buyers and three Flat options for your international buyers with each one specific to a range of international locations.

If you select "Worldwide," it means that you are offering this service to anyone around the world, regardless of location.

If you select "Choose custom location" for any of the international Ship To options, a set of locations with check boxes will appear.

International shipping ⑦

Flat: same cost to all buyers ▾

Ship to ⑦	Services ⑦ 🖾 Research rates	Cost ⑦
Choose custom location ▾	- ▾	$
☐ N. and S. America ☐ Europe ☐ Asia		
☐ Canada ☐ United Kingdom ☐ Australia		
☐ Mexico ☐ Germany ☐ Japan		
- ▾	- ▾	$
- ▾	- ▾	$

If you opt for "Choose custom location," make sure to select at least one location for the list.

If you select Canada, then the selected service applies only to Canada.

If you are willing to ship to some areas but only if the buyer in that country or geographical area contacts you first for shipping costs, indicate those countries or areas by checking the appropriate boxes in the Additional Ship To Location—Buyer Contact for Costs section.

Also note that both the domestic and international shipping sections have separate settings for Insurance and Handling Time (if you have selected Flat Rate, then Handling Time is displayed only for domestic shipping) and Insurance, Handling Time and Handling Cost (if you have selected Calculated Rate). To set the domestic flat rate handling and insurance options, click the "Change" link:

Domestic shipping ⑦

Flat: same cost to all buyers ▾

Services ⑦ 🖺 Research rates

Standard Flat Rate Shipping Service ▾

- ▾

- ▾

Domestic options ⑦
- Insurance: Optional
- Handling time: Not Specified
- Get It Fast: No

Change

Enter the appropriate information as required.

Shipping ⑦

Domestic shipping ⑦

Flat: same cost to all buyers ▾

Services ⑦ 🖺 Research rates   Cost ⑦

Standard Flat Rate Shipping Service ▾ $ [   ]   ☐ Free shipping ⑦

- ▾ $ [   ]

-

Domestic options ⑦
- Insurance: Optional
- Handling time: Not Specifi
- Get It Fast: No
Change

Domestic options   ✕

Insurance ⑦

Optional ▾ $ [   ]

Handling time ⑦

Select a time period ▾

Get It Fast ⑦

☐ Seller must offer a domestic overnight shipping service and 1 day handling
time.

International shipping ⑦

Flat: same cost to all buye

Ship to ⑦

Worldwide ▾

- ▾

- ▾

Additional ship to locations

Will ship worldwide

☐ N. and S. America
☐ Canada
☐ Mexico   ☐ Germany   ☐ Japan

[Save] | Cancel

Click the "Save" button to close the pop-up window. To set the domestic calculated rate handling and insurance options, click the "Change" link:

449

Shipping ⑦

Domestic shipping ⑦

Calculated: Cost varies by buyer location ▾

Package ⑦   Weight ⑦

Package (or thick envelope) ▾   Custom weight ▾

☐ Irregular package

Services ⑦ 🖼 Research rates

- ▾

- ▾

- ▾

Domestic options ⑦

- Insurance: Optional
- Handling time: Not Specified
- Handling cost: US $0.00
- Get It Fast: No

Change

Enter the appropriate information.

Shipping ⑦

Domestic shipping ⑦

Calculated: Cost varies by buyer location ▾

Package ⑦   Weight ⑦

Package (or thick envelope) ▾   Custom weight ▾   0   lbs.   0   oz.

☐ Irregular package

Services ⑦ 🖼 Research

-
-
-

Domestic options ⑦

- Insurance: Optional
- Handling time: Not Specifi
- Handling cost: US $0.00
- Get It Fast: No

Change

International shipping ⑦

Flat: same cost to all buye

Ship to ⑦

Worldwide ▾

- ▾

- ▾

Domestic options   ⊗

Insurance ⑦

Optional ▾

Handling time ⑦

Select a time period ▾

Handling cost - Calculated shipping only ⑦

$ 0.00

Get It Fast ⑦

☐ Seller must offer a domestic overnight shipping service and 1 day handling time.

Save | Cancel

Click the "Save" button to close the pop-up window.

One extremely important aspect of the Shipping section to keep in mind: If you choose to exclude certain countries from your shipping options by not checking them, you can prevent eBay buyers registered in those countries from bidding on or purchasing items from you by selecting the Buyer Requirement (defined later in this section) for "Block bidders/buyers who are registered in countries to which I do not ship" in order to exclude these buyers.

Caution! As displayed above, eBay provides a data box for sellers to include a handling cost for their shipping. eBay expects that any handling charge you provide will be reasonable and of an amount that covers the supplies used in packing the item. Inflated or unreasonable handling costs can result in the removal of the listing from eBay and possible sanctions against the offending seller.

To learn more about eBay's policies regarding excessive shipping charges, visit the eBay Help pages by clicking "Help" on the top of any eBay page. Then click "A–Z index," "S," and then "Shipping and Handling—Excessive Charges."

GRIFF TIP! eBay is a worldwide marketplace. To sell successfully in this marketplace, an eBay seller should be willing to sell to anyone, anywhere on the planet, and not limit his potential customer base to only those living within the United States. There are eager, honest eBay buyers around the world for your item. Don't cut them off! Selling and shipping to international eBay buyers is not difficult or complicated. In fact, it's easy. (More on international shipping in chapter 4.)

Additional Information

This section contains settings for Buyer Requirements and your Return Policy. Both are important.

Buyer Requirements

The default setting for buyer requirements is "None: allow all buyers." To view and add selected buyer requirements, click the "Add buyer requirements" to display the settings box.

451

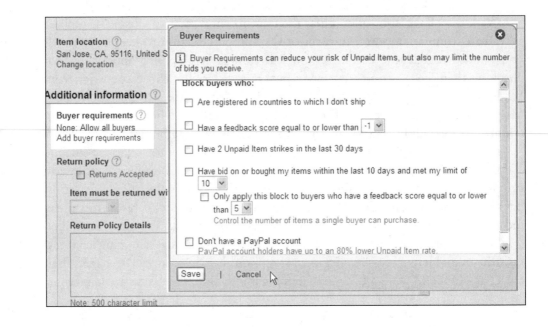

There are five requirements from which to choose in order to block buyers who:

1. **Are registered in countries to which I don't ship.** If there are countries you exclude from your shipping options in the Shipping Calculator, you must check this requirement in order to prevent buyers in those countries from bidding on or buying your item.

2. **Have a feedback score equal to or lower than –1, –2, or –3.** This requirement will block anyone with a negative feedback score from bidding on or buying your item. Note: This does not block buyers with one, two, or three negative comments. This requirement will only block buyers with a total displayed negative feedback score—for example, "myuserid (–2)."

3. **Have two Unpaid Item strikes in the last thirty days.** Self-explanatory.

4. **Have bid on or bought my items within the last 10 days and met my limit of X number of items bid on or bought.** You can also apply this block to only those buyers with a feedback score equal to or lower than 5, 4, 3, 2, 1, or 0. Some sellers employ this requirement to block what might be described as "exuberant" new buyers who may be bidding frivolously.

5. **Don't have a PayPal account.** Think of this requirement as unofficial buyer verification (since PayPal requires valid, verifiable personal information upon registration). This requirement can help dramatically reduce

the incidence of Unpaid Items or attempts at buyer fraud. This requirement does not mean your buyer must pay you with PayPal. It means only that he or she must have a PayPal account in order to bid on or buy your item.

Return Policy Considerations

Should you have a return policy? The short answer: yes. In fact, it doesn't matter if you are selling one or one million items on eBay. Each item you list on eBay should display your return policy.

"But Griff," I hear you saying, "I don't want to take my item back. I just want to sell it. Can't I say 'Item sold as is; no returns or refunds'? After all, my goal is to turn the item into money, not to list the item only to have to take it back and refund the buyer's payment."

Yes, that is your goal: sell the item. But the only way to reach that goal without hassles or difficulties is to have a clear, equitable return policy. Of course, you are free to employ an "As is—no returns" policy. But get ready for lots of unhappy buyers, disputes, and negative feedback if you do.

Will you have to take an item back now and then? Possibly. If you are selling part or full time on eBay, returns are a fact of life, just as they are in any retail business. Never worry over one single transaction. The most successful businesses on eBay align all of their business practices to benefit the buyer. No matter what anyone else may tell you, the customer (buyer) is king. The quality of your customer service strategy will determine your level of selling success on eBay, and the keystone of any customer service strategy is a clear and equitable return policy.

Besides, an equitable return policy is good business because eBay buyers are a savvy lot. Given the choice between two otherwise identical listings, they will always go with the seller who has the best return policy.

If you opt to accept returns, check the box labeled "Returns accepted" and select a duration for the options under "Item must be returned within." The choices are three, seven, fourteen, and thirty days. Then choose an option under "Refund will be given as": exchange, merchandise credit, or money back. Type the details of your return policy into the box provided.

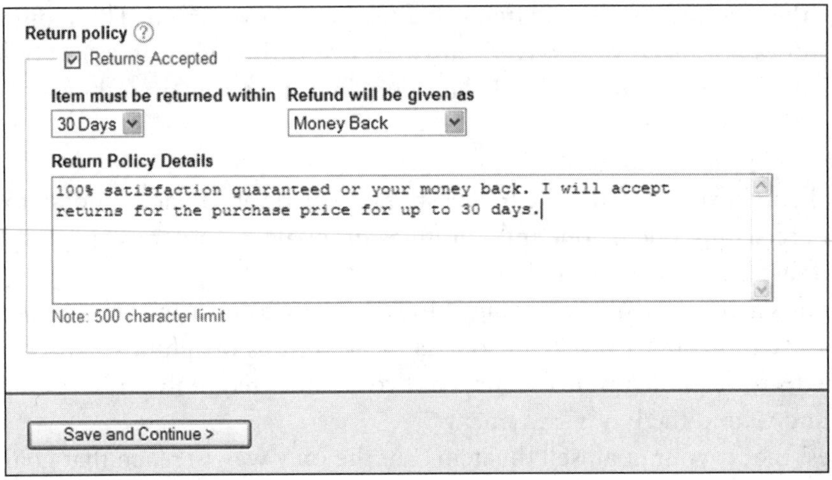

Return policy (?)

☑ Returns Accepted

Item must be returned within **Refund will be given as**

30 Days ▼   Money Back ▼

Return Policy Details

100% satisfaction guaranteed or your money back. I will accept returns for the purchase price for up to 30 days.|

Note: 500 character limit

Save and Continue >

Click the "Save and continue" button.

PROMOTE AND REVIEW YOUR LISTING

In the next section, you can select from several features to promote your item more effectively.

Sell: Promote and Review Your Listing

Make your listing compelling
Review how your listing will appear to buyers and add features to help you sell successfully.

[Edit Listing] [Help]

[i] Click Edit Listing to go back to the previous page rather than using your browser **Back** button.

Make your listing stand out ⑦

value pack   [i] **Value Pack is not applicable**
You've already selected an option that contains Gallery.

Gallery picture ⑦
☑ Add a small version of your selected picture to search results

[Picture 1 ▾]

Gallery Plus ($0.75) ⑦
☐ Display multiple larger pictures in search results when buyers mouse over "Enlarge". Free Gallery Picture included.

Subtitle ($0.50) ⑦
☑ Give buyers more information in search results (searchable by item description only)

[Free Shipping with Buy It Now]

Gift Icon ($0.25) ⑦
☐ Promote your gift service with a 🎁 icon next to your listing in search results

Bold ($1.00) ⑦
☐ Attract buyers' attention by making the title of your listing appear in **Bold**

Border ($3.00) ⑦
☐ Outline your listing with an eye-catching frame

Highlight ($5.00) ⑦
☐ Make your listing stand out in search results with a brightly-colored band

Gallery Featured ($19.95) ⑦
☐ Showcase your item in search results with an enlarged picture and close up views. Free Gallery Picture included.

How your listing will appear in search results ⑦

Item Title	PayPal	Price	Shipping	Bids	Time Listed ▾
Honiton Collard Poole Devon Pitcher Jug Creamer Exton Free Shipping with Buy It Now	🅿	$0.99 $14.00	$5.00	- =Buy It Now	Jan-27 17:00

🔍 Preview your listing | Edit listing

Promote Your Listing

Gallery Picture

Displays a thumbnail next to your item title in search results and category lists. A Gallery image will cost 35¢, but eBay statistics show that listings with Gallery pictures get more traffic and more bids. In fact, Gallery listings are shown to increase the final price by an average of 11 percent. That's 35¢ well spent.

If you still are unsure of the value of a Gallery thumbnail, put on your buyer's hat and visit any category list or title keyword search result list. Which items tend to catch your eye first? Which items do you tend to overlook?

I thought so.

Gallery Plus

This is a new feature at eBay. When a buyer hovers his mouse cursor over a Gallery image that includes Gallery Plus, a larger version of the smaller Gallery thumbnail will appear. Gallery Plus costs 75¢ per Gallery image.

Gallery Plus includes a Gallery picture, so if you opt for Gallery Plus, don't check the box for Gallery picture.

Subtitle

We saw this feature in the Title section at the beginning of the Sell Your Item form. If you didn't select this feature then, here is your chance to reconsider.

Gift Icon

If you have an item that would make a great gift or if you are willing to promote your item with special services such as gift wrapping or express shipping, you might opt for this feature. For a quarter, this feature places a blue Gift icon next to your item title in category and search result lists. In addition, your item is searchable using the Gift icon filter from the Advanced Search page.

Show only

☐ Buy It Now items　　　　　☐ Items listed wi

☐ Free Shipping

☐ Get it Fast items

☐ 🌐 Gift items　　　　　　☐ 🎗 eBay Giving
　　　　　　　　　　　　　Search for items th

☐ Best Offer

☐ Classified Ads

☐ Store Inventory Items only　　☐ All items inclu

☐ Listings
　[Ending within ▾] [1 hour ▾] Change to

Bold

Draw additional attention to your listing by bolding the text of your item's title as it appears in category or search result lists. Bold listings are shown to increase final price by an average of 25 percent.

Border

The Border option showcases your listing by surrounding it with a colored band.

Highlight

Highlight employs a colored band behind your item title to emphasize the listing in the search results and category lists.

GRIFF TIP! Although Bold, Border, and Highlight are excellent features, it is important to use them wisely. Before selecting any of the three options, check out your category or search to determine how many listings are already using them. For example, if you find that the category or search result lists for your item shows that no one is using Bold, it might be a wise investment to use it on your listing to help promote it. However, if you discover that many listings already have Bold, then perhaps there is less value in the feature for this particular instance.

Gallery Featured

Provides prominent placement of your item and Gallery image at the top of the Gallery view pages. With Gallery Featured, your listing will periodically appear in the special Featured section above the general Gallery. Here is an example:

Gallery Featured includes a Gallery image and the Gallery Plus feature.

NOTE: The exact position of your listing and the number of times it appears at the top of the page are affected by factors such as the timing of your listing and the number of other Gallery Featured items in your category. Because of this, eBay cannot guarantee that all Gallery Featured listings will receive the same exposure.

Our new User ID has a feedback score of 0; therefore, the next two features will not be available to us. However, if your feedback score is 10 or more, you will also see the following upgrade features.

Featured Plus

With Featured Plus, a copy of your listing title is placed within the Featured Items located in the top section of the listing and search results pages that buyers see first. Your item also appears in the general listings and search results, for double the exposure. Featured Plus listings are 28 percent more likely to sell!

3 items found in **Rugs Finder**   Add to f

Show only: Age: **1940-1969**, Shape: **Rectangle**, Size: **8' x 10', 8' x 11'**, Style: **Persian**, Background Color: **Blues** Show all

List View | Picture Gallery   Sort by: Time: newly listed

⤢	Compare	Item Title	PayPal	Bids	Price*	Shipping to 95116, USA

Featured Items

| ☐ | | INCREDIBLE BLUE 12'4x8'10 Kerman Persian Rugs W-1614 Free Shipping- Free Insurance- Free Pad- $7000 Value | ⒫ | - | $999.95 | See description |

Optimize your selling success! Find out how to promote your items

☐		TABRIZ 10.4 x 7.5 Semi Antique Hand Knotted Persian Rug	⒫	- ꜛBuy It Now	$900.00 $1,249.00	$89.00
☐		INCREDIBLE BLUE 12'4x8'10 Kerman Persian Rugs W-1614 Free Shipping- Free Insurance- Free Pad- $7000 Value	⒫	-	$999.95	See description
☐		Area Rugs Meduim Persian Wool Kerman 8 X 11 Persian Rug	⒫	- ꜛBuy It Now	$3,275.00 $3,850.00	Free

Home Page Featured

This upgrade places a copy of your item's title in the eBay Featured Listings section, which you can reach from the eBay home page. With Home Page Featured, your listing has a chance to rotate into a special display on eBay's home page. The Home Page Featured fee is charged per listing and is in addition to other fees, such as Insertion Fees and Final Value Fees.

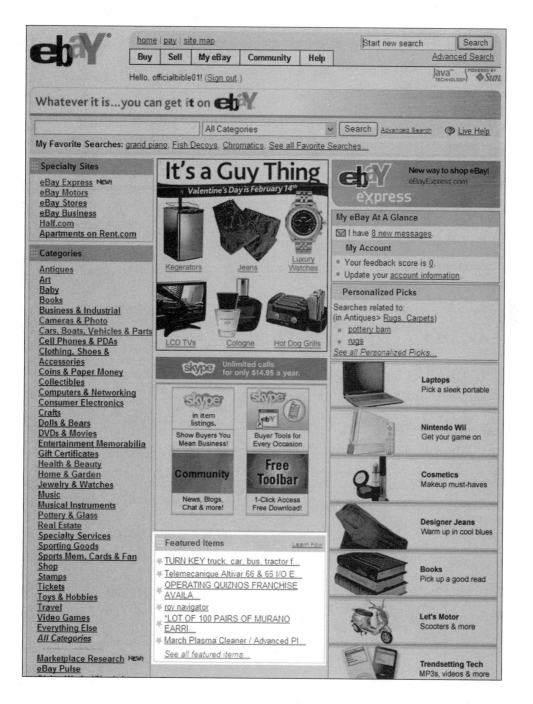

NOTE: You need a feedback score of at least 10 to use Featured Plus or Home Page Featured.

How Your Listing Will Appear in Search Results

This feature gives you a preview of how your listing will appear in search results, allowing you to view all the upgrade features you selected (or not).

Recommendations for Your Listings

Once you reach this stage of the SYI form, eBay reviews your listing and provides a series of recommendations to increase your chances of a successful sale. If you are open to some helpful suggestions, click "Edit Listing" to view each specific recommendation.

Recommendations for your listing

You can increase your chances of success by taking the following steps:

Add Item Specifics
Add Item Specifics so that more buyers can find your listing.

Have the shipping cost calculated automatically
Allow buyers to see the shipping cost for their location. Save time and money, especially on international shipping.

Edit Listing

Otherwise, it's now time to preview your listing, make any corrections or edits as needed before submitting it to the site.

Preview Your Listing

Scroll through the box to view your listing as it will appear on the site.

Preview your listing (?)

🏺 **Honiton Collard Poole Devon Pitcher Jug Creamer Exton**   Item number: --
Free Shipping with Buy It Now

This item is being tracked in My eBay | Email to a friend

Visits: 00001

Starting bid:	US $0.99	Place Bid >	**Meet the seller**
			Seller: officialbible01 (0)
Buy It Now price:	US $14.00	Buy It Now >	Member: since Nov-27-06 in United States
			▪ Read feedback comments
			▪ Ask seller a question

Preview | Edit Listing

You can also click the "Preview" link on the bottom of the window to see the listing in a bigger scrolling window.

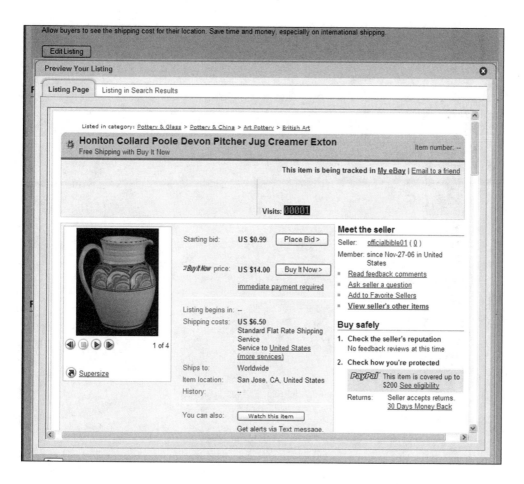

Click the "Listings in Search Results" tab to view how your listing will look in a category or search result list.

Edit Listing

Preview Your Listing

Listing Page | Listing in Search Results

☑ Subtitle ($0.50) ⑦
Free Shipping with Buy I

☐ Bold ($1.00) ⑦   ☐ Border ($3.00) ⑦   ☐ Highlight ($5.00) ⑦   ☑ Gift Icon ($0.25) ⑦

Item Title	PayPal	Price	Shipping	Bids	Time Listed ▾
Honiton Collard Poole Devon Pitcher Jug Creamer Exton ⊘ Free Shipping with Buy It Now	⊘	$0.99 $14.00	$5.00	≡Buy It Now	Jan-27 17:00
19thC Antique Stoneware "Doulton Lambeth Toby Jug" Perfect Condition w/ Hand Worked Details #3726	⊘	$9.99	See description	-	Jan-21 19:20
Plichta Wemyss Pig with Shamrocks, London England	⊘	$29.99	Calculate	-	Jan-21 19:03
Maryleigh Pottery Wine Bucket/Planter " Cottage Rose"	⊘	$13.99	$16.95	-	Jan-21 18:45
*UNUSUAL ART DECO BRITISH ART POTTERY JUG w SHIP N/R	⊘	$9.99	$17.99	-	Jan-21 18:31
Royal Tara CELTIC ILLUMINATIVE ART Bk Kells Design MUG	⊘	$5.99	$6.95	-	Jan-21 18:24

Save and Close | Cancel

Before your listing goes live, you have the chance to review and change the information and features for each section. This is an important step! Please don't rush through it. Check each section to make sure that the information is correct.

Make it a habit to carefully review the entire listing preview. If you find something that needs correction, click the "Edit Listing" link.

Preview | Edit Listing

Fees ⑦

Fees

For example, I have decided to reschedule my listing to go live in two weeks instead of one week. I click the "Edit Listing" link and go directly to the Scheduled Start area of the SYI form.

To schedule the listing to start at a later date and time, I select the duration and time from the Scheduled Start feature:

Scheduled start ($0.10) ⓘ

| Sunday, Feb 11 ▾ | 5:00 PM ▾ | PST |

Sunday, Jan 21
Monday, Jan 22
Tuesday, Jan 23
Wednesday, Jan 24
Thursday, Jan 25
Friday, Jan 26
Saturday, Jan 27
Sunday, Jan 28
Monday, Jan 29
Tuesday, Jan 30
Wednesday, Jan 31
Thursday, Feb 01
Friday, Feb 02
Saturday, Feb 03
Sunday, Feb 04
Monday, Feb 05
Tuesday, Feb 06
Wednesday, Feb 07
Thursday, Feb 08
Friday, Feb 09
Saturday, Feb 10
Sunday, Feb 11

Make sure to scroll down to the bottom of the page and click the "Save and continue" button.

Fees

Review the fees for each of the listing features or upgrades that either you selected or were required.

Fees ⑦	
Fees	
Insertion fee:	$0.20
Buy It Now Fee:	$0.10
Picture Pack:	$1.00
Subtitle:	$0.50
Scheduled start time :	$0.10
Listing Designer:	$0.10
Gift Services:	$0.25
Total:	$2.25

If your item sells, you will be charged a final value fee based on a percentage of the final sale price. Estimate final value fee | Review account balance

Attention Sellers:

Add Bold!
BOLD Go for the **bold**! Item titles with **bold** (see example) sell for 39% more, on average. A wise investment for $1.00.

Add It Now!

These amounts will be added to your Seller Account invoice for the current month once the item is listed live to the site. If you have scheduled the listing for sometime in the future, the fees will be added to your invoice at that time.

Note that if your item sells, a Final Value Fee (based on a percentage of the final bid or purchase price—more on fees later in this chapter) will be added to your monthly invoice at the time of sale or listing closing.

LIST YOUR ITEM

One last step: Click the "List your item" button to list the item on eBay.

Total: $2.25

If your item sells, you will be charged a final value fee based on a percentage of the final sale price.
Estimate final value fee | Review account balance

Attention Sellers:

Add Bold!
Go for the **bold!** Item titles with **bold** (see example) sell for
39% more, on average. A wise investment for $1.00.

Add It Now!

(e11853-109158-5653)

By clicking **List Your Item**, you agree to pay the fees above and assume full responsibility for the cont

☐ Save this listing as a template

List Your Item | Edit listing

Our listing is now queued on eBay as a Scheduled or Pending listing. It will go live on the date and at the time we selected.

Only the seller can view a scheduled listing. Click the linked title to view the pending listing.

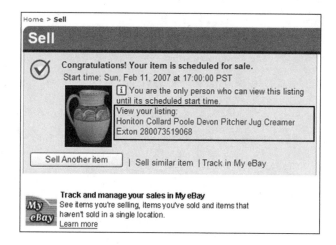

Home > **Sell**

Sell

✓ **Congratulations! Your item is scheduled for sale.**
Start time: Sun, Feb 11, 2007 at 17:00:00 PST
ⓘ You are the only person who can view this listing until its scheduled start time.
View your listing:
Honiton Collard Poole Devon Pitcher Jug Creamer Exton 280073519068

Sell Another item | Sell similar item | Track in My eBay

Track and manage your sales in My eBay
See items you're selling, items you've sold and items that haven't sold in a single location.
Learn more

Here it is!

ebaY®

home | pay | register | sign out | site map

Buy | Sell | My eBay | Community | Help

Start new search | Search
Advanced Search

Java™ TECHNOLOGY | POWERED BY ◆Sun

🔙 Back to My eBay   Listed in category: Pottery & Glass > Pottery & China > Art Pottery > British Art

Honiton Collard Poole Devon Pitcher Jug Creamer Exton
Free Shipping with Buy It Now

Item number: 280073519068

You are signed in

This item is being tracked in My eBay | Email to a friend | Printer Version

This auction has not yet started.

Revise your item
Promote your item
Sell a similar item

Want to sell more quickly and efficiently? Learn about how Turbo Lister can help you save time.

Visits: 00001

Starting bid: US $0.99   [Place Bid >]

≡Buy It Now price: US $14.00   [Buy It Now >]

immediate payment required

Listing begins in: Feb-11-07 17:00:00 PST
Shipping costs: US $6.50
Standard Flat Rate Shipping Service
Service to United States
(more services)
Ships to: Worldwide
Item location: San Jose, CA, United States
History: --

◀ ⏹ ▶ ⏭   1 of 4

🔍 Supersize

You can also: [Watch this item]

Get alerts via Text message, IM or Cell phone
Sell one like this

Meet the seller
Seller: officialbible01 (0)
Member: since Nov-27-06 in United States
» Read feedback comments
» Ask seller a question
» Add to Favorite Sellers
» View seller's other items

Buy safely
1. Check the seller's reputation
   No feedback reviews at this time
2. Check how you're protected

   PayPal This item is covered up to $200
   See eligibility

   Returns: Seller accepts returns.
              30 Days Money Back

Listing and payment details: Hide

Starting time: Feb-11-07 17:00:00 PST   Payment methods: **PayPal**
Starting bid: US $0.99   See details
Duration: 7-day listing

Description

Honiton Exton Small Pitcher

I was culling treasure from the china closet and found this Honiton pitcher, 4 1/2 inches tall, circa 1950's. White clay. Exton shape. Pitcher is in excellent condition; no cracks, breaks, chips or stains. Embossed mark on bottom: "Honiton Potteries Exton England" with a black hand painted "t."

A Brief History of Honiton Pottery: Honiton pottery was (and is) located in the town of Honiton in Devon, England. The pottery was started by Foster and Hunt at the turn of the 19th/210th century. It was purchased by Charles Collard shortly after WWI. In 1947, Collard sold the pottery to Norman Hull and Harry Barratt who ran it until 1961 when it was sold to Paul Redvers. All production ceased in 1997 and the pottery was shuttered. The premises were recently reopened as pottery and craft shop.

Check out my other items!

- **Payment Terms:** I accept and prefer payment through PayPal. I also accept personal checks (items shipped immediately after check has cleared) or money orders.
- **Shipping:** I will ship this item anywhere to anyone. International bidders and buyers welcome. Please enter your zip code in the box provided below this description. This will provide you up to three shipping options and costs from which you may select one.
- **Return Policy:** If you win or purchase this item from me through this listing and upon receiving it are not 100% satisfied, you may return it to me within 14 days from the close of the listing for a full refund of the winning bid plus shipping.

Larger Picture

Select a picture

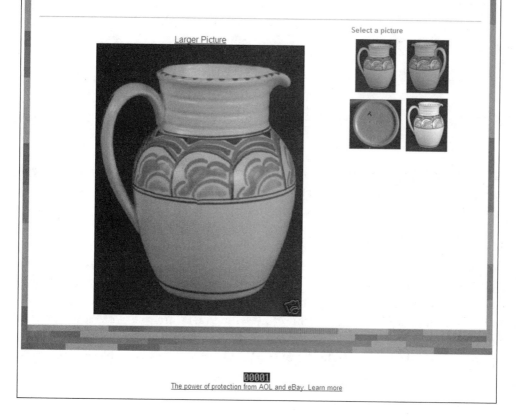

00001
The power of protection from AOL and eBay. Learn more

Shipping, payment details and return policy

Ships to
Worldwide

Country: United States

Shipping and Handling	To	Service
US $6.50	United States	Standard Flat Rate Shipping Service

Domestic Handling Time
Will usually ship within 2 business days of receiving cleared payment.

Shipping insurance
Domestic: Included (in the shipping and handling cost)
International: Not offered

Seller's return policy:
Item must be returned within: 30 Days   Refund will be given as: Money Back
Return Policy Details: 100% satisfaction guaranteed or your money back. I will accept returns for the purchase price for up to 30 days.

Payment methods accepted

Payment method	Preferred/Accepted	Buyer protection on eBay
PayPal MasterCard VISA AMEX DISCOVER eCHECK	Accepted	PayPal This item is covered up to $200 See eligibility

Learn about payment methods.

You can also manage this pending listing from My eBay, All Selling, Scheduled.

NOTE: We can reschedule the listing to a later or earlier date or time, we can schedule it to go live immediately, or we can simply delete it. If we delete it before it goes live, we will not incur any insertion fees.

Congratulations! If you have followed along with the instructions and steps of this chapter, you should have listed your first item on eBay. There's nothing quite like the thrill and satisfaction you feel when you have completed your first eBay listing. Take a moment to relax and savor the accomplishment.

But don't get too relaxed. Your eBay selling tasks are not over. You still have to be available for buyer e-mails, and if the item sells, you will have to accept payment and ship the item. In the meantime, here are a few troubleshooting tips.

Selling Troubleshooting

EBAY PICTURE SERVICES PHOTOS ARE NOT SHOWING ON THE REVIEW LISTING PAGE

This is a rare problem, but it does happen. Usually, this is due to a faulty connection between your computer and eBay. If your images are not showing up on the Review page, go back and start your listing again from the beginning.

CHANGING SOMETHING IN A LIVE LISTING

You can make major changes to your listing after it has gone live to the site, but only before it actually receives a bid. Since items do not usually receive bids for at least thirty minutes after they are listed, this gives you some time to revise your item.

To make revisions to a live item where no bids have been placed, go to the Item Description page. Click the link "Revise your item" on the top section of the item page.

This will take you to the Revise Your Listing page, where you can change almost anything about your listing.

REVISING AN ITEM AFTER BIDS ARE RECEIVED— ADDING TO AN ITEM DESCRIPTION

In cases where bids have been received and you need to correct an error but the error is not so serious as to warrant ending the auction early, you can always add to the listing's description. There are two pathways for adding to your item's description. The first is to click the "Revise item" link on the top of the listing page and follow the instructions from there. If a bid has been placed on your item, you will only be able to revise by adding text. Follow the prompts to do so.

Or go to the My eBay All Selling page. Find the column labeled Related Links, and click "More . . ." on the bottom of that column:

This will open the page Selling-Related Links. Look for the link "Add to item description."

Follow the instructions from there. (You will need the item number.) This feature is handy for adding information about the item.

ENDING A LISTING EARLY

A seller may, at any time and entirely at her discretion, end an auction listing early. This might occur if the item is damaged or stolen after being listed, or if the seller inadvertently described the item incorrectly.

From My eBay, click the "All Selling > Scheduled" link. Locate the item title, scroll to the right, and click the down arrow in the box located in the Action column. Select the "End item" option.

Follow the instructions from there. Again, you will need the item number of the listing you wish to end. If there are active bids on the listing you wish to end early, the system will cancel them before you end the listing. You should also, as a courtesy, e-mail all bidders whose bids were canceled to inform them of the reason.

RELISTING AN ITEM USING THE RELIST FEATURE

Once a listing has ended, there are two ways to relist the item quickly and easily: from My eBay or from the Closed Item page. To relist from My eBay, go to the My eBay Selling, Sold, or Unsold page. Find the listing, look under the Action column, and select "Relist."

You can also relist an item by clicking the "Relist" button on the closed (sold or unsold) listing page.

If you are using the Relist feature, the fee for relisting may be waived if the item sells on the second attempt. When you relist, if your previous item had a reserve, you will have to lower the reserve price for your listing to be eligible for the listing-fee credit. If your item did not have a reserve, you will need to lower the opening bid amount to qualify for the listing credit.

You can also use the Relist feature to list a new, similar item and save yourself a lot of typing. If you use the Relist feature to sell a similar item, make sure you change the appropriate information (pictures, text, title, etc.) before submitting the listing.

A BIDDER RETRACTED HER BID!—IS THIS ALLOWED?

Yes, it is, but only under certain circumstances. If a bidder has made an error in her bid amount, she may retract her bid and reenter the bid correctly. A bidder may also retract due to extraordinary circumstances that place an unreasonable burden on the bidder should he or she win the item.

A bidder may not employ the bid-retraction privilege for frivolous reasons—for example, a change of heart or finding the item someplace else for less.

All bid retractions are tracked on a user's Feedback Profile card.

Chronic bid retractions are routinely investigated by eBay and can result in suspension of the retracting bidder's eBay registration.

The ability to retract a bid is limited by the time left in an auction and the time between your first bid and the next. Bid retraction rules are explained in detail in Section One, chapter 7.

BIDDER IS NOT RESPONDING TO E-MAIL

How to Contact a Bidder

First, don't panic! Sometimes bidders find themselves unexpectedly pulled away from their computers for a time. Bidders can experience crises. Always give your bidder a few days before moving to the next step.

If your buyer hasn't responded to your e-mail within three to five days, then you should attempt to contact him by phone. You can obtain the phone number of any high bidder on your listings by clicking on "Advanced search" and then "Find a member." Then click on "Find contact information."

Enter the buyer's User ID and the item number in the box provided for Contact Information. (Note: Only the high bidder(s) and the seller in a specific eBay transaction can obtain each other's phone numbers.)

Reporting an Unreachable Bidder

If a bidder's phone number is not valid or if a e-mail sent to a bidder is bounced back to you as undeliverable, you should report the bidder to eBay. Click on the "Security & Resolution Center" link found on the bottom of any eBay Web page.

Select the option for "Report another problem" and follow the instructions from there.

BIDDER BACKED OUT

Sometimes a winning bidder may back out of a sale. If a bidder contacts you with extenuating circumstances and asks to be relieved of her bidder obligation, you may agree to do so. If the backing out is for reasons you consider frivolous or if the bidder does not respond to repeated e-mails or phone calls, you may want to report the sale as an Unpaid Item.

In either case, if the transaction is not completed, you can and should file for a Final Value Fee credit by filing an Unpaid Item claim.

Go to the Security & Resolution Center (look for the link on the bottom of any eBay page), select the option for Unpaid Item, and click the "Report problem" button.

SECOND CHANCE OFFER

Sometimes a buyer may back out, leaving you with an unsold item—one for which you have paid insertion and other fees. Instead of relisting the item (and incurring more fees) you might want to try the Second Chance Offer feature.

Second Chance offers can be sent to any of the nonwinning bidders if the high bidder does not buy the item, if a seller has duplicate items, or if the reserve price is not met in a reserve price auction. Second Chance offers can be created immediately after a listing ends and for up to sixty days. Please note that Second Chance offers will not be sent to bidders who have opted not to receive them.

Before sending a Second Chance Offer because of an Unpaid Item (see above), a seller should be sure that everything has been done to resolve the issue with the original buyer. Also, the number of offers you send can't be more than the number of items you have for sale.

There are no insertion fees for using the Second Chance Offer feature on an unsold item. In addition, all the regular eBay features such as Feedback and Buyer Protection are available to both the buyer and the seller in a Second Chance Offer transaction.

To learn more about the Second Chance Offer feature, go to the My eBay page, click on the link to the All Selling page, scroll down to Related Links, and expand the list if necessary by clicking "More. . . ." Then click "Send a Second Chance Offer." Follow the instructions from there.

GRIFF TIP! Do you notice a pattern here? Almost everything you may need to accomplish as a seller, be it filing an Unpaid Item claim, ending a listing, or relisting an item, can be done through My eBay. If you ever have a question about your items, your Seller's Account, or your eBay preferences or information, go to My eBay first!

Now that you have your first item listed, you'll find the rest are a snap. Who knows? This may be the start of your business on eBay!

Before we move on to the next chapter, eBay seller Robert Sachs has a great selling tip to share. He employs it around the holiday sales season, but any eBay seller could use it anytime:

I found a neat little trick to help boost my holiday sales enormously: free shipping!

I combined Buy It Now with free shipping and came up with a killer offer. If the buyer used Buy It Now, I would zero out the shipping charge. I changed the heading for my auctions to be sure to include "FREE SHIP" in each one. My auctions, normally set for five days, would close within twenty-four hours! This allowed me to post more without flooding a particular item. And posting more meant more sales!

My normal closing rate for a recent year averaged around 45 percent. My closing rate during November and early December of that year pushed closer to 80 percent with this special offer, with the vast majority being Buy It Now sales!

4

After the Sale

In 1998, Mike Driscoll was selling restaurant equipment and antiques out of an old 1880 home he had recently purchased. On weekends, he would move most of his inventory outside to attract roadside attention, and he was lucky if he sold $500 in two days—not nearly enough to survive, and certainly not worth the strain of moving furniture in and out of his home shop every weekend.

Then in 1999 Mike found eBay, started selling, and, in his own words, "fell in love with eBay."

"I now own three computers. I never sat at one until thirteen months ago. I no longer open my front door to my antiques store, as I sell all my antiques, and even some restaurant equipment stuff that sat downstairs in my basement for years, on eBay."

Today, Mike has an average of two hundred items up for sale or bid on eBay. His feedback stands at 4,450 and is climbing. He is also a member of the eBay Power-Seller team. eBay has indeed changed his life, but not only in a business sense.

"I sold an item that was not as I described. It was an ice cream syrup pump that I sold as a catsup, mustard, and relish pump."

The buyer contacted Mike to alert him to his error, and he immediately obtained the buyer's contact information so that he could quickly refund the buyer's money without even waiting for the item to be returned.

"She surprised me by showing up at my doorstep one day." They started dating, and, as Mike says, the rest is history.

"I thank you, eBay, for changing my life! I have been richer in money, romance, and confidence since finding eBay."

Your item sold! Congratulations! Now, the after-sale tasks begin:

> Invoicing the Buyer
> Leaving Feedback
> Shipping

Invoicing the Buyer

When one of your items has sold on eBay, the next step is to send the lucky winning buyer an e-mail invoice or notice. You can send an invoice manually, or if you set up your eBay selling preferences appropriately, eBay will automatically send out an invoice with a total that includes shipping, handling, sales tax (if applicable), and your payment instructions. In addition, if you integrated PayPal fully into your listings (per the previous instructions), the automatic invoice will contain a clickable "Pay now" button that will take the buyer directly to his PayPal account.

SENDING AN INVOICE—MY EBAY

My eBay provides the quickest and easiest method for manually sending an invoice to a buyer. Navigate to the page view for My eBay, All Selling, Sold.

Send Invoice to Buyer

Review or update the information below. When you're done, click the **Send Invoice** button and eBay will email an invoice to your buyer.

Buyer: pnirchy (12 ☆)

Zip Code:

Enter Payment Details

Select	Item #	Item Title	Qty.	Price	Subtotal
✓	4960205182	PS/2 Model 90 XP 486 Quick Reference & Guide	1	US $14.99	US $14.99

recalculate

Subtotal: US$14.99

Shipping and handling: [Standard flat rate shipping service ▼] US $ [4.00] 🖩

Add another

Shipping insurance: [Required ▼] US $ [0.70]

Sales tax: [California ▼] [8.25] %

☐ Apply sales tax to subtotal + shipping and handling.

Enter Payment Instructions & Personal Message

Give clear instructions to assist buyers with payment, shipping, and returns.

Note: 500 character limit

Select Payment Methods for this item

You can choose additional payment methods you will accept.

PayPal (MasterCard VISA DISCOVER AMEX eCHECK)

✓ PayPal - payment will go to: [   ]

✓ Money order or Cashiers check
✓ Personal check

Merchant credit card
Only for sellers accepting credit card purchases through their own merchant account.

    ✓ Visa / Mastercard   ☐ Discover   ☐ American Express

☑ Copy me on this invoice

[Send Invoice]

After you click this button, your buyer will be emailed an invoice.

Click "Send invoice" to the right of the item for which you need to send an invoice. This will display the invoice for this item.

Make additions or changes as needed and click "Send invoice."

(I've blocked out any personal information out of respect for my buyer's privacy.)

SENDING AN INVOICE—PAYPAL

If you have integrated your PayPal account into your eBay Selling, you can also send an invoice using PayPal.

Log in to *www.paypal.com,* click the "Auction tools" tab, and click the "End of auction email" link.

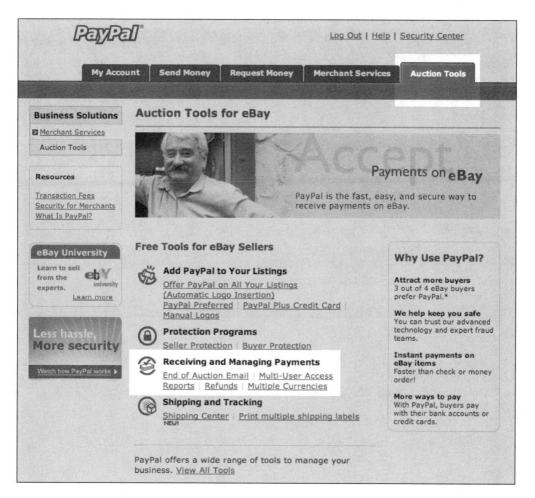

In the next window, select your eBay User ID from the drop-down box and select the "On" option for "Select your preferences . . ."

My Account	Send Money	Request Money	Merchant Services	Auction Tools

| Overview | Add Funds | Withdraw | History | Resolution Center | Profile |

End of Auction Email

How It Works

eBay automatically sends an End of Auction email to your winning buyers, informing them they've won your item and enabling them to pay you. You can customize this email for listings which offer PayPal as a payment method.

To customize your End of Auction emails, sign up and enter the information below or select an existing account.

eBay User ID: uncle_griff (eBay) ▼ Add

Your preference to customize End of Auction emails is currently **On**.

Select your preference to customize End of Auction emails:
⊙ On ○ Off

If you do not see your User ID in the drop-down box, click the "Add" link and follow the instructions for adding your User ID to your PayPal profile.

Scroll down the same page to the section Customize End of Auction Email.

Customize End of Auction Email

The email always includes item information, your payment instructions from the listing, as well as a **Pay Now** button. Create your custom message below. Use the AutoText drop-down menu to insert personalized information (such the buyer's User ID). If you sell internationally, be sure to add information about international shipping, handling, and insurance charges.

Customize Your Email Message
AutoText

[Buyer User ID ▾]   [Insert]

AutoText glossary   See message examples

> For more information on my shipping,
> insurance, and other policies, or if
> you would like to pay for this item
> with a method other than PayPal, please
> see the item listing for details.

2,000 character limit, no HTML   Reset to standard

Sample Email

(+) See a Larger View

Display Your Logo

Display your logo on your customers' payment pages by entering the URL of the image. Logo must be 310 X 90 pixels, 10 KB or smaller, in GIF, JPG, or PNG format, and on an unsecure server.

[http://]   [?]
Click here to test your logo

Receive a copy of End of Auction emails

☑ Send me a copy of the custom email when it's sent to a winning buyer.

[Submit]   [Cancel]

Here you can customize the end-of-auction e-mail with AutoText inserts for Buyer User ID, item number, item title, and so on. You can also type default text into the box provided. I have typed in the default text message for my buyers and inserted the appropriate AutoText for Buyer User ID and so on.

Receive a copy of End of Auction emails

☑ Send me a copy of the custom email when it's sent to a winning buyer.

Submit   Cancel

Mobile | Mass Pay | Money Market | ATM/Debit Card | Referrals | About Us | Accounts | Fees | Privacy |
Plus Card | Security Center | Contact Us | Legal Agreements | Developers | Shops |

I have checked the box for "Send me a copy . . ." Now, click the "Submit" button. This will store your customized invoice on PayPal and an automatic PayPal invoice will be sent out to all your winning bidders and buyers. Here is a copy of what a buyer will receive:

NOTES ON INVOICING A BUYER

As a professional eBay seller, you should always take the initiative and send any e-mails or invoices to your buyer immediately after the listing closes.

Nothing is less professional or more annoying to a buyer than receiving an e-mail invoice from a seller containing little or no information or instructions about what to do next. Even if you have stated all terms and instructions explicitly in your listing description, *repeat them in your invoice e-mails to bidders and buyers*. Some eBay members have bids out on ten, twenty, or more items and may not recall your payment options, instructions, or general terms. You have nothing to lose and everything to gain by repeating your complete list of terms and options for your buyer. Believe me, we eBay buyers *really* appreciate those sellers who do.

To this end, your e-mail invoice should contain all the information the buyer needs to complete his transaction obligations. This should include:

- All payment options with detailed instructions for each
- Links to payment services wherever possible
- Shipping options and costs
- Your full name, address, and phone number
- Any reminders regarding your terms of sale

Here is an e-mail sent by an eBay seller:

```
Congratulations!

You have won the bid on this item. The total is:

Bid:  $616.01
S&H:  $60.00
==================
      $676.01 Total


Please read the following notes about payment carefully:

++++++++++++++++++++++++++++++++++++++++++++++
We do not accept personal or business checks.
++++++++++++++++++++++++++++++++++++++++++++++

If you are a resident of state of Georgia please add 7% tax to Bid
amount.
If you have already made your payment just reply that you  have.

Thank you.

persianmasterpiece.com


=================================================
```

The seller omitted any payment instructions, which could hamper the buyer in completing the transaction.

Note that the PayPal invoice explained in the previous section contains a "Pay now" button, which makes the payment process easier for both buyer and seller.

A responsible bidder should and will respond to your e-mail invoice as quickly as she can. In fact, if you accept PayPal and have it fully integrated into your listing page, and if you have used set shipping rates with the Flat or Calculated shipping feature, you will find that many of your buyers will not wait for an invoice but will instead simply complete the transaction immediately, without further input from you.

However, in those cases where buyers are slow in responding, do not, I repeat, do not berate, lecture, or criticize them in an e-mail. Always, always, always maintain your professional poise and courtesy when corresponding with a customer.

If you need to send them, your payment reminders should be informative and polite, even if you are informing a customer that you are about to file an Unpaid Item alert.

Your nonresponsive, nonpaying buyer may eventually respond with either an apology or a diatribe. If you receive an apology, accept it and move on either with the transaction or, if necessary, with the Unpaid Item process. If you receive a diatribe, avoid responding with a diatribe of your own.

Buyers can find themselves in the most unexpected of circumstances. eBay seller Barry Lamb sent me this amusing tale:

> *In well over five thousand transactions on eBay, there's one that I'll always remember.*
>
> *I had a buyer purchase a set of car speakers from me. The first e-mail, where she replied to my congratulations e-mail, she wrote, "I can't pay you now, I have to go to the hospital." In her second e-mail, she wrote, "I'm having a baby, my boyfriend will send you the money." Her third e-mail: "My boyfriend is an idiot, he didn't send you no money." Then nothing for about four days, and then, "I have a 6½-pound baby boy, I'm sending it to you."*
>
> *Boy, was I glad when it was the payment showed up and not the baby.*

The rule in brief: There is never a reason or excuse for any seller to behave unprofessionally. You never know what the situation might be on the buyer's end!

ACCESSING PAYPAL PAYMENTS

One of the never-ending joys of selling on eBay and receiving payment through PayPal is how quickly you have the cash in your PayPal account. Buyers who pay with PayPal tend on average to pay faster than buyers who must send mailed payments (checks or money orders).

Once a buyer pays you with PayPal, your options are as follows:

Leave the Payment Proceeds in Your PayPal Balance

All payments made to your PayPal account sit in your PayPal balance until you act on them. Many sellers prefer to leave the bulk or even the entirety of their payments in their PayPal balance. Then they either use the funds to pay for items on eBay through other merchant PayPal accounts or access the funds through the special PayPal debit card (available to all qualified PayPal members).

Another benefit of leaving funds in PayPal: You can opt into the PayPal Money

Market Fund and possibly earn a return on your PayPal balance. To learn more about the PayPal Money Market fund and the PayPal Debit Card, click the "Help" link on the top of any PayPal page. Then click the "Features" folder in the Categories window and click the subfolder "Money Market or PayPal Debit Card."

Transfer the Proceeds (in Part or in Total) to a Bank Account

To transfer funds from PayPal to a bank account listed in your PayPal profile, log in to PayPal and click the "Withdraw" tab under the My Account tab on the top of the PayPal page.

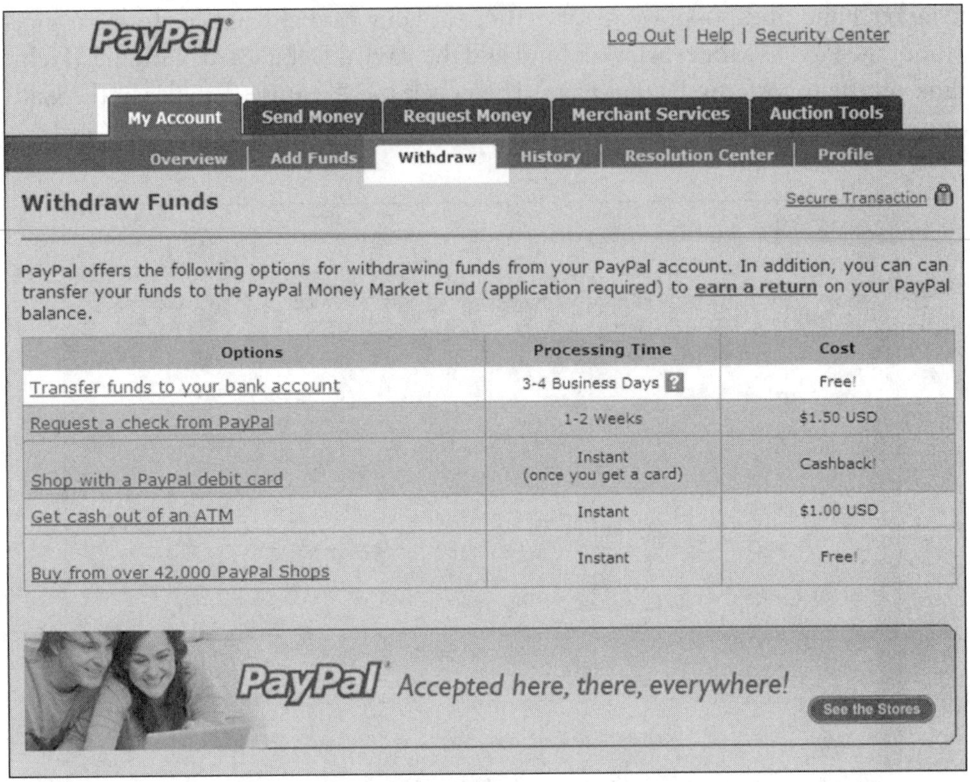

PayPal

Log Out | Help | Security Center

| My Account | Send Money | Request Money | Merchant Services | Auction Tools |

| Overview | Add Funds | Withdraw | History | Resolution Center | Profile |

Withdraw Funds

Secure Transaction

PayPal offers the following options for withdrawing funds from your PayPal account. In addition, you can can transfer your funds to the PayPal Money Market Fund (application required) to **earn a return** on your PayPal balance.

Options	Processing Time	Cost
Transfer funds to your bank account	3-4 Business Days ?	Free!
Request a check from PayPal	1-2 Weeks	$1.50 USD
Shop with a PayPal debit card	Instant (once you get a card)	Cashback!
Get cash out of an ATM	Instant	$1.00 USD
Buy from over 42,000 PayPal Shops	Instant	Free!

PayPal Accepted here, there, everywhere!

See the Stores

Click the option for "Transfer funds to your bank account." On the next screen, enter in an amount to transfer, and from the drop-down list select the bank account that will receive the funds.

PayPal®

Log Out | Help | Security Center

| My Account | Send Money | Request Money | Merchant Services | Auction Tools |

| Overview | Add Funds | **Withdraw** | History | Resolution Center | Profile |

Withdraw Funds by Electronic Transfer

Secure Transaction 🔒

Please indicate the amount you want to withdraw and which bank account to credit. Withdrawals from your PayPal account to your bank account must meet the minimum withdrawal amount.

It can take 3-4 business days to complete the transfer, depending on your bank's policies. You can get instant access to your funds with a PayPal Debit Card once you receive the card.

From This Balance: $0.00 USD

Amount: [   ]

To: [Bank Checking (Confirmed) XXXXX1887 ▼]

Add Bank Account

Note: If your bank information is incorrect, your withdrawal will be returned and a fee will be charged. See the fees table. Additional bank fees may apply. Please contact your bank directly regarding additional fees.

[Continue]

Mobile | Mass Pay | Money Market | ATM/Debit Card | Referrals | About Us | Accounts | Fees | Privacy |
Plus Card | Security Center | Contact Us | Legal Agreements | Developers | Shops |

NOTE: The transfer will be complete in three to four business days. Fund transfers from your PayPal account to a bank account are, by law, routed through the ACH (Automated Clearing House) Network—the same network that processes your written checks. PayPal is not responsible for the delay in clearing and cannot speed up or override this feature of the ACH system.

If your PayPal account has only a bank account attached as the sole funding method, all payments you receive in PayPal that are funded from a buyer's checking account will immediately show as "Pending" until the three to four days it takes for the funds to clear the ACH path. Pending funds are not available for use or transfer until they have cleared.

However, you can avoid the "Pending" status of a bank-account-funded PayPal payment by adding a credit card to your PayPal Premier or Business account. The credit card is used as backup insurance against any returned checks. In return, PayPal will credit your account balance immediately for any payments sent to you that were funded by a bank account. (Payments to your account that were funded by a credit card are always applied immediately to your balance.)

Leaving Feedback

If you are an eBay seller, chances are you will previously have received feedback as an eBay buyer. You know how important leaving feedback can be. As an eBay seller, you may find that many of your buyers are relatively new to eBay and do not quite understand how to leave feedback or, if they do, are not familiar with the protocol of leaving feedback.

Your eBay duty is to help educate your buyers on how eBay feedback works. eBay user Carolyn Lanzkron has an unusual but effective method for reminding her buyers about the importance of leaving feedback:

> *"I'm a new seller, and I'm hungry for feedback. I'm hoping my gimmick will help. In the package with the item I put a candy bar, with a wrapper that says, 'Thank you for making this eBay transaction such a sweet experience,' with my eBay ID. On the back of the candy bar, I put the following: 'Ulterior motive disclaimer: Now that I've fed you, I'm hoping that you'll feedback! (Pretty please?)'*

> *"I'm not sure how successful this will be, but the idea is to demonstrate that I'm willing to deliver more than was in the original bargain."*

Carolyn is going to be a very successful eBay seller. Not only is she giving a little extra gift to her buyers, she is showing by example how feedback works at eBay.

FEEDBACK—WHO LEAVES IT FIRST?

In the early days of eBay, the accepted protocol was for the seller to leave feedback immediately upon receiving payment. This has—unfortunately, I believe—changed. Many sellers wait until the buyer has left feedback before they will leave feedback in kind. I've been told by some of these sellers that this is a defensive strategy they employ to protect themselves in cases where a buyer leaves them negative feedback. By waiting, they are in a position to leave negative feedback in kind for the buyer. It is not against any eBay rules to practice this strategy, but I believe it is an unfortunate and misguided practice.

Consider: A buyer's transaction obligations to the seller end when she sends payment for the item. A buyer is not obliged to alert a seller that the item has arrived or that she is happy with the item (though it is definitely good eBay etiquette to do so). Thus, once the seller receives payment (the check has cleared, or the PayPal payment has been transferred to the seller's PayPal account, etc.) he should really leave appropriate feedback for the buyer . . . first. Interestingly, I have found that most sellers who do not receive feedback from their buyers also, as a rule, do not leave feedback first.

As for the buyer leaving the seller feedback, the seller's transaction obligations are not complete until the buyer has received the item and is satisfied with it. Only then should the bidder be expected to leave feedback.

FEEDBACK—WHAT SHOULD IT SAY?

You have eighty-five character spaces in which you may type a comment. If the bidder has paid for the item and sent payment quickly, make sure to mention this. Nothing makes a bidder happier than to have an eBay seller tell the world that he or she is quick to send payment.

Here are some samples:

"Excellent transaction. Buyer sent payment immediately."
"A reputable eBay buyer. Always pays fast and is cordial in e-mails. A+"
"Great to do business with! A definite asset to eBay! WE HIGHLY RECOMMEND!!!"
"Outstanding eBay buyer, sets the ultimate standard. Amazing!"

FEEDBACK—WHAT NOT TO SAY

As a seller, you may run into the occasional difficult customer. Unless the buyer has backed out of the sale, you should avoid leaving a negative feedback comment for paying customers. Instead, consider leaving feedback that is neutral or positive but subdued. The customer will get the message.

Either way, avoid using inflammatory language. Regardless of how much you believe the person deserves it, refrain in your feedback comment from calling a customer "a real jerk" or something equally pejorative. Why? Because calling someone "a jerk" or "an idiot" or worse in your feedback ends up reflecting more on you than the other party. Coarse language is unprofessional and will put potential customers off doing business with you.

Instead, use unemotional, reasoned comments to let the rest of the community know about the transaction. You have an unpleasant customer who nonetheless sent payment immediately? Leave a positive or, if really deserved, a neutral saying something like: "Some misunderstanding at first but it all worked out in the end. Thanks!"

or

"Very happy to have finally satisfied this customer. Thank you!"

If a bidder backs out for no reason or is unreachable via e-mail or phone, leave a neutral or negative with a comment along the lines of "Not a serious bidder. Recommend avoiding" or "Unable to contact buyer. Avoid their bids" or "Bidder refused to complete transaction."

Of course, in all these situations, the bidder can and just might leave you a neutral or negative in kind. Don't sweat it. Your calm and reasoned words will speak volumes about your integrity and professionalism. You can and will weather the occasional retaliatory negative comment. The only words you need to be concerned with are your own.

FUTURE CORRESPONDENCE WITH YOUR EBAY BUYERS

A good customer is an asset to an eBay seller. It's a smart strategy to keep good customers coming back to your eBay listings. A good way to do this is through a mailing list. There are, however, some important concerns to keep in mind about formulating mailing lists of your eBay customers.

Once another eBay member has purchased an item from you, you may, in your first e-mails to her, ask for her permission to add her to your mailing list for future eBay listings of interest. In fact, you mustn't add your eBay customers to your mailing list without their permission. You are also only allowed to e-mail your eBay winning bidders or buyers. You must never e-mail another seller's bidders with solicitations to bid on your items or requests for their permission to place them on your mailing list. These are serious rules at eBay. Breaking them can result in the suspension of your eBay registration!

Shipping

Our listing has ended and we have a high bidder. It's time to ship the item. The last item on the list of your seller obligations is sale fulfillment, that is, sending the item to the winning buyer.

The ultimate success of your eBay transaction depends on quick and secure fulfillment. How well you pack the item and how quickly you ship it can make all the difference in buyer satisfaction. The most common reasons for buyer-seller disputes are slow or seriously delayed shipping and items damaged in transit due to poor or inadequate packing.

WHEN TO SHIP

The standard protocol at eBay is for the seller to ship the item to the buyer once payment has been received and cleared. Most sellers wait for personal checks to clear before shipping. Nearly all sellers ship immediately upon receiving payment via PayPal, credit card, or money order.

Once you have received payment, it's your duty to get the item on its way to the happy buyer.

Speed is important. The most successful eBay sellers send the buyer's merchandise out the very day payment is received. The best sellers have the item packed before the listing has closed so that they can go into action the very second the payment is in their hands. For those bidders who pay via PayPal, this can be mere minutes after the listing has closed.

If you scan through the feedback comments for longtime eBay sellers, you will find that the most common praise is for fast or quick shipping. 'Nuff said?

PACKING SLIPS AND INVOICES

Using packing slips is one more step toward ensuring your item ships safely. In some instances, they are required. Regardless, providing a packing slip with the item shows that you are a true eBay professional.

As a bidder, I always appreciate those sellers who include a printout of the item page along with the item. Since I tend to buy a lot at eBay, a copy of the item page helps me to remember who sent the item, when I bought it, and how much I paid. In the case of similar items, I know to leave feedback for the correct seller.

SHIPPING LABELS

The outside of the package is the first thing your buyer is going to see. If you want to be perceived as a professional seller, make sure you use professional-looking shipping labels.

In the old days, eBay sellers had to create their own shipping labels either using a word processor or by hand. Now, any eBay seller can use the Print Label feature in My eBay. Go to My eBay > All Selling, Sold and check the item for which you wish to create and print a shipping label. Click "Print shipping labels," or click the button under "Action" and select "Print shipping label."

This will take you to PayPal. Log in to continue (use the same e-mail address that is connected to your eBay Seller's Account and registration).

Payments by **PayPal**

Print Shipping Labels with eBay & PayPal   See Demo

Simplify your shipping! eBay and PayPal have teamed up with the U.S. Postal Service and UPS to provide integrated shipping tools.

Now you can use your PayPal account to:

- Calculate shipping costs
- Buy and print shipping labels
- Track packages online

If you have never paid through PayPal,   Click Here

PayPal Login
If you already have a PayPal account, enter your log-in details below

Email Address: jimgr   net   Problems logging in?

PayPal Password: | Forget your password?

Continue   Back to eBay

The fields on the next page should fill in automatically. If not, type in the address and other information as requested.

PayPal®

Log Out | Help

My Account | Send Money | Request Money | Merchant Tools | Auction Tools

U.S. Postal Service - Print Your Label

See Demo

Create, purchase and print U.S. Postal Service® shipping labels from your PayPal account. Enjoy the affordable Postal Service rates without having to leave your desk.

Shipping tools with U.S. Postal Service are currently only available for transactions where both the sender's and recipient's addresses are in the United States.

Address Information

Ship From: Jim Griffith
Edit this Address   eBay Inc
2145 Hamilton Ave
San Jose, CA 95125
United States

Ship To: Jim Griffith

Address 1: eBay Inc

Address 2: 2145 Hamilton Ave
(optional)

City: San Jose

State: CA

ZIP Code: 95125   (5 or 9 digits)

Country: United States

Shipment Options

Shipment Options FAQ

Service Type: Parcel Post®   Choose a different shipper

Package Size: Package/Thick Envelope   Learn More About Package Sizes
☐ The packaging is irregular or unusual

Mailing Date: 1/17/2005

Weight: 1 lbs. ___ oz.

Label Printer: Laser/Ink Jet Printer Edit Printer Settings

Delivery Confirmation: $0.13 USD

Note: Delivery Confirmation is FREE with the purchase of Signature Confirmation.

Label Processing Fee: $0.20 USD

Signature Confirmation: ● Yes ($1.30 USD)   ○ No
Note: Signature of receipt is available upon request for Express Mail®.

Display Postage Value on Label: ☐

Email message to Buyer: (optional)

USPS® Insurance

USPS® Insurance FAQ

Purchase Insurance: ● Yes   ○ No

Insured value: 9.99   USD
Provides coverage up to $200.00 USD

USPS® Insurance, available at Post Office™ locations, provides coverage up to $5,000.00 USD Insurance purchased online cannot be combined with insurance purchased at a Post Office™. When I select **Continue** to purchase insurance, I agree that my package is not perishable, flammable, or too fragile to withstand normal mail handling.
Terms and Conditions

Item(s) Being Shipped to Your Buyer

Note: If you have multiple packages for this transaction, you can print multiple labels by clicking the **Ship multiple boxes for this order** link after creating the current label.

Item #	Item Title	Qty
4351318564	PS/2 Model 90 XP 486 Quick Reference & Guide	1

Continue   Cancel

Click "Continue" to move to the confirmation screen.

PayPal®

| My Account | Send Money | Request Money | Merchant Tools | Auction Tools |

U.S. Postal Service Shipping Confirmation

Please confirm your shipping details below. To make changes, click **Edit Shipment Details**. To process your order, click **Pay and Continue**. When you click the button, the Total Shipping Cost (below) will be deducted from your chosen source of funds. You will then be taken to a page where you can print the shipping label.

Address Information

Ship From: Jim Griffith
Edit this Address eBay Inc
2145 Hamilton Ave
San Jose, CA 95125
United States

Ship To: Jim Griffith
Edit this Address eBay Inc
2145 Hamilton Ave
San Jose, CA 95125
United States
Status: Unconfirmed address

Source of Funds

Instant Transfer: $5.61 USD from ▓▓▓▓▓▓▓▓▓▓▓XXXX1887
Back Up Funding Source: Visa XXXX-XXXX-XXXX-6921
More Funding Options

Shipment Details

Service Type:	Parcel Post®
Mailing Date:	1/17/2005
Package Size:	Package/Thick Envelope
Label Printer:	Laser/Ink Jet Printer[?]
Actual Weight:	1 lbs. 0 oz.
Package Cost:	$2.81 USD
Delivery Confirmation:	FREE
Label Processing Fee:	$0.20 USD
Signature Confirmation:	$1.30 USD
Display Postage Value on Label:	NO
Insured Value:	$9.99 USD
Insurance Cost:	$1.30 USD
Total Shipping Cost:	$5.61 USD

Edit Shipment Details

Item(s) Being Shipped to Your Buyer

Note: If you have multiple packages for this transaction, you can print multiple labels by clicking the **Ship multiple boxes for this order** link after creating the current label.

Item #	Item Title	Qty
4351318564	PS/2 Model 90 XP 486 Quick Reference & Guide	1

| Pay and Continue | Cancel |

United States Postal Service, the Eagle logo, and their combined form, as well as U.S. Postal Service, Parcel Post, Priority Mail, First-Class Mail and Express Mail, are registered trademarks, and Media Mail, Delivery Confirmation and Signature Confirmation are trademarks, owned by the United States Postal Service.

Double-check that everything is accurate. If you need to make changes, click the appropriate edit links. Do not navigate back one page or you will lose all the information and have to start all over from My eBay.

Once you are satisfied that everything is correct, click "Pay and continue." The next screen is a preview of your label.

Make sure your printer is set up and loaded with paper or printing labels.

 GRIFF TIP! There are self-adhesive labels that are perfect for printing out using the PayPal label feature. The USPS Click-N-Ship label is one option, but any eight-by-ten-inch single-label sheet should work.

When you are ready to print the item, click the "Print label" button. Once printing is complete, the browser will display a confirmation page with instructions for voiding labels in case of error.

PayPal®   Log Out | Help

| My Account | Send Money | Request Money | Merchant Tools | Auction Tools |

U.S. Postal Service Shipping Label Completed

Shipment Details

Shipping Method: Parcel Post®

Total Shipping Cost: $5.61 USD

Your **buyer** will receive an **email receipt** with a **tracking number**, to confirm that the item is being shipped. You will also receive an email for this transaction shortly.

Items Being Shipped to Your Buyer

Item #	Item Title	Qty
4351318564	PS/2 Model 90 XP 486 Quick Reference & Guide	1

Voiding a Shipping Label

You may request a refund for the shipping label you just created within the next **48 hours**, if necessary. To request a refund, click on the Void Label link in the <u>Transaction Details</u> page for this transaction, or in the Shipping Confirmation Email.

What do you want to do next?

- Reprint this label
- Ship multiple boxes for this order

Take advantage of these free shipping products and services!

- Request a <u>free carrier pickup</u> and the U.S. Postal Service® will pick up your package, or locate a <u>Post Office</u>™ and drop your package off yourself
- Order free U.S. Postal Service® <u>shipping supplies</u> online
- <u>Create a Packing Slip</u> instantly that summarizes your transaction and includes a personalized message to your buyer

[Account Overview]   [Back to eBay]

United States Postal Service, the Eagle logo, and their combined form, as well as U.S. Postal Service, Parcel Post, Priority Mail, First-Class Mail and Express Mail, are registered trademarks, and Media Mail, Delivery Confirmation and Signature Confirmation are trademarks, owned by the United States Postal Service.

GRIFF TIP! If you use plain paper, cut the printed sheet in half and keep the right-hand side as your receipt. You can then paste or tape the left-hand side onto your package. Use clear tape to fasten the plain-paper shipping label to your package, but make sure not to cover the bar-code area with tape. Tape can sometimes make the bar code unreadable, which could result in shipping delays (and consequently an unhappy buyer).

SHIPPING METHODS

Most of the items sold at eBay are small enough to pack and ship through one of the major delivery services:

> USPS (United States Postal Service)
> UPS (United Parcel Service)
> FedEx
> Others (DHL, etc.)

If you are planning on selling regularly, schlepping boxes back and forth to pickup locations could end up taking much of your day. You will want to open an account with either UPS or FedEx for regular pickup services and invoicing.

USPS does not provide accounts, but it does have a free pickup service. This covers an unlimited number of boxes. For pickup, your packages have to have postage prepaid and at least one of the packages has to be either a Priority Mail or Express Mail package. The USPS pickup service is available in most zip codes, but check its Web site for more information.

USPS offers two solutions for prepaid postage:

> Click-N-Ship (prints out postage over the Internet)
> Postage meters (prints out on a meter)

If you have a postage scale, you can purchase shipping postage over the Internet from USPS. Visit the USPS Web site for more information: *www.usps.com*. Look for the link for Click-N-Ship and follow the instructions from there.

Another postage option is to purchase or lease a postage meter. You then purchase postage by connecting the meter to a phone line, dialing a special number, and downloading postage directly to the meter. Visit the USPS Web site for more information: *www.usps.com* and *www.usps.com/postagesolutions*.

UPS is popular with high-volume sellers. UPS offers a regular pickup service and a wide range of shipping options. You can create an account on the UPS Web site, and just as with USPS, you can print UPS postage labels on your computer for your parcels so they are ready for pickup. UPS also has some shipping supplies. Visit its Web site for more information: *www.ups.com*.

FedEx is also a popular shipping option with online shipping tools similar to UPS. Account creation can be done on its Web site: *www.fedex.com*.

USPS, UPS, FEDEX . . . WHICH ONE SHOULD I USE?

The three major carriers are fairly competitive when it comes to fees and shipping services. Depending on your location and the type of items you sell, one of the three may work best for you.

Investigate each of the services thoroughly before you pick one. Or, as eBay seller Peter Cini advises, offer your customers *all* of them:

"Empower the customer by offering as many shipping options in your listing as is feasible for your business. Customers love options and it gives them a feeling of control over the outcome."

TOOLS AND SUPPLIES YOU WILL NEED FOR SHIPPING

You should have the following tools and supplies handy:

- Printer
- Postage scale adequate for parcels
- Yardstick or tape measure (to weigh and measure the dimensions of each parcel accurately)
- Clear packaging tape
- Packaging tape holder/dispenser
- Packing materials (bubble wrap, packing peanuts, excelsior, etc.)
- Boxes (different shapes and sizes)

CALCULATING COSTS

Nothing pleases customers more than knowing exactly what shipping costs will be *before* they bid. There are many ways to help customers determine costs quickly and accurately.

One option is simply to state flat shipping costs. Here is a table with shipping costs from an actual eBay listing:

Ship To Location	Shipping (USD)
US	$5
Canada	$8
UK	$10
All Others	$15

An even better option is to utilize the free eBay Shipping Calculator for indicating flat costs. Either way, flat shipping costs are an ideal solution for small, lightweight items. No calculations for the buyer or the seller to make, no possibility of confusion or mistakes.

GRIFF TIP! Keep your buyers happy! Provide estimated and flat rate shipping costs as accurately as possible.

Important: It is against eBay rules to inflate shipping costs past a reasonable amount (use common sense to determine what constitutes "reasonable"). In addition, your shipping costs cannot be based on the final price of your item; that is, you cannot employ a sliding scale or percentage of the final price to determine shipping.

For items weighing more than, say, a pound, use the free eBay Shipping Calculator to calculate rates. All you need is a scale to weigh the item and a tape measure to measure the dimensions of the package (for some shipping services).

INSURANCE

The best insurance is to overpack your item. Still, even the best-packed items can suffer damage (or worse, loss) in transit.

To safeguard the parcel, you should insure it with the carrier. In fact, you should make insurance mandatory for all your eBay sales. In your item description, state something along the lines of "All eBay item parcels will be insured for the selling price."

You can pay for the insurance yourself or state it as a buyer cost. Whatever option, always state it explicitly and clearly in your listing description!

Insurance costs should always be based on the selling price of the item, not its market value.

There are many ways to insure your packages. For example, USPS has several options. One is actual insurance. It also provides special delivery and delivery confirmation services to help ensure that the intended recipient receives your package:

> Certificate of Mailing
> Certified Mail
> Collect on Delivery (COD)

Delivery Confirmation
Insured Mail
Merchandise Return Service
Registered Mail
Restricted Delivery
Return Receipt
Return Receipt for Merchandise
Signature Confirmation
Special Handling

You can learn more about these services at the USPS Web site.

NOTE: Collecting on a shipping insurance claim isn't always easy. Each shipper has different criteria that must be met before a claim can be granted. Meet with an authorized representative of the shipping or carrier company and ask for specifics regarding their company's insurance and claims policies.

Keep all documentation regarding the item's condition and the security of the packaging and store them with your insurance and delivery confirmation receipts in a safe place.

CRATING AND FREIGHTING LARGE ITEMS

Furniture, machinery, appliances, farm equipment, autos, boats, Learjets . . . if your item is larger or heavier than the limits set by USPS, UPS, or FedEx, you will have to send it through a shipping company as freight. Don't let this discourage you! Many sellers routinely sell huge and heavy items on eBay. As long as they know the details before they bid or buy, savvy eBay buyers fully understand that they will foot the shipping and handling bill for larger items. Your duty as a seller is to fully research crating and shipping services in your location before you list a large item. Select those companies with the best reputations and prices, and list them in your item description. Start with the yellow pages under Shipping or Freight. Contact different freight companies and get good estimates or quotes for crating and shipping. Provide all of this information in your listing description.

Although it is not always the case, freight items usually need to be crated. Proper crating involves using wood and plywood to create a custom-built box large enough to ship the item safely. Unless you are a whiz with a power saw and don't mind hammering a crate together, you'll probably do better handing this chore off to a professional crater/shipper.

NOTE: If your item is too large to ship via standard post or delivery and thus will need to be crated for freight, make certain you state this in your item description!

You can usually obtain a good estimate of crating and shipping costs from a local freight company by describing the item's size and weight. You can then pass this information along to potential buyers by including it in your item description.

Several crating and shipping companies have Web sites for calculating costs. For example, see Craters and Freighters at *www.cratersandfreighters.com.*

In addition, on eBay one can now visit the Freight Resource Center at *http://ebay.freightquote.com.*

In fact, make it a point to visit the Shipping Center as well. It's easy to reach from the Site Map. Just look for the "Shipping Center" link under Selling Resources:

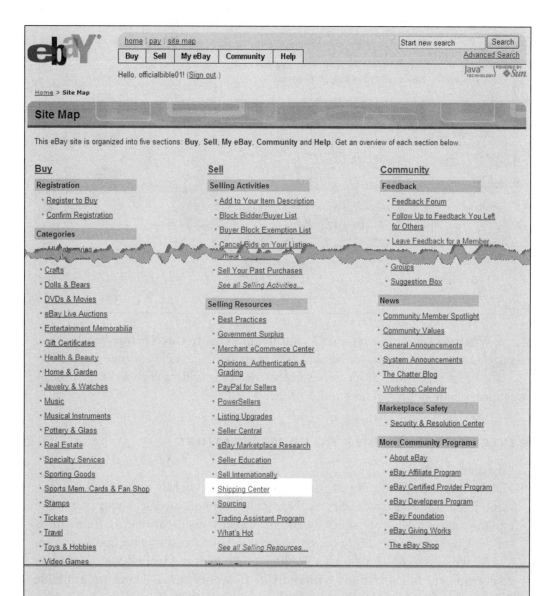

Click it to reach this page:

Whatever the size or weight of your item, do the research before you list, and provide as much information about cost, companies, and delivery time as possible.

It bears repeating: You can never provide your bidders with too much information about shipping costs and options.

INTERNATIONAL SHIPPING CONSIDERATIONS

Customs

For the most part, shipping an item overseas is only slightly more involved than shipping within the United States. Normally, shipping overseas will cost more and take longer. All other shipping and insurance considerations are the same as for the United States, except you may have to fill out a customs declaration form.

As the sender of an item to a country other than the United States, you are responsible for filling out any required U.S. Customs forms. These are available at any post office or from the carrier of your choice (UPS, FedEx, etc.). You can also download the appropriate forms directly from each of the above carriers' Web sites.

Make sure you fill out all forms accurately and honestly. Sometimes an international bidder will ask you to fudge a customs declaration in order to save on duty (which is paid by the package recipient). Don't do it. If a customs official decides to open your package for inspection and determines that your declaration is intentionally inaccurate, you could find yourself in hot water with customs (and customs could also confiscate the item).

In fact, it would be prudent for all eBay sellers to state clearly in their Terms of Service exactly who is responsible for paying any customs duties. Sellers should also state that they will not falsify a customs declaration under any circumstances.

In fact, for all international shipments of items sold on eBay, you should print out the item description page showing a photo of the item and the actual sold price or high winning bid. Include the printout in the customs envelope along with the necessary customs forms. This will not only help speed your package through customs but also make it less likely that customs officials will need to open the package for inspection.

Tracking for International Shipping

Sellers should always utilize whatever tracking services a particular carrier offers. FedEx, UPS, and DHL offer the most robust and thorough tracking and delivery confirmation services for overseas shipping, but they are often more expensive than USPS.

If the item you are shipping to an overseas location is valued at more than a few hundred dollars, you may want to ship it via FedEx, UPS, or DHL. The costs for these services are usually higher than USPS, but in a case of nondelivery, damage in transit, or loss in transit, you will stand a better chance of weathering a complaint listed by the buyer if you have full tracking and insurance to prove that the item was in fact sent and at least delivered to some location after it left you.

Insurance for International Shipping

If you are shipping a valuable item overseas, you should make sure the item is fully insured for the value as indicated on eBay as the "sold" price. As stated above, you should include in the customs envelope a printout of the listing page showing the sold price on eBay. This will help facilitate any possible claims you may need to file with the carrier.

Import and Export Restrictions

Although the vast majority of items sold on eBay are not restricted for sale to most countries around the world, there are certain types of items that are either restricted or in some cases prohibited. It is important to learn about import and export restrictions and prohibited items for international shipments.

Each shipping carrier has a page on its Web site that explains what is and isn't allowed for export out of the United States to specific countries. For example, the UPS Web site has an excellent page called Verify for Export.

You can reach it by going to *www.ups.com*. Select your country from the drop-down list. Click the "Support" tab on the top of the screen. Click through the following links from the menu on the left-hand side of the Support page: "Global Advisor > Ship Internationally with UPS > Quick-Reference Guide for Avoiding Delays > Verify for Export."

FedEx also has an excellent page with information at *http://www.fedex.com/ us/promo/regulatoryupdate.html*.

These last few chapters have covered the eBay selling basics necessary for every seller—part time to full time. The next chapter will help you find ways to build and grow your eBay business.

5

eBay Business Tips and Tools

Owning and running your own business—what could be more exciting or more fulfilling? How many times have you dreamed of being your own boss? Who among us hasn't come this close to marching up to that boorish supervisor to announce, "I quit"?

Many new eBay sellers began as eBay buyers who started a small eBay selling business out of a room of their home. Still other eBay sellers are self-employed business owners who have moved a part or all of their off-line business online through eBay. Whether you already own a business or are starting a new business, using eBay for some or all of your business will help that business grow.

Of course, there are risks. No one can guarantee that every new business venture will be a raging success, but there are potential rewards aplenty for those who at least give it a try.

Here's a simple checklist of the things you will need in order to take your eBay selling from an occasional pastime to a real part-time or full-time business:

- ✔ A business structure
- ✔ Product(s) to sell
- ✔ A place from which to sell (a business location)
- ✔ Computer and office equipment (a computer, digital camera, printer, desk, shelving, lights, etc.)
- ✔ A bookkeeping system
- ✔ Office and packing supplies (tape, peanuts, boxes, printing paper, etc.)

The first step is to determine the optimum structure for your eBay business.

Business Structures for eBay Sellers

No business can grow if it cannot be managed. No business can be managed if it cannot be measured. For your eBay business to be properly measured, it will need an appropriate business structure.

The short list of possible structures:

> Sole proprietorship
> Partnership
> Corporation

Each option has its advantages and disadvantages. A partnership may be perfect for some businesses, whereas a corporation may be ideal for others. How do you determine which business structure is right for you? You should always get professional advice before making any decision as to how you set up your business. For a start, the Internet is a great place to get accurate and helpful information quickly (and without cost) if you stick with trusted Web sites. For example, look for more information about business structures on the IRS Web site, *www.irs.gov.* Hey, it's the IRS. How could they be wrong? In the search box provided on the IRS home page, try searching for Publication 334: Tax Guide for Small Business. Read the introduction page for links to publications for partnerships, corporations, S corporations, direct selling, and record keeping.

In addition, check out the Small Business Administration Web site at *www.sbaonline.sba.gov.* Specifically, look for the SBA Small Business Startup Kit.

For more specific information about corporations, try the National Business Incorporators Web site at *www.nationalbusinessinc.com.*

"But Griff," I hear you say, "I've only just started to figure out how to list on eBay. Isn't it a bit premature for me to start thinking of business concerns?"

No. It is never too early to plan. Too many people on this planet (eBay sellers included) seem to live their lives based on the "planning to plan" plan. That is, they continually put off taking action on matters such as losing weight, building that addition to the house, taking that trip to Italy, or, for our purposes, setting up a business on eBay. Sure, figuring out how eBay works and listing your first item on eBay can seem overwhelming enough. Why else would you have bought this book? Certainly it's too early to become the CEO of your own company.

No, it isn't. In my experience, people who think "success" eventually realize success. You have to imagine your business on eBay and then start building it, from this very moment. Now. Right this minute.

Motivated? Good. Let's continue.

THE ADVANTAGES OF INCORPORATION
VS. SOLE PROPRIETORSHIP

You should contact a business consulting expert or tax attorney for all your specific business structure and incorporation questions.

The majority of regular sellers on eBay operate as sole proprietors. No surprise. In lieu of an actual business structure such as a corporation (or even a partnership), a business is, by default, a sole proprietorship.

Here is a perfect example of where the majority is not necessarily right. A sole proprietorship may have its upside, but anyone operating as a sole proprietor needs to understand the pitfalls of doing so.

The primary advantage of a corporation business structure is protection against liability. Let's face it—we are probably the most litigious society that has ever graced this planet. If you operate your business on eBay as a sole proprietor, you may be exposed to damages in a lawsuit brought against you by another party. For example, if a buyer or another seller or even someone from outside of eBay should ever name you as a party in a lawsuit and you are operating as a sole proprietor, both your business and your personal assets may be at risk of seizure or forfeiture if a court should issue a judgment in the plaintiff's favor. However, incorporation can protect your personal assets in the event of a judgment against your business. This is because the corporation's assets (cash, real estate, securities, accounts payable, etc.) do not include your personal property and assets such as your car, your house, your bank account, and other personal property. Your personal property is considered separate from the property and assets of your incorporated business.

A second advantage of incorporation over sole proprietorship is organization and efficiency. No matter what form your business takes, keeping your personal and business finances and assets separate is crucial to the survival of your business. Remember the maxim stated earlier: "No business can grow if it cannot be managed. No business can be managed if it cannot be measured." If your business and personal finances are intertwined, it will prove difficult and eventually impossible to sort them out to the satisfaction of, say, banks and other financial institutions where you might be applying for business loans (or worse, to the satisfaction of Uncle Sam on April 15).

A third advantage: saving money. There are myriad instances where, as a corporation, you may be able to save on business costs—savings that might otherwise be unavailable to you as a sole proprietor. For example, business equipment amortization IRS allowances and schedules are generally more favorable for corporations than for individuals (i.e., sole proprietors). Also, financial institutions tend to give more favorable credit and lending rates to corporations as opposed to individuals.

These are only general points to keep in mind. For specific advice regarding your business and incorporation needs, you should contact a tax attorney.

COSTS OF INCORPORATION

There are costs associated with incorporating your business. They vary depending on where you incorporate and who assists you in the process. If you have never incorporated a business, you may want to consult with a tax attorney. There are forms to fill out and file with state agencies. There are also fees for filing the forms. Incorporating should not be attempted as a do-it-yourself project. Don't risk making a mistake by doing it yourself. Hire an expert and do it right the first time. Remember, the cost of consulting a tax attorney is probably deductible as a business expense at tax time. Oh, and while we are on the subject . . .

A FEW WORDS ABOUT TAXES

Pay them.

All kidding aside, first let me state that I am not a tax attorney and that everything I tell you in this section is from my perspective as a citizen taxpayer and does not necessarily represent the actual word of the law.

You should contact a tax accountant or tax attorney for all your tax liability questions.

Sorry to bring you down after giving you such a great pep talk a page ago, but "What about taxes?" is one of the top five questions I am asked by new and experienced eBay members alike. Now that we have that little disclaimer out of the way, let me dispel a popular and rather distressing myth: There is no such thing as an exemption from tax reporting for "hobby selling," on eBay or anywhere else.

Contrary to the beliefs of some eBay members with whom I have spoken in the past six years, all businesses and individuals—big or small, successful or not, online and off-line—must report their income to the IRS (and possibly their state and even their city or county). Yes, eBay seller, that means you! In fact, even if you sell only one thing this year, you are by law required to report the income of that sale on your state and federal tax returns.

This doesn't mean that you will necessarily owe taxes on that sale. However, unless your relish risking the unique and exquisite instrument of torture otherwise known as an audit, and the ensuing wrath of the IRS—heavy fines and penalties, and even possible jail time—you'd better make darned sure that all of your eBay sales are reported to Uncle Sam.

Now, wipe the sweat off your brow and let's get back to our discussion on business structures.

Different business structures use different forms for reporting income from sales. Most sole proprietorships fill out a Schedule C (Profit and Loss) along with their regular Form 1040. Partnerships use IRS Form 1065. Corporations must use Form 1120. Some eBay sellers will have to pay their taxes in quarterly estimated installments, depending on their past tax liabilities.

Does all of this sound confusing? Don't worry. It is confusing. That's why I strongly suggest that all new or existing eBay business owners educate themselves about their tax reporting and filing responsibilities. You can get helpful information on the Web sites listed in this chapter, and of course you should always contact a tax attorney and an accountant.

YOUR STATE SALES AND INCOME TAX DEPARTMENT WEB SITES

Depending on the state where your business is located, you may be responsible for charging, collecting, reporting, and sending in sales tax. In addition, some local municipalities levy business or inventory taxes or require local businesses to be licensed. How do you determine if you are responsible for collecting sales tax and possibly other taxes? What are your licensing requirements? Most state government Web sites supply all this information along with the necessary forms and applications.

What is your state's tax Web site? I found this handy URL: *www.taxsites .com/state.html*. Find the site for your state sales tax department and read up. Or you can look up the phone number for your state tax department in your local yellow pages.

If your state has a sales tax, you may have to apply for a state tax resale number. You would then collect sales tax for all eBay sales made to buyers who are residents of your state as well as in any state in which your business has a "nexus" or business office, store, warehouse, or agent.* Depending on your state, you may have to file sales tax returns monthly, quarterly, or yearly. You may also have to send the collected sales taxes to the state sales tax department.

Finally, if your business on eBay is not new but is, in fact, established and growing and you are uncertain as to your sales and income tax liabilities and responsibilities, you should contact a local tax accountant for assistance immediately. It is money well spent.

EBAY MAIN STREET

The eBay marketplace may be the fastest-growing marketplace in history. Many have taken notice of this fact, including other marketplaces, some of which have petitioned their local and state governments and even the federal government for protection or sanctions against fast-growing marketplaces such as eBay.

eBay's Government Relations team has created a project called eBay Main Street, a Web page where eBay buyers and sellers can learn about recent state and federal legislative initiatives that could impact their business and buying on eBay. Go to *www.ebaymainstreet.com.*

---

* Currently, a seller on eBay is not responsible for paying sales tax to states in which they do not reside or do not have a business nexus. However, several states are working together to pass an initiative known as the Streamlined Sales Tax Project. As currently written, the Streamlined Sales Tax would negatively impact most eBay sellers in the United States. To learn more about this and other important government issues of concern to all eBay buyers and sellers, visit the eBay Main Street site, the link to which can be found in the next section, "eBay Main Street."

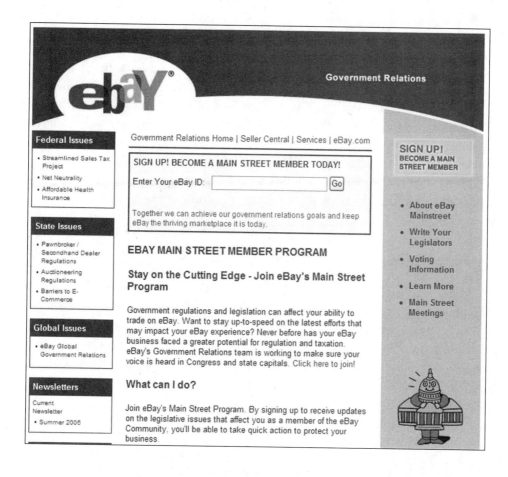

Take a moment to visit eBay Main Street and learn what is happening in the world of e-commerce and legislation and what you can do to make your voice heard by your local government representatives.

What to Sell?

It's a common question: "I want to start a business online at eBay but I don't know what to sell."

The possibilities are practically endless. Just about anything you can think of has a potential market on eBay. Many new sellers come to eBay knowing exactly what products they want to sell. Having a product source in place before you start on eBay certainly gives you an advantage. But for those who don't have a product in mind, don't let this stop you. Start listing items from your possessions until you figure out exactly what your niche will be. The worst possible strategy is paralysis. So dig out stuff to list on eBay, and while you are busy photographing, describing, listing, packing, shipping, and leaving feedback, you may find yourself creating a niche or selling a product line you might otherwise never have even considered.

It pays to like, or even love, what you sell—to have a "feel" for it. Although it is possible to be successful selling a line of wares for which you have absolutely no passion, where's the fun in that? So let's start off by asking some questions: What type of merchandise interests you? Do you collect? If so, what do you collect?

Many of the more successful eBay sellers I meet in my travels started out as buyers or collectors at first and then started selling on eBay, either out of sheer interest or by necessity. Unless you are filthy rich, collecting as a full-time pastime tends to deplete one's resources rather quickly. To keep collecting, many collectors are compelled to sell off lesser pieces of their collection. Soon they find themselves bona fide dealer/sellers.

Many eBay sellers don't start out as collectors per se—they might just enjoy shopping at tag or garage sales, picking up items along the way because they are new and cheap or unusual.

If nothing comes to mind or if you don't collect or have a fancy for certain types of merchandise but you are determined to be a market force on eBay, then you will need to start researching the supply-and-demand situation both on eBay and in your local area.

What types of items are readily available in your locale? For example, Vermont is home to the world's best maple syrup (sorry, Canada—Griff's a Vermont boy at heart). Maple syrup is usually cheapest and most plentiful in New England, but it can be extraordinarily difficult to find in other parts of the world. Some savvy Vermont maple syrup producers have realized this and have started offering their maple harvest on eBay with great results. Does that mean that you should start selling maple syrup on eBay? Not necessarily. A little sleuthing on eBay may show serious competition in the maple syrup business. I searched on *maple syrup*, and many more sellers are offering this product now compared with when I wrote the first edition of this book.

ENTERING AN ESTABLISHED EBAY CATEGORY

So you research eBay and find that lots of sellers are offering items similar to those that you were planning to sell on eBay. Should the threat of competition stop you? It should give you pause, of course. Competitive markets are not always easy to join. But the possibility of stiff competition in an established eBay market niche or category should not prevent you from trying to enter that market if:

✔ You are the type of person who enjoys and relishes competing.
✔ You fully understand and accept the risks inherent to business competition.
✔ You are ready to match and beat the competition at their own game.
✔ You are the type of person who relishes a good fight.

If you are planning to sell in a highly competitive category (jewelry, for example), you need to follow a game plan that includes (but is not limited to) the following aspects:

Watch Your Competitors

Visit their listings every day! Check their pricing strategies, their special promotions. Sometimes the tipping point for a buyer considering two similar items can be as simple as a few cents difference in shipping fees. Or better photos. Or clearer Terms of Service. Or even just the friendlier tone or more professional look of one seller's description. Visit your competition every day, note what they are doing, and go back to your listings and make yours better, more appealing, and more successful than theirs.

Never Stop Hunting for Better Sources of Product

If your products come from a wholesaler, keep searching for other sources, even if you are happy with your current source. Business is dynamic. Sources that are good today can dry up tomorrow, leaving you in the lurch. The best insurance is to have a second or even third or fourth possible source that you can rely on if your current source grows unreliable or, heaven forfend, disappears.

Expand Your Product Line and Lines

You sell one thing on eBay that no one else sells. Let's call it a doohickey. You have established and cornered the doohickey market on eBay. You are riding high, living large, buying property. Congratulations! Now, just how long do you think you can keep the top-dog position in the doohickey market? Do you think other sellers aren't figuring out how successful doohickeys have been for you? Make no mistake: When it comes to business, the wolves are always at the door. They are watching your eBay listings every day, ready to pounce without warning, unleashing a torrent of doohickeys on eBay at even lower prices! With free shipping! And quantity discounts! (What? Do you think you are the only eBay seller reading this book?) The problem with a sudden torrent of doohickeys is that they tend to flood a marketplace with oversupply, which subsequently satiates demand, which subsequently lowers prices, which subsequently lowers your bottom line.

Don't panic. You can ensure your survival with two strategies.

First, expand your product line beyond doohickeys. Find a product that is related to doohickeys and start offering it on eBay. Let's look at specific examples. You sell jewelry, specifically imported jewelry from a closely guarded source. That is all you sell. No one else sells the type of jewelry that you do. The market is all yours, for now. But competition in the eBay jewelry market can be tough and someone will eventually discover your source.

Before that happens, add to your product line. Perhaps you should start offering jewelry cleaning products or jewelry boxes or display cabinets. Maybe they are custom-made! Or maybe you add watches or other pieces to your eBay jewelry listings. Now, when someone searches for *diamond ring cleaner*, she finds your diamond cleaner, and follows the links in your eBay listing to your eBay Store, where all of your items are on full display, including a ring she is just mad for.

Or, even more drastic, you start adding new product lines that are completely unrelated to jewelry. Garden supplies! They all live in your eBay Store. Someone searching for a trowel spots one of your diamond rings, and before you know it, you've sold a trowel and a ring. (What? You don't wear your jewelry while gardening? You never know who might stop by for tea.)

Seek Out Market Trends Outside of Ebay

The eBay marketplace reflects the world at large, especially when it comes to trends. Starting with Beanie Babies back in 1996, eBay sellers have been extraordinarily savvy when it comes to predicting the next hot market. Don't keep your head buried in eBay. Subscribe to trade publications and attend trade shows that relate to your product line. Search for news of upcoming new products.

In fact, search out new products before they are released and make deals to purchase them in bulk prior to public release. That's what hundreds of eBay sellers did with the first release of the Sony PlayStation 2 a few years ago. They "knew" the new PlayStation would be a hot item; that is, they bet on their intuition about the new device's appeal to gamers, and they committed to purchase as many units as they could from retailers across the country before the actual game consoles hit the stores. I talked to several sellers who wrote checks to retail store managers for several thousand dollars, buying up the store's entire allotment of PlayStation 2 consoles before the public could get them. The result? For about three months prior to the holidays that year, the only place you could purchase a PlayStation 2—the hottest new toy on the market that year— was on eBay. Prices soared. Sellers were the beneficiaries of the craze and shortage.

GRIFF TIP! Want to know what's hot on eBay right now? Visit eBay Pulse at *http://pulse.eBay.com.*

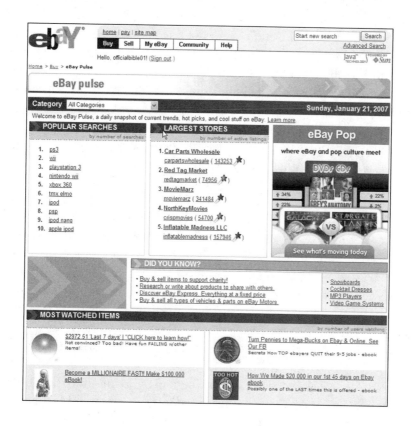

At eBay Pulse, you can see the current top ten most popular search terms on eBay. This list provides an excellent snapshot of what eBay buyers are looking for.

By the way, the PlayStation 2 craze didn't last. Crazes never do. That's why they call them crazes, because, just like a long night of carousing, the "craze" wears off and people come to their senses. ("Twenty-five hundred dollars for a two-hundred-dollar game console? What was I thinking?") By spring of the following year, you could find lots of PlayStation 2 consoles on eBay at no more than $250 each. That leads us to our next item.

Prepare for the End of a Market Trend

Risks are always inherent in any marketplace strategy, and the same holds true for eBay strategies. If the trend subsides before your supply does, you could end up holding a lot of doohickeys that no one wants. Thus, timing is everything. You may ride the crest of a trend to great selling success, but you can still end up with too much product as the trend subsides.

How do you best avoid winding up with useless or devalued inventory? Easy! Just remember this rule: The best time to sell is when you have a buyer.

At the height of the trend, sell as much of your inventory on eBay as possible, even at prices lower than the going price (as long as you are still making a viable profit). Your competitors may realize greater per-unit profit than you do, but the equation could change if they end up with units that don't sell.

Later, as the market for your items cools, keep selling, even if it means lowering your sell price to the point where you are taking a loss on some of the items. If you still have a market—that is, if you have buyers—sell the items. Sell. Sell. Sell. Whatever happens, do not wait for the market to rise again. Sitting with devalued inventory can be deadly. The longer it sits, the more it costs you. Unless you have invested in items that are traditionally viewed as having a long-term gain in value, such as expensive fine art or antique furniture or rare collectibles and memorabilia, your unsold inventory can kill your business. Get what cash you can out of dying inventory so you can reinvest it in new stock, new stock that, if you plan and market properly, can realize enough profit to offset any loss you sustained in unloading the old inventory.

All this sounds risky, doesn't it? Business is by its nature risky. If it weren't risky, everyone and her mother would be running a successful business with no worries or cares. But don't let the threat of risk paralyze you into not trying. Make your first move! Get that first listing up! Remember, first movers are not always winners, but most winners were first movers.

Be Gone, Inefficient Markets . . . eBay to the Rescue!

In the old days before eBay, sellers had to rely on traditionally inefficient markets to sell and liquidate inventory. Take the antiques business, for instance. My partner and I used to be in the antiques business. I remember once in the late 1970s we found ourselves needing a quick cash infusion. We had a lot of valuable stock. In the summer show season, we could have sold it all quickly to collectors for big bucks, but it was midwinter in New England—stormy, dark, and icy. With no other viable avenues of quick liquidation, we loaded up our pickup truck the next morning with choice items from our inventory and drove four hours to a well-known auction house that took consignments up to and during the day of sale. Luckily for us, a sale was scheduled for that evening. After unloading our truck, we grabbed a cup of coffee, took our seats, and watched in horror as our merchandise sold for pennies on the dollar. Normally, this auction house would have been teeming with other dealers and collectors, but the weather had kept them away. I would rather have forgotten this humiliating and depressing experience, thank you, but I dredge it up now to make a point. All this happened before the Internet and eBay. This was the time of creaking, inefficient, and unfair marketplaces where buyer and seller found each other in a hit-or-miss process with great expenditures of time, gasoline, money, and mental health. Sometimes you hit, sometimes you broke even, and many times you lost.

That's the beauty of eBay the marketplace. Reaching it doesn't require driving. It doesn't matter where you live, East Coast, West Coast, Ivory Coast, Amalfi coast . . . eBay is always only a few clicks of the mouse away. And it's always open, twenty-four hours a day, seven days a week, all year long. Best of all, eBay's scope is not limited to a single trading location or commodity-market bullpen. eBay is literally everywhere there is an Internet connection. In offices, homes, and hot spots across the planet, at any given moment, millions of eBay buyers are online, with cash at the ready, eager to buy, regardless of the day of the week, time of day, or even the weather. In fact, business on eBay is usually booming when the weather is at its worst. It only makes sense; where else can one go when the weather outside is too frightful for driving? Might as well hunker down with a cup of hot coffee, fire up the old PC, and browse eBay.

FINDING PRODUCT

A few years back, I met a woman in the Midwest who lived close to a factory that made maternity clothing. Many manufacturers routinely offer their seconds at bargain prices or, worse, toss them into the Dumpster. Most discarded seconds have fairly noticeable flaws, but many of the seconds tossed out are guilty of one or two practically imperceptible imperfections. Where the manufacturer saw throwaways, this plucky woman saw opportunity. She arranged with the manufacturer to purchase all of their seconds at mere pennies on the dollar. She then carefully sifted through the lots, culling those items whose flaws were inconsequential. She then offered the merchandise at eBay, as seconds, and soon made a viable business out of the venture.

You may not be as lucky as this woman. You may not live near an untapped source of practically free product. Even if you did, it would most definitely dry

527

up over time. Finding good product to sell on eBay involves a combination of hard work, sleuthing, experimenting . . . and luck and timing. Many eBay sellers travel the globe in search of good product at attractive prices. Some actually succeed. Others come up with an idea for a product, patent the idea, find a manufacturer, and start listing the items on eBay, all the while doing what they can to market and promote their new item on eBay.

GRIFF TIP! Many sellers find product in the most unusual places, for example, unclaimed merchandise from self-storage bins. The owners of self-storage companies hold auctions to liquidate unclaimed or abandoned storage bin contents. (They also liquidate the contents of bins whose renters have become seriously delinquent in rent payments.) Buyers usually cannot look through or examine the contents of the bins—they must bid for the stuff blind. It is a risky proposition but one that can pay off handsomely if the contents turn out to be treasure.

OFFLINE PRODUCT SOURCES

There are literally thousands of sources for product offline. Here are some good starting points.

Classifieds

Your city's newspaper classified section will usually have notice of any local liquidation or closeout sales.

Yard, Tag, Estate Sales

This is where many of us got our start selling on eBay. In fact, on any given Saturday across the United States, there are armies of eBay sellers trolling yard and tag sales looking for affordable product to sell on eBay. The competition can be fierce, but that doesn't discourage some of us (yes, I still hunt sales occasionally) from trying. The hunt is part of the appeal!

Auctions

Look online for locations of off-line government and police auctions. A good place to start: *www.policeauctions.com.*

Public Storage

Public storage companies routinely sell off the contents of abandoned bins or bins where the renter has gone into serious arrears with the monthly rental payments. Search Google or Yahoo for *public storage auctions*.

Trade Shows

Wholesaler trade shows are an excellent solution for finding new and unusual products. There are several well-known, regularly scheduled trade shows, but none bigger or more well known than the ASD/AMD shows held by the Merchandise Group. Visit *www.merchandisegroup.com* for more information.

Other Countries

Fabrics from India, silver jewelry from Thailand, toys from China, crafts from Africa, food products from Italy . . . yes, that's right, some of the best sources for new and unusual product are beyond the borders of the United States. Of course, a trip abroad takes time and money, but if it is a business trip, you might be able to write off most if not all of the expenses incurred as business expenses. (And have a great time as well!)

Manufacturers

This is one option few sellers consider. Instead of dealing with middlemen, why not simply contact directly the manufacturer of a specific product that you are interested in reselling on eBay? The steps are easy. Locate the phone number for the sales department of the particular manufacturer. Call them and inquire about setting up a purchase account to buy in bulk. Have at the ready your sales tax resale number and your federal tax ID. One trick for cold calls: Let the person in sales with whom you are dealing know that you are interested in a cash account, as opposed to setting up a credit account. It is usually easier to get a foot in the door as a new, unknown account if your arrangement with the sales department is on a cash basis. Later, after you have established a working relationship with Sales, you can, if needed, request an application for opening a credit invoice account.

FINDING PRODUCT SOURCES ON THE INTERNET (AND EBAY)

Yes, it is still possible to find great sources of product on the Internet. In fact, you can find product to sell on eBay . . . on eBay. eBay provides a new top-level category called Wholesale, available from the eBay home page.

Many eBay sellers find products to sell by browsing the Wholesale category. More and more wholesalers and liquidators are listing bulk quantities of items in this category: DVDs, home building supplies, business and industrial equipment, health and beauty items, cell phones, jewelry, computers, consumer electronics . . . the eBay Wholesale category is chock-full of potential inventory for resale on eBay.

Another recently introduced wholesale source is called Reseller Marketplace. In order to buy in this special forum, you must be an eBay PowerSeller. (Sellers who sell at least $1,000 a month over three months and who meet specific feedback and member qualifications are invited to join the eBay PowerSeller program. The full list of qualifications for and the benefits of the PowerSeller program are outlined in detail later in this section.) However, anyone with bulk product can sell in this forum. Learn more at *http://reseller.ebay.com*.

Another trick to finding product wholesale on the Internet is to use the word *pallet* and a product name to search Google, Yahoo, and other search engines. For example, try searching Google using *pallet shoes*. You will find thousands of results! Other words to use: *liquidation, liquidators, closeout, closeouts*.

DROP SHIPPERS AND OTHER SUPPLIERS

Many sellers offer items on eBay that are drop-shipped to the buyer. That is, the seller has made an arrangement with a wholesaler or manufacturer to purchase items they actually never take possession of. Instead, the seller lists the items on eBay, and the wholesaler or manufacturer drop-ships the item directly to the winning buyer. Although there are many obvious advantages to a drop-shipping arrangement (no warehousing of inventory, no fulfillment and shipping tasks, etc.), there are also many potential pitfalls as well. Any seller entering into a drop-shipping arrangement must be fully aware of the possible downsides.

For one, if the quality of the items suddenly dips or if the drop shipper's delivery times start to lag seriously (or if the drop shipper suddenly stops fulfilling eBay purchases), it's your reputation and account status that are on the line, not the drop shipper's.

Still, for some sellers, the drop shipper option can work.

Finding Reliable Drop Shippers and Suppliers

Literally thousands of sellers are seeking out undiscovered or underutilized drop shippers around the world. This is not to say that you won't find a good drop shipper—just be prepared for a potentially long hunt. A few well-known drop-shipping-resource Web sites offer to help connect a seller with a drop shipper.

In addition, many businesses that offer drop-shipping services have joined the eBay Solutions Directory. You can reach the directory by clicking the "Site map" link on the top of any eBay page. Look there for the link for the eBay Solutions Directory.

What to Avoid

Searching Google for *drop shipper* will bring up over a hundred thousand sites. Surely they can't all be reliable. Whenever you are considering entering into any purchasing agreement with a wholesaler, you should first do a little research. For example, a drop shipper's product may sound affordable at their offered price but you should probably search eBay before you commit. You may find similar product on eBay that is selling for close to or even less than the price the drop shipper is offering to you.

Use caution whenever a drop shipper or wholesaler demands a sizeable commitment up front in either purchased product or contract duration. A reliable supplier will always work with new clients to help assure them of the product quality and value as well as the supplier's own business integrity.

Be wary of any business that requires a sizeable investment in cash up front—for example, one-day seminars that come to your town and offer a complete "out-of-the-box" package for selling online or on eBay. These companies usually require a few thousand dollars up front for purchasing the package. If you are considering such a proposition, make sure the company offering you the deal has a reasonable escape clause in the way of a trial period or money-back policy. As always, read the fine print before you sign any contract.

What's my take on these businesses? Every single successful eBay seller that I have met in the last eleven years (and I have met thousands of them) started off from scratch. Remember the old maxim: "If sounds too good to be true, it probably is."

We've covered a lot of information in this section. Again, don't be overwhelmed to the point of inaction. If you don't have product to sell, go grab an unwanted item from your attic or basement and start listing it on eBay. Many eBay sellers start off this way. In fact, eBay seller Tim Burnett started out with only four items!

> My wife and I were trying to work out a way of increasing our income, so we decided to try our hand at selling on eBay. We looked for suitable products we could get at a reasonable price that we could ship easily and would possibly not be widely available. We started off on eBay on a shoestring budget of $15 with four items. We listed our items on eBay for the princely sum of $2.65 (at the time we didn't have a scanner, so we had to scan our pictures at the local Kinko's for $2.10). Out of the four products, one got six bids and sold much higher than we had guessed, one sold at a reasonable profit, and the other two didn't sell at all. So we had found our market, art supplies.
>
> At that time the only mode of transport we had was a 1969 VW camper bus, which my wife would drive twenty miles each way to work. This left me with a two-mile walk each way to the local post office, which I trudged three times a week to make sure our shipments went out on time. Now, less than six months down the line, we are buying our products direct from the manufacturer, and our eBay sales are going toward building our business. We are planning to introduce many new products in the near future, and it's all thanks to eBay!
>
> If we can start up on a total outlay of less than $20, you can do it too!

In my tenure at eBay I have seen just about anything you can imagine offered for sale. Art supplies, new and vintage clothing, old computers, new kitchenware, auto parts, golf clubs, time-shares, homemade crafts, brand-new electronic equipment, domain names . . . the list is endless.

There are even eBay businesses that offer fresh-baked goods custom-made and shipped overnight to your location.

With a little ingenuity and research, you may just find available sources of interesting or unusual products right in your own neighborhood—products you can then turn around for a potential profit on eBay.

If after giving it a lot of thought you still cannot come up with a product yourself, maybe you should consider selling items for others on consignment. That's where the eBay Trading Assistants program might help.

Trading Assistants

Trading Assistants are eBay sellers who sell for others on a consignment or fee basis. Selling on consignment at eBay can be a terrific business opportunity. Lots of folks have heard of eBay. Many of them have things they would like to sell on eBay, but sometimes the process is too overwhelming for them or they don't have the time to list their items themselves. That's where you, as a Trading Assistant, fit in.

To become a Trading Assistant, you must meet the following requirements:

- You've sold at least four items in the last thirty days.
- You have a feedback score of 50 or higher.
- Ninety-seven percent or more of your feedback is positive.
- Your eBay account is in good standing.

To remain in the Trading Assistants Directory, you need to meet the following requirements:

- You've sold at least one item in the last thirty days.
- You have a feedback score of 50 or higher.
- Ninety-seven percent or more of your feedback is positive.
- Your eBay account is in good standing.

If you meet those requirements, you can create a Trading Assistant account by clicking the "Become an assistant" link from the Trading Assistants Directory. Your eBay User ID will then be added to the Trading Assistants Directory and will be searchable via your region or location.

Folks in your region who want to sell an item on eBay but are not set up for selling can locate you by searching the Trading Assistants Directory. They then contact you and make arrangements for you to sell their item for them on eBay.

Joining the directory is a privilege, not a right, and eBay can remove you from the directory. This might happen, for example, if clients started complaining about your service as a Trading Assistant.

Including yourself in our Trading Assistants Directory is a lot like running a classified ad for your services. Trading Assistants are not employees or independent contractors of eBay. Nor does eBay endorse or approve them. Each Trading Assistant runs his or her own independent business free from any involvement by eBay.

As a Trading Assistant, you are free to run your business as you see fit. You may set your own fee schedule, and you may limit the types and quantities of items you are willing to sell on consignment. All sales at eBay are under your Seller's Account. You are charged all eBay fees but are free to pass these fees on to your clients as you see fit. All negotiations are between you and your clients.

You can learn more about the Trading Assistant program on the eBay Web site. Click the "Site map" link on the eBay Navigation Bar. The link for Trading Assistants Program can be found in the center column of links on the site map page, under the section for Selling Resources.

I meet with several Trading Assistants every month. Two of my favorites are Peter Becker and Erik Holcomb, who are partners in a very successful eBay drop-off store business. Here's what they told me about their business on eBay:

We opened the Global Garage Sale eBay drop-off store in Winooski, Vermont, in December 2003. We were buying and selling on eBay just for fun when a friend asked us to sell some musical instruments for him in exchange for a commission. After several successful listings, and some cash in our pockets, we realized that more people must need a similar service. We registered our business name and eBay user ID and we were off and running. Due to a shoestring budget and minimal advertising, we spent each weekend that first summer going to garage sales to find merchandise to sell. The word rapidly spread and we were soon too busy selling items for our clients to go out hunting anymore.

As more merchandise started coming through the door, we recognized the need to keep track of Global Garage Sale's clients and all of their items. We ordered some used steel shelving and developed a proprietary Web-based software system to control all aspects of our business. The software is directly connected to eBay *and Paypal, giving us the information we need when we need it. This makes the whole operation easier for us to control and expand as we continue to grow. We've based our business on customer service with a company motto: "If we do good work the people will come back." We now have a client return rate of over 25 percent, with some customers coming back every few months for almost three years.*

All in all, providing great customer service to both our sellers and our buyers is what keeps them spreading the word about "the eBay Guys" and coming back to Global Garage Sale.

Proof again that the key to running a successful business on eBay is to provide excellent customer service.

Your Business Location

You have selected your business structure and you've a pretty good idea of what types of items you are going to sell on eBay. Now it's time to locate a place for your selling.

SELLING FROM YOUR HOME

Home-based selling has several advantages over separate retail-location selling, the most obvious being cost savings of not having to rent and run a separate location. There are also tax advantages. In most cases, you may be able to deduct a percentage of your regular home expenses (rent or mortgage, heat, electricity) as business expenses. You can work in your bathrobe and slippers. You can take coffee and cigarette breaks when you like. Best of all, if you are a stay-at-home parent, you can keep an eye on the little ones while you work (and once the little ones are able, you can recruit them into your home business workforce).

The disadvantages of selling from your home will grow exponentially as your eBay business starts to take off. It may become impossible to keep the physical parts of your business from commandeering all of the space in your home.

If you don't have the luxury of a second building, select one area of your home for eBay selling. It doesn't have to be much—a spare bedroom or basement or garage. If you cannot give over a complete room, then use a part of a room. For most eBay selling, you will find that a space roughly four feet deep by eight feet long will be more than adequate. Here is a real-life example of an eBay seller home office sent in by eBay seller Anita (beachbadge). Notice how well organized Anita keeps her home office.

Within your home office space, designate separate areas for your computer, for digital photography, for item storage, and for packing and shipping. The key is organization. If you keep your eBay office space strictly organized, you'll be better prepared for any growth of your business, and your business will run more efficiently.

Keep pace with your business. Don't cram your growing, successful business into a space too small to contain it, or else your business will suffer. If you are selling from your home and your eBay business is growing by leaps and bounds, you will know when it is time to move your eBay home business to a separate and bigger location.

GRIFF TIP! Don't set up your eBay business where there are smokers. Nothing turns off a buyer like opening a package and having the odor of stale cigarette smoke come wafting up from the box. If you or anyone in your household smokes, you should designate a well-ventilated, smoke-free room for the storage and packing of your eBay items.

ITEM STORAGE

Whether you are selling knickknacks or airplanes, merchandise takes up space. Depending on the type, size, and volume of merchandise you plan on selling, you will need an appropriate means of storage. In most cases, simple metal, plastic, or wooden shelving will do (airplanes will need hangar space, of course).

Label and mark all items with an identifying number. This will help prevent mix-ups later.

Avoid wasted storage space. Adapt your shelving or storage system to suit your needs. For example, if your store-bought shelving has shelves spaced every twelve inches and your items are only three inches tall, add more shelves. eBay user beachbadge keeps her smaller items on a set of hardware shelves.

eBay seller Karen Gray keeps her fabric items in sealed plastic bins.

Your Office Equipment

There isn't much to say about office equipment that isn't obvious, except maybe that good new equipment isn't cheap, so consider used if budget is a concern. New or used, here is a checklist of the basic equipment you will need for your eBay business.

✔ *A computer with an Internet connection.* Although you can get by with using a four-year-old or older computer, it is best to have the most up-to-date system you can afford. If you can afford it and it is available, get a high-speed Internet connection.

✔ *A printer to print out invoices, listing pages, shipping labels, and so on.* Again, if you can afford it, purchase two printers—a black-and-white one and a color bubble jet. Print out your listing pages on the color printer and everything else with the black-and-white.

✔ *A digital camera.* Buy the best you can afford. I suggest 2.0 megapixels or higher, and make sure it has a macro feature for extreme close-ups. Refer to Section Two, chapter 3, for more information on digital cameras.

✔ *A flatbed scanner.* You may not use it all the time, but when you do need it, you will be glad you have one. Sellers of flat items such as comic books, post-cards, coins and stamps, etc., simply must have one. Refer to Section Two, chapter 2, for more information on scanners.

✔ *A good desk and chair.* Pretty obvious, but I cannot tell you how many eBay seller homes I have been in where the desk was something like an old door on milk crates set too low or too high and the chair was a hard stool—neither item coming close to anything that could be considered ergonomically sound. If you are selling on eBay, you will be sitting in front of a computer for long stretches. Don't hurt yourself by sitting incorrectly. Obtain a good desk and the best chair you can afford.

✔ *A filing cabinet.* Two drawers at least. What with listing pages, invoices, letters, and every thing else, you are going to have a lot of paper to file. Keep it organized right from the start.

✔ *Good lighting for both the office space and for taking digital pictures.*

Other various office necessities such as printer paper, labels, and pens are obvious. You can get great deals for office equipment and supplies of all types at . . . hmmm, I wonder where?

Bookkeeping

One of the most common and, in some ways, distressing questions I field from both new and seasoned eBay sellers goes something like this: "I sell on eBay primarily as a hobby, so I don't have to keep books, right?"

Wrong.

Whether you're a sole proprietor or multinational corporation, you must keep accurate records of your business activity. As I wrote earlier, you cannot manage what you cannot measure, and no business can survive and thrive without management. Your eBay business is no exception.

Now, don't you wish you had paid better attention during Accounting 101? Not to worry. Several excellent bookkeeping software programs are available that not only will help you track your business but are actually fun to use.

Two popular applications for small businesses are Intuit's QuickBooks and Microsoft's Money. Both applications are excellent tools that allow you to record costs and income, track and manage expenses and accounts receivable, print invoices, and create custom reports to show the state of your business. Most important, come April 15, both applications will help you determine your tax liabilities.

In addition, for the budget-conscious, there are many free and shareware accounting applications. You can find some by going to *www.tucows.com* and searching their application library using the word *accounting*.

If you sell even one item at eBay, you should create and keep a record of the sale by at the very least saving:

- A printout of the item page taken immediately after the listing closes
- A photocopy of the check or money order used to pay for the item (or, if you are using an online payment service to accept credit cards, a printout of the payment page)
- A receipt showing your purchase price or cost for the item
- The e-mail and mailing address of the buyer

TRACKING EBAY EXPENSES WITH YOUR EBAY SELLER ACCOUNT

If you are running a business on eBay, your eBay selling fees may be tax-deductible operating or business expenses. You can view and print out past eBay invoices by month and keep this information for your records. Go to My eBay and click the "Seller account" link under the My Account section. Then click "View invoices."

Select a month from the drop-down box.

This will display that month's invoice for printing or saving to your hard drive.

Or click "View account status" to see your current activity.

You can print out or, better, download this information to your computer as a CSV (Comma Separated Value) file and use it within your bookkeeping software.

TRACKING EBAY SALES WITH YOUR PAYPAL ACCOUNT

One of several advantages of accepting only PayPal payments is that all of your sales data will be kept in your PayPal History view. From there you can access the details of any payment you have made or received through PayPal. Best of all, you can download the history directly to your computer as a spreadsheet-compatible or QuickBooks or Quicken file!

Click the "History" tab under the "My account" tab in PayPal. Then click the link for "Download my history" in the History box on the left.

Select from the available download options to customize the data you wish to download and save, and then click the "Download history" button.

GRIFF TIP! I strongly recommend eBay's Accounting Assistant tool. It works with QuickBooks to help sellers download and organize all their eBay selling data.

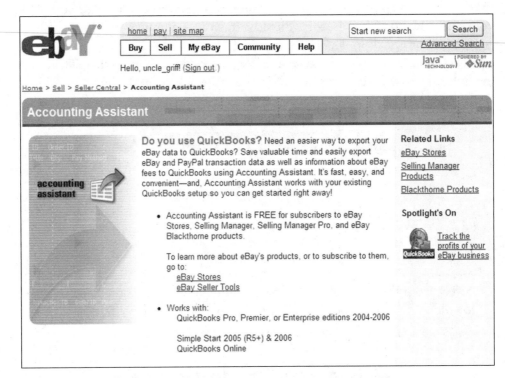

Home > Sell > Seller Central > Accounting Assistant

Accounting Assistant

Do you use QuickBooks? Need an easier way to export your eBay data to QuickBooks? Save valuable time and easily export eBay and PayPal transaction data as well as information about eBay fees to QuickBooks using Accounting Assistant. It's fast, easy, and convenient—and, Accounting Assistant works with your existing QuickBooks setup so you can get started right away!

- Accounting Assistant is FREE for subscribers to eBay Stores, Selling Manager, Selling Manager Pro, and eBay Blackthorne products.

  To learn more about eBay's products, or to subscribe to them, go to:
  eBay Stores
  eBay Seller Tools

- Works with:
  QuickBooks Pro, Premier, or Enterprise editions 2004-2006

  Simple Start 2005 (R5+) & 2006
  QuickBooks Online

Related Links
eBay Stores
Selling Manager Products
Blackthorne Products

Spotlight's On

Track the profits of your eBay business

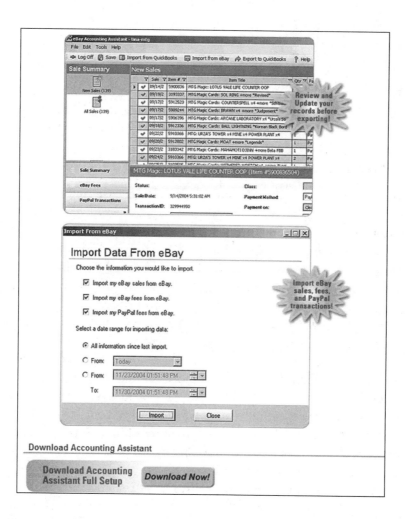

To download Accounting Assistant, go to *www.ebay.com/accounting assistant*.

WHY KEEP RECORDS? THREE REASONS

1. Taxes. Even though you might not actually owe taxes on the proceeds of an eBay sale, you are obliged to report the income. Thus for your own peace of mind and to make sure you are in full compliance with all tax laws, create and save a complete record of every eBay sale as well as all your business expenses. They will come in handy in the event of a tax audit.

2. Access to business capital loans. If you decide to grow your business, you will need a record of your previous business activity when applying for business loans or establishing business lines of credit.

3. If you want to grow your business, you must have an accurate way of measuring it. Good bookkeeping will provide the blueprint for building your business plan from quarter to quarter and year to year.

WHICH BOOKKEEPING METHOD IS RIGHT FOR ME?

There are two basic methods of business accounting: cash and accrual.

The cash method of accounting is the simplest system. Every time you receive payment for an item or pay out an expense, you immediately record it (keep a ledger book or use accounting software). Using the cash method of accounting, most of your expenses and nearly all of your income are recorded the moment the cash for them is spent or received. The exceptions for expenses would be some capital expenditures for, say, office equipment (computers, printers, etc.) that need to be amortized or depreciated over time. If you sell services instead of items on eBay or if your eBay goods are custom-made or if you are an artist or photographer or writer who is selling his own work on eBay, then you might be able to use the cash method.

The accrual method of accounting is more complex than the cash method. In brief, when you use the accrual system, you record sales when they are made, not when the cash for them is actually received or spent. If your business involves inventory, then you may be required to use the accrual method of accounting.

Either way, if you are in doubt or have questions, consult an expert accountant.

A few good online bookkeeping resources are the Business Owners Toolkit, *www.toolkit.cch.com*, and of course the IRS, *www.irs.gov*.

In summary, if you plan on selling regularly on eBay, you really must set up a simple bookkeeping system both to adequately record your business activity and to help your business grow. And it bears repeating: Educate yourself about your tax and accounting responsibilities both on your own and through the services of a tax accountant or attorney.

Using Auction Management Tools

KEEPING TRACK OF YOUR LISTINGS USING MY EBAY FOR LOW-VOLUME SELLERS

Once you get your eBay selling started, the processes for taking digital pictures and writing excellent descriptions become almost second nature. If you sell only a few items a week, then using the Sell Your Item form with a text-file template of your standard payment, shipping, and other terms is probably the easiest way to go. You can also keep track of your listings with My eBay.

In Section One, chapter 2, I outlined and described each section of My eBay. The Selling, Account, and Feedback pages of your My eBay page are invaluable for managing your eBay listings.

- The Selling tab shows you all of your items currently up for sale. It can also show all of your recent (past thirty days) closed listings.
- The Account tab displays all of your eBay Seller's Account information, including your last invoice and your to-date selling activity, with all fees displayed in a ledger form.
- The Feedback tab allows you to view feedback left for you. More important, clicking a button on the My eBay Feedback page shows you all the feedback you need to leave for others.

For the low-volume seller, these My eBay features may be more than adequate to meet sales-tracking needs.

EBAY SELLER TOOLS FOR HIGH-VOLUME SELLERS

If you list ten or more items a week, you will want to employ a listing management tool to make listing easier. eBay provides four basic listing management tools. They are:

- Turbo Lister
- eBay Selling Manager (Basic and Pro versions)
- Blackthorne (Basic and Pro versions)
- eBay Stores

These tools provide various features that help eliminate as much repetitive data entry (typing) as possible and keep listings, invoices, e-mails, inventory, and accounts organized and manageable.

Each tool is tailored to fit the needs of all types of eBay sellers.

Turbo Lister

Turbo Lister is a free, downloadable auction management and bulk-uploading tool created by eBay. It is best suited for those sellers who list ten to one hundred

or more items a week. However, you may find it helpful even if you are only listing one item at a time.

Turbo Lister provides all of the following features:

- Preview listings before submitting.
- Schedule listings in bulk.
- Easily create HTML-formatted descriptions using the built-in WYSIWYG
(what you see is what you get) interface—no need to know HTML. You
"draw" your description as you would create a document in a word
processor.

Here is the Turbo Lister main window:

Turbo Lister helps you create a set of listings off-line that you can store as a
collection for uploading to eBay at a later time. Turbo Lister also helps to eliminate most of the repetitive typing and feature selection one encounters when using the eBay Sell Your Item form.

Click the "New" button to create a new listing in Turbo Lister:

Select "Create New Item."

This will bring up a new item window.

Once you fill this form out, you can save it for future use and use it for listing brand new items, making any edits as necessary.

Where do I get Turbo Lister?

Turbo Lister is available for free as a download on the eBay Site Map page. Click on the "Site map" link on the top of any eBay page. Scroll down the page to the Seller Tools section and click the link for "Turbo Lister."

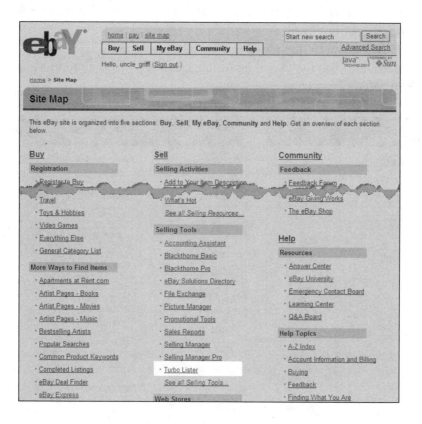

Turbo Lister is easy to download, install, and use. Once you have the application installed, click the Turbo Lister icon on your desktop or task bar and follow the wizard instructions to set up your copy of Turbo Lister with your eBay account information.

SELLING MANAGER (BASIC AND PRO)

If you are selling a hundred items a week or more, you should give Selling Manager a try.

Selling Manager provides a comprehensive suite of listing management tools including e-mail management, invoicing, feedback alerts, payment status, and basic accounting tools as well as many other features tailor-made for the high-volume eBay seller. Selling Manager is a subscription-based tool, that is, you pay a small monthly fee ($4.99 for Basic, $15.99 for Pro) to use it. All new subscribers receive a thirty-day free trial.

Selling Manager Basic is free to all sellers who have a Basic eBay Store subscription. Selling Manager Pro is free to all sellers with Featured or Anchored eBay Store subscriptions.

There is nothing to download and install. Selling Manager works inside My eBay. Once you subscribe to Selling Manager, the All Selling tab in My eBay will change to Selling Manager.

Although it can be used alone, Selling Manager was designed to work in tandem with Turbo Lister. Together, they provide an excellent bulk-upload and listing-management solution for the full-time eBay seller.

Selling Manager comes in two versions, Basic and Pro. Both Selling Manager Basic and Selling Manager Pro have helpful features to make your selling experience easier and more enjoyable:

- Easy access from My eBay. Selling Manager replaces the All Selling page view in My eBay.
- Monitor your active listings in real time and keep up to date on all sales at a glance.

- Manage post-sale activities. Send and track buyer e-mails, bulk relist sold and unsold items, mark which buyers have paid and left feedback, let buyers combine payments and print invoices and shipping labels.

To subscribe to Selling Manager Basic or Pro, click the trusty "site map" link on the top of any eBay page. Scroll down to Seller Tools under Sell. Click "Selling Manager" and follow the instructions for subscribing.

You can also subscribe to Selling Manager from the Selling tab on your My eBay page by clicking the "Subscriptions" link under "My Account."

BLACKTHORNE BASIC AND PRO VERSIONS (FORMERLY KNOWN AS SELLER'S ASSISTANT)

Where Selling Manager is a server-side tool—that is, there is nothing to download on your end—Blackthorne (Basic and Pro) is an actual application that, like Turbo Lister, you download, install, and run from your computer. Here's the Blackthorne main window:

The functionality of Blackthorne is similar to Selling Manager except Blackthorne is more robust and can handle a higher volume of listings, e-mail, and inventory management. Blackthorne can also automate tasks such as sending invoices and leaving feedback.

You can learn more about Blackthorne by going to both the Blackthorne Basic and Pro hub pages. To access them, click the "Site map" link on the top of any eBay page. Scroll down the center column of links to the Selling Tools section. Click either "Blackthorne Basic" or "Blackthorne Pro."

WHICH SELLING TOOL IS BEST FOR ME?

Hard to tell. Luckily, all of these products come with a thirty-day free trial period. However, eBay does have a feature called Tools Recommendations that can help guide you to the right tools based on your responses to a series of questions.

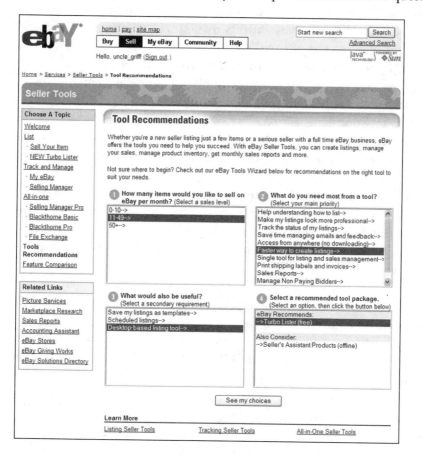

You can find this tool at *http://pages.ebay.com/sell/toolrecommendations.html.*

555

In addition to these, eBay Stores is the tool that establishes your customized e-commerce presence on eBay. No seller on eBay should be without one!

eBay Stores

In 2001, eBay introduced a new selling format called eBay Stores. eBay Stores offer the eBay seller an effective channel for growing a business on eBay, with various features to help sellers promote and market their eBay items to the rest of the world.

With an eBay Store you can:

- Create up to three hundred custom categories exclusive to your eBay Store. Your eBay Store comes with its own search engine, which will search for items only in your eBay Store.
- Customize your business by adding your own business logo to your eBay Store pages or by choosing one of eBay's online image templates.
- Describe your business in depth on your About My Store page.
- Market your items across eBay by using the built-in cross-promotion tools that come as a part of your eBay Store.
- Receive monthly sales reports that provide a checkup on the effectiveness of your business.
- Access Store Traffic Reporting, which includes real-time data on page views and visitors for all of your listings and Store pages as well as information on search terms used by visitors in your Store.
- Create and send your own custom marketing e-mails directly to your buyers.

If you are a regular eBay seller, there are definite advantages to setting up an eBay Store, especially if you offer a large inventory of items. All of your eBay items—eBay Store, Auction format, and Fixed Price format—will display within your eBay Store, making it the ideal destination to send your eBay buyers.

Before you set up an eBay Store, you must:

- Have an eBay Seller's Account with a credit card on file.
- Have a minimum feedback rating of 20 or be ID Verified ($5 charge).
- Accept credit card payments via an online payment service such as PayPal or through a merchant account.

eBay Store fees are separate and different from those for regular eBay listings. eBay Stores are a subscription-based service. There are three levels of eBay Stores, each with its own suite of tools and features:

- eBay Stores Basic—$15.95 per month
- eBay Stores Featured—$49.95 per month
- eBay Stores Anchor—$499.95 per month

Insertion fees for eBay Store items are significantly lower than regular eBay listing insertion fees. In brief, eBay Store format items are charged an insertion fee of 2¢ per thirty days, and a seller can opt to list an eBay Store item for thirty days or as "good until canceled."

An eBay Store is an attractively priced solution if you have a large number of listings or a large inventory. However, eBay Store items do not show up in regular (non–eBay Store) categories. eBay Store items also do not appear by default in keyword search-result lists; however, eBay Store items will appear in eBay keyword search results under certain circumstances. Store Inventory listings appear in the main search results when thirty or fewer Auction and Fixed Price results surface in the following areas:

- eBay search and browse results
- Product Details (Catalog) pages (when the seller uses Pre-filled Item Information)

Store Inventory listings always appear in the main search results at the end of Auction-style and Fixed Price results when:

- The Store Inventory check box in the Search Options box is selected on the search and browse pages.
- The buyer clicks the Buy It Now tab at the top of every search results page.

Store Inventory listings are included in specialized Stores searches in the following areas:

- Search for Items in Stores box at *stores.ebay.com*
- All searches within a single Store
- Seller's Other Items page
- Searches for Store Inventory listing only

We covered browsing and buying through eBay Stores in Section One, chapter 3. Setting up an eBay Store is a snap. Go to the eBay home page and click on the link "eBay Stores" (located in the box on the top left-hand side of the page).

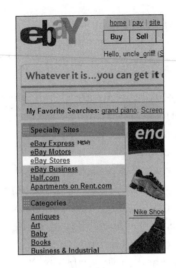

This will take you to the Stores home page.

On this page, click "Open a Store" on the top right-hand side of the page.

Follow each of the three easy steps for setting up a Store. You can change any selection after your Store has been set up.

eBay Store Setup Tips

1. Pick a catchy, memorable name for your Store, preferably one that relates in some way to your business or the items you sell.
2. You will be asked to create a short description of your Store. In addition, you can create a special header for each of your eBay Store pages. Your eBay Store description will appear under your Store name in the lists of Stores as well as at the top of your Store page. Your eBay Store page headers will appear on the top of each eBay Store page. The words you supply in your Store description and page headers will be the words that search engines such as Google use to pick up your eBay Store pages. Thus, you should make sure your eBay Store description and page headers contain descriptive keywords that will help it show up in a Google search.
3. Create up to three hundred customized categories on three levels to help organize and display your items with maximum effectiveness. Note that these categories are for your eBay Store only. Whenever you list an item at eBay—whether in your Store or as a regular listing—you will be prompted to select one of your eBay Store custom categories for your item.

Why the special search engine and customized categories? Some eBay Store sellers have thousands of items listed in their eBay Store. The personalized categories and personal search engine help their buyers find items more effectively in their eBay Store.

You can learn more about eBay Stores by going to the Stores page as described above and clicking on "More FAQs."

GRIFF TIP! Items that you list exclusively in your eBay Store will not show up in a regular title search (although they do show up in a title search of eBay Stores). A trick that many sellers use is to list most of their inventory in an eBay Store and always have one or two similar items for sale in a regular (non–eBay Store) auction or Buy It Now. These sellers then cross-promote their eBay Store in their regular listings to help drive traffic to their store items.

EBAY CROSS PROMOTIONS TOOL

Many cool features come with an eBay Store, but a real favorite is known as eBay Cross Promotions. With Cross Promotions, you have the ability to create and manage specific cross-promotional marketing of your Store items so that these select items (up to twelve items) appear in key buyer locations such as on the Bid Confirmation and Winning Buyer Confirmation pages.

Here's an example of an active item listing page where the seller is using Cross Promotions to promote other items she has for sale.

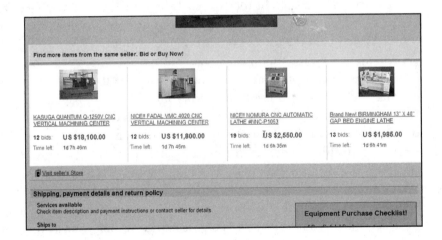

Cross Promotions can be a great boost for your eBay business. For example, say you are selling digital cameras at eBay and you also have digital camera accessories in your eBay Store. If someone bids on or buys one of your digital cameras, you can use Cross Promotions to have your digital camera accessories show up on the Bid Confirmation or Winning Bidder or Winning Buyer Confirmation page, both to entice the buyer into purchasing more items from you (he might just need a digital camera bag) and to help lead him to your eBay Store.

To set up your eBay Store Cross Promotions, go to "My eBay" and click "Marketing tools:"

Click the link for "Item promotion" and click the "Manage" link to change your defaults.

Or click the "Edit" link to change your Cross Promotion settings:

Now you can make changes or edits to suit your promotional needs. Then click "Save settings" at the bottom of the page.

eBay Sales Reports

eBay sellers generate tremendous sales volume, with millions of items sold on the site every day. Tremendous sales volume generates stupendous amounts of sales data. Until recently, sellers had limited access to this data, and the format was not easy to plot into a graph. eBay sellers have enough on their hands without having to create, from scratch, comprehensive reports with graphs and charts showing their eBay selling activity.

With the recent introduction of eBay Sales Reports, sellers can now track and analyze all their eBay selling activity. Sales Reports compiles a seller's past activity by quarter and displays it in easy-to-read graphs, charts, and reports.

Why is this important? Remember our mantra: You cannot grow a business unless you can manage it effectively. You cannot manage a business effectively if you cannot measure it. As eBay's marketplace evolves, you'll need the most effective measuring tools available so you can identify new opportunities as they arise and plot a course to success.

eBay Sales Reports is the perfect business measuring tool for all your eBay selling activity. eBay Sales Reports comes in two flavors: a basic version called Sales Reports and an enhanced version named Sales Reports Plus.

SALES REPORTS

Sales Reports is free by subscription to all eBay sellers. It provides data for:

- Sales
- Ended listings
- Successful listings (by percentage)
- Average sale price
- eBay and PayPal fees

SALES REPORTS PLUS

Sales Reports Plus includes all features of Sales Reports, plus:

- Data for sales and listings by category
- Data for sales and listings by format (Auction, Fixed Price, Store, etc.)
- Data for sales and listings by ending day or time

- Buyer counts
- Detailed eBay fees
- Unpaid Item credits requested

Sales Reports Plus costs $4.99 per month with a free thirty-day trial but is free to all eBay Store sellers.

Sales Reports Plus provides four views: Sales Summary, Sales by Category, Sales by Format, and Archived Sales. The following screens show examples of each view:

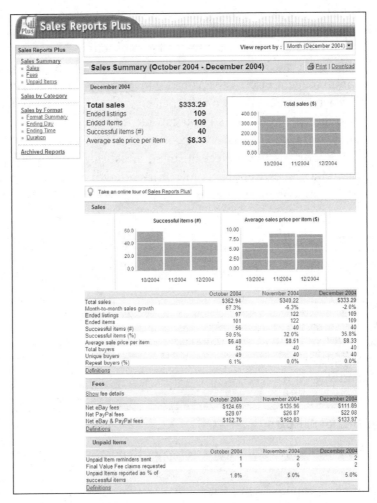

Sales Summary

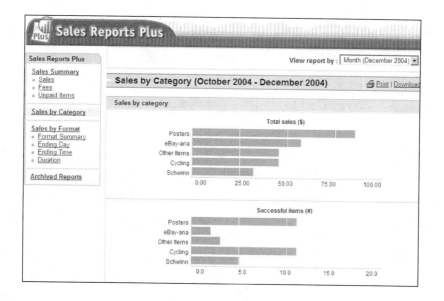

Sales by Category

Sales by Format

Sales Reports Plus

Archived Reports

Your Sales Report Plus will be available for 24 months after they have been generated. they expire.

← Back to your current reports

Monthly Reports

2004

Sales Reports Plus, September 2004
Sales Reports Plus, October 2004
Sales Reports Plus, November 2004

Weekly Reports

2004

Sales Reports Plus, Week 10/24/04 - 10/30/04
Sales Reports Plus, Week 10/31/04 - 11/06/04
Sales Reports Plus, Week 11/07/04 - 11/13/04
Sales Reports Plus, Week 11/14/04 - 11/20/04
Sales Reports Plus, Week 11/21/04 - 11/27/04
Sales Reports Plus, Week 11/28/04 - 12/04/04
Sales Reports Plus, Week 12/05/04 - 12/11/04
Sales Reports Plus, Week 12/12/04 - 12/18/04
Sales Reports Plus, Week 12/19/04 - 12/25/04
Sales Reports Plus, Week 12/26/04 - 01/01/05

Archived Sales

To learn more about and subscribe to Sales Reports, click the "Site map" link on the top of any eBay page and click the link for "Sales Reports" in the Selling Tools section.

Promoting Your eBay Business with Your About Me Page

The About Me page is probably the most underused feature at eBay. I am constantly amazed at how many sellers do not take advantage of this excellent feature.

An About Me page is your eBay home page. Any eBay member can create and maintain an About Me page all on her own.

Building an About Me page is easy. To build yours, click the "Site map" link on the top of any eBay page. Then click the "About Me" link under the Connect section.

This brings you to the About Me hub page.

Follow the instructions from here. Note: You can change your About Me page at any time simply by returning to this page or by clicking "Edit your page" on the bottom of your About Me page.

You can select from the HTML templates eBay provides to simplify the process, or you can enter your own HTML in the text box provided. Learn more about HTML commands in the next chapter.

GRIFF TIP! If you are creating your own HTML-formatted text for your About Me page using a Web editor such as FrontPage, only copy and paste the HTML between and excluding the <body> and </body> tags.

You can talk about practically anything you like on your About Me page. You can describe your business, and unlike the restrictions against linking to your personal Web site from your item page, you can link to your own Web site from your About Me page. You can talk about the items you sell (though you mustn't offer items for sale from your About Me page). You can even tell the world about your family, your favorite charities, your hobbies, and your collecting interests.

Once your About Me page is up, you can link to it from your item listing descriptions with a simple hypertext link along these lines: "Visit my About Me page to learn more about my eBay business."

Growing Your eBay Business

You have done everything right so far, and your eBay business is now thriving and growing. A growing business is usually most vulnerable once it starts to really take off. Often, an eBay seller will find a successful business strategy and will grab on to it tightly, sometimes so tightly that when the business climate changes, he doesn't. This inflexibility can be deadly to a business.

You can avoid these pitfalls by staying nimble in your business strategies and by always keeping one step ahead of the market.

How? Research! Never take your eye off your competition. Learn what makes them successful—or not—and incorporate the lessons into your own business. Stay ahead of market trends for the items you list.

For example, it is the middle of June and you just got a great deal on a big lot of assorted batteries from a local store that is going out of business. Do you sell the lot off right away? Or do you hold on to it and sell it later? When do you think the demand for batteries is highest, on the Fourth of July or in December? You might have a hunch that your batteries will do better in December, but you may need to turn merchandise over sooner rather than later.

And there are other factors to consider. Who else is currently offering batteries at eBay? What are their starting prices? Are they aggressively marketing them in the middle of the summer? If not, maybe you could offer a portion of them now and reserve the rest of the lot for the upcoming holiday season.

A good business is never static. Stasis is the sure death of any business.

I met an eBay seller a few years ago who was offering a type of item that no other eBay seller had. Let's call this seller Pat. Pat was doing a great business. Pat had an extremely inexpensive source for these items and invested heavily in stocking up her inventory. Buyers interested in these items went to her listings, as she had the market cornered. All was profits and bliss until eventually another seller (let's call him Sam) discovered the market in these items simply by doing a little browsing in the eBay category where the items were listed. Sam did some research and discovered Pat's source. Sam began buying from the same source and offered the items at a slightly lower opening bid than Pat. That meant lower margins for Sam, but Sam was banking on making up for the lower margin of profit with a higher volume of sales.

Pat was suddenly faced with competition, and her sales started to slow. Pat faced a dilemma. If she lowered her opening bid prices, it would mean lower profits, but a higher volume of sales might offset this, just as Sam had gambled.

So what did Pat do? Nothing. Pat decided that lowering the prices of the items she had in inventory would be too big a risk, so she chose to wait out Sam's aggressive marketing attack, hoping that the market would expand enough to include both sellers. And it did, at least for a while, but within a few months, other sellers started moving into the same line of merchandise until there were several different sellers of the item. This was great for buyers, who could now shop by price as well as by item. It was not good for the sellers, as they watched their gross sales drop.

Sam saw the writing on the wall and unloaded his inventory of items for a small loss by dumping them on eBay for a penny opening bid each. Sam then took the cash and went searching for other wares—wares with not many sellers. Pat stuck it out, refusing to adjust prices or to expand her line of eBay merchandise, and was eventually out of business.

The moral of the story: If you choose to take a risk and move ahead, you may make the wrong choice and you may fail—but you may also win. If you don't at least try to move ahead but instead remain in place, you will definitely fail.

The eBay PowerSeller Program

To recognize and reward with respect those sellers who generate a consistently high volume of sales, eBay created a program known as PowerSeller.

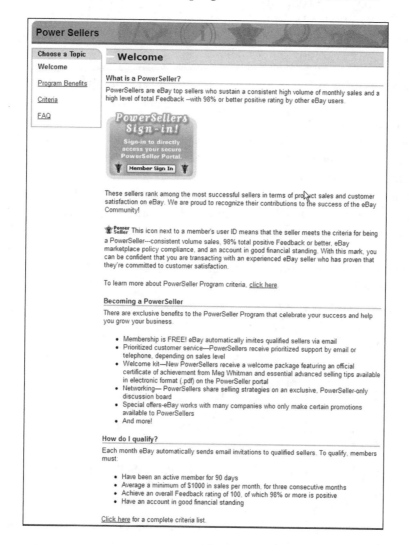

NOTE: You can reach the PowerSeller page above by clicking the "PowerSeller" link on the "Site map" page (located under the Selling Resources section). You probably know how to reach the Site Map page by now, but just in case . . . the "Site map" link is on the top of every eBay page.

The PowerSeller program is divided into five levels. Eligibility for each level depends on monthly gross merchandise sales (indicated below in parentheses next to the level name).

- Bronze ($1,000–$3,000)
- Silver ($3,000–$10,000)
- Gold ($10,000–$25,000)
- Platinum ($25,000–$150,000)
- Titanium ($150,000+)

There are benefits for those who join the PowerSeller program:

✔ Membership in the program is free.
✔ The PowerSeller Portal and Forum, which let all PowerSellers log in and network with other PowerSellers. PowerSellers also enjoy the benefits of a special recognition and rewards program.
✔ A banner-ad tool to create, target, and monitor their own eBay banner ads.
✔ Exclusive invitations to eBay-sponsored educational or special events.
✔ Monthly newsletters and program updates featuring new products, benefits, and policies.
✔ Exclusive PowerSeller offers from eBay designed to help PowerSellers save time and money.
✔ All PowerSellers receive a PowerSeller icon next to their User ID.

The special benefits for each level of the PowerSeller program include:

✔ Bronze PowerSellers: 24/7 e-mail support.
✔ Silver PowerSellers: All of the Bronze PowerSeller benefits plus free phone support during business days and hours (PST).
✔ Gold PowerSellers: All of the Silver PowerSeller benefits with the addition of access to a pool of account managers.
✔ Platinum PowerSellers: All of the Gold PowerSeller benefits plus 24/7 phone support and a dedicated support account manager.

✔ Titanium PowerSellers: All of the Platinum PowerSeller benefits plus immediate phone contact from eBay for any listing issues or questions.

You can find out more about the PowerSeller program requirements, levels, and benefits on the PowerSeller page.

Successful Business Practices—Treating Your Customers Like the Priceless Assets They Are

A time-honored golden rule of bricks-and-mortar business says, "The customer is always right." Actually, there are two rules of business. Rule number one: "The customer is always right." Rule number two: "When the customer is wrong, see rule number one."

eBay sellers with the most successful businesses all apply this rule to each and every customer. During my tenure at eBay Customer Support, I received many e-mails from sellers embroiled in disputes with their buyers, most of which stemmed from simple misunderstandings due to either an ambiguous e-mail or confusion over an item description or terms. Many, if not most, of these disputes resulted in negative feedback for both buyer and seller, as well as unnecessary additions to the world's already-too-large pool of ill will.

Here are my seller tips for nearly trouble-free eBay transactions.

BE EXPLICIT, POLITE, AND PROFESSIONAL IN YOUR LISTING TERMS

You cannot provide too much information in your item descriptions. Note every quality and every flaw of your item. If you don't have much information, do some research and provide what you find. State your payment and shipping terms with as much detail as possible, in neutral and polite language.

Nothing turns a potential buyer away from your listing faster than a list of harsh rules and regulations for bidders. This is not to say that you shouldn't state your rules, only that you should do so in polite and friendly language. Here's an example of text from an actual eBay listing followed by my rewording:

If you have any negative feedback, DO NOT BID! I will not accept any bids from a bidder with negative feedback, and I will cancel your bids AND I WILL CONTACT EBAY and you will be thrown off. So DON'T BID unless you UNDERSTAND THESE TERMS!

Makes me want to run and hide instead of bid. Wouldn't it sound better this way?

If you have any recent negative feedback, we still want your bid. However, please contact us via e-mail so we can discuss the reasons for the negative feedback before you bid. Thanks! We appreciate your cooperation!

DON'T TURN OFF POTENTIAL GOOD BIDDERS WITH HARSH REGULATIONS AND TERMS

Yes, you can use eBay's Bidder Management Tool to block the bids of an unwanted bidder, but unless you know the User ID of a bidder beforehand, you cannot block him in advance. Also, using negative feedback alone as a guide to a bidder's reliability or seriousness of intent can be misleading. Each case where negative feedback has been left is different. There may be extenuating circumstances. Give your bidders a chance to explain themselves if necessary. If you are unhappy with a bidder, quietly and without rancor cancel his bid, then add him to your item's blocked list.

PROVIDE A REFUND OPTION FOR YOUR BUYERS

Although eBay allows you as a seller to adopt a policy of "all sales as is, no returns or refunds," please don't do it. As efficient and fun as the eBay marketplace is, eBay buyers don't receive and have the chance to examine items with their own hands and eyes until they have already paid for them. Even with the most explicit description and pictures, sometimes a well-meaning buyer simply isn't happy with an item once he receives it. Put yourself in a buyer's shoes. Would you want to be stuck with something you bought in good faith but found you didn't like once you received it? Of course not!

In the world of off-line retail, returns are an accepted way of life. If you want to succeed at eBay, offer a 100 percent satisfaction-guaranteed policy with no such conditions as "I'll take the item back this time, but don't ever bid on my items again!" In fact, if a bidder asks to return an item, not only should you cheerfully agree to take it back, but you should also encourage the bidder to come back and shop with you again. Your bidders will love you for it.

If you still decide not to provide a 100 percent satisfaction-guaranteed policy, you should spell out your "no returns" policy in clear and concise language within your item description so that bidders are fully informed before they decide to bid. And, oh, best of luck. You'll need it.

MAINTAIN YOUR PROFESSIONALISM AND POISE

Another fact of life in business is that you will now and then run into a difficult customer. I don't mean the nonpaying bidder. These are a separate problem dealt with in a separate way. By "difficult," I mean the customer who sends churlish or abrupt, demanding e-mails. We get them occasionally at eBay Customer Support. We never respond in kind but instead always respond politely and professionally. We simply ignore any inappropriate or inflammatory language and focus only on the crux of the e-mail, responding to the complaint itself and not to its tone—no matter how nasty or unpleasant.

You should always do the same. Your response to an angry customer e-mail reflects directly on you. Think of yourself as the Customer Support representative for your eBay business. Do what you can to calm and placate an angry customer. If you are unable to satisfy him, in spite of offering a refund or kind, polite words, send one last e-mail with your regrets and offer of future assistance if needed.

If anyone sends you harassing e-mails you should contact the sender's Internet Service Provider (ISP) and forward them a copy of the e-mail with full headers attached. Then add the sender's e-mail address to your e-mail application's spam filter program. Remember, you are under no obligation to open, read, or respond to an e-mail sent to you. If all else fails, delete any and all e-mails from the sender without opening them.

"What if a customer sends me an e-mail threatening to come find me and do me bodily harm?" We believe people are basically good. However, you might want to keep a closer eye on some people out there. The lion's share of e-mail threats are hollow, but if someone threatens you with bodily harm, you may want to contact the local law enforcement authorities in your and the sender's locale and alert them to the threat.

GO THE EXTRA MILE

Your customers are your most valuable business assets. Treat them like royalty. Always give at least a little more than expected. The most memorable experiences I have had at eBay as a buyer have been with those sellers who have sent refunds for unintentional overcharges for shipping or handling, or who have included some small but thoughtful extra with the item. Offer free gift wrapping and shipping directly to a gift recipient, and pay for a delivery confirmation option. Again, your goal should be happy customers. Do whatever it takes to reach your goal. Here's what eBay seller Mike Ford has to say on going the extra mile:

If you are selling an item that requires batteries, you can add a brand-new pack of batteries to the item and tell your potential buyers that in the auction! You can increase your sales just by including batteries. . . . You can get a brand-new pack of the batteries (any size) that item requires from top brands like Panasonic and Energizer for as low as $1 for a pack of four at most dollar stores! Be smart! Little things like this will give you the advantage over someone selling the exact same thing.

OFFER AUTHENTICATION SERVICES FOR YOUR ITEMS

If you plan on selling items such as comic books, trading cards, Beanie Babies, rare books, stamps, coins, jewelry, sports autographs, Native American artifacts, or political or sports memorabilia, you should offer them authenticated or graded by one of the recognized and trusted authentication or grading services on eBay's list of recommended vendors. Authentication or grading will instill confidence in your bidders and establish a sense of security and trust that your item is genuine as described.

You can find a page of all the eBay-reviewed and approved authentication and grading services by clicking the "Site map" link on the top of any eBay page. Then scroll down to the "Seller central" link:

On the Seller Central page, click the "Resource" link to reach:

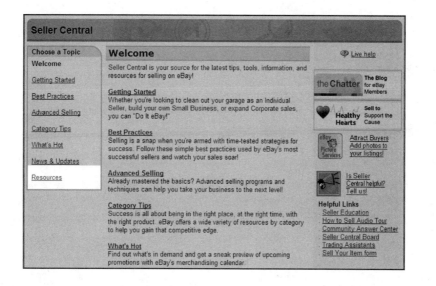

On the Resources page (you may want to bookmark this page for quick reference), click the link for "Opinions, authentication, and grading" under the section labeled Third Party Services.

This will lead you to the Opinions, Authentication, and Grading page.

OFFERING ESCROW

If you are a brand-new seller and offering expensive items, you may want to provide an online escrow option for your bidders. Escrow acts like a trusted middleman between buyer and seller.

Once a listing has ended, the buyer sends payment to the escrow company, which verifies and holds the funds and then notifies the seller, who then sends the merchandise to the buyer. Once the buyer receives, inspects, and accepts the item, she notifies the escrow company, which then sends the payment to the seller.

If the buyer doesn't accept the item, she sends it back to the seller, who inspects the item and alerts the escrow company that the item has arrived in the same condition it was sent. The escrow company then refunds the funds to the bidder. Everyone is protected!

eBay's preferred and recommended escrow partner is Escrow.com.

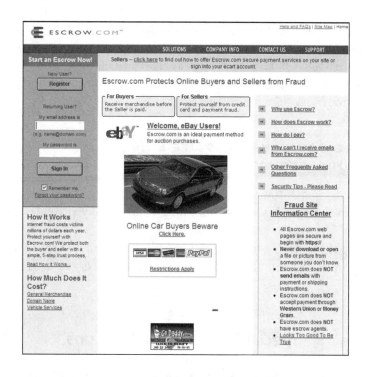

Caution: The only eBay-recommended online escrow service is Escrow.com. Be wary of any other seller- or buyer-suggested online escrow services. There have been incidents of fraud involving spurious online escrow services. If, as a buyer or a seller on eBay, you decide to use an escrow service, only agree to use only Escrow.com!

Escrow.com charges a small percentage fee based on the final bid amount (with a minimum fee of $25). It is customary for the buyer and the seller to split the fee.

Finally, here is what one eBay seller had to say about the road to successful eBay selling:

Give your buyers more than they expect. Just an example in one area: I've made quite a few purchases online with major retailers. You pay your money and they ship in seven to ten days.

I control all aspects of my small empire, so when a buyer pays me, they have their item in their hands in two to three days. They get their feedback immediately. They get a notice that the item is being shipped and the tracking number when it applies. Many of my feedback comments are from buyers surprised at how quickly they have their purchases.

This seller has learned that there is nothing more valuable to one's business than a happy and satisfied customer.

A happy, satisfied customer is usually a loyal customer who will return to shop with you again and again. Loyal customers are the backbone of your business. You cannot survive without them.

PROMOTING YOUR BUSINESS OFF-LINE AND ON YOUR WEB SITE

Most eBay sellers have their own commercial Web sites. You can promote your eBay items on your Web site by including a link—eBay provides preapproved links and logos for users.

To access these links and logos, go to the eBay Site Map and look under Manage My Items for Sale to find the "Promote your listings with link buttons" link.

Special Selling Considerations

SELLING CARS, TRUCKS, BOATS, AND SIMILAR ITEMS ON EBAY

eBay is the online destination of choice for those looking for new, used, and collector cars as well as trucks, motorcycles, and boats. Many used-car sellers have moved some or all of their entire inventory to eBay Motors.

Click the "eBay Motors" link on the eBay home page.

This will take you to the eBay Motors hub page.

If you plan on selling a car or passenger vehicle, boat, or motorcycle, click the "Sell" link on the top of the eBay Motors hub page.

Selling a vehicle on eBay is similar to selling any other type of item, with a few extra concerns.

First, the fee schedule is different. The transaction service fee for all passenger vehicles and motorcycles is fixed. It costs $40 to list a passenger car or other type of vehicle. It costs $30 to list a motorcycle.

In addition, if the item sells, there's a fixed $40 transaction services fee (similar to the eBay final value fee) for passenger vehicles and other vehicles, and a $30 transaction services fee for motorcycles. Again, this fee applies only if there is a successful high bid on the item.

All other fees are the same as for a standard eBay listing.

Some other tips for selling vehicles:

1. Take many photos. (You can show up to twenty-four photos when selling a vehicle.) A car has many sides and facets—inside, outside, and underneath. Make sure that you have a digital image for all views of the vehicle, including both sides, front, back, inside trunk, under hood, front and back seats, dashboard, and undercarriage.

2. You should have the title certificate for the car in your possession. Indicate this in the item description.

3. Be extra explicit in listing the details. Note and include a picture of every imperfection. Include the blue book values for the same car in conditions directly above and below the condition of your vehicle.

4. Be clear about your shipping terms. Most online car buyers understand that they will have to pay for shipping the car and that often this can cost several hundred dollars, but make sure to state this clearly in your listing.

5. When you list the item, you will be prompted to select a category for the vehicle and an item title. You can also provide a subtitle, which you should create carefully! This is the text that is searched when using keywords, so remember to limit your eBay Motors item subtitle to only those keywords that relate to your vehicle. Try to avoid descriptive terms such as *choice* or *rare* or *must see*. No one goes to eBay Motors and searches for all the must-see items, and no one will be compelled to open your listing because you have ordered them to do so. By using these useless words or phrases, you are wasting space. However, do feel free to use the subtitle for mention of miles on the odometer or maybe as a place to state "no reserve" if the item is indeed a no-reserve item.

Selling to the World

If you are going to sell on eBay, you have to decide right off whether you are going to welcome international eBay members to bid on or purchase your items. Let me try to help you make the right decision: Sell to anyone, anywhere.

Wasn't that easy?

Yes, there are special considerations for selling, accepting payment, and shipping items internationally, but don't forget, you are doing business on eBay, the most vibrant and far-reaching marketplace mankind has ever created. eBay is a worldwide phenomenon. Millions of people around the world are ready to shop and buy from you! They have cash they are ready to spend and in some cases, where the U.S. dollar trades lower against their own currencies, your wares are irresistible bargains! You have to ask yourself, "Do I really want to cut out such a vast, wealthy potential customer base?" If you are a smart, savvy business owner, the answer should be a resounding no!

If, however, the above has failed to move you, then move on down a few paragraphs to the section "I Won't Sell Internationally." The rest of you savvy businesspeople, follow me. . . .

Don't pay attention to those 'fraidy cats I just sent on. Selling to international buyers on eBay is easy. Besides, opening your business on eBay to the world will give you a competitive edge over those sellers who, for whatever reason, have closed their markets to millions of potential loyal return buyers around the world. Here is a list of tips and issues to keep in mind when dealing with international buyers.

- Accept payment through an online payment service such as PayPal. Currently, the PayPal network includes 103 countries. By accepting payment via PayPal, you forgo the need for cumbersome currency conversion (PayPal makes the conversion for you at the current rate of exchange), and you don't have to worry about clearing checks. In addition, you get paid fast, so you can ship the item fast—making for a happy seller and a happy buyer.
- Accept international money orders in lieu of checks or online payment from international buyers. However, you may want to consider limiting all international buyers to PayPal. In any event, never accept cash for any listing—domestic or international.
- Investigate all shipping options. Go to the USPS, FedEx, UPS, and DHL Web sites and learn how each one works for international shipping from the United States. Then, in your shipping terms, offer your international bidders a choice of those services that you have selected.
- For large or heavy items, have a good estimate of the weight and dimensions of the item once it has been packed and post these in your item description. Include links to the rate or postage calculators on the Web sites for your preferred shipping and freight services so that international bidders can calculate the approximate cost for shipping to their country before they bid.
- For smaller, lighter items, use the built-in, free eBay Shipping Calculator, which offers international shipping services options.

- When you ship internationally, you will have to fill out a customs form. Familiarize yourself with the various forms (they aren't complicated), and if possible, keep a stack of them handy in your office. Note: Never deflate an item's value on a customs declaration when shipping internationally, no matter how hard the buyer insists. See the last tip below for more information on detailed payment and shipping terms for international buyers.
- Make insurance mandatory for all bidders and buyers.
- Use a packing list, invoice, and envelope as well as a shipping label. Make sure the invoice is complete.
- Always obtain a tracking number or (for the USPS) use Delivery Confirmation. Always require a signature upon delivery.
- Finally, make your item description and terms for shipping, payment, and returns as explicit and detailed as possible for both international and domestic buyers—but even more so for international bidders.

For more tips and advice for selling to buyers around the world, visit the eBay International Trading page. Click the "Site map" link on the top of any eBay page and look for "Selling internationally" under the Selling Resources section in the middle column of links . . .

. . . to reach the Global Trade page:

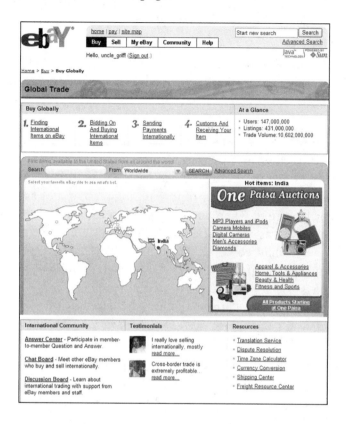

I WON'T SELL INTERNATIONALLY

And no one can force you to do so. In fact, as we saw in the Sell Your Item form, eBay actually provides you with the option of blocking members from buying or bidding on your items if they are registered in countries to which you will not ship.

In the first edition of this book, I stated, "Do keep in mind that eBay does not (and probably will never) provide a mechanism that automatically blocks international buyers from bidding or buying." Well, I was wrong. eBay now provides a mechanism to block buyers in countries to which you will not ship from bidding on or purchasing your items. The feature, known as Buyer Requirements, was described in Section Two, chapter 3. Use it if you must; however, I strongly urge you to reconsider.

Even with Buyer Requirements set to block international buyers, you should still state your shipping terms in clear, explicit language and large, bold text in all your listing descriptions.

GRIFF TIP! If you decide to limit your sales to the United States only, make sure your Terms of Service do not offend! Use something along the lines of:

"We do not ship to locations outside the United States."

SELLING ON THE EBAY INTERNATIONAL SITES

Most of you reading this are registered on the U.S. eBay site, *www.eBay.com*, but did you know that once you are registered on eBay, regardless of which site you used to register, you can list on any of international eBay sites as well?

There might be a time when you will want to list on an international eBay site. For example, Italians are fanatic philatelists (they collect stamps, specifically Italian stamps). You may come across some Italian stamps someday, and you may realize a higher price if they are listed on the eBay Italian site, *www.eBay.it*. Of course, it pays to have some grasp of the language, and your description should be in Italian, but these are small obstacles if you use an online translation site such as AltaVista's Babel Fish at *babelfish.altavista.com*.

NOTE: Online translators offer extremely rudimentary translations and do not take into consideration nuances and untranslatable idioms unique to each language. Thus, you should keep the descriptions for foreign-language listings as simple and basic as possible.

One more thing—when you list on an international site, you will be paid in the currency of that country. For the eBay Italian site, you would be paid in euros, and your Seller's Account will be charged fees based on euros (but converted to dollars), so your fees may be at the mercy of the conversion rate between the two currencies at the time the fees are charged.

Happy international selling!

We've now covered just about every aspect of selling on eBay that one can imagine. The rest of the chapters in this section cover lots of extra tips, tricks, and skills that can help make you a better eBay seller.

6

HTML for eBay Sellers

This chapter covers several HTML tags that you will find useful in creating a professional eBay item description.

Even if you currently use a Web editor to create and format your item description text with HTML or if you rely on the built-in Description Editor on the Sell Your Item form, I strongly suggest you read through this chapter. Understanding how HTML works from the bottom up will help you troubleshoot potential HTML snafus that might show up later in your eBay descriptions.

Bob Bull (bobal) is a popular chat-board regular who has found great satisfaction teaching others about HTML. Bob, who is sixty-five, suffers from several serious disabilities.

"I was so lonely staying home alone while my wife, Alice, went to work every day. At one point, I didn't care if I lived or not."

But Bob did not give up, and in April 1998 he discovered eBay. At first, he bought and sold small lots of items, always watching and learning from other savvy eBay members. Bob had a lot of questions about selling and began asking for help from other eBay members on the eBay chat boards. Over time, Bob asked so many questions and garnered so much helpful information that he became an HTML expert, answering newbie questions on the chat boards.

"I now live my life on eBay helping others. eBay has changed my life completely. When I can help a new user, I am on top of the world and I feel like my life is still worth living."

Today, Bob is a legend on the eBay chat boards and continues to help others figure out the ins and outs of selling. And he continues to make new friends every day. As he says: "No matter how many disabilities you have, you can help make a difference in someone's life."

Once you have finished this chapter, I guarantee that you will experience a great sense of accomplishment. Playing with HTML is fun!

What Is HTML?

HTML (hypertext markup language) is the language of the Internet, specifically that part of the Internet known as the World Wide Web (or the Web for short).

HTML was developed in 1990 by Tim Berners-Lee while working at the European Organization for Nuclear Research (known as CERN, the acronym of its old French name, Centre Européen pour la Recherche Nucléaire) in Geneva, Switzerland. I wonder if Tim ever imagined his little invention would literally change the world.

HTML is an easy-to-learn, universal formatting language that allows anyone to create text files called Web pages, which, when placed on a Web server, can be viewed by anyone else on the Web using any type of computer and a Web browser.

What Exactly Are Web Pages?

Web pages are text documents consisting of nothing but a simple text type called ASCII (American Standard Code for Information Interchange). Since all computer systems can read ASCII text, HTML documents can be created and viewed on any type of computer (IBM, Mac, Unix, Linux, etc.). This is what makes the Web accessible to anyone, regardless of what type of computer she uses. All of the pages you see on eBay are, at their core, text documents that have been "marked up" with HTML (along with other bits of special coding in a language called JavaScript).

GRIFF TIP! You can view the "source" text document behind any Web page by using your web browser's "View Source" or "Page Source" command, usually found under "View" on the browser's main menu bar.

What Is the Web?

The Web, or World Wide Web, consists of a vast network of special computers called servers. Web servers are located across the planet in universities, ISPs, telephone companies, businesses, homes, and of course in huge private-industry complexes called server farms. These servers are all connected through various channels including regular phone lines, special phone lines, fiber-optic cables, and even, in some cases, microwaves or radio waves.

Although they are not technically the same thing, many people use the names Internet and Web interchangeably. Actually, the Web is only a part of the Internet, which includes many other parts, such as e-mail, FTP, IRC chat, and so on. Anyone with a computer and an Internet connection can access the Web.

There are basically two types of computers on the Web: the specially configured, aforementioned Web servers and "user" computers (for lack of a better word). Your user computer can be a Mac, a PC, a Unix computer, a laptop, a PDA, a Smartphone, a Pocket PC, and the like.

Web servers are where all Web pages are stored. Hundreds of thousands of Web servers are connected to the Web, containing millions and millions of Web pages. Millions of people like you across the globe are accessing the Web with their Mac or PC or Linux computer or handheld PDA or cell phone.

An extremely important feature of the Web bears emphasizing: For a Web page or picture to be seen by everyone on the Web, the page or picture must live on a Web server. The contents of your computer, unless it is a connected Web server, are not viewable on the Web! You can create Web pages or digital pictures on your computer and you can see them in your browser, but until you upload them to a Web server, no one will ever see them. This includes your eBay pictures!

GRIFF TIP! Anytime the address for a Web page looks like this—

| File | Edit | View | Favorites | Tools | Help | | Back | F |

Address | C:\Documents and Settings\griff\Desktop\test.html

—that is, the address starts with "C:\" (or sometimes "File|\\\"), you are viewing a file from your hard drive. No one else but you will be able to view it.

What Is a Web Browser?

A Web browser is a special type of application designed for viewing Web pages. The two most popular Web browsers are currently Internet Explorer and Netscape Navigator. All of our examples employ Internet Explorer but can easily be adapted to work with Netscape.

A Web browser has the built-in ability to read any text file with the extensions .htm, .html, and .txt. Web browsers can also read picture files of the types .gif and .jpg. Using special "plug-ins," Web browsers can also read Word files, Adobe Acrobat files, and special multimedia files such as Flash Graphics.

Oh, Come on, Griff. Do I Really Need to Know All This HTML Stuff to Sell on eBay?

Thankfully, you don't. Now that the handy eBay Description Editor is built in to the Sell Your Item form, anyone can create a clean and professionally formatted item description without having to delve into HTML. However, the more knowledgeable you are about areas such as HTML, the better prepared you will be to troubleshoot problems that might pop up later. Besides, you should really explore how HTML can make your listing description even more professional and dressy. At the least, it helps to know exactly what goes on behind a Web page, since your items will be viewed as Web pages. Plus, learning HTML can provide a lasting sense of accomplishment, as eBay seller Pat Fulton discovered:

Because I can't stand to leave things alone nor can I see any reason at all for anything to be just plain vanilla, I decided that if I was going to sell on eBay, my auction pages just had to be fancy! Having young males in the house can be very helpful when you want to learn such things, as their youthful minds obviously work in a totally different direction from that of their elderly parents. Of course, as a backup plan, I bought a book on HTML as, more often than not, I have no idea at all what the boys are saying when it comes to computer stuff.

Book in hand and a son nearby, I bravely dove into HTML. Opening, closing, a <br> here and an <hr> there, tables, fonts, and colors. It was like I'd suddenly turned into Houdini doing magic tricks! Colors, lines, pictures! Amazing!

Of course there were mistakes here and there, and that's where the kid came in handy. "What's wrong with my creation? It's all weird." My son would scrutinize the page, fingers flying, clicking, shortcutting, and scrolling. "You didn't close the table" or "You put the line break in the wrong place again" was frequently the answer.

I finally got that very first item description all written up in HTML, and it had taken me days to do. Things went along very well, and as each item was listed, it sold!

Sound like fun? Let's try it and see!

Creating an HTML-Formatted eBay Description from Scratch

You don't need special software to create an HTML page or to format your eBay item description—all you need is a text editor (Notepad for Windows, Text Edit for Mac), a Web browser, and some basic HTML. And basic HTML is easy!

OPENING A TEXT EDITOR

PC users: To start, we open a blank Notepad file. Notepad can be started form the Windows Start menu at "Programs > Accessories > Notepad."

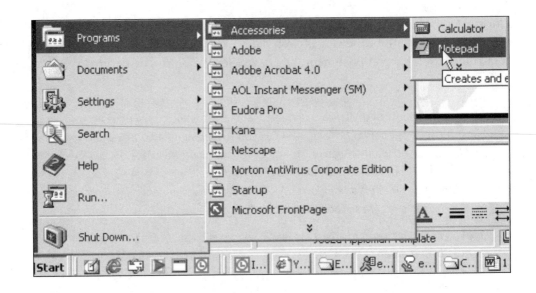

MAC users: Look for and open a program in your Applications folder called TextEdit. Follow along with us here, substituting Mac TextEditor for Notepad.

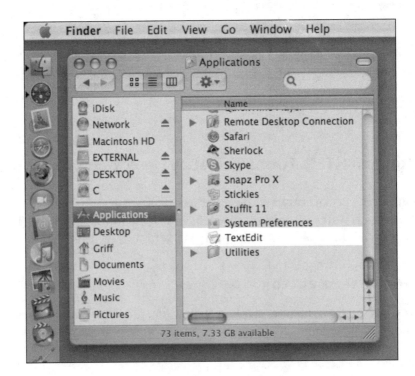

Back to Windows . . . we've clicked on and opened an Untitled text editor (Notepad or TextEdit) window.

For the remainder of this chapter, you will type everything into this text file window.

Next, we open up a fresh new browser window. For Windows, click "Start, Programs, Internet Explorer" or click the Internet Explorer icon on your desktop or toolbar.

For Mac users, click either the Safari or Firefox icon in your Dock or in the Application folder.

A browser window:

NOTE: I have resized our browser window down to a size suited for our purposes. Your browser window may be full-size. Also, I have typed "about: blank" into the Address window to show a blank (white) page.

This web browser window is where we will view the text we input into our text file window. Think of it as our "view" window.

TYPING THE DESCRIPTION

Here we will use the same item description for the small pottery pitcher I photographed in Section Two, chapter 2. It describes the item by type, age, condition, and size and also includes detailed payment instructions and shipping terms and costs.

```
Untitled - Notepad                                              _ □ ×
File  Edit  Format  Help  🖉Send
Honiton Exton Small Pitcher

I was culling treasure from the china closet and found this Honiton pitcher, 4 1/2 inches
tall, circa 1950's. White clay. Exton shape. Pitcher is in excellent condition; no cracks,
breaks, chips or stains. Embossed mark on bottom: "Honiton Potteries Exton England" with a
black hand painted "t".

A Brief History of Honiton Pottery: Honiton Pottery was (and is) located in the town of
Honiton in Devon, England. The pottery was started by Foster and Hunt at the turn of the
19th/20th century. It was purchased by Charles Collard shortly after WWI. In 1947, Collard
sold the pottery to Norman Hull and Harry Barratt who ran it until 1961 when it was sold
to Paul Redvers. All production ceased in 1997 and the pottery was shuttered. The premises
were recently reopened as pottery and craft shop.

Payment Options:

Credit/debit card
Checks (item shipped immediately after check has cleared)
Money Orders


Shipping Terms:

I will ship this item anywhere to anyone. International bidders welcome. High bidder to
pay winning bid plus USPS priority or global priority shipping and insurance as shown
below.

US bidders: $5 USD
Canadian bidders: $8 USD
UK bidders: $10 USD
All others: $15 USD

Refunds, Returns, Regrets:

If you win this item and upon receiving it, are not 100% satisfied, you may return it to
me for a full refund of the winning bid and shipping. (Returning buyer pays for shipping
back to me.)
```

Important: Notice that whenever I need to create a new paragraph, I hit the Enter key on my keyboard twice to move down two lines.

SAVING THE DESCRIPTION AS A SPECIAL TEXT FILE

Now that the content of my description is finished, we want to view the description through a Web browser. Remember, for this HTML exercise, the text file is the "input" window and the Web browser is the "output" window.

Viewing the text description through our Web browser will show us exactly how it will look on the eBay Item Description page when we list my item.

But to view the text file containing the description in another application, we first must save it to our computer's hard drive. As it stands now, the file exists only in the computer's memory.

Why We Must Save First . . .

Computer memory or RAM (random-access memory) is divided into little sections using a special type of addressing plan. For example, when you open a text editor application such as Notepad or TextEdit, your computer assigns a block of addresses in its memory where the application loads and waits to do its job. For the text editor app, that job is accepting input from your keyboard and displaying it on your computer monitor as words.

Once a set of addresses in RAM is filled with data, nothing else can read from or write to those addresses. This is a built-in memory-protection mechanism used by all operating systems—Windows, Mac, Unix, and so on. If this memory protection were not in place, any program could overwrite data in RAM at any time, making it impossible to use a computer securely.

Here's what happened when we opened a blank text editor window. First, the computer code that makes up the application was loaded up from the hard drive into a section of RAM addresses that the computer assigned. Then, we typed in some data (our description), which was also loaded into addresses within the space the computer originally allotted to the text editor application when we started it. That data is staring at us from the computer monitor.

We now want to read that data in a Web browser, but the rules of computer memory won't let any application read a memory address that is currently in use. The only application that can read the data is the one that loaded into that space—in this case our text editor application (Notepad or TextEdit).

For another application to read the data from the text editor, we need to first save the data to the hard drive. Once it is saved safely on our hard drive, a Web browser can then access, read, and display that same data by pulling it from the hard drive.

To create a computer file that a Web browser can read, we need to save the data to the hard drive by selecting "File, Save As . . ." from the our text editor toolbar.

Follow these steps exactly!

For Windows

1. Select "File" and "Save As . . ." from the text editor application toolbar.

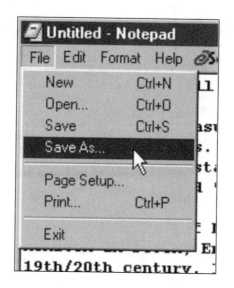

2. Choose a location on your hard drive for the new file. We will use the desktop.

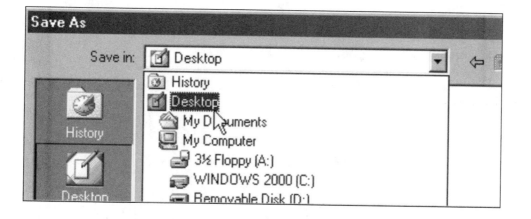

3. In the box labeled "File name," type "test.html." Locate the box for "Save as type," click the arrow on the right of the drop-down box and select "All files." Ignore any box labeled Encoding.

4. Click the "Save" button.

For Mac

1. Here is the text inside a TextEdit window:

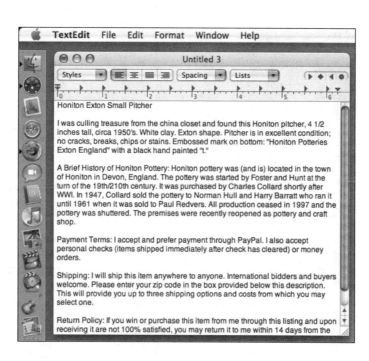

2. On the TextEdit tool bar, click "Format" and select "Make plain text."

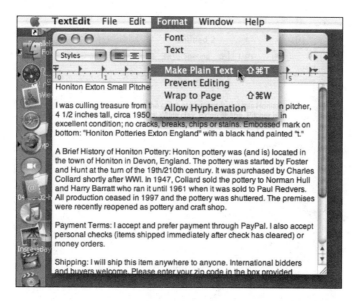

3. If prompted, click "OK" for "Convert this document to plain text?"
4. Click "File" and then "Save as."

5. Select "Desktop" as the destination.

6. In the "Save as" box, type "test.html."

7. For "Plain text encoding," select "Western (Mac OS Roman)."

8. Click the "Save" button.

9. Choose "Use .html" for the dialog box "You have used the extension . . ."

You have now saved a copy of this file to the hard drive. Note that I said "copy." There is a copy still in RAM. The copy on the hard drive is set in stone. The copy in RAM can be changed while it is open. Both copies have the same file name, in this case *test.html*.

By the way, you could name the part of this file before the dot anything you like. We chose *test*. What is important is what comes after the dot. This must be *html* or our exercise will not work.

Let's open our test.html file in a Web browser—our "output" window.

For Windows

1. Go to your fresh, new browser window. Click "File" and then "Open . . ."

2. For Windows, this will bring up an Open box. Click the "Browse . . ." button.

This will bring up another dialog box:

3. In the box labeled "Look in," click and select "Desktop" from the list of choices. This will display a list of the files on your desktop, filtered so that only HTML files are displayed. (You will notice that the box "Files of type" is set to HTML.)

4. Look for the file named *test* and double-click it.

5. In the next box, click OK.

And here's our description, displayed in the browser window exactly as it would appear in an eBay item description.

Honiton Exton Small Pitcher I was culling treasure from the china closet and found this Honiton pitcher, 4 1/2 inches tall, circa 1950's. White clay. Exton shape. Pitcher is in excellent condition; no cracks, breaks, chips or stains. Embossed mark on bottom: "Honiton Potteries Exton England" with a black hand painted "t". A Brief History of Honiton Pottery: Honiton Pottery was (and is) located in the town of Honiton in Devon, England. The pottery was started by Foster and Hunt at the turn of the 19th/20th century. It was purchased by Charles Collard shortly after WWI. In 1947, Collard sold the pottery to Norman Hull and Harry Barratt who ran it until 1961 when it was sold to Paul Redvers. All production ceased in 1997 and the pottery was shuttered. The premises were recently reopened as pottery and craft shop. Payment Options: Credit/debit card through eBay Payments (BillPoint) only Checks (item shipped immediately after check has cleared) Money Orders Shipping Terms: I will ship this item anywhere to anyone. International bidders welcome. High bidder to pay winning bid plus USPS priority or global priority shipping and insurance as shown below. US bidders: $5 USD Canadian bidders: $8 USD UK bidders: $10 USD All others: $15 USD Refunds, Returns, Regrets: If you win this item and upon receiving it, are not 100% satisfied, you may return it to me for a full refund of the winning bid and shipping. (Returning buyer pays for shipping back to me.)

For Mac

1. Open a browser window (Firefox or Safari) and click "File" and then "Open File . . ."

2. In the Open window, click the Desktop icon and double-click the *test.html* file.

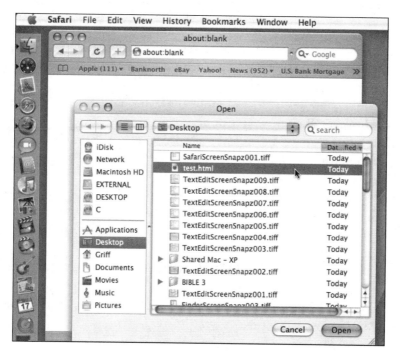

And our description is now displayed in our browser window exactly as it would appear on an eBay item description!

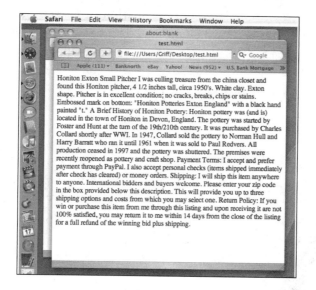

OUR TEXT IS DISPLAYED

Notice something odd? All of the line and paragraph breaks we placed in our description are gone. Our description is still readable, but it certainly doesn't look professional or easy to parse. If you go back and check the Notepad file, you will see that they are still there. So why are they missing from our description when it is viewed through a Web browser?

Web browsers are built to read all of the text characters on your computer keyboard. However, Web browsers do not recognize the Enter command used in Notepad to break a new line, so they simply ignore it, running all the text together in one continuous line that breaks only when it reaches the right-hand side of the Web browser window.

How do we get the Web browser to recognize a line or paragraph break? We need to talk to it in its own language, HTML!

HTML Tags

HTML is made up almost entirely of bits of text called tags. The simple syntax for an HTML tag looks like this:

<tag_name>

That's a lesser-than character, a tag name, and a greater-than character.

The tag name can be a letter, a combination of letters, or a word. The tag name is also case-insensitive, which means it can be upper- or lowercase and still be read as the same tag. For visual consistency, we will use uppercase for all of our tag names.

The first tag we will use looks like this:

<P>

P is the tag name, and it stands for *paragraph*. We need to type a <P> tag at every location in our description where we wish to insert a paragraph. The <P> tag will tell the browser, "Hey, browser, put a paragraph right here."

Let's type in a paragraph tag for each place in the *test.html* file where a new paragraph appears.

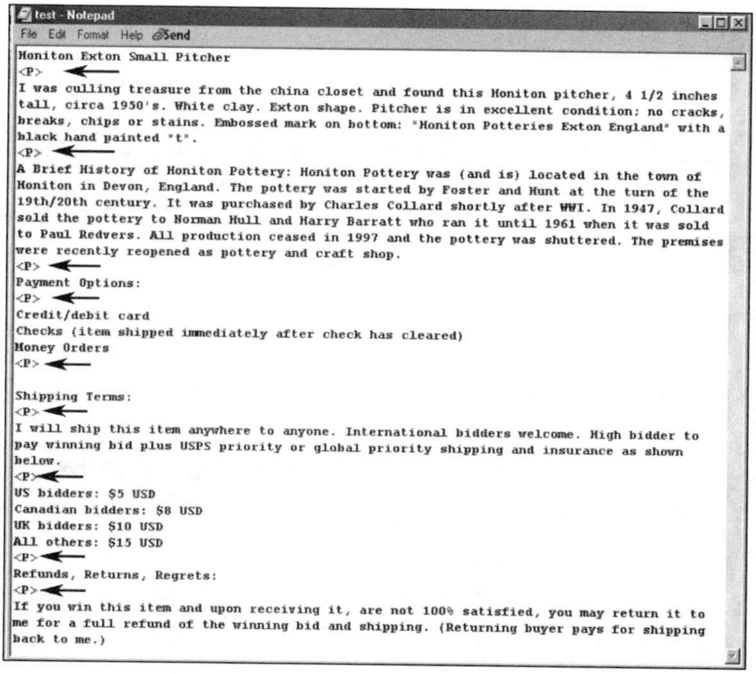

We have inserted the <P> tag in all the right places in our description. To see what these tags do to our description when viewed through a Web browser, we must resave the file to the hard drive.

Click on "File" on the text editor menu command bar and then click "Save."

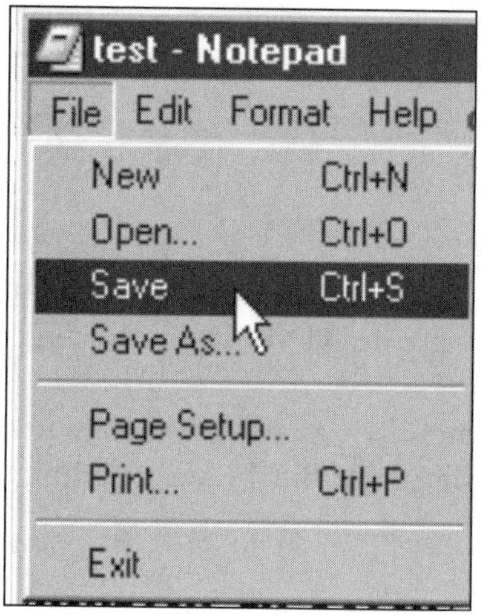

Windows

Mac

Now go back to the Web browser window and click the Refresh icon on the Web browser toolbar.

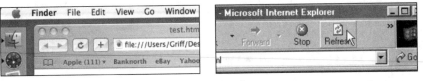

Mac   Windows

Magically, where once there were no paragraphs, there are now several!

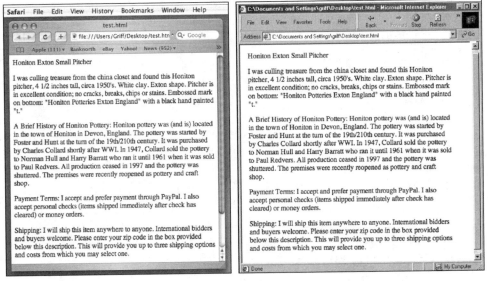

Mac   Windows

That's it. That's how HTML works. The <P> tag is just one tag out of many, but almost everything you need to know about HTML from here on is based on this simple exercise.

You could stop here and use only the <P> tag and your eBay item descriptions would be perfectly readable, if a bit plain. But I have a feeling you aren't satisfied with just the <P> tag.

Let's learn some more tags!

LINE BREAKS

The <P> tag works for double line breaks, but what about those places where we only want to break to the next line (for example, our list of payment options)?

Payment Options:

Credit/debit card Checks (item shipped immediately after check has cleared) Money Orders

Although it's readable, it would be much cleaner if each option were on a separate line. The tag we need is the <BR> or "break" tag. Let's type one in after each of the payment options and the shipping costs in our text editor file.

```
Payment Options:|
<P>
Credit/debit card <BR>
Checks (item shipped immediately after check has cleared) <BR>
Money Orders
<P>

Shipping Terms:
<P>
I will ship this item anywhere to anyone. International bidder:
pay winning bid plus USPS priority or global priority shipping
below.
<P>
US bidders: $5 USD <BR>
Canadian bidders: $8 USD <BR>
UK bidders: $10 USD <BR>
All others: $15 USD
<P>
```

Once we have typed in all of the <BR> tags we need, we must save the changes in the text editor application and refresh the web browser window. From now on, I will refer to these two steps as "save and refresh," since we will be saving changes many times in the rest of this chapter.

NOTE: For brevity, from here on we will use the Windows examples only. Mac users can follow along substituting the Mac versions of save and refresh.

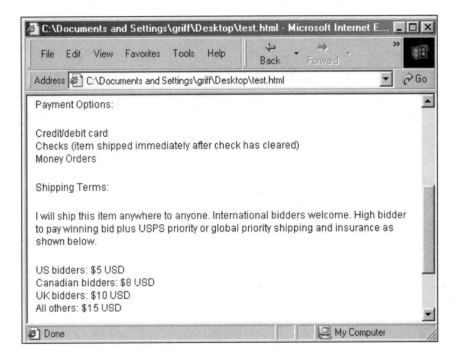

Here's what our description looks like in Internet Explorer with the added <BR> tags:

Our payment options and shipping costs are now a lot easier to understand. So, should we stop here or do you want to learn more tags?
I thought so.

BOLD

I like to emphasize titles and important words in my eBay listing descriptions. One way to do so is to use the <B> tag, which stands for boldface. Let's add it to the header line at the top of our description.

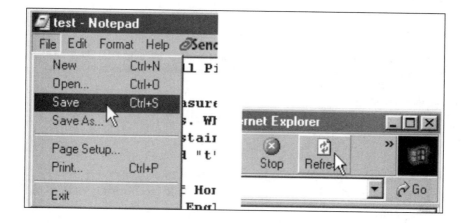

Save and refresh! (Save in our text editor, refresh in our Web browser.)

Here's what bold formatting using the <B> tag looks like:

```
C:\Documents and Settings\griff\Desktop\test.html - Microsoft Internet Explorer

File   Edit   View   Favorites   Tools   Help      Back   Forward   Stop   Refresh

Address   C:\Documents and Settings\griff\Desktop\test.html                    Go
```

Honiton Exton Small Pitcher

I was culling treasure from the china closet and found this Honiton pitcher, 4 1/2 inches tall, circa 1950's. White clay. Exton shape. Pitcher is in excellent condition; no cracks, breaks, chips or stains. Embossed mark on bottom: "Honiton Potteries Exton England" with a black hand painted "t".

A Brief History of Honiton Pottery: Honiton Pottery was (and is) located in the town of Honiton in Devon, England. The pottery was started by Foster and Hunt at the turn of the 19th/20th century. It was purchased by Charles Collard shortly after WWI. In 1947, Collard sold the pottery to Norman Hull and Harry Barratt who ran it until 1961 when it was sold to Paul Redvers. All production ceased in 1997 and the pottery was shuttered. The premises were recently reopened as pottery and craft shop.

Payment Options:

Credit/debit card
Checks (item shipped immediately after check has cleared)
Money Orders

Shipping Terms:

I will ship this item anywhere to anyone. International bidders welcome. High bidder to pay winning bid plus USPS priority or global priority shipping and insurance as shown below.

US bidders: $5 USD

```
Done                                                    My Computer
```

Uh . . . so much for bold emphasis. We wanted only the top line of the description to appear bold, but now everything is bold, so nothing stands out! Why did this happen?

When you insert a text formatting tag into a text document, the Web browser that reads the document starts the formatting at the exact spot in the text where you placed the particular formatting tag, and it doesn't stop formatting until either it comes to the end of the document or you tell it where to stop.

Clearly, we need to tell the Web browser where to stop with the boldface. We do this by inserting a close tag. A close tag for a specific tag is the same tag with a forward slash before the name: </B>.

Let's type a bold close tag right after the word *pitcher*.

Save and refresh!

Here's the result in our browser window:

Honiton Exton Small Pitcher

I was culling treasure from the china closet and found this Honiton pitcher, 4 1/2 inches tall, circa 1950's. White clay. Exton shape. Pitcher is in excellent condition; no cracks, breaks, chips or stains. Embossed mark on bottom: "Honiton Potteries Exton England" with a black hand painted "t".

A Brief History of Honiton Pottery: Honiton Pottery was (and is) located in the town of Honiton in Devon, England. The pottery was started by Foster and Hunt at the turn of the 19th/20th century. It was purchased by Charles Collard shortly after WWI. In 1947, Collard sold the pottery to

Exactly what we wanted!

Let's add bold tags to other important words in our description.

```
<P>
<B>Payment Options:</B>
<P>
Credit/debit card
Checks (item shipped immediately afte
Money Orders
<P>

<B>Shipping Terms:</B>
<P>
I will ship this item anywhere to any
pay winning bid plus USPS priority or
below.
<P>
US bidders: $5 USD <BR>
Canadian bidders: $8 USD <BR>
UK bidders: $10 USD <BR>
All others: $15 USD
<P>
<B> Refunds, Returns, Regrets: </B>
<P>
```

Save and refresh!

Here's how our item description would look on our eBay listing:

```
C:\Documents and Settings\griff\Desktop\test.html - Microsoft Internet Explorer

File    Edit    View    Favorites    Tools    Help        Back    Forward    Stop    Refresh

Address   C:\Documents and Settings\griff\Desktop\test.html                         Go
```

Honiton Exton Small Pitcher

I was culling treasure from the china closet and found this Honiton pitcher, 4 1/2 inches tall, circa 1950's. White clay. Exton shape. Pitcher is in excellent condition; no cracks, breaks, chips or stains. Embossed mark on bottom: "Honiton Potteries Exton England" with a black hand painted "t".

A Brief History of Honiton Pottery: Honiton Pottery was (and is) located in the town of Honiton in Devon, England. The pottery was started by Foster and Hunt at the turn of the 19th/20th century. It was purchased by Charles Collard shortly after WWI. In 1947, Collard sold the pottery to Norman Hull and Harry Barratt who ran it until 1961 when it was sold to Paul Redvers. All production ceased in 1997 and the pottery was shuttered. The premises were recently reopened as pottery and craft shop.

Payment Options:

Credit/debit card
Checks (item shipped immediately after check has cleared)
Money Orders

Shipping Terms:

I will ship this item anywhere to anyone. International bidders welcome. High bidder to pay winning bid plus USPS priority or global priority shipping and insurance as shown below.

US bidders: $5 USD
Canadian bidders: $8 USD
UK bidders: $10 USD
All others: $15 USD

Refunds, Returns, Regrets:

```
Done                                                          My Computer
```

Now our description is starting to look like something. Still, there is so much more we can do to dress it up. For other different emphasis, we can use the <U> and <I> tags (underline and italics).

```
<B>Payment Options:</B>
<P>
Credit/debit card<BR>
Checks (item shipped <U>immediately</U> after chec
Money Orders<BR>
<P>
<B>Shipping Terms:</B>
<P>
I will ship this item <I> anywhere </I> to anyone.
welcome. High bidder to pay winning bid plus USPS
```

Save and refresh. Here is what the <I> and <U> tags do in the Web browser:

Payment Options:

Credit/debit card
Checks (item shipped <u>immediately</u> after check ha
Money Orders

Shipping Terms:

I will ship this item *anywhere* to anyone. Internatior
winning bid plus USPS priority or global priority sh

Our description is looking more and more professional. What? You want more? Then more you shall have!

LIST TAGS

List tags come in handy when composing an eBay item description. They are actually a set of tags that work together to create lists:

<UL> </UL>
<LI>

Let's use them for our payment options. We will first need to remove the <BR> tags we typed in earlier. Then we place an opening <UL> tag before the items on the list of payment options and a closing </UL> tag after the last payment option on the list. Finally, we place a <LI> tag before each option on the list.

```
<UL>
<LI>Credit/debit card
<LI>Checks (item shipped <U>immediately</U> after check has cleared)
<LI>Money Orders
</UL>
```

Save and refresh!

Here's what our list will look like in our item description:

THE FONT TAG

Up to now, the tags that we have used in our item description have consisted of a name between lesser-than and greater-than characters. Some tags have more than just a name inside the lesser- and greater-than characters. One of them is the <FONT> tag.

The <FONT> tag is used to change either the size, color, or typeface of text. To make these changes, there needs to be more information inside the brackets than just *FONT*. This information is added after the name using the following syntax:

<name attribute=value>

Looks a little like algebra, but don't panic—it's not complicated. An attribute is some aspect of the name. For example, in HTML, FONT has a few common attributes. Two of the most commonly used are *size* and *color*. A value is assigned to an attribute using the = (equals) sign in order to change that particular attribute.

The first attribute we will change using the <FONT> tag is SIZE. In HTML, the attribute for SIZE can take as a value any number from 0 to 7.

<FONT SIZE=6>

To close out the FONT tag, we use a closing tag:

</FONT>

Note that the closing </FONT> tag does not include the attribute value pair SIZE=6. Attribute/value pairs are only indicated in the opening tag, never the closing tag.

Let's add it to the title on the top of our item description.

To make it clearer, I have placed the tags above and below the line to be formatted. Let's save and refresh and view the change in our Web browser.

Amazing, isn't it? Well, there's more! Not only can we change the size, we can change the color of the font as well!

The attribute is COLOR and the value can be one of two types. The simplest type of values to use for COLOR are common color names like *red*, *blue*, *green*, *orange*, *yellow*, *purple*, *white*, *black*, and so on. Note that some not-so-common color names such as *maroon* and *fuchsia* will work, as will some combination words such as *lightblue* or *lightgreen*. Uncommon names such as *bruise*, *oatmeal*, and *monkeyspit* won't. There is another type of value that uses hexadecimal numbers, which I will tell you more about shortly. For now, we will use a common color name for a value. I'll use *yellow*, which will show up gray in our black-and-white illustration.

```
<FONT SIZE=6 COLOR=yellow>
</FONT>
```

Note that a tag can have more than one attribute value pair. When adding attribute value pairs, make sure that there is one space and only one space between them. More than one space will "break" the tag and it won't work. Let's add this attribute value pair for COLOR to our item description.

```
text.html - Notepad
File  Edit  Format  Help  Send

<FONT SIZE=6 COLOR=yellow>

<B>Honiton Exton Small Pitcher</B>

</FONT>
```

Save and refresh . . .

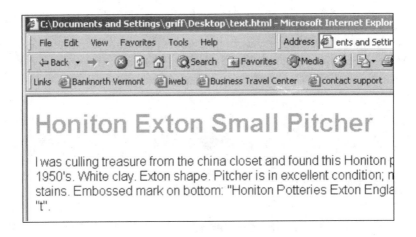

. . . to view the changes in the Web browser window.

This is the easiest way to indicate a color, but it limits us to a narrow range of colors. There is, however, another type of value for the COLOR attribute that provides literally thousands of colors. It involves a special type of number called hexadecimal. Let's talk a little about hexadecimal numbers before we see them in action as a color value.

Our everyday number system is based on a decimal system, that is, a numbering system based on 10 (most likely because we have five fingers on each hand to work with when counting).

1 2 3 4 5 6 7 8 9 0

A hexadecimal number system is one based on 16. (Imagine if humans evolved with eight fingers on each hand. We would most definitely be using a hexadecimal number system instead of the decimal system we have always used.)

Since our everyday numbering system has only ten number symbols, we have to borrow other symbols to accommodate a hexadecimal system. Our hexadecimal numbering system uses the digits 0 through 9, plus it "borrows" the first six letters of our alphabet:

0 1 2 3 4 5 6 7 8 9 A B C D E F

We use a six-place hexadecimal number with a pound sign before to represent a COLOR value in HTML, for example:

<font color=#FF33EE>

This number, #FF33EE, will give you a particular shade and hue of a color. The hexadecimal numbers for a color value are not random, though. Here is how they work.

The six-place hexadecimal color value number can be pictured as three separate two-place values, for example:

FF 33 EE

The three parts of the six-place number represent three values for colored light indicated as RGB (red, green, blue).

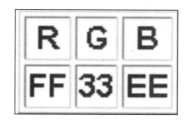

The value FF represents the strength of the red component of light, the 33 represents the strength of the green component of light, and the EE represents the strength of the blue component of light.

The values of the two-place hexadecimal numbers increase in strength from 00 (no value) up to FF (highest value). Here is an abridged scale from 00 to FF:

00 01 02 03 04 05 06 07 08 09 0A 0B 0C 0D 0E 0F 10 11 12 13 14 15
16 17 18 19 1A 1B 1C . . . and on up to . . . 98 99 9A 9B 9C 9D 9E
9F AF BF CF DF EF FF

An interesting fact about light color: Equal amounts of full-strength red, green, and blue light produce white light. A zero value of red, green, and blue light equals black (no light). Therefore:

<font color=#FFFFFF> equals the color white
<font color=#000000> equals the color black

With all the other thousands and thousands of colors in between! Many Web pages on the Internet display color charts with each color's respective hexadecimal numbers. To find them, go to *www.google.com* and search on the words *"HTML color chart."*

HTML Character Entities

Many folks e-mail or ask me at eBay University how to go about inserting a special symbol such as ™ into their Item Description pages or About Me page. It's nothing complicated—it's all done with character entities.

A character entity is a small set of keyboard characters that make up a numeric or text code that stands for a special symbol. When a Web browser parses these sets of characters, it will display a related special symbol or character not found on your computer keyboard. For example, to insert a ™ into your listing description, you would type:

™

That's an ampersand, followed by a pound sign, the a 1, a 5, a 3, and finally a semicolon.

Here are some other popular character entities that rely on numeric codes:

¢ = ¢ (cent sign)
£ = £ (pound sterling)
¥ = ¥ (yen sign)
© = © (copyright)
® = ® (registered trademark)

Some character entities utilize ISO Latin 1 codes instead of numeric codes. Here is a good example using the ISO Latin code for "nonbreaking space." If you type more than one space between words or objects into an HTML document, all Web browsers will ignore any spaces after the first one. For example, if I type

word   word

with six spaces between each word, the Web page will still display

word word

To add the extra spaces, we need to insert a special character entity for the nonbreaking space. It looks like this:

** **

If we type five of these character entities between each *word*—

word   word

—we get this

word   word

Another good use of ISO character entities is for displaying actual HTML formatting tags on a Web page. Let's say you wanted to show someone on one of eBay's chat boards how to create a hyperlink using HTML. You might type the following into your chat board post:

<A href=http://www.eBay.com> Visit eBay! </A>

But, of course, when others viewed your post, they would see

Visit eBay!

instead of the actual HTML. That's because the viewers' Web browsers parse and format the text based on the tags you provided. To display the actual HTML link tags within a Web browser, you would need to substitute character entities for the lesser-than and greater-than tags. Those character entities look like this:

< (which equals the "<" character)

That's an ampersand followed by the lowercase letter *l*, the lowercase letter *t*, and finally a semicolon.

> (which equals the ">" character)

That's an ampersand followed by the lowercase letter *g*, the lowercase letter *t*, and finally a semicolon.

By substituting these character entities, you effectively "break" the ability of the Web browser to parse and display the HTML as an actual link. This is good, since your intention is not to create a link but to display the HTML needed to create a link! With the character entity substitutions, you would type

<A href=http://www.eBay.com> Visit eBay! </A>

and the Web browser would parse this and display it as

<A href=http://www.eBay.com> Visit eBay! </A>

QUIZ QUESTION

When I was a regular on the eBay chat forums, I would use this character entity trick to display HTML tags for users who had questions about how to create a link. Other users would notice that I had effectively displayed HTML tags without the tags being parsed by the Web browser. They would ask me, "How did you do that?" I would then show them how. Again, note that if I type what I typed to create the "inactive" HTML link—

<A href=http://www.eBay.com> Visit eBay! </A>

—the following would display:

<A href=http://www.eBay.com> Visit eBay! </A>

What would one type into an HTML text document to display the following text inside a Web browser?

<A href=http://www.eBay.com> Visit eBay! </A>

(Hint: It involves a character entity substitution for one of the characters within the character entities < and >.)

Can you figure it out?

The answer: To display the actual character entity without the Web browser parsing the entity and displaying the character, you substitute a character entity for one of the characters inside the original entity. In this case, we substituted the character entity for ampersand—&—for the "&" character. This could go one forever in an endless regression of nested character entities, but I will assume you got the point and will spare you the tedium of actually printing out an endless regression of nested character entities, but I will assume you got the point and will spare you the tedium of actually printing out an endless regression of nested character entities, but I will assume you got the point and will spare you the tedium of actually printing out an endless regression of nested character entities, but I will assume you got the point and will spare you the tedium of actually printing out an endless regression of nested character entities . . .

Character entities also come in handy when you need to insert special non-English-alphabet characters into your text, for example, *ä* or *ö* (*a* and *o* with an umlaut).

You can find many complete lists of other numeric code and ISO Latin 1 HTML character entities by going to any good search engine (such as my favorite, *www.google.com*) and searching on the phrase "*character entities.*"

You probably never thought you could do so much with a description. You're learning fast!

So far, we've only been formatting text. HTML can do much more.

Hyperlinks

One of the most important features of the Web is the ability to click a text link to go to another Web page. The Web would be almost impossible to navigate without these links (imagine having to type in a Web address for every page on the Web you wanted to visit).

Links, or more properly hyperlinks, are easy to add to your item description. The tag for creating a hyperlink is the <A> tag.

The *A* stands for "anchor." The <A> tag never stands alone—it always contains an attribute-value pair where the attribute is *href* and the value is a URL (Universal Resource Locator, or Web address) for a file somewhere on the Internet. The opening and closing <A> tags surround some text that you have selected to be the actual clickable link.

<A HREF=some URL> type text here that will be the clickable link </A>

Let's add a link to the item description. This link will take our bidders to our other eBay listings.

Click on "Advanced search" on the top of any eBay page. Then on the left click "Items by seller." Finally, enter your User ID into the box provided.

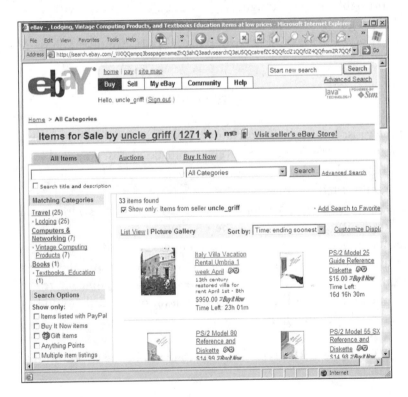

Click "Search." This takes us to the list of current listings by uncle_griff.

Thirty-three listings are currently open for uncle_griff, but even if there were no current listings, it wouldn't matter. All we need is the URL for this page and the trick will still work.

Find the Address box on the Internet Explorer menu bar. Click once inside the box to highlight the entire URL (address). Keeping your mouse cursor over the highlighted URL, click the right button on your mouse and select "Copy" from the pop-up menu.

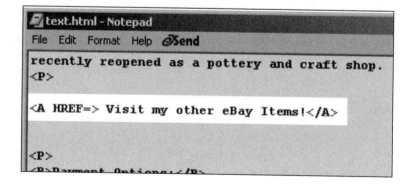

This copies the complete URL in the Address box to the operating system's Clipboard function.

Go back to the item description in the text editor file. At the end of the second paragraph of our description, before Payment Options, we'll add the following line of HTML-formatted text.

<A href=> Visit my other eBay Items! </A>

Once you have typed the line of HTML text into the description, place your mouse cursor so that it blinks right between the = and the > after *HREF*.

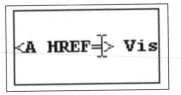

Now, without moving the cursor, click the right mouse button and select "Paste" from the pop-up menu.

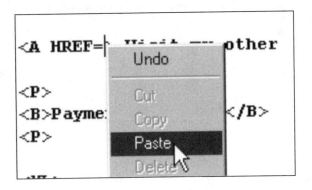

This will paste the entire search URL into the appropriate space in the <A> tag:

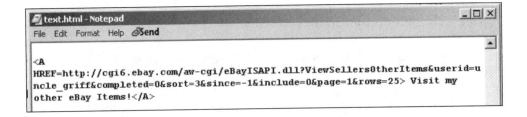

Save and refresh!

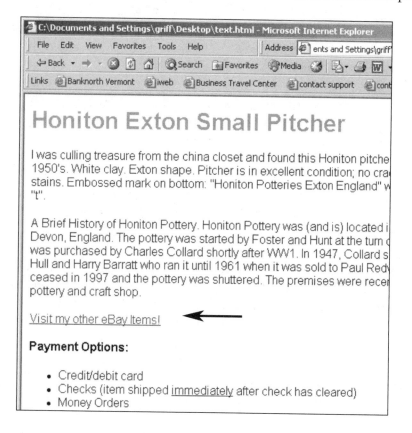

Go to your Web browser window to view the link in the item description.

Now you know how to create and insert any hyperlink into an item description. Quite an accomplishment, but before we move on to embedding images . . .

A FEW IMPORTANT CONSIDERATIONS ABOUT LINKS

eBay does not allow links from your item description to your personal or commercial Web page. In fact, every seller should know exactly what is and what isn't allowed in the way of links in an item description so, this is an excerpt from the eBay site regarding links policy:

eBay allows sellers to place only certain types of links within an item description. (See the Links Frequently Asked Questions for the definition of a link.) Links that are permitted are listed below; sellers should review the specific link's policy by clicking on it to ensure any links included in the listing adhere to the policies outlined.

- *One link to a page that further describes the item being sold in that listing*
- *One link to your e-mail address that opens an e-mail client for potential buyers to ask questions about the item in that listing*
- *Links to photos of the item for sale*
- *Links to your eBay (including your eBay Store) or Half.com listings*
- *Links to your About Me page (in addition to the About Me icon already provided by eBay)*
- *Links to your "Add to My Favorite Sellers and Stores" page*
- *Links that provide credits to third parties*
- *One link to your listing terms and conditions (providing that the most relevant information is within the listing itself and that this page does not include any links off of the eBay Web site)*

A logo used for any of these links may be no greater than 88x33 pixels and it may not flash or otherwise move. (The exception to this guideline is links to your eBay or Half.com listings.) A URL used as a static or clickable link may not represent, brand, or advertise a homepage URL outside of eBay, except in listings offering a domain name for sale.
Linking to Web sites that offer to trade, sell, or purchase goods or services, or including links for any purpose other than those listed above is not allowed. Prohibited links include, but are not limited to:

- *Links to Web pages that offer to trade, sell or purchase goods or services outside of eBay. This applies whether it is a static URL or an active link*

- *Links to Web sites or pages offering merchandise not permitted on eBay*
- *Links to sites that solicit eBay User IDs, passwords or e-mail addresses from buyers*
- *Links that encourage buyers to place their eBay bids through a site other than eBay*
- *Links or other connections to live chat systems*
- *Links to subscribe to newsletters or mailing lists hosted outside-of-eBay*

When linking to the "Add to Favorite Sellers and Stores" page, references to the Favorite Sellers Top Picks email are permitted. If you have an eBay Store, references to your Store newsletter and mailing list names are permitted, provided that your inclusion of the mailing list names does not constitute keyword spamming or violate any other eBay policy.

Just look at our eBay item description. We've gone from a single block of text to a professional-looking layout with a link in just a few minutes!

And you thought this was going to be hard. But wait! There's more. . . .

The Image Tag

In the previous chapters, when we actually listed our item live on eBay, we relied on eBay Picture Services, since it's a quick, no-fuss way to place digital pictures on your listing.

Still, it's important to know just how digital pictures are placed onto an eBay item page.

All Web page graphics—JPEGs, GIFs, pictures, icons, and so on—are embedded in a Web page using the <IMG> tag.

The <IMG> tag does not have a closing tag. It does not format text but it "does" something. That is, it tells the Web browser to go fetch a copy of a digital picture file somewhere on the Internet. Here's how the <IMG> tag works.

The <IMG> tag, like the <FONT> tag, cannot live on its tag name alone. It needs an attribute-value pair. For the <IMG> tag, this attribute-value pair looks like this:

<IMG SRC=url>

where *url* is a valid URL that points to either a JPEG or GIF file.

Here is a URL that points to a picture of someone you might know:

http://www.unclegriff.com/images/feb-19-02-headshot05.jpg

Let's use it for our listing. Here is the complete URL.

<IMG SRC=http://www.unclegriff.com/images/feb-19-02
-headshot05.jpg>

We will place it at the very bottom of our item description in Notepad, save and refresh, and check to see the results.

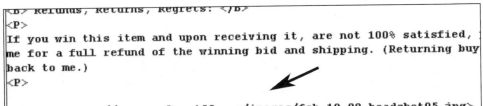

```
<b> Refunds, Returns, Regrets: </b>
<P>
If you win this item and upon receiving it, are not 100% satisfied,
me for a full refund of the winning bid and shipping. (Returning buy
back to me.)
<P>

<IMG SRC=http://www.unclegriff.com/images/feb-19-02-headshot05.jpg>
```

Save and refresh!

And here's our description with a shot of yours truly:

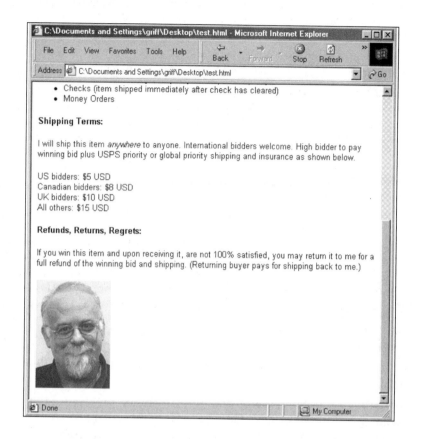

If you know the URL to a picture, you can link to it using the <IMG> tag. The linking is the easy part. Placing a digital picture file on a Web server is a bit harder but not impossible. Again, we will use eBay Picture Services when we list our item in the next chapter. I will also show examples of using other options for digital picture hosting at the end of the next chapter.

A NOTE ABOUT "BORROWING" PICTURES

As I mentioned earlier, if you know the URL for an image file, you can embed it into a Web page (such as your eBay Item Description page) by using the <IMG> tag. That means it's technically possible to link to any image on the Web. However, this doesn't mean that it's okay to do so without permission.

Never link to another person's or company's images or graphics without first asking their permission. This is especially important on eBay.

Table Tags

Tables are simply grids made up of one or more cells. Here is a typical (non-HTML) four-cell table created in Microsoft Word.

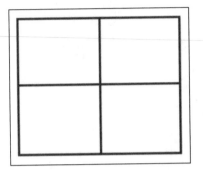

In Web pages (and especially in eBay item descriptions), HTML tables come in handy for creating layouts for text and pictures. We can place tables in our item description by using the <TABLE> tag set.

<TABLE> tags never act alone—they are used in sets just like <UL> (list) tags. The other tags that <TABLE> needs to do its job are <TR> (table row) and <TD> (table data).

HTML table cells can contain text, links, or images. HTML tables can also have visible or invisible borders. Here is an example of the HTML formatting used to create a four-cell table. Each cell contains the word *eBay*:

```
<TABLE BORDER=1>
<TR> <TD>eBay</TD> <TD> eBay</TD> </TR>
<TR> <TD>eBay</TD> <TD> eBay</TD> </TRB>
</TABLE>
```

The above HTML, when we copy it into our *test.html* document, save the changes, and then refresh our browser, creates the following table:

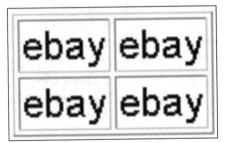

Every HTML table starts with a <TABLE> tag and ends with a </TABLE> tag. *This is extremely important!* If you use tables in your description and do not close them with the proper number of </TABLE> tags, your item description will not appear in some types of Web browsers!

The <TABLE> tag may include an attribute-value pair for BORDER=value. A value of 0 will make the border invisible. Any other value will show a border of increasing size. We will use a value of 1.

Every row in our table is indicated by <TR> and </TR> tags. (Again, *TR* stands for *table row*.)

Within every set of table row tags, table cells are created by inserting <TD> and </TD> tags for each cell. (To repeat, *TD* stands for *table data*.)

TEXT PLACEMENT USING TABLE TAGS

Tables can be useful for laying out text as data in cells. For example, our various shipping costs per location will look better if we place the data in a table. Here's how that section of our eBay item description looks now:

```
US bidders: $5 USD
Canadian bidders: $8 USD
UK bidders: $10 USD
All others: $15 USD
```

We have four rows of data for each location. Each row contains two parts: one for location and one for cost. Thus, we need a table of four rows with two columns for a total of eight cells. I like to type out the table tags first before typing in the data. Each row starts with an opening <TR> tag and ends with a closing </TR> tag. In between the <TR> and </TR> for each row, there are two sets of table data tags <TD> </TD>—one for each cell. (Remember, we need two cells for each row.) I am also going to add a fifth row for our headers: "location" and "shipping costs."

```
<TABLE BORDER=1>
 <TR> <TD> </TD> <TD> </TD> </TR>
 <TR> <TD> </TD> <TD> </TD> </TR>
 <TR> <TD> </TD> <TD> </TD> </TR>
 <TR> <TD> </TD> <TD> </TD> </TR>
 <TR> <TD> </TD> <TD> </TD> </TR>
 <TABLE>
```

Let's fill in the data for each cell. We carefully type it in between each <TD> and </TD> tag:

<TABLE BORDER=1>
<TR> <TD>Ship To Location</TD> <TD>Shipping (USD)</TD>
</TR>
<TR> <TD>US</TD> <TD>$5</TD> </TR>
<TR> <TD>Canada</TD> <TD>$8</TD> </TR>
<TR> <TD>UK</TD> <TD>$10</TD> </TR>
<TR> <TD>All Others</TD> <TD>$15</TD> </TR>
</TABLE>

I say *carefully* because if you type the data in the wrong place, your table will be a mess.

We now type this set of table tags with data into our eBay item description in our Notepad file in place of the original shipping costs.

```
<TABLE BORDER=1>
<TR> <TD>Ship To Location</TD> <TD>Shipping (USD)</TD></TR>
<TR> <TD>US </TD> <TD>$5 </TD> </TR>
<TR> <TD>Canada </TD> <TD>$8 </TD> </TR>
<TR> <TD> UK </TD> <TD> $10 </TD> </TR>
<TR> <TD>All Others </TD> <TD>$15 </TD> </TR>
</TABLE>
```

Save and refresh!

Here's what our new tabled shipping costs look like viewed through our Web browser:

Ship To Location	Shipping (USD)
US	$5
Canada	$8
UK	$10
All Others	$15

Data such as our shipping costs is much easier to read when it is displayed in a table.

Creating tables bigger or fancier than a few rows and columns is difficult to do "by hand" without making simple errors created by mistyping a tag name or leaving off a closing tag. If you create HTML tables by hand for your eBay listing description (and I urge you to do so), keep them simple. Two columns and two to five rows should be easy to handle.

PICTURE PLACEMENT USING TABLE TAGS

The following HTML sample shows how to use a simple two-cell table to align two images in an eBay item description. Between each <TD> and </TD> tag, there is a complete <IMG SRC> tag for a valid digital picture file. (These are digital pictures of our item that I uploaded to a Web server—*www.sover.net*—back in my old home state of Vermont. How to upload digital pictures to a server is covered in the next chapter.)

```
<TABLE BORDER=1>
<TR>
<TD> <IMG
SRC=http://www.sover.net/~jimgriff/images/honiton03.jpg> </TD>
<TD> <IMG
SRC=http://www.sover.net/~jimgriff/images/honiton04.jpg> </TD>
</TR>
</TABLE>
```

Let's paste the above HTML formatting into our item description before the brief history section. Bidders like to see pictures ASAP!

```
text.html - Notepad                                               _ □ ×
File   Edit   Format   Help   ✒Send
<B>Honiton Exton Small Pitcher</B>

</FONT>

<P>
I was culling treasure from the china closet and found this Honiton pitcher,
4 1.2 inches tall, circa 1950's. White clay. Exton shape. Pitcher is in
excellent condition; no cracks, breaks, chips or stains. Embossed mark on
bottom: "Honiton Potteries Exton England" with a black hand painted "t".
<P>

<TABLE BORDER=1>
<TR>
<TD><IMG SRC=http://www.sover.net/~jimgriff/images/honiton03.jpg></TD>
<TD><IMG SRC=http://www.sover.net/~jimgriff/images/honiton04.jpg></TD>
</TR>
</TABLE>


<P>
A Brief History of Honiton Pottery. Honiton Pottery was (and is) located in
the town of Honiton in Devon, England. The pottery was started by Foster and
Hunt at the turn of the 19th/20th century. It was purchased by Charles
Collard shortly after WW1. In 1947, Collard sold the pottery to Norman Hull
and Harry Barratt who ran it until 1961 when it was sold to Paul Redvers. All
```

Save and refresh . . . and here's our item description viewed in our browser:

There is a big advantage to embedding digital image files into a table as opposed to including them without a table. When a Web browser gets to an <IMG> tag, it stops loading the rest of the page as the pictures download. For fast Internet connections, this is not a big issue, but for those with slow dial-up connections, the wait can be annoying. Placing your image URLs in an HTML table helps to remedy this problem. Web browsers will load the table and keep loading the rest of the item page while the pictures load into the table cells, allowing the potential bidder to read the rest of the contents of the item description while the pictures load.

Other HTML Tags

CENTER

To center text or a picture on a Web page, use the <CENTER> tags:

```
<CENTER>
</CENTER>
```

Let's use the <CENTER> tag to center my picture on the item description page:

```
<P>
<CENTER>
<IMG SRC=http://www.sover.net/~jimgriff/images/feb-19-02-headshot05.jpg><BR>
Thanks for shopping with Uncle!
</CENTER>
```

Save and refresh!

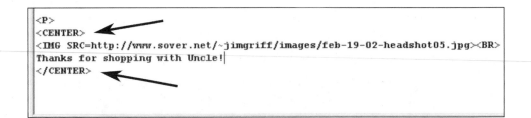

View the changes in Internet Explorer:

Within the browser window:

I will ship this item *anywhere* to anyone. International bidders welcome. High bidder to pay winning bid plus USPS priority or global priority shipping and insurance as shown below.

Ship To Location	Shipping (USD)
US	$5
Canada	$8
UK	$10
All Others	$15

Refunds, Returns, Regrets:

If your win this item and upon receiving it, are not 100% satisfied, you may return it to me for a full refund of the winning bid and shipping (Returning buyer pays for shipping back to me.)

Thanks for shopping with Uncle!

THE HORIZONTAL RULE TAG

The <HR> tag places a horizontal rule into the Web page. It comes in handy for separating sections of a Web page or eBay Item Description page. Let's slip one in our item description to see what it does.

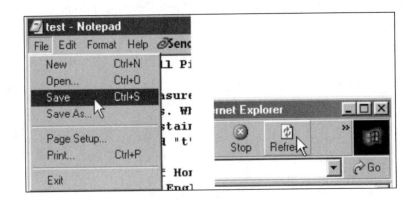

```
test - Notepad
File  Edit  Format  Help  Send

Paul Redvers. All production ceased
shuttered. The premises were recent.
<P>


<A
HREF=http://cgi6.ebay.com/aw-cgi/eB
Items&userid=uncle_griff&include=0&
other eBay Auctions! </A>


<HR>   <----


<P>
<B>Payment Options:</B>
<P>


<UL>
```

Save and refresh!

```
test - Notepad
File  Edit  Format  Help  Send
New        Ctrl+N    l Pi
Open...    Ctrl+O
Save       Ctrl+S    asure
Save As...           s. Wh
                     stair
Page Setup...        "t'
Print...   Ctrl+P
                     Hor
Exit                 Engl
```

```
rnet Explorer        _ □ ×
  Stop    Refresh    »
                          ▼   Go
```

Ta-da! A horizontal rule!

A Brief History of Honiton Pottery. Honiton Pottery was (and is) located in the town of Honiton in Devon, England. The pottery was started by Foster and Hunt at the turn of the 19th/20th century. It was purchased by Charles Collard shortly after WW1. In 1947, Collard sold the pottery to Norman Hull and Harry Barratt who ran it until 1961 when it was sold to Paul Redvers. All production ceased in 1997 and the pottery was shuttered. The premises were recently reopened as a pottery and craft shop.

Visit my other eBay Items!

Payment Options:

- Credit/debit card
- Checks (item shipped immediately after check has cleared)
- Money Orders

Using simple HTML tags, we've turned a boring, hard-to-read block of text into a polished and professional-looking eBay item description.

There's an additional benefit to creating our eBay item description in a separate text file. We can now save this file and use it over and over again as a template for future eBay listings, effectively avoiding endless retyping of our payment options or shipping and return policies. Saving the description also preserves our layout for future use.

That wasn't so difficult, was it? I told you HTML would be a snap.

Now that we've finished this chapter, though, I have to 'fess up. Few sellers actually work through HTML the way we just did. Most sellers rely on the Description Editor, which is built into the eBay Sell Your Item form. Many eBay sellers purchase predesigned templates with fancy borders, backgrounds, and shapes and simply fill in their text for each listing. Some eBay sellers use specialized applications called Web editors to create their item descriptions. Web editors are like word processors for Web pages. They allow you to create a Web page without typing a single HTML tag.

So why did I put you through this HTML tutorial? Because, if you know how the HTML behind Web pages, and specifically eBay Item Description pages, works, you'll be better prepared to troubleshoot problems as they might arise.

Plus, you have to admit—this has been fun! You've accomplished something solid and useful that you can immediately put to use in your eBay listings.

GRIFF TIP! In the beginning of this chapter, we named our file *test.html*. This file can be saved for use as a template for future eBay listings. One problem: If we save and close this file and then subsequently click on it to reopen it, it will open in either Internet Explorer or Netscape (depending on which browser you use), not Notepad. We can make changes in this file only when it is open in Notepad. If we open it in Internet Explorer, we won't be able to edit it since IE is an "output" window and doesn't accept input.

In Windows, to force our *test.html* file to open in Notepad, we need to follow these steps:

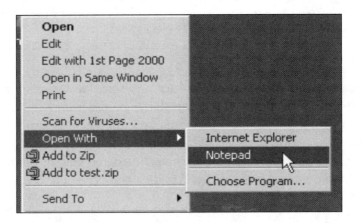

Go to your desktop, hover the mouse cursor over the icon for *test.html,* and click the mouse's right-hand button to display a pop-up menu containing special commands.

Select "Open with" and then select "Notepad" from the pop-up menus. This will open the *test.html* file in Notepad.

Advanced Image Hosting Solutions

Four years ago, Chris Spencer was a publicist and personal manager for actors.

"I had a very stressful job working twelve- to fourteen-hour days for unappreciative clients who would whine because they were only making $12,000 a week. I was miserable and unhappy."

But then Chris decided to take charge of his life. He started selling antiques and collectibles on eBay.

"I know virtually nothing about antiques and I don't own any inventory. I work with very honorable and reputable dealers in the L.A. area who provide me with accurate, honest descriptions for the items that I take on consignment. Last year, I sold over $400,000 worth of antiques and collectibles on eBay."

Today, Chris is not only a Gold-level eBay PowerSeller (borntodeal), he's also a regular instructor at eBay University seminars.

"I like to teach others how to use the site so that they can make their business better and see the money I am seeing. It is a really fun life!"

eBay Listings and Digital Pictures—Advanced Solutions

For the first-time eBay seller, eBay Picture Services is invaluable. In our earlier example listings, we relied on eBay Picture Services to host (upload, store, and display) our digital pictures in our eBay listing. As a digital-picture hosting option, eBay Picture Services is simple and fast; most important, it automatically and seamlessly places our pictures on our listing page.

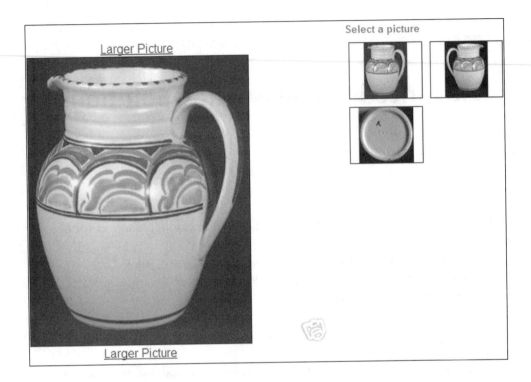

You can employ other digital-picture hosting solutions either in place of or in combination with eBay Picture Services. These hosting solutions have solid advantages: You can add more than six pictures to a listing, you have more options regarding the placement and layout of your images, and if you are a subscriber to an Internet service provider, it may not cost you anything extra.

PICTURES ON A WEB PAGE—HOW DOES THAT WORK?

Before we explore other digital-picture hosting solutions, we need to examine a few Internet and digital-pictures basics.

eBay item pages are Web pages that contain text and images. To our eyes, the text and images on an eBay item page make up one complete Web page on our computer screen, and in fact though they do "live" together as a single Web page in our Web browser, they didn't start off that way.

Usually, the two major components of a Web page—text and pictures—start out as separate files stored in separate locations on the Internet. That is, the text for the Web page is stored on one Web server, while the digital-picture files may be stored on another Web server (which could be halfway around the world!). It's the job of your Web browser to collect copies of all these components and put them together on your computer screen for you to view as one complete page.

I put up a simple Web page to illustrate how displaying a Web page with images works. If you are near a computer connected to the Internet, go to *http://xmission.com/~jimgriff/book/bookexample.html* and follow along. (Make sure you type in the tilde character before the user name *jimgriff*.)

The Web page at the end of the URL above is a single file called *bookexample.html*. It looks like this:

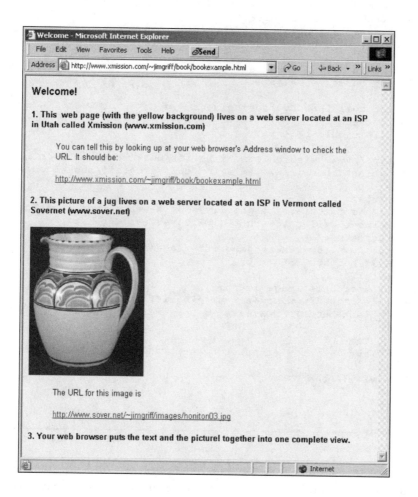

The Web page is actually a simple text file almost exactly like the one we created in the last chapter. (It has a few added HTML tags that are necessary for making a true Web page.)

Here is a copy of the text file I created in Notepad. It contains the HTML-formatted text that makes up our Web page.

```
bookexample[1] - Notepad                                           _ □ X
File  Edit  Format  Help  Send
<html>
<head>
<title>Welcome</title>
</head>

<body vlink="#551a8b" alink="#ff0000" link="#0000ee"
text="#000000" bgcolor="#F8F1A5">
<p><font size="4"><b>Welcome!</b></font> </p>
<p><b>1. This  web page (with the yellow background) lives on
a web server
located at an ISP in Utah called Xmission
(www.xmission.com)</b></p>
<blockquote>
<p>You can tell this by looking up at your web browser's Address
window to check
the URL. It should be:</p>
<p><a
href="http://www.xmission.com/~jimgriff/book/bookexample.html"
target="_blank">http://www.xmission.com/~jimgriff/book/bookexample
.html</a></p>
</blockquote>
<p><b>2. This picture of a jug lives on a web server located at an
ISP in Vermont called Sovernet (www.sover.net)</b></p>
<p><img border="0"
src="http://www.sover.net/~jimgriff/images/honiton03.jpg"
width="189" height="236"></p>
<blockquote>
<p>The URL for this image is</p>
<p><a href="http://www.sover.net/~jimgriff/images/honiton03.jpg"
target="_blank">http://www.sover.net/~jimgriff/images/honiton03.jp
g</a></p>
</blockquote>
<p><b>3. Your web browser puts the text and the picture together
into one
complete view.</b></p>
</body>

</html>
```

Some of this should look familiar. There are <P> and <B> tags as well as some new tags not covered. Scroll through the file to find the <IMG> tag.

```
            ... in Vermont called Sovernet (www.sover.net)</b></p>
<p><img border="0"
src="http://www.sover.net/~jimgriff/images/honiton03.jpg"
width="189" height="236"></p>
```

I have underlined the URL within the <IMG> tag: *http://www.sover.net/ ~jimgriff/images/honiton03.jpg*.

The complete HTML tag is:

<img border="0" src="http://www.sover.net/~jimgriff/images/honiton03.jpg" width="189" height="236">

There are attributes inside this <IMG> tag for border, width, and height, as well as the familiar "SRC." The URL after SRC points to a picture file called honiton03.jpg,

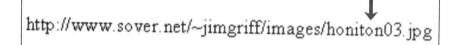

which "lives" in a folder called *images,*

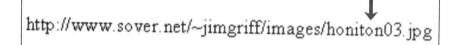

which is nested inside a folder called *~jimgriff,*

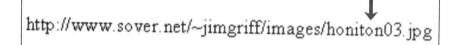

which lives on a Web server called *www.sover.net.*

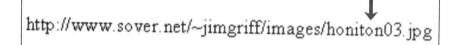

The *www.sover.net* Web server is physically located at an ISP called Sovernet, which is nestled in the beautiful Green Mountains of Vermont.

I have an ISP account with Sovernet. As part of that account, I have "space" set aside in my user name for storing files. I moved (uploaded) a copy of the *honiton03.jpg* picture from my computer, over the Internet, to the Sovernet Web server using a special type of application on my computer known as an FTP client. (More on FTP later in this chapter.)

Once I uploaded a copy of the picture file to *www.sover.net*, I then uploaded a copy of the text file *bookexample.html* to another Web server called Xmission, which is located in Salt Lake City, Utah. I also have an account with Xmission.

I needed to upload a copy of this text file to make it a Web page that can be accessed by anyone on the Internet (like you, if you navigated to it earlier as part of this exercise). Again, we'll explore uploading in depth later in this chapter.

The URL for my little yellow Web page is:

http://www.xmission.com/~jimgriff/book/bookexample.html

The HTML file *bookexample.html* "lives" inside a subfolder called *book*, which is nestled inside another folder called *~jimgriff*, which is located on the *www.xmission.com* Web server.

All my components are in place. The picture file lives on a server in Vermont. The little yellow Web page lives on a server in Utah. Here's what happened when you opened the link *http://www.xmission.com/~jimgriff/book/bookexample.html* in your Web browser:

1. Your Web browser immediately sent a request through the Internet for the file name located at the end of the URL.
2. The Web server at Xmission, on which the requested file resides, then sent a copy of the HTML file back to your computer, and it opened up in your Web browser.
3. The browser then started to "parse" (scan) and convert the HTML-formatted text in the file into viewable text, which is displayed in the Web browser's window.
4. While parsing the HTML file, the Web browser came across the <IMG> tag for the picture file located in Vermont. The Web browser read the URL.
5. The computer then sent a request for a copy of the picture file to the location indicated by the URL in the <IMG> tag.
6. The Web server back in Vermont received and granted the request for a copy of *honiton03.jpg* and sent a copy of the digital picture back to your computer.
7. The computer hands the copy of the digital picture to the Web browser, which embeds the copy of the digital picture file into the exact place on the page where the original <IMG> tag lives.

You have a complete Web page with text and picture in your Web browser!

Every time you open a Web page in your Web browser, this same process occurs. If there are no pictures or files embedded into the page, then only one request is made—for the Web page HTML file itself. For each image file embedded in the HTML text file, your computer needs to make a request out to the Internet for a copy of the file. This is why a page with several pictures located in different physical locations can sometimes take a while to display completely.

Now that you have a better understanding of how digital pictures are retrieved from the Internet and displayed in your Web browser window, we can explore other digital picture options besides eBay Picture Services.

Digital Picture Hosting (Image Hosting)

First, some definitions.

Digital picture hosting (otherwise known as image hosting) is the moving (uploading) of a copy of your digital picture file from your computer to a remote Web server on the Internet, where it is stored (hosted) for retrieval by any other Internet user.

The digital picture is then displayed on an item page by typing (embedding) the digital picture Internet address (URL or Uniform Resource Locator) into the item text. The embedded URL is said to "reference" the actual image file.

eBay Picture Services is an automatic image-hosting service. You only need to point to a picture on your hard drive and eBay Picture Services does the rest (uploads the file to a Web server, hosts the file, embeds the URL for your picture at the bottom of your listing, and displays the picture file on your item page).

As I mentioned earlier, there are definite advantages to hosting image files using solutions other than eBay Picture Services. To repeat: You can host more than six pictures, you can place the images wherever you choose inside your item text, and it may not cost you, since you may be paying for the hosting service already!

Hosting an image file is a three-part process:

1. Acquiring hosting space on a Web server.
2. Moving copies of your picture files to a Web server.
3. Embedding copies of these picture files in your eBay Item Description text by using special HTML to go get the picture file and display it in the item page.

The first step is to find hosting space on the Internet.

1. ACQUIRING HOSTING SPACE ON A WEB SERVER

Your ISP

If you are paying an Internet service provider (ISP) to access the Internet, you most likely have file hosting space set aside for your use as a part of your service package. For example, if you are an AOL user, you automatically have 12 megabytes set aside on the AOL Web servers for your exclusive use. I use an ISP in Vermont called Sovernet. As part of my monthly dial-up access plan, Sovernet provides me with several megabytes of Web server space where I can store my image files. Most every local-based ISP will provide hosting space. Contact your ISP for more information.

Other Hosting Services

Many online companies provide image hosting services. Most charge a small fee. You can view a vast list of them by going to *www.google.com* and searching on "*image hosting.*"

2. MOVING COPIES OF YOUR PICTURE FILES TO A WEB SERVER

Once you have acquired space for image hosting, the next step is to upload copies of your digital pictures from your computer to this image hosting space. Moving copies of your digital picture files from your computer to a Web server requires file transfer protocol, or FTP. Note this term—I will use it frequently in the next few pages.

For some ISPs, you will need a special FTP application to move copies of digital picture files from your computer to your Web server space. Other ISPs (such as AOL) have FTP software embedded within their own software, so you don't need a separate FTP application. You can download one of several popular freeware and shareware FTP client applications from any of the download sites on the Internet. Try *www.tucows.com* and type in *FTP* as a search for programs to download.

I am using a popular FTP application called WS_FTP from Ipswitch.com. I start the application by clicking its icon on my Start menu. This is the application interface for the most recent version of WS_FTP:

Most FTP applications look something like this. FTP applications usually have two windows. The one on the left shows the contents of my computer's hard drive. The one on the right is empty now, but once I connect to Sovernet, it will show the contents of my personal Web server space there.

To connect, I click "Connect" on the bottom left-hand corner of the application window:

This brings up a dialog box where I can enter a new site connection. Sovernet's Web site has all the information I need for establishing an FTP connection.

GRIFF TIP! Your ISP will post on its Web site all the information you need for configuring the FTP connection to your Web server space.

I select the folder MySites, then click "Create site . . ."

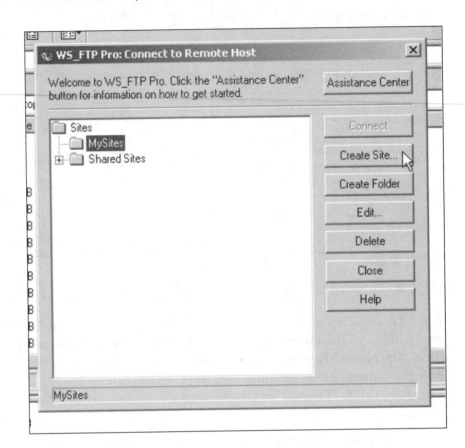

On the following screens, I enter the requested information in the spaces provided. I enter a name—Sovernet—for the new profile and opt to have it placed in the folder MySites.

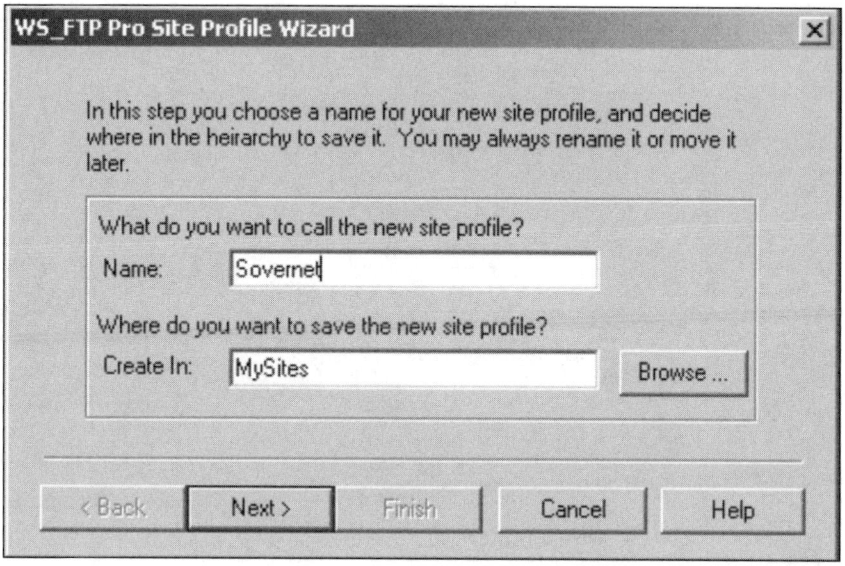

I click "Next," and in the next screen, I enter the host name (as provided to me by the folks at Sovernet—again, you must obtain your host name from your ISP).

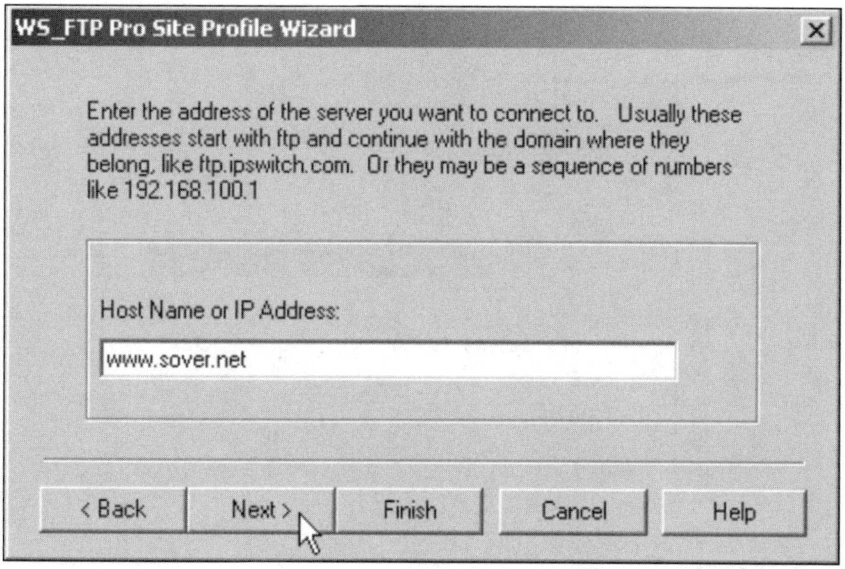

I again click "Next" to move to the next screen, then enter my User ID and password. (Your ISP will tell you if you need an account with a User ID and password.)

I click "Next" to select the server type, which in most cases will be FTP, and then I click "Finish."

My connection profile is now recorded for quick future access. To connect to my FTP space at Sovernet, I click "Connect."

Since I didn't provide my password when I created my profile for Sovernet, the system will prompt me for one before it will complete the connection.

Login Information

Last Message: 331 Password required for jimgriff.

Remote Host Login:

Host: www.sover.net

User Id:

*Password:

Account:

Connect   Cancel   Help

Click "Connect" and the right-hand FTP window will display the file contents of the remote Web server back in Vermont.

WS_FTP Pro

File Edit View Sites Options Tools Help

Address ftp://jimgriff@www.sover.net/

Local system

C:\Documents and Settings\griff\Desktop

Name	Size	Type	Mi
PR		File Folder	1C
Tiff Files		File Folder	1C
AOL Instant Messenge...	1KB	Shortcut	6/
arrow4_black.gif	2KB	Binary file	1C
bookexample.html	2KB	HTML Document	1C
ebay_links.htm	1KB	HTML Document	1C
EPSON Digital PhotoL...	2KB	Shortcut	1C
Graphic Workshop.lnk	1KB	Shortcut	1C
honiton.txt	2KB	Text Document	9/
imagelink.html	1KB	HTML Document	1C
IrfanView.lnk	1KB	Shortcut	1C
itemtext.txt	2KB	Text Document	9/

28 object(s)   54KB

Remote system

/www

Name	Size	Type	
09-16-02-ebayimages		Folder	
09-18-02-ebay		Folder	
aboutme		Folder	
book		Folder	
ebay		Folder	
ebaylive		Folder	
ebayimages		Folder	
files		Folder	
images		Folder	
italy99		Folder	
mascio		Folder	
mickeypics		Folder	

59 object(s)   1,345KB

ChgDir MkDir View Execute Rename Delete Refresh DirInfo

150 Opening ASCII mode data connection for '/bin/ls'.
transferred 3809 bytes in 0.240 seconds, 123.809 Kbps (15.476 KBps), transfer succeeded.

Disconnect   Cancel   Help   Options...   About   Exit

Using this FTP application, I can now create folders or delete folders or files on my Web server space almost as if it were a separate hard drive on my own computer! I can also move files back and forth from one window to the other. To move a copy of an edited digital picture of my eBay item from my computer to my Web server space, I locate the file on my hard drive in the left-hand window and either drag and drop it or highlight it and click the right arrow between the windows. I first have to make sure the source directory on my computer and the target directory or folder at Sovernet are both open in their windows.

Now I can upload a copy of any file on my computer to my Web server space at Sovernet.

First, in the left-hand window, I locate the file on my computer I wish to upload (by clicking through the folders and/or using the green arrow to move up one level in the folder hierarchy on my hard drive). I am looking for a picture file called *honiton03.jpg*. I find and then highlight the file.

Name	Size	Type
Tiff Files		File Folder
AOL Instant Messenge...	1KB	Shortcut
arrow4_black.gif	2KB	Binary file
bookexample.html	2KB	HTML Documen
ebay_links.htm	1KB	HTML Documen
EPSON Digital PhotoL...	2KB	Shortcut
Graphic Workshop.lnk	1KB	Shortcut
honiton.txt	2KB	Text Document
honiton03.jpg	23KB	Binary file
imagelink.html	1KB	HTML Documen
IrfanView.lnk	1KB	Shortcut
itemtext.txt	2KB	Text Document
Kana Power Client.lnk	1KB	Shortcut

C:\Documents and Settings\griff\Desktop

1 object(s) selected 22KB

226 Transfer complete.
Transfer request completed with status: Finished

Disconnect   Cancel

Next I must navigate to the folder into which I want to place the copy of *honiton03.jpg*. In the right-hand window, I locate and double-click the *images* folder to open it.

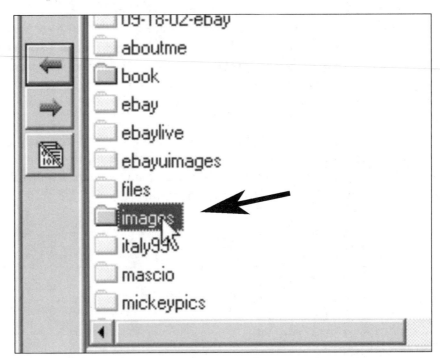

Once the *images* folder is open, I can click the right-hand arrow to move a copy of the *honiton03.jpg* file from the left-hand window to the right-hand window.

This will tell the FTP application to send a copy of the selected file through the Internet to the *images* folder in the *~jimgriff* directory on the Sovernet Web server. A status window shows the progress of the file transfer:

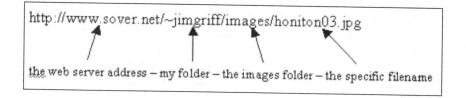

Once the transfer is complete, a copy of the *honiton03.jpg* file will live on the Sovernet Web server and will be accessible to the entire Internet using its unique URL or address to locate it. In this case, the URL is:

> http://www.sover.net/~jimgriff/images/honiton03.jpg
>
> the web server address – my folder – the images folder – the specific filename

I can also check the URL to make sure it is valid by typing it into my Web browser and hitting Enter.

If the image displays, then the URL is correctly typed and valid. It is a good habit to check your picture URLs in a Web browser. Better to correct a mistake in a URL before you list the item than to have to revise the item after it is listed.

Using Internet Explorer as an FTP Client

A little-known feature of the latest version of Internet Explorer is that it can be used as an FTP client!

If you have FTP space somewhere (check with your Internet service provider) and you have a user ID and password, you can use your Internet Explorer Web browser along with a Windows Explorer window to move files to and from your computer and a remote FTP location:

1. Open a Web browser window.

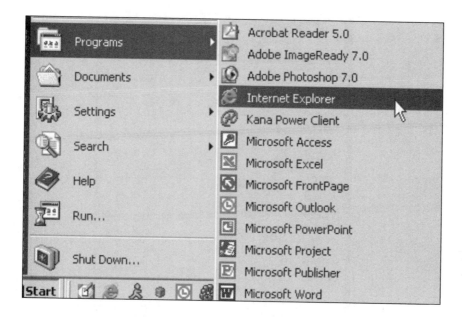

2. Type the following into the Address window, substituting your actual user name and password for *username* and *password* and your ISP's domain name for *domain.name*.

ftp://username:password@ftp.domain.name

Here is an example:

ftp://jimgriff:**********@ftp.sover.net

(No, I won't tell you my password, thank you very much.)

3. Open a My Computer window.

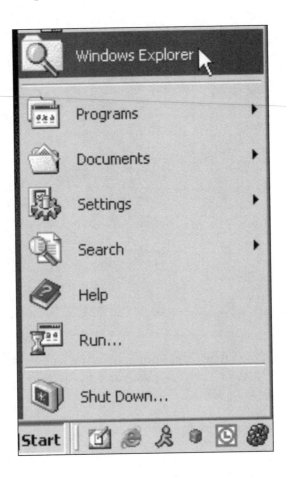

4. Position the two windows so that you can drag and drop files back and forth from either window.

5. You can create and delete directories (folders) on your remote FTP space by using the "File, New" command on the Internet Explorer menu bar.

6. You can also rename, move, and delete files on your FTP space.

Hosting Digital Picture Files at AOL

First, you'll need to have an AOL account. Many eBay sellers already do, but the majority of them are unaware that along with their monthly AOL access and AOL e-mail, they are also paying for 12 megabytes of AOL Web space. Twelve MB of server space can come in real handy for hosting eBay image files.

The steps for uploading your digital pictures onto your space at AOL are easy to find.

Open your AOL software and search using the keywords *"my ftp space"* to bring up the My FTP Space box.

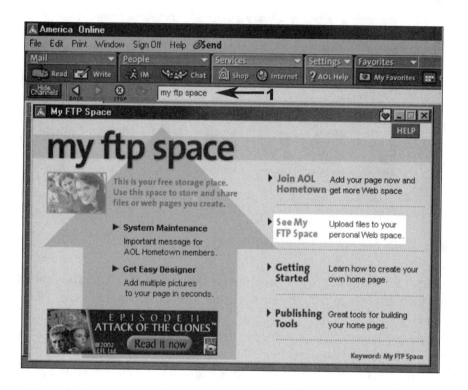

This is AOL's built-in FTP application. (Note: You don't need to download and install an application such as WS_FTP when using your AOL account for hosting.)

Click on See My FTP Space to see the current contents of your AOL FTP space.

NOTE: AOL's built-in FTP application has only one window.

Using this window, you can create new directories (folders) and upload files from your computer to AOL by clicking the "Upload" icon. Let's click "Upload" to start.

Next, you have to type a name for the file. This is an unusual procedure and different from the way most other FTP applications work. With AOL's FTP procedure, you are, in effect, creating an empty file on the AOL server and giving the empty file a name into which the file on your computer will be placed once you begin the uploading. It's confusing. To prevent any mixups, I usually type in the same name as the file on my hard drive I want to upload. I suggest you do the same.

I type in the name *honiton03.jpg,* and then click "Continue." In the Upload File window that pops up, I click the "Select File" icon to choose a file on my hard drive.

This brings up an Attach File window. I navigate through my hard drive to the file I wish to upload.

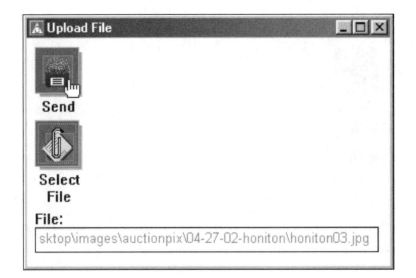

Once I have located the file, I double-click it to open it. The path of the file will show up in the File box on the Upload File window. Next, I click the "Send" icon:

The file will upload to your FTP space at AOL. A message will alert you when the transfer is complete. Click "OK" and you are nearly done.

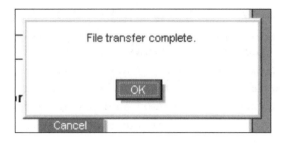

To check whether the file was successfully uploaded into the proper directory, I click on the *images* directory to find the file.

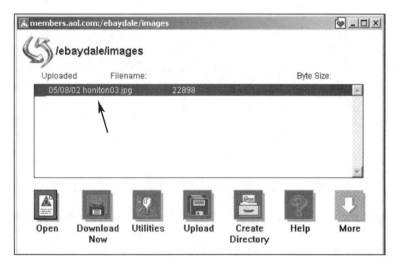

There it is!

Whenever I use AOL to host images or files, I always double-check the directory into which they were uploaded to be sure that they were uploaded correctly.

Now, let's test the image in a browser and get its URL. Go to any Web browser, type in *http://members.aol.com/*, and put your AOL user name after the last forward slash. Here's mine: *http://members.aol.com/ebaydale*. If you haven't previously set up an actual AOL member's hometown Web page, the URL with your AOL user name will display the contents of your AOL FTP space:

If I click the link for the *images* folder, I should see my file, *honiton03.jpg*. And there it is:

If I click the image name, it should display the actual digital picture . . .

. . . and it does.

GRIFF TIP! You can usually view the file contents of any Web folder if that folder does not contain a file named "index.html." Some Web servers (such as *www.xmission.com*) are set up so that the contents of a user's Web folders are not ever readable, even if they do not contain an "index.html" file.

This ability to read the contents of another user's Web folder can come in handy should you need to troubleshoot one of your own URLs.

3. EMBEDDING DIGITAL PICTURE FILE URLS IN YOUR EBAY ITEM DESCRIPTION

You have uploaded your item pictures to your own Web server space and you have the URLs (addresses) for each.

The last step in the process is to embed your digital pictures in your item description. You do this by typing the URL for each digital picture you uploaded in Step 2 into the item description. Each URL must be placed inside an HTML <IMG> tag.

In the previous step, I uploaded a file to my Web server space at Sovernet. Here is the URL for that digital picture:

http://www.sover.net/~jimgriff/images/honiton03.jpg

Here is how the URL looks when used as the value for the attribute SRC inside an <IMG> tag.

<IMG src=http://www.sover.net/~jimgriff/images/honiton03.jpg>

Let's review what happens when the Web browser gets to an <IMG> tag with a URL as the value for an src attribute. Our URL shows the address location for the file *honiton03.jpg*, which lives in a directory or folder called *images*, which in turn lives inside a directory folder called *~jimgriff*, which in turn lives on a Web server called *www.sover.net*.

GRIFF TIP! Think of any URL as a file's mailing address, only in reverse. In a mailing address, the most specific final destination—the name of the recipient of the letter—is always on the top of the address:

Mr. Honiton03 JPG
Image Street
Jimgriff, sover.net, www

However, in a URL, the final destination—the file name—is always at the end of the address: *http://www.sover.net/~jimgriff/images/ honiton03.jpg*.

When the browser gets to the "<IMG" part of the <IMG> tag, it knows that special instructions will follow.

The browser looks next for the SRC attribute and reads, from left to right, the URL after the equals sign. The URL tells the browser where on the Internet it needs to send a request for a file. Again, the actual file name is always at the very end of the URL. So reading from left to right, the browser tells the computer to go to a Web server called *sover.net* and ask if there is a file named *honiton03.jpg* in a subdirectory called *images* in a next-level directory called *~jimgriff*, and if there is such a file in such location, would the Web server be so kind as to send a copy of the file back through the internet to your computer?

If the URL is correct, the Web server "serves" a copy of the digital picture named *honiton03.jpg* through the Internet back to your computer, which passes the file to your Web browser, which then displays the copy of the digital picture by embedding it within the Web page at the very spot in the HTML document behind the page where the <IMG> tag appears.

ANOTHER GRIFF TIP! Using a special feature of Internet Explorer, you can quickly find the URL for any picture on the Web by hovering your mouse over the picture and clicking the right-hand button on your mouse. Then select "Properties" from the pop-up menu:

In the Properties box, there is a field for Address: (URL). Highlight the URL by holding down your left mouse button and dragging the mouse cursor over the URL itself. Once it is entirely highlighted, click the right mouse button and select "Copy."

The URL for the picture is now copied to your Windows (or Mac) Clipboard, ready to paste into any text document. Using the "Save picture as . . ." menu option in the same pop-up window,

you can also save a copy of the digital picture somewhere on your computer!

Save Picture	? ×

Save in: My Pictures

Sample.jpg

History
Desktop
My Documents
My Computer
My Network P...

File name: honiton03   Save

Save as type: JPEG (*.jpg)   Cancel

AND YET ANOTHER GRIFF TIP! For consistency, create all your file names in lowercase. *honiton03.jpg* and *honiton03.JPG* are two different files as far as a Web browser is concerned, and one cannot be used to reference the other.

eBay's Picture Manager

eBay recently introduced an eBay-based image hosting solution called Picture Manager. You can subscribe to Picture Manager from My eBay, Manage Subscriptions:

Once you subscribe to Picture Manager, you can add multiple pictures to all of your listings without paying any extra fees. Picture Manager offers three levels of storage space:

- 50 MB for $9.99 per month
- 125 MB for $19.99 per month
- 300 MB for $39.99 per month

Your monthly subscription fee is automatically added to your eBay account and will appear on your monthly invoice.

All eBay Store sellers receive one megabyte of storage free with their Store subscription to host their Store logo and Store layout pictures. Featured and Anchored Store sellers also can benefit from the following discounted pricing:

Featured Store Sellers

- 50 MB for $4.99 per month
- 125 MB for $14.99 per month
- 300 MB for $34.99 per month

Anchored Store Sellers

- 50 MB free per month
- 125 MB for $4.99 per month
- 300 MB for $14.99 per month

I subscribe to Picture Manager. Here is what the interface looks like:

With Picture Manager, you can add, name, and edit folders, upload images from your computer, and move and rename them. One feature, Web Links, comes in handy. Here's how it works.

Check the images for which you need to obtain URLs and click the "Web links" button.

This pops up a window containing the URL for each image, which you can then copy and paste into your listing description using the <IMG> tag that we learned about in the previous chapter on HTML.

In addition, you can add Picture Manager photos into your item description via eBay Picture Services. I strongly recommend Picture Manager as the best integrated photo hosting solution on eBay.

Help!

Our last chapter covers all aspects of obtaining help for a myriad of potential eBay situations. Let's start off with Trust and Safety.

Trust and Safety for Sellers

Selling on eBay can be great fun as well as potentially profitable. I hope this book proves to be of some help to you on your path to successful eBay selling. However, before you start out, there is one area of selling that many sellers don't give due consideration, even after they have been selling on eBay for months or years.

THE RULES

Yes, Virginia, there are rules for selling on eBay, and all eBay sellers are expected to become fully acquainted with the rules before they start selling.

As of this writing, "the rules" are better known on eBay as Trust and Safety. We will cover the most common topics of eBay Trust and Safety as they relate directly to sellers. I strongly suggest that you visit the site as soon as possible and read them all in greater detail.

Not all the rules are obvious! There are many procedural ins and outs to eBay selling, and it would be foolish for any eBay seller to assume she knows and understands all the rules without reading them carefully.

So unless you don't mind having your listings ended, receiving warnings for prohibited activity, or having your registration on eBay suspended, possibly forever, this chapter is an absolute must-read.

EBAY TRUST AND SAFETY—A HISTORY AND OUTLINE

In 1997, we in eBay Customer Support created a special department called SafeHarbor. SafeHarbor's mission was to explain and apply the rules, processes, and policies governing all eBay members' activity on the eBay site. In the very beginning, the SafeHarbor team had jurisdiction over all potentially prohibited site activity, from bidding and feedback offenses to prohibited items.

In 1999 eBay entered its most frenetic period of explosive growth, and with this growth came whole new areas of prohibited activities and items. The number of new offenses, such as feedback abuse and spam, rose along with the exploding number of new users who registered on eBay each day. It soon became apparent to all of us in Customer Support and on eBay in general that one department alone could not adequately handle these increasingly complex issues and their attendant questions. Thus, in early 1999, a decision was made to split SafeHarbor into four separate departments—SafeHarbor, Community Watch, Fraud, and VeRO.

These separate teams have grown and changed since 1999, but they are still staffed by specially trained eBay Customer Support reps who have experience with all the rules governing activity on the eBay site, and certain eBay member activity off the eBay site. All four of the teams now exist under the umbrella of the customer-support metateam Trust and Safety.

QUESTIONABLE OR PROHIBITED PRACTICES AND ACTIVITIES

All eBay community members—buyers and sellers alike—are expected to adhere to certain standards of business conduct when using eBay. However, since the typical eBay transaction usually has the buyer sending payment to the seller before goods are shipped, eBay sellers bear a larger share of responsibility when it comes to staying within the rules.

Most of the rules pertaining to eBay selling are based on good old common sense. Before you initiate any action at eBay—writing out an item description, constructing terms of service for your buyers, and so on—ask yourself this question: "Will my action provide my listings or my online business with an unfair advantage over other sellers?" If the answer is yes or even maybe, then you need to check the list of policies and offenses on the eBay Rules and Safety page (navigation road map below).

For example, you might think that a great way to promote your business would be to link to your personal Web site directly from your eBay Item Description page. After all, why shouldn't you take advantage of the traffic that your eBay item is bound to receive? With hundreds of potential visitors to your eBay listing, a link to your Web site would indeed be to your benefit. However, linking to your Web site from your eBay listing description is strictly prohibited. You may not have realized this, but ignorance will be little comfort when all of your offending listings are ended early by eBay.

Your best protection against having all of your eBay listings ended is to know the rules! Safeguard the time and effort you put into listing your items at eBay by reading through all of the eBay selling rules and selling policies before you list an item for bid or sale.

GRIFF TIP! You can navigate to any of the Trust and Safety Rules for Sellers pages by following these steps:

Click the "Help" link on top of any eBay page. On the Help page, look for Rules and Policies toward the bottom of the topics.

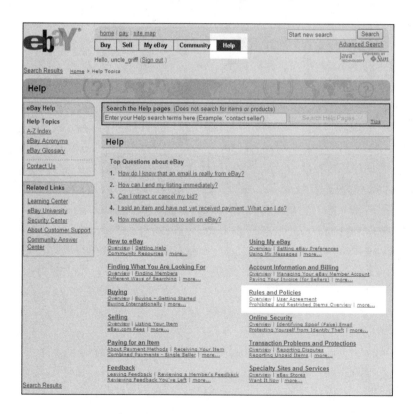

Click "Rules for Sellers."

Review the topics and their contents by clicking on each one and reading it carefully.

You will need this page in the future. Remember where it is. Bookmark it for safekeeping.

A Few of the Rules

The Trust and Safety team handles reports of selling abuses or seller rule violations including, but not limited to, the following areas:

> Bidding offenses
> Feedback
> Unpaid Items (aka UPIs)
> Listing violations

BIDDING OFFENSES—SHILL BIDDING

Simply put, sellers are not allowed to inflate the bid for their items by employing second accounts or agents to bid on their items. This activity is known as shill bidding. Not only is shill bidding strictly prohibited on eBay, but since it may include violations of local, state, or federal laws, you could find yourself in need of a good bail bondsman.

You can get a fairly good picture of the seriousness of shill bidding by going to *www.google.com* and typing in *"shill bidding."* Read some of the archived news articles about past shill bidders who are now punching out license plates instead of eBay listings.

FEEDBACK

Certain activities are prohibited within the Feedback Forum. For example, you may not post another member's contact information—in part or in whole—within a feedback comment or, for that matter, anywhere else on eBay. This includes, but is not limited to, the other party's first name, phone number, e-mail address, city, or state.

Also, you may not leave profanity or obscenities in another person's feedback file. And using altered spellings or substituting punctuation marks does not excuse the offense, so *as**ole* is equally as unacceptable as the same word fully spelled out. Rules and policies aside, your words reflect your character. You should choose them with the utmost care as they are going to tell the world who you are. You may believe the other party in a transaction to be an *as**ole,* but don't think for one minute that anyone reading your comment isn't going to say to herself, "Hmmm . . . sounds like whoever wrote this comment is the real *as**ole.*"

Finally, if the other party reports such a comment to eBay, we will remove the entire comment and serve a warning to the poster of the offending remark.

The upshot? Leave feedback that you would have others leave for you.

UNPAID ITEMS

Buyers are obligated to follow through with their purchases after a listing has closed. The vast majority of bidders are, to paraphrase eBay founder Pierre Omidyar, basically good, but sometimes a buyer bids on and purchases an item and a real-life crisis takes him away, often to a place where he is unable to make contact with you or pay for the item. It happens.

Other times, a buyer may have intended to pay for the item if she won, but she suddenly found herself in unexpected dire financial straits. This doesn't automatically excuse the buyer from her obligation to follow through on her purchase, but you might work out a payment schedule or some other solution.

The point? Always give Unpaid Item buyers the benefit of the doubt. If they don't respond to your e-mails, try calling them. You can obtain their contact information by clicking on the "Advanced search" link on the top of any eBay page and then clicking the "Find members" link in the left-hand column. Scroll down and enter the buyer's User ID in the box marked Contact Information.

On occasion, a new member will traipse around the site randomly and frivolously bidding away on things he has no intention of buying. You try to contact him and he ignores your e-mail, or you attempt to phone him and he doesn't answer his phone or, worse, the line has been disconnected. These deliberately frivolous bidders are not welcome on eBay.

We cannot hold these bidders upside down and shake the funds out of them. We cannot force them to pay for your item. However, we can show them the exit—but only with your help.

You can help rid eBay of these nuisance bidders by reporting them to eBay through the Unpaid Item process. Simply follow the instructions on the Unpaid Item page:

1. Click the "Security center" link on the bottom of any eBay page.

2. Select the option for "Unpaid item" and follow the steps from there.

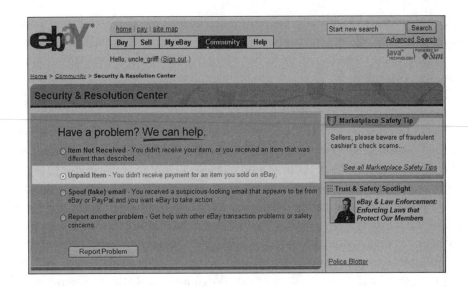

Each Unpaid Item alert is recorded on the buyer's eBay account. On the third report, the buyer is automatically suspended from the eBay site.

Note that the Unpaid Item process has built-in safeguards to prevent sellers who are not basically good (they aren't reading this book, remember) from abusing it. Thus, if you should ever have to use this process, you must take specific steps before you will be allowed to file an Unpaid Item report, such as attempting to contact the bidder via e-mail, waiting a fair amount of time for a reply, and so on.

You may be impatient to file your report ASAP, but we are certain that if the shoe should ever be on the other foot, you would want these safeguards in place to prevent you from being the subject of a hastily filed UPI report that could result in the suspension of your eBay registration.

LISTING VIOLATIONS

The Trust and Safety team also fields all reports of listing violations. These include items that are prohibited or restricted on eBay, and reports of such activities as keyword spamming (the inclusion of words or phrases into a listing title or description intended to give the listing an unfair advantage in search results), links to a seller's Web site included in item pages, and payment surcharges.

Not all otherwise legal items can be listed on eBay, so don't automatically assume yours is okay. For example, although it is perfectly legal to sell a bear rug in the rest of the United States, it is not legal in California. eBay headquarters are located in California; thus all eBay members are bound by the California state laws prohibiting the sale of bears or bear parts.

Trust and Safety also has jurisdiction over the contents of an item description. On the same Rules for Sellers page mentioned earlier, you will find the link "Listing policies," which contains a list of all eBay listing policies and prohibited listing activities.

Note that practically all reports of prohibited listings, or listings with prohibited activities, are sent to eBay Customer Support by other eBay members.

All activities that eBay considers reportable to Trust and Safety can be found on the eBay Security & Resolution Center, accessible by a link on the bottom of every eBay Web page.

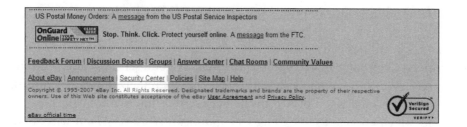

This takes you to the Security & Resolution Center.

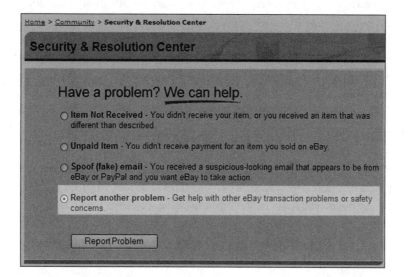

Read through the procedures on the Security & Resolution Center pages at least once.

EBAY AND PAYPAL BUYER PROTECTION

We (eBay and your fellow buyers and sellers in the eBay Community) believe you are basically good. Give yourself a hearty pat on the back. Or a hug.

How do we know that you are basically good? For nearly a decade, despite what they cynics predicted, you have proven your goodness and honesty by speeding an item to your buyer once she has submitted payment. How can we be so certain that people are indeed basically good? Because you are an honest and considerate seller whose primary concerns—in order—are:

- Happy, satisfied buyers
- Your sterling eBay reputation (as exhibited by your feedback)
- The viability and continued success of your eBay business

You, like all basically good sellers, only have the best of intentions for your customers. They come first! You, like all basically good sellers, want to avoid disputes with your buyers. Sometimes this becomes extremely difficult to do. Sometimes an item is damaged or lost in the mail. Other times you might mistakenly have described an item as one thing when, unbeknownst to you, it was quite another thing entirely. No big sin. You didn't mean it. You really thought it was solid gold when it was, in fact, plated. We are all only human and we are all prone to the rare error in attribution. That's why you always immediately take back that gold-plated-but-mistakenly-sold-as-solid-gold item and quickly and cheerfully refund the buyer's money.

If any of these unfortunate mishaps should happen to you and your buyer, we are sure that you are going to bend over backward to make it right.

But then there are some other sellers. (They are not reading this book, so we can talk behind their backs.) They are not numerous. In fact, they make up less than .001 percent of all eBay sellers. But no matter—these sellers are sadly, tragically, not basically good. Oh, they were good once. They tried, really they did. But somewhere along the line they decided being basically good wasn't worth all the diligence, the excellent feedback, the happiness of their customers, and the eventual long-term success of their businesses. These sellers, who are not basically good, go for the quick return with no concern at all for their buyer's satisfaction or to the consequences. These sellers say, "Your item was damaged in shipping? Too bad for you. It's not my problem. Your package never arrived? Blame it on the mailman. It's not really solid gold after all? The ad said 'as is,' so tough cookies."

Oh, these poor, sad sellers. They have no idea what tragic fate awaits them.

Outraged and angry buyers who have tried to get some satisfaction from these sad sellers usually quickly alert eBay by filing for PayPal Buyer Protection.

By default, PayPal offers $200 of protection for all PayPal transactions for tangible goods in the United States (excluding vehicles).

In addition, PayPal Buyer Protection provides coverage to buyers for up to $2,000 for all tangible items listed by qualified sellers in the United States. Qualified items will clearly indicate the amount of coverage available in the Meet the Seller box on the item page. Both protection plans cover buyers if they paid for an item and never received it, or received an item that was less than what was described—such as winning a solid-gold necklace but receiving a plated one instead.

If a buyer is awarded payment from either protection program, the seller at fault runs the risk of immediate suspension from eBay. Thus it behooves any seller to do whatever it takes to satisfy a filed complaint, including refunding the buyer's money or exchanging the plated-gold item for a solid-gold example.

You can learn more by visiting the eBay Security & Resolution Center and following the links there to the Selling, Rules & Policies page and for the Item Not Received process.

LISTING COPYRIGHTED OR TRADEMARKED ITEMS ON EBAY

Offering items that infringe upon an owner's trademark, copyright, or other intellectual property rights is strictly prohibited on eBay.

Believe it or not, some sellers (again, not you, of course) find sources for counterfeit items and offer them on eBay—for example, handbags that bear the name or logo of a well-known designer or company brand name or trademark, except that the handbag is actually not genuine. Or a wristwatch that was made offshore somewhere but is inaccurately and dishonestly labeled as an expensive, famous brand name watch.

Important note! These items, if not manufactured by the trademark holder, are infringing on the trademark holder's rights, and the seller of said counterfeit items can be suspended from eBay for offering them. In addition, sellers of counterfeit items run the serious risk of civil or criminal prosecution.

When I first started on eBay back in 1996, I would occasionally field reports from concerned eBay members about fake brand-name watches on the site. They were easy to spot. The sellers of such items would use words like *faux* (French for "false") in their titles. We would (and still do) quickly remove these items from the site and send the sellers a stern warning about the consequences of future activity of this sort.

More times than not, the offending sellers respond with surprise that what they were doing was in any way wrong. "But I was not being dishonest! I stated that they were fakes/knockoffs/copies/reproductions! I demand that you reinstate my listing."

Our reply to protestations of this type is that our decision is final. We also advise the seller of said clearly stated infringing items (aka "fakes," "knockoffs," etc.) to contact the trademark or copyright owner and ask them for their opinion and counsel.

Property rights are just that—property rights. Just as something you own is yours, copyrights, trademarks, and intellectual property also belong to owners who are entitled to protect their property against damage or loss. In fact, the owners of intellectual property and trademarks are actually required by law to protect and defend their property against misuse and infringement or risk losing control or even ownership of those rights! This is why companies (eBay included) will often go to court against those who are, by their actions, damaging or degrading their brand names or trademarks.

Copyrighted material is not limited to just trademarks or name brands. Copyrights cover all sorts of intellectual property, including but not limited to video, film, music, software, and books.

THE EBAY VERO PROGRAM (VERIFIED RIGHTS OWNERS)

If you are a trademark or copyright holder, you may want to join the eBay VeRO Program. To learn more about the VeRO Program, click the "Help" link on the top of any eBay page and follow the links for "Online Security and Protection > Protection Programs > Protecting Intellectual Property > eBay's Verified Rights Owner."

The VeRO program works like this: The owner of a brand name or intellectual property rights owner contacts eBay and joins the VeRO program. Once in the program, she is provided with a reporting pathway for alerting eBay of any items she finds listed on the site that she believes infringe on her property rights. Once eBay is alerted by the rights holder, they take the listing down and alert the seller of the action.

Except for listings that state or imply that the item for sale is a fake, knockoff, faux, replica, look-alike, and so forth, eBay does not proactively look out for items that are infringing and then remove them from the site. As a rule, eBay will remove an item that is potentially violating property rights only at the request of the rights holder, and only through the VeRO reporting process.

LISTING BRAND-NAME AND COPYRIGHT-PROTECTED ITEMS ON EBAY

If you have genuine, verifiably authentic designer or brand-name merchandise or copyright-protected items, and you want to list them on eBay, you need to bend over backward in your listing descriptions to assure both your potential buyers and the agents and representatives of the brand's owners that the items are indeed the real McCoy. How?

If you purchased a so-called brand-name item from a secondary market, such as a thrift store, mall, street vendor, or online store, or if someone has given you a designer bag or expensive designer brand name watch or piece of jewelry and you are uncertain as to its authenticity, you should have it appraised by an expert or a representative of the company that owns the brand name. If you cannot have the item authenticated—that is, if a representative of the brand name will not authenticate the item—**do not list it on eBay!** If you do, you risk having the item removed and having possible sanctions taken against your eBay registration.

Claiming "I didn't know" or "I never said it was genuine" or "I never stated anything either way about the item's authenticity" will not exempt your listing from removal or your registration from possible sanctions.

"But Griff, I am certain that the item is genuine! What do I do to prove it?" Take these precautions when listing the item on eBay:

- In your listing description, you need to state, unambiguously and clearly, that the item is 100 percent genuine. If you cannot honestly and unambiguously state that the item is 100 percent genuine, **do not list it on eBay!**
- If you have a receipt from the store where the item was purchased, include a scan in your listing description.
- If you have any documentation from the brand owner stating that the item is authentic, include a scan of that as well.
- Include close-up shots of the inside of a handbag, the stitching, the fabric, any rivets or metal clasps, and the like. If the item is a piece of jewelry, take a macro close-up of any marks, engraving, stone settings, or other relevant feature.
- The rule of thumb: With a brand-name item, you can never provide too much textual and photographic proof of authenticity.

I repeat: If you cannot unequivocally state in your listing description that the brand name item or copyright item is 100 percent authentic, **do not list it on eBay!**

I hope I made my point.

APPEALING VERO ACTIONS

What if you list an absolutely authentic brand-name item and the brand-name owner has the item removed as counterfeit? If your listing was removed through VeRO and you believe that it was removed in error, eBay suggests that you first try to contact the rights owner directly. (The e-mail notifying you that your listing had been removed should have included the rights owner's e-mail address or a link to the VeRO About Me page where you can find the specific rights holder's contact address.) Only the rights owner understands her products and intellectual property rights. If the rights owner agrees that she made a mistake, have her e-mail eBay and eBay will allow you to relist your item.

Learn more about the VeRO program by visiting the VeRO-related Help pages:

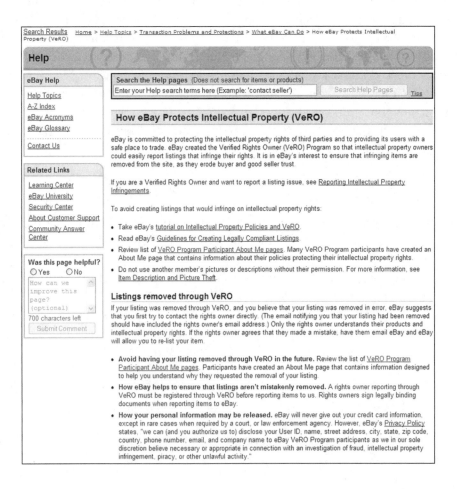

You can also find more information about a VeRO member on the Copyright, Trademark, and Other Intellectual Property Rights Owner About Me pages. The URL for this page is *http://pages.ebay.com/help/community/vero-aboutme. html.*

DISPUTE RESOLUTION

Some buyer and seller disputes are, to a great extent, no-fault disputes—that is, no real fraud was intended on the part of either the seller or the buyer. Something just went terribly, horribly wrong. And then communications went awry.

If you are the seller in a dispute case, you should, as the professional, take the initiative and squelch the dispute before it grows out of control. Make a genuine and generous offer of resolution to the buyer. Don't rely on e-mail alone! I have learned that most disputes are easier solved by phone. Call your buyer or seller and try to work it out voice to voice.

If you need third-party assistance in a dispute case with another member, consider using eBay's resolution dispute partner, SquareTrade.com.

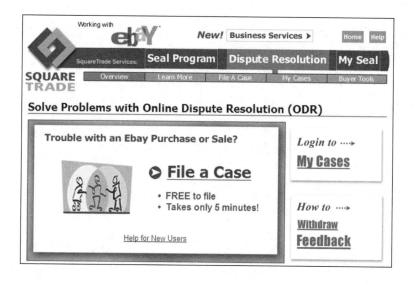

SquareTrade can help resolve disputes by facilitating communication between trading partners. SquareTrade will even provide a professional mediator (for a fee).

HOW TO GET ASSISTANCE AT EBAY

Although this book should prove to be useful, there is a seemingly infinite number of topics and potential issues regarding how to use eBay, and it would be impossible for one book to cover them all in detail.

Not to despair! The eBay Web site is a virtual treasure trove of valuable information, tips, answers, and clarifications. However, just as with any treasure, one has to hunt a little to find it. I hope that this last section will serve as a handy road map for finding answers to nearly any question, issue, complaint, or concern you might have about eBay.

Here are a few starting points for finding help, information, and general eBay knowledge right on the eBay Web site.

ON-SITE HELP

You can find the answers to most common eBay procedure and policy questions quickly and easily by clicking "Help," on the top of most eBay pages. We've seen the eBay Help page many times already, but let's give it one more visit:

On the Help portal page, you can type into the box one or more keywords that relate to your query or you can scroll and click through the list of Help topics. Either method turns up a treasure trove of help, answers, and explanations of policies and procedures. In fact, I use the eBay Help pages myself whenever I am stumped for an answer. I even keep a browser window open to the eBay Help A-Z index page during the broadcast of eBay Radio (more on eBay Radio at the very end of this chapter).

More often than not, I can find accurate answers to caller questions quickly in the eBay Help index!

The keyword method of searching Help will search the entire Help database for matches and return a list of links with the most relevant first.

The topic method of searching Help allows you to drill down an intuitive pathway, starting with high-level topics and progressing down to detailed subtopics.

MY EBAY

Your My eBay All Buying, All Selling, Favorites, and Account pages each contain lists of related links at the bottom in the left-hand column. For example, the bottom left-hand side of the Selling page has the box Selling Links, with selling-related links covering nearly every aspect of selling on eBay.

Click the "More . . ." link to expand the view to the complete list of selling-related links.

If you have a selling, buying, account, or preferences-related question, check the bottom of the appropriate page in My eBay before sending an e-mail to Customer Support or contacting Live Help.

GETTING HELP FROM OTHER EBAY MEMBERS

eBay members are an invaluable source of eBay-related knowledge. Lucky for us, most expert eBay members are eager to dispense their wisdom, free of charge!

I have mentioned the chat boards in previous chapters, but it bears repeating here that the smartest eBay members in the world hang out on one or more of the many eBay chat boards. You can find the chat boards under Community on the eBay Navigation Bar.

Click on "Discussion boards" to begin. This displays the various Community help boards and category-specific discussion boards.

Discussion Boards

eBay's discussion boards are a great place to find information on everything from art to travel. Browse the discussion boards below and see what you discover.

Community Help Boards

About Me Pages
Auction Listings
Bidding
Buyer Central: Professional Buying
Checkout
eBay Blogs Help NEW!
eBay Express NEW!
eBay My World NEW!
eBay Stores
eBay Wiki NEW!
Escrow/Insurance
Feedback
Half.com
International Trading
Live Auctions
Miscellaneous
My eBay
Packaging & Shipping
PayPal
Photos/HTML
Policies/User Agreement
Registration
Reviews & Guides NEW!
Search
Seller Central
Skype
Technical Issues
Trading Assistant
Trust & Safety (SafeHarbor)

eBay Tools Boards

eBay Board Usage Policy explanation
Accounting Assistant & Record Keeping
Blackthorne Basic/SA Basic
Blackthorne Pro/SA Pro
eBay Marketplace Research and Sales Reports
eBay Picture Services and Picture Manager
eBay Toolbar
File Exchange
Selling Manager
Selling Manager Pro
Turbo Lister

Category Specific Discussion Boards

Animals
Antiques
Art & Artists
Bears and Plush
Book Readers
Booksellers
Business & Industrial
Children's Clothing Boutique
Clothing, Shoes & Accessories
Coins & Paper Money
Collectibles
Comics
Computers, Networking & I.T
Cooks Nook
Country/Rural Style
Custom Made Items and Services NEW!
Decorative & Holiday
Disneyana
Dollhouses and Miniatures
Dolls
Dolls Artists and Limited Edition NEW!
eBay Motors
Handmade/Custom Clothing for Kids
Health & Beauty
Historical Memorabilia
Hobbies & Crafts
Home & Garden
Jewelry & Gemstones
Mid-Century/Modern
Motorcycle Boulevard
Movies & Memorabilia
Music & Musicians
Needle Arts & Vintage Textiles
Outdoor Sports
Photography
Pottery, Glass, & Porcelain
Products & Accessories for Infants NEW!
Science & Mystery
Scrapbooking
Shoes, Purses, and Fashion Accessories
Sports Cards, Memorabilia & Fan Shop
Toys & Hobbies
Victorian/Edwardian
Vintage
Vintage Clothing & Accessories
Watches, Clocks & Timepieces

I will select "Packing and Shipping."

Community Help Boards

About Me Pages
Auction Listings
Bidding
Buyer Central: Professional Buying
Checkout
eBay Blogs Help NEW!
eBay Express NEW!
eBay My World NEW!
eBay Stores
eBay Wiki NEW!
Escrow/Insurance
Feedback
Half.com
International Trading
Live Auctions
Miscellaneous
My eBay
Packaging & Shipping
PayPal
Photos/HTML
Policies/User Agreement
Registration
Reviews & Guides NEW!
Search
Seller Central
Skype
Technical Issues
Trading Assistant
Trust & Safety (SafeHarbor)

This displays the page of threaded discussions for the topic Packing and Shipping.

Each "title" is a separate thread started by either an eBay member or, in some cases, an eBay employee. Anyone—registered eBay member or not—can read the contents of any of the threads. Only registered members can start a thread or post responses to a thread. To start a thread or post a response, a member must first log in with her registered eBay User ID and password.

To read a thread, simply click on its title. Let's check out the thread for "A Buyer's Tutorial to Shipping and Handling" (sellers should read it also).

This opens the thread for reading and posting.

Packaging & Shipping

Sign in to the community boards.

Discussion   Post a reply | Print

A Buyer's Tutorial to Shipping and Handling (Sellers Should Read Also)

rswagner (3337 ★) me View Listings | Report   Apr-15-01 05:46 PDT

OK people. There are too many threads bashing handling, supporting
hanlding, complaining about overcharges, etc. that buyers have a very
hard time finding out what is really expected and what to do. Here are
some common sense (for those that appreciate common sense over
bashing)
approaches on how to handle shipping and handling.

(1) Handling is a charge that is generally used by sellers to offset
the cost of packaging and shipping items. Generally, handling charges
on ebay include packaging costs (boxes; packaging materials - peanuts,
bubblewrap, etc; and miscellaneous office supplies; handling (time or
wages to package; time to deliver to the shipper; etc); and
miscellaneous expenses as applicable (cost of storage for shipping
supplies; expenses to operate the shipping area; etc.).

(2) Although the above is typically the definition of handling, sellers
have a right to charge whatever they wish for handling. eBay will not
get involved in this aspect of a seller's operation unless it is an
obvious case of fee avoidance.

(3) If a seller is charging handling, it should be posted in the
auction, either in the form of a fixed shipping amount, or by adding a
statement "Buyer pays actual postage plus x.xx handling", or something
along those lines.

(4) By bidding on an auctions, buyers are agreeing to the terms of the
auction.

(5) If a fixed shipping amount is posted, it should not be assumed that
the posted shipping amount is going to be the same as actual postage

Note the "Sign in to the community boards" link in the upper left-hand corner. If you want to post a query or answer, you need to click this link and log in
first. Follow the instructions from there.

The members that hang out on these topic-specific chat boards provide a
great service to other members. It's a subject near and dear to my heart, since I
got my start at eBay by answering questions on the first eBay chat board. The
tradition continues!

LIVE HELP

eBay Customer Support recently initiated a project called Live Help to quickly
respond to new-customer queries. Live Help is similar to an instant message service. You—the brand-new eBay member—look for and click the "Live help"
icon, which brings up a messaging window. For those unfamiliar with the

instant-messaging format, the concept is simple. You type your query into the window, and within moments an expert eBay support representative receives it and is assigned to your case. Then the two of you conduct an online conversation using text in real time.

eBay Live Help is intended primarily as a resource for new eBay buyers and sellers with questions about registration, bidding, and selling, along with some basic computer and Internet technical questions. However, the expert specialist reps on staff for Live Help can often assist with questions regarding Community Watch, account security, eBay policies and procedures, user-to-user disputes, or the eBay VeRO Program.

Here's the step-by-step process for using Live Help:

1. Locate a Live Help icon on the eBay home page.

2. Depending on how your Web browser is configured, you may see an alert that asks whether you want to accept a cookie. If so, you must accept this cookie to use Live Help. (A cookie is a small text file stored by a Web site on your computer to keep track of information about your browsing on that site.)

3. In the next window, you type in a chat name. It can be just about anything. You also select a topic from the drop-down list.

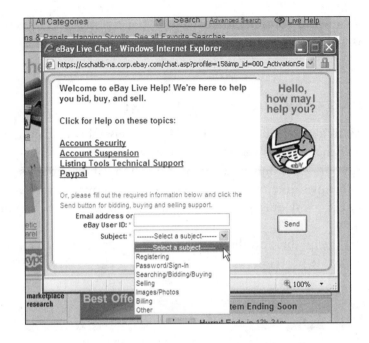

I have selected the topic "Other" for other questions. Click "Send" to begin the chat session.

4. Type your question into the box at the bottom of the next window. Once a support rep is free, he or she will respond.

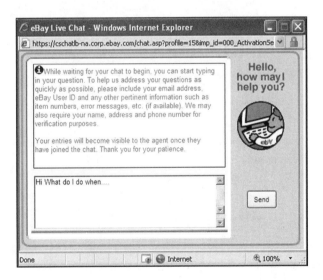

5. You can then continue to chat until your question is answered to your satisfaction.

CONTACTING EBAY CUSTOMER SUPPORT

If the information provided through the eBay site, eBay Live Help, or eBay members doesn't adequately answer your question, you should send an e-mail to eBay Customer Support—but only after exhausting all the above options.

It can sometimes take twenty-four to forty-eight hours to receive a response to an e-mail. For many questions, you can find an answer on the site in less than a few minutes.

Click the "Help" link on the top of any eBay page and then click "Contact Us" under eBay Help.

Help

eBay Help

Help Topics
A-Z Index
eBay Acronyms
eBay Glossary

Contact Us

Related Links

Learning Center
Security Center
About Customer Support

Contact Us

① Select a Category   2. Select a Subtopic   3. Review Help and Email Us

Select the category that best matches your question or concern, and click the **Continue** button. Then follow the pages to select the appropriate topics. If you have a PayPal question, please contact PayPal Customer Support.

Note: Selecting the most appropriate topic will enable us to assist you more quickly and prevent delays.

○ **Listing Violations**
Report a listing violation or prohibited (banned) item

◉ **Buying and Finding**
Ask about searching, bidding, paying for an item, or dispute resolution

○ **Account Security**
Report fake eBay emails, unauthorized account activity, or other safety concerns

○ **My Account, Registration, and Password**
Ask about My eBay or changing your contact information

○ **Selling and Managing Your Item**
Ask about photos, fees, tools, Stores, unpaid items, or problems with a buyer

○ **Suspension**
Ask about a suspended account, notices you've received from eBay, or sign-in problems

○ **Feedback**
Ask about eBay's Feedback system, or about feedback you've left or received

○ **View and Report Site Issues**
Examples include error messages, functionality that is not working, and pages that do not display. Please ch policy violations or specific issues with your eBay account.

[Continue >]

Select the appropriate topics and subtopics. Let's select "Buying and Finding" and click the "Continue" button.

Select the topics in each step box and click the "Continue" button.

HELP!

713

Click "Email us" under Contact Customer Support.

Fill in each of the boxes and click the "Send" button.

And a last word . . .

EBAY RADIO

Launched at the 2004 eBay Live Community Conference in New Orleans, eBay Radio is broadcast on the Internet every Tuesday from 11:00 A.M. to 2:00 P.M. Pacific Time, and a special, call-in-only eBay Radio show titled *Ask Griff* is broadcast every Sunday from 3:00 P.M. to 5:00 P.M. Pacific Time.

Our Tuesday show includes a roster of guests and topics all related to eBay buying and selling, with a particular emphasis on starting and running a successful business on eBay. We also take calls for thirty minutes of every hour during the three-hour broadcast.

Our Sunday show is devoted entirely to your phone calls.

It's easy to tune in to a live show. Just go to *www.wsradio.com/ebayradio*

and follow the instructions for listening live. In addition, you can listen to any of our past shows by searching through the archives by date or topic. You can even download past shows as podcasts on iTunes!

Sign up with the eBay Radio eBay Group to receive e-mail reminders for up-coming shows. Click the "Community" link on the top of any eBay page and click the "Groups" link:

Locate and click the "eBay Radio" link under News & Events. Follow the in-structions from there.

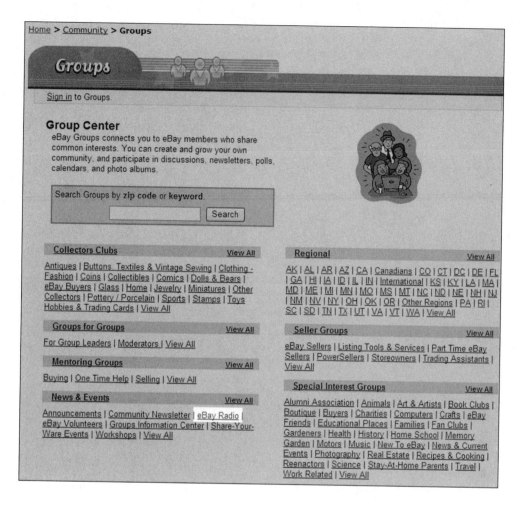

Home > Community > **Groups**

Groups

Sign in to Groups.

Group Center

eBay Groups connects you to eBay members who share common interests. You can create and grow your own community, and participate in discussions, newsletters, polls, calendars, and photo albums.

Search Groups by **zip code** or **keyword.**

[   ] [Search]

Collectors Clubs   View All

Antiques | Buttons, Textiles & Vintage Sewing | Clothing - Fashion | Coins | Collectibles | Comics | Dolls & Bears | eBay Buyers | Glass | Home | Jewelry | Miniatures | Other Collectors | Pottery / Porcelain | Sports | Stamps | Toys Hobbies & Trading Cards | View All

Groups for Groups   View All

For Group Leaders | Moderators | View All

Mentoring Groups   View All

Buying | One Time Help | Selling | View All

News & Events   View All

Announcements | Community Newsletter | eBay Radio | eBay Volunteers | Groups Information Center | Share-Your-Ware Events | Workshops | View All

Regional   View All

AK | AL | AR | AZ | CA | Canadians | CO | CT | DC | DE | FL | GA | HI | IA | ID | IL | IN | International | KS | KY | LA | MA | MD | ME | MI | MN | MO | MS | MT | NC | ND | NE | NH | NJ | NM | NV | NY | OH | OK | OR | Other Regions | PA | RI | SC | SD | TN | TX | UT | VA | VT | WA | View All

Seller Groups   View All

eBay Sellers | Listing Tools & Services | Part Time eBay Sellers | PowerSellers | Storeowners | Trading Assistants | View All

Special Interest Groups   View All

Alumni Association | Animals | Art & Artists | Book Clubs | Boutique | Buyers | Charities | Computers | Crafts | eBay Friends | Educational Places | Families | Fan Clubs | Gardeners | Health | History | Home School | Memory Garden | Motors | Music | New To eBay | News & Current Events | Photography | Real Estate | Recipes & Cooking | Reenactors | Science | Stay-At-Home Parents | Travel | Work Related | View All

GLOSSARY

About Me: A page you can create on eBay that tells other members about you and your eBay business. You'll see the About Me icon next to the User ID of anyone who has an About Me page.

Administrative Cancellation: The cancellation of a bid by eBay due to administrative circumstances, such as when a bidder becomes unregistered.

Account Guard: The security feature of the eBay Toolbar that identifies when toolbar users are on an eBay or PayPal Web site, and warns them when they are on a potentially fraudulent (spoof) Web site.

Announcement Boards: Special pages where eBay posts current news and information. You'll find announcements about new features and promotions, policy changes, special event information, and notices about system issues. (For access, click "Community" on the top of any eBay page.)

Answer Center: Special pages where you can ask questions and get help with using eBay from other members of the eBay community.

Auction-Style Listing (Online Auction Format): The basic, most common way to sell an item on eBay—listing the item for sale, collecting bids for a fixed length of time, and selling the item to the highest bidder.

Authentication Services: Provided by third-party companies, authentication services offer everything from opinions to certified authentication and grading for items like jewelry, books, stamps, coins, comic books, and trading cards. (For access, click the Services link on the top of any eBay page.)

Best Offer: This feature allows sellers to receive price-based offers from buyers which can be accepted at the discretion of the seller. This feature is available for listings in the Fixed Price format, and once a buyer's best offer is accepted by the seller, the listing ends.

Bid Cancellation: The cancellation of a bid by a seller during an auction-style listing. In general, you should not cancel bids in your listings. However, you might cancel a bid if you are unable to verify the identity of the bidder. Once a bid is canceled, it cannot be reinstated by the seller. However, the bidder may bid again. (Click "My eBay > All Selling > Seller-Related Links.")

Bid Increment: The amount by which a bid must be raised in order for it to be accepted in an auction-style listing. For example, if the current bid for an item is $5.00, and the bid increment is 50¢, the next bid must be at least $5.50. The bid increment is automatically determined based on the current high bid.

Bid Retraction: The cancellation of a bid by a buyer during an auction-style listing. In general, a retraction may be allowed only under special circumstances. For example, if you accidentally enter the wrong bid amount (entering $99.50 rather than $9.95), you may retract it and enter the right bid amount as long as you do so immediately. (Click "My eBay > All Buying > Buyer-Related Links.")

Bidder Search: A search for all the items that a member of eBay has placed bids on. You can use this feature to see what another member has bid on during the last thirty days. All you need is the member's User ID.

Block Bidders/Buyers: A feature that lets you create a list of specific eBay members who are not allowed to bid on or buy items you list for sale. People on the list will be blocked from participating in all of your items until you take them off the list. (Click "My eBay > All Selling > Seller-Related Links.")

Buy It Now: A listing feature that lets a buyer purchase an item immediately for a price the seller has set. Items with this feature will display the icon and the Buy It Now price in the seller's listings.

Buyer Requirements: Special preferences any seller can set through My eBay that will block a buyer from bidding on your item based on four criteria: location, feedback score, unpaid item strikes, and PayPal. (Click "My eBay > All Selling > Seller-Related Links.")

Category Listings: The set of categories by which items are organized on eBay, such as Antiques, Books, Computers, Sporting Goods, and so on.

Changed User ID Icon: Indicates that the member has chosen a new User ID within the past thirty days. (Click "My eBay > Accounts > Personal Information.")

Completed Listings (Search): A search for items that have ended over the last fifteen days. (Click "Advanced search.")

Digital Picture Host (or Hosting): A Web server location, accessible by computer to anyone through the World Wide Web, where digital photos are stored for viewing.

Discussion Boards: Special pages where members can post messages to the eBay community about various topics. (Click "Community" on the top of any eBay page.)

Dispute Console: Accessible through My eBay, the Dispute Console helps buyers and sellers manage, track, and take action on disputes related to their transactions, such as the Unpaid Item process and the Item Not Received process.

Dutch Auction (Multiple-Item Auction): A listing in which a seller offers multiple identical items for sale. For example, 500 pens, each at a starting price of 99¢.

eBay Picture Services: An effective and easy-to-use picture uploading tool available through the eBay Sell Your Item form. (Available in the Sell Your Item form.)

eBay Sales Reports: Helps sellers track and record their selling activity quarter to quarter. Metrics include listings and sales by category and format, average sales price, conversion rates, and more. (Click the "Site map" link on the top of any eBay page.)

eBay Shop: A Web site offering officially licensed, quality merchandise with the eBay logo. eBay Shop offers great items for you to purchase—from apparel to office accessories to cool collectibles.

eBay Stores: Special pages on eBay featuring all the items offered by an individual seller, including Buy It Now items not available in regular eBay listings. (Click the "eBay Stores" link on the eBay home page.)

eBay Time: The official time of day at eBay headquarters in San Jose, California, in the United States. This location is in the Pacific time zone.

eBay Toolbar: A free eBay buying tool that you can add to your Web browser, which tracks items you're bidding on or watching, alerts you when listings are about to end, and offers simple yet powerful ways to search for items. (Click the "Site map" link on the top of any eBay page.)

Escrow: A procedure in which a third party holds a buyer's payment in trust until the buyer receives and approves the item from the seller. Escrow is recommended for purchases of $500 or more. eBay recommends that you use Escrow.com as your escrow company. If a seller suggests a different company, please use caution. (Click the "Site map" link on the top of any eBay page.)

Feedback: A system that eBay members use to rate their buying or selling experience with other eBay members. The feedback system helps you build your reputation on eBay and helps you check the reputation of other members of the community.

Feedback Score: A number used to measure a member's reputation on eBay. After a listing is completed, the buyer and seller can leave a rating (positive, neutral, or negative) for each other. Members receive points as follows:

> +1 point for a positive rating
> 0 points for a neutral rating
> -1 point for a negative rating

The feedback score is the sum of all the ratings a member has received from unique users. Every member of eBay has a feedback score. You'll find it in parentheses next to the User ID. Click on the feedback score to see that member's entire feedback profile.

Feedback Star: Indicates that an eBay member has achieved a certain feedback score. The star will vary according to the feedback score of the member:

Yellow Star: 10 to 49
Blue Star: 50 to 99
Turquoise Star: 100 to 499
Purple Star: 500 to 999
Red Star: 1,000 to 4,999
Green Star: 5,000 to 9,999
Yellow Shooting Star: 10,000 to 24,999
Turquoise Shooting Star: 25,000 to 49,999
Purple Shooting Star: 50,000 to 99,999
Red Shooting Star: 100,000 or higher

FTP: File Transfer Protocol. A service that allows a person to transfer files between his computer to another computer on the Internet, typically a Web server.

Final Value Fee: A fee or commission that eBay charges to a seller when a listing ends. This fee is based on the "final value" of the item, which is the closing bid or sale price.

Fixed Price Format: A selling format that lets you list an item for an unchanging, set price, with no auction-style bidding.

Gift Services: A listing option that lets you promote the item you're selling as something that would make a great gift. When you use this feature, an eye-catching gift box icon appears next to your listing on search and browse result lists. You can also promote gift-related services, such as gift wrapping and shipping to the gift recipient.

Giving Works: eBay Giving Works is the dedicated program for charity listings on eBay. When you list an item through eBay Giving Works and donate 100 percent of the final sale price to a nonprofit member organization, eBay will donate the insertion fee and the final value fee to the nonprofit selected in the listing. (Click the "Giving works" link on the eBay home page.)

HTML: Hypertext Markup Language. The formatting system that "marks up" the plain text that makes up a web page. For example, <B> Make me bold </B>. The bracket characters, <B> and </B>, markup the plain text "Make me bold" so that it appears on a web page as **Make me bold**.

Hyperlinks: Text or images on a web page which are marked up with HTML to make them "clickable," that is, by clicking the formatted text or image, the viewer is taken to another Web page somewhere on the Internet. Hyperlinks are usually, but not always, indicated on a web page with colored and underlined text.

ID Verify: Indicates that the identity of a seller has been confirmed, giving buyer an extra measure of security. To ID Verify a seller, a third-party company works with eBay to cross check the seller's contact information across consumer and business databases. (Click the "Site map" link on the top of any eBay page.)

Insertion Fee: The fee that eBay charges to a seller for listing an item. This fee varies by the type of listing and is nonrefundable. Please see the Fees page to learn more about how the insertion fee is determined in different types of listings.

ISP: Internet service provider. Any individual or company that provides other individuals or companies access to the Internet. In addition to dial-up and broadband internet access, ISPs typically offer a suite of other common services such as e-mail and Web hosting. ISP can be any size, from a telecom such as ATT to a local small business such as Vermont-based Sover.net (a small provider of Internet access and services).

Item Not Received: eBay's new online tool for resolving transaction disputes, problems, or miscommunication. Use this process when you've paid for an item but didn't receive it, or when you've paid for and received an item but it was significantly different from the item's description. (Click the "Security & Resolution Center" link on the bottom of any eBay page.)

Learning Center: eBay Education's hub page containing links to eBay University, online tours and tutorials, and the eBay Education Specialist program. (Click the "Help" link on the top of any eBay page and then click the link for "Learning center.")

Member Profile: A page showing all of a member's feedback information, including ratings and comments from others who have bought or sold with that person before. To see a member's profile, just click on the feedback score in parentheses, next to the User ID.

Merge Accounts: To combine your eBay accounts when you have more than one. If you've created two eBay accounts (with two User IDs) during the time you've used eBay, merging them can simplify your buying and selling activities.

Multiple-Item Auction: See Dutch Auction.

My eBay: A central place on eBay where you can manage all of your activities, including buying, selling, feedback, and general account preferences.

New Listing Icon: Indicates that the item has been listed within the last twenty-four hours. If you search or browse for the same kind of items repeatedly, this icon helps you spot items you may not have seen before.

New Member/User Icon: Indicates that the user has been a registered member of eBay for thirty days or less.

Online Auction Format: See Auction-Style Listing.

PayPal: A fast, easy, secure payment method offered by most eBay sellers for purchasing items. When you use PayPal, your payment is sent from your credit card or bank account without giving your account information directly to the seller.

PayPal Buyer Protection: A buyer-protection program that offers up to $2,000 of free coverage for buyers who pay with PayPal on qualified listings. Listings are qualified if the seller has a feedback score of 50 (98 percent positive) and meets other transaction-related requirements. Items that qualify for PayPal Buyer Protection are denoted by the PayPal Buyer Protection shield on the View Item page.

Picture Icon: Indicates that the listing has a picture of the item in its description. This icon appears in browse and search result lists.

Picture Manager: eBay's own picture-hosting service, available to all sellers at a low monthly subscription price. Works in conjunction with eBay Picture Service.

PowerSeller: A seller on eBay who has maintained a 98 percent positive feedback score and provided a high level of service to buyers. (Click the "Services" link on the top of any eBay page.)

Pre-Approve Bidders/Buyers: A feature that lets you create a list of specific eBay members who are allowed to bid on or buy an item you're listing for sale. Each preapproved list applies to only one item, so you can restrict bidding or buying on one of your listings without changing the others.

Private Auction Listing: A listing in which the User IDs of bidders are not displayed to others. When a private auction listing ends, the seller and high bidder are notified through e-mail.

Proxy Bidding: The feature of an auction-style listing in which eBay automatically bids on your behalf, up to the maximum amount you set.

Real Estate Advertisement Format: A listing format used for advertising real estate to eBay's audience without having to hold an auction-style listing or conduct the sale on eBay. There is no bidding with this format—interested buyers provide their contact information to the seller through the listing.

Registered Member/User: A person who has registered with eBay by providing basic contact information.

Relisting: Listing an item for sale again after it did not sell the first time.

Reserve Price: The lowest price at which you're willing to sell your item in an auction-style listing. When you list your item, you can set a secret reserve price. If the highest bid does not meet your reserve price, then you're under no obligation to sell the item to the bidder.

Second Chance Offer: A feature that lets you make an offer to a nonwinning bidder when either the winning bidder has failed to pay for your item or you have a duplicate of the item.

Secure Server: A special server used for processing credit card and other sensitive information that you submit. This server uses Secure Sockets Layer (SSL) encryption to keep your information private and safe.

Secure Sockets Layer (SSL): An industry-standard encryption protocol that is used to transmit users' personal or credit card information securely and privately over the Internet. eBay uses this technology to keep your information safe.

Security & Resolution Center: The central location on the eBay site for members to report problems, as well as for members to learn how to stay safe on eBay and online. (Click the "Security & Resolution Center" link on the bottom of any eBay page.)

Sell Similar Item: A feature that lets you list a new item based on the information you've previously entered for another item.

Seller's Return Policy: A feature in the Sell Your Item form that enables sellers to specify their product return policy. This feature includes a set of preformatted policies from which the seller can choose.

Seller Search: A search by User ID for a specific seller on eBay.

Seller's Assistant (Blackthorne): An advanced eBay selling tool that helps frequent sellers create professional listings in bulk, track them at eBay, and manage customer correspondence. (Click the "Site map" link on the top of any eBay page.)

Selling Manager: An advanced eBay selling tool that lets you perform all of your listing- and sales-related activities from one location in My eBay. (Click the "Site map" link on the top of any eBay page.)

Selling Manager Pro: An eBay selling tool that has all the features of Selling Manager, but has additional capabilities to track inventory, list items in bulk, send feedback and e-mails in bulk, and generate profit-and-loss reports. (Click the "Site map" link on the top of any eBay page.)

Shill Bidding: The deliberate placing of bids to artificially raise the price of an item. This practice is not permitted on eBay. Family members, friends, and individuals living together, working together, or sharing a computer should not bid on one another's items.

Shipping Calculator: Free seller tool that provides accurate, calculated shipping amounts to buyers based on parcel origination and destination zip codes.

Sniping: Placing a bid in the closing minutes or seconds of an auction-style listing. Any bid placed before the listing ends is allowed on eBay.

SquareTrade: Third party vendor that offers dispute resolution and identity verification services for all eBay members. (Click the "Site map" link on the top of any eBay page.)

Starting Price: The price at which you want bidding for your item to begin in an auction-style listing.

Store Inventory Format: A selling format that eBay Store sellers can use to list items in their Store for a fixed price.

Tags: Bits of special text that form the "language" of Hypertext Markup Language (HTML). For example, <B> is the HTML tag that formats any text after it as bold.

Title Search: A method of finding items on eBay by entering keywords that match the title of the items.

Trading Assistants: Trading Assistants are experienced eBay sellers who will sell your items on eBay for a fee. Find them in the Trading Assistants directory at *www.ebay.com/ta.*

Turbo Lister: An advanced, free desktop-based eBay selling tool that helps you create multiple eBay listings quickly and easily offline from your computer. (Click the "Site map" link on the top of any eBay page.)

Unpaid Item Process: The dispute resolution process used by sellers when they have not been paid for their item. The Unpaid Item Process provides sellers with a method for obtaining a refund for a Final Value Fee credit from eBay. (Click "Help" and "A–Z index.")

URL: Uniform Resource Locator, more commonly known as "Web address." URL's take the following form: *http://www.ebay.com.*

User Agreement: The terms under which eBay offers registered members access to eBay services. (Click "Help" and "A–Z index.")

User ID: The "nickname" you choose to identify yourself to other eBay members. You choose a User ID when you register on eBay.

VeRO: eBay's Verified Rights Owner (VeRO) program facilitates cooperation between eBay and rights owners who wish to protect their intellectual property rights. (Click "Help" and "A–Z index.")

Want It Now: A section of the eBay site where buyers can tell sellers exactly what they want. Buyers post a message to Want It Now with a description of what they'd like to buy. Sellers can review these posts and respond to buyers with items they are selling on eBay. (Click "Help" and "A–Z index.")

INDEX

A

abbreviations, 86
About eBay page, 39
About Me page, 68–69, 163–64, 295, 568–69, 634
Account Guard, 287–88
account information, 54, 68–78
accounting, 539–46
Accounting Assistant tool, 544
account managers, 572
account status, 76
ActiveX controls, 406
address information, 18, 69, 70, 310
Ad Format auctions, 254
adjectives, 400
age restrictions, 14
alerts, 149, 173
All Buying, 54, 55
All Categories, 48
All Favorites, 54
All Items, 99, 105
All Selling, 54, 62
America Online (AOL), 671–78
amortization, 546
Anchored Stores, 552, 684
Answer Center, 34
arbitration and mediation, 279, 701. *See also* disputes and dispute resolution
archiving, 237–41, 368–71, 566
articles, 128, 129, 400

artwork, 373–74. *See also* photographs and images
ASCII, 588
assistance, 702
asterisks, 128, 129
attributes of items. *See* finder tool
auction formats, 4–5, 328
auction management services, 222
AuctionPix, 304
Auctions tab, 99
auction status, 58
AuctionWeb Bulletin Board, 5, 296
audits, 519
authentication services, 576–78, 699, 700–701. *See also* VeRO Program
Automated Clearing House, 495
automobiles, 139, 249–53, 580–82. *See also* eBay Motors
AutoText inserts, 487–88

B

Babel Fish, 263, 586
backdrops, 337–39, 345
background of eBay, xix, 3–5, 6–8
bank accounts
    bank-to-bank transfers, 185, 235
    and PayPal, 22, 25–26, 26–27, 493–95
    and seller's accounts, 307–12
Becker, Peter, 534
Berners-Lee, Tim, 588
Best Offer feature, 138, 232, 436–37

bidding
  bidding history, 171–72, 214
  bidding offenses, 692
  bid increments, 197, 198
  bid retractions, 81, 475–76
  bid screen, 193, 196
  bid values, 214
  blocking bidders, 451–53
  canceling bids, 474
  Confirm Bid screen, 194
  confirming bids, 194, 195, 197, 207–10, 220
  Dutch auctions, 214
  and eBay Motors, 250
  homework before, 151
  increments for bids, 197, 198
  maximum bid, 199, 206
  multiple items, 211–14
  and My eBay, 56
  options for, 52
  Place Bid button, 205
  proxy bidding, 191–99, 199–211
  retracted bids, 272–74, 475–76
  and Safe Trading Checklist, 160–90
  searching by bidder, 141
  shill bidding, 276, 692
  sniping, 200–211
  tie bids, 199
  volume of, 328
  winning bids, 214
big-ticket items, 186–87, 248–55, 580–82.
    See also eBay Motors
billing address, 69, 70
Blackthorne (Basic and Pro), 554
blocking bidders/buyers, 451–53
blogs, 34, 35
boats, 580–82
bold text, 458, 615–20
bookkeeping, 539–46
books, 247
borders, 458
boxes, 383–84
brand names, 245, 334, 699
browsing. *See also* navigating eBay
  and adding pictures, 403
  and categories, 43–46, 96–104, 153,
    391–93
  and eBay stores, 110–18
  featured items, 105–8
  product finder, 108–10

bubble wrap, 382, 388
Bull, Bob, 587–88
bulletin boards, 4
business loans, 518
business tips and tools, 515–86
  and auction management tools, 546–56
  and bookkeeping, 539–46
  and business location, 535–38
  business structures, 516–21
  and eBay Stores, 556–62
  and growth, 569–70
  and international selling, 582–86
  and market efficiency, 526–33
  and office equipment, 538–39
  and PowerSeller Program, 571–73
  product selection, 521–26
  and promotion, 568–69
  and sales reports, 563–67
  selling considerations, 580–82
  successful practices, 573–80
  and Trading Assistants, 533–35
Buyer Service & Protection hub page,
  251–52
Buyer Trust and Safety Checklist, 270,
  271–76
buying
  backing out of sales, 478–79
  blocking bidders, 451–53
  Buyer Guides, 255
  buyer notifications, 60–61
  buyer protection, 107, 173, 176–77, 246,
    251–52, 696–97
  buyer requirements, 398, 451–53, 585
  Buying Resources link, 288
  buying totals, 56
  correspondence with buyers, 498
  homework before, 151
  overview, 151–60, 190–220
  portal page, 31
  reminders, 56
  restrictions on buyers, 275
  rules for, 269–70, 272–76
  Safe Trading Checklist, 160–90
  special requirements for, 161, 188
Buy It Now
  described, 214–17, 433–34
  and eBay Stores, 557
  and fixed-price listings, 436
  and item descriptions, 52, 99, 107

and payment terms, 217–20, 441–42
and Safe Trading Checklist, 161, 166–68
and searching, 102, 154
and shipping, 152, 480

C

California state law, 276, 694–95
cameras, digital, 333–34, 538. *See also* photographs and images
capital expenditure, 546
cars, 249–53, 580–82
cashier's checks, 185, 228, 397
cash payments, 185, 236, 442, 532
cash transfer services, 442
categories
    All Categories, 48
    browsing, 96–104, 153, 391–93
    Category Portal pages, 47
    and community help, 706–7
    and completed listings, 327, 329
    and customization, 556, 559
    and discussion boards, 35, 298
    eBay Express, 245
    eBay Motors, 139, 250
    eBay Stores, 112–16, 399, 556, 559
    and favorites, 65, 67
    and finder feature, 108
    hierarchy of, 41–46, 96–104
    and item descriptions, 48–53
    navigating with, 41–46, 46–48
    and product selection, 522
    recently used, 394
    and researching items, 325
    and sales reports, 565
    and searching, 102, 120–21, 123–24
    and selling, 390–94
Cawlfield, Bill, 210–11
cell phone alerts, 173
centering tags, 643–45
certified checks, 185
character entities, 626–29
charity, 440
chat forums, 34, 628, 635, 704–9. *See also* discussion boards
The Chatter, 35
checking accounts, 184–85, 228, 235–36, 307, 311, 397
checklists, 152
civility, 86

classified ads, 528
Click-N-Ship, 504–5, 506
closed items, 84
collectibles, 201, 299, 522
color of text, 623–26
commissions, 534–35. *See also* fees
community. *See* discussion boards
Community Watch Department, 688, 710
comparing items, 156–59
competition, 523, 569–70
completed listings, 74, 121, 169–81, 222–36, 323–30, 326
conference (eBay Live), 299–300
conjunctions, 128, 129
consignment items, 533–35
contacting buyers and sellers. *See also* feedback
    and canceled bids, 474
    changing contact information, 17–19
    and completing transactions, 229, 230–32
    and customer support, 712–14
    and difficult transactions, 280
    and eBay guidelines, 272
    and e-mail, 232
    and feedback, 87–88, 692
    and invoicing, 482–84, 484–89, 489–92
    and My Account page, 68
    nonresponsive bidders, 476–77, 478
    and preferences, 72
    and receiving won items, 242
    and return customers, 498
    and Safe Trading Checklist, 188
    and searches, 143–44
    and shipping options, 448
    and spoof e-mails, 281–89
    tips, 11
    and unpaid items, 693
containers for shipping, 383
copy feature, 416–17, 417–23
copyright issues, 637, 697–98, 699, 700–701
corporations, 516
counterfeit items, 697–98, 700–701
counteroffers, 436
counters, 430
country listings, 256, 259
Craters and Freighters Company, 510
crating, 509–12

credit, 518
credit cards
    and buyer protection, 177
    and currency conversion, 261–62
    and difficult transactions, 281
    and eBay Stores, 556
    and My Account page, 68, 69
    online payment services, 233
    payment with, 235
    and PayPal, 22, 25–26, 495
    and premier PayPal accounts, 318
    Safe Trading Checklist, 184, 185
    and security, 189–90
    and seller's accounts, 307–12
credits, 453. See also refunds
cross promotions tools, 560–62
currency options, 136, 260–62, 586
customer policies, 228
customer service and support
    and authentication services, 576–78
    and buyer protection, 696–97
    contacting, 712–14
    and eBay guidelines, 267
    escrow services, 578–80
    importance of, 535, 573–80
    and Live Help, 709–12
    Safe Trading Checklist, 188–89
customization
    and categories, 556, 559
    and comparing items, 156–59
    and My eBay, 56–57
    and searches, 103–5, 131–32
    and shipping options, 448
customs, 263, 264, 512–13, 584
cut feature, 416–17, 417–23

D

damaged items, 242
dealers, 253, 522
debit cards, 69, 185, 318
delivery policies, 229
deposits, 251
depreciation, 546
description of merchandise
    and completed listings, 327–28
    Description Builder, 396
    Description Editor, 415–16, 423–29, 587,
        647

and eBay Stores, 114
    searching, 120–21, 128
    title, 399–400
design of eBay, 4
DHL, 513, 583
diacritical marks, 629
difficult transactions, 280–81. See also
        arbitration and mediation; disputes and
        dispute resolution
digital images. See photographs and images
Digital Photography Review Web site, 335
directories, 111–14
discussion boards. See also chat forums
    and category discussion boards, 35, 298
    Community portal page, 34
    and eBay Radio, 716–17
    and eBay's origins, 7
    generosity of, 222
    help and assistance, 35, 296–99, 704–9
    portal page, 34
    tools boards, 35
disputes and dispute resolution, 78, 87–89,
        277, 279, 280–81, 573, 701, 710. See
        also feedback
donations, 440
double-boxing, 384–87
drag-and-drop file management, 352–55
Driscoll, Mike, 481–82
drop shippers, 531–33
dual-format listings, 442
duration of listings, 434–35
Dutch auctions, 168–69, 211–14
duties, 264, 513

E

eBay Express, 72, 244–47
eBay Giving Works, 138
eBay Help, 290
eBay Italia, 257
eBay Live, 299–300
eBay Main Street, 520–21
eBay Motors, 139, 249–53, 580–82
eBay MyWorld, 34
eBay Picture Manager, 682–85
eBay Picture Service, 401–5, 405–9,
        409–13, 471, 649–55
eBay Pulse, 525
eBay Radio, 714–17

eBay Stores
  browsing, 110–18
  categories, 112–16, 399, 556, 557, 559
  and cross promotions tools, 560–62
  and item description page, 52
  and links, 634
  searching by, 142
  and selling formats, 430
  and Selling Manager, 552–54
  setting up, 558–60
eBay Toolbar, 287–88
eBay University, xxi, 292–93
eBay Web site
  and the Feedback Forum, 78–92
  and My eBay, 53–78
  navigating, 29–53
editing images. See photographs and images
editing listings, 454–66, 462, 464–65, 471
education on eBay, 291–96
efficient markets, 526–33
electronic checks, 184, 185
e-mail
  alerts, 149, 173
  changing, 19, 20
  and contacting sellers, 232
  and difficult transactions, 280
  and eBay's origins, 4
  and invoicing, 487–88, 489–91
  and links, 634
  and My Account page, 68, 69
  and My eBay, 55
  phishing and spoof e-mails, 281–89
  preference settings, 72
  and receiving won items, 242
  and registration, 13–16
  spoof e-mails, 64, 281–89
  support, 572
  and watched items, 60–61
embedding, 655, 678–82
encryption, 189–90
ending listings, 169–81, 473–74
Ending Soonest, 100
Ending Today, 100
environmental practices, 387
escrow services, 186–87, 578–80
estate sales, 528
exact phrasing, 128, 129, 134
exporting, 264, 513–14

F
fake merchandise, 697–98, 700–701
favorites
  All Favorites page, 65–67
  searches, 132–34
  sellers, 52, 426–29, 634
Featured Items, 105–8, 459
Featured Stores, 552, 684
FedEx, 263, 506–7, 513, 583
feedback
  and bidding restrictions, 315
  and buyer safety, 271
  and buyers restrictions, 275, 452–53
  content of, 497–98
  and eBay Stores, 556
  and escrow services, 579
  Feedback Forum, 73–74, 78–92
  Feedback Profile, 475–76
  leaving for buyers, 496–98
  and Meet the Seller page, 175
  offenses, 277
  order of, 496–97
  and PowerSellers, 530
  prohibited activities, 692
  and receiving shipments, 242
  removal of, 277
  and Safe Trading Checklist, 160,
    161–63
fees
  and completing transactions, 229
  and eBay Motors, 582
  and eBay Picture Service, 402, 404
  and eBay Stores, 557
  excessive charges, 451
  and image options, 414, 456–57
  and item description page, 378
  and mediation, 701
  and multiple categories, 393
  and Picture Manager, 683–84
  and sales reports, 564
  sample invoice, 466
  and Second Chance offers, 480
  and seller's account, 310–11
  and shipping calculators, 230, 263, 380,
    442–51, 451–53, 507–8
  and Trading Assistants, 533–35
file management, 347–52, 352–55, 368–71,
  663–66, 682–85

file transfer protocol (FTP), 656–66,
    666–70, 671–78
filtering options, 45, 101–3, 128, 137,
    154–56
financial information, 18, 69, 307
finder tool, 101–2, 108–10, 142, 154–56
Find Items page, 119
Firefox Web browser, 595
fixed-price listings, 168–69, 215, 328, 430,
    436–37, 437–38. *See also* Buy It Now
flat-rate shipping, 443–44, 508
flexibility, 569–70
font tags, 621–26
Ford, Michael, 383–84, 575–76
formats of auctions, 137, 430–38, 565
formatting text, 423–29, 458
fragile items, 265
Fraud Department, 688
free shipping offers, 480
Freight Resource Center, 510
freight shipping, 443–45, 509–12
Frequently Asked Questions (FAQs), 634
frivolous bidders, 693. *See also* unpaid
    items
Fulton, Pat, 591

G
galleries. *See* photographs and images
garage sales, 534–35
generosity of eBay community, 222
Get It Fast option, 137
gift items, 137, 457
Giving Works, 440
Global Garage Sale, 534–35
government auctions, 528–29
Government Relations team, 520
grading services, 576–78
Gray, Karen, 538
green practices, 387
groups, 34, 716–17. *See also* discussion
    boards
growth of eBay, xxi, 6–7, 569–70
guidelines for eBay use, 267–79
guides, 77

H
Half.com, 75, 247–48, 634
handing costs, 448, 451
harassment, 575

hard-to-find items, 245
hard-to-ship items, 265
Heidner, Tim, 88
Help, 687–717
    accessing, 268, 289–300, 702
    boards, 298
    and buyer protection, 696–97
    and Customer Support, 712–14
    and dispute resolution, 701
    and eBay community, 704–9
    and eBay Radio, 714–17
    and intellectual property, 697–98, 699,
        700–701
    and Live Help, 709–12
    and My eBay, 703–4
    on-site help, 702–3
    portal page, 36
    and rules overview, 691–95
    trust and safety for sellers, 687–90
hexadecimal color system, 623–26
hierarchy of categories, 41–46, 96–104
high-bidder field, 172
hit counters, 329–30
Holcomb, Erik, 534
home businesses, 535–36
Home Page featured, 460–61
homework before buying, 151
horizontal rule tag, 645–48
Hornyak, Melissa, 380
HTML (hypertext markup language),
    587–648
    and About Me page, 568–69
    and character entities, 626–29
    described, 588
    and hyperlinks, 629–35
    and ISO character entities, 627–29
    and item descriptions, 388, 415–16,
        428–29, 548, 591–610
    and tags, 610–26, 635–37, 638–43,
        643–48, 652–55
    and text formatting, 615–20
    and web pages, 588, 589–90
Huffman, Linda, 93
Hurricane Katrina, 440
hyperlinks. *See* links

I
identity theft, 64
ID Verify, 313–15, 430, 433, 556

images. *See* photographs and images
import restrictions, 513–14
income tax, 518–20
incorporation, 516, 517–18
indexing, 101
index pages, 40, 678
inefficient markets, 526–33
initial public offering of eBay, 7
insertion fees, 480, 557
inserts, 426–29, 487–88
instant messages, 60–61, 173
instant purchases, 52. *See also* Buy It Now
insurance, 242, 448, 508–9, 513, 584
intellectual property, 697–98, 700–701
interference in transactions, 272–74
Internal Revenue Service (IRS), 516, 518–19
international buying and selling
   advantages of, 582–86
   international eBay sites, 586
   overview, 256–64
   payment options, 262
   and shipping, 187–88, 446–47, 448, 512–14
   as source for products to sell, 529
Internet, 4, 200–201, 530, 538, 643, 651–52
Internet Explorer
   and ActiveX controls, 406
   and centering tag, 644–45
   and HTML, 590, 594, 614, 648
   and image hosting, 666–70, 679
   and item descriptions, 422
   and saving auctions, 241
Internet service providers (ISPs), 656–66
inventories, 557
invoices, 76, 482–96, 499, 540–42, 683–84
Irfanview, 347, 351, 352
ISO character entities, 627–29
item descriptions
   and bidding, 196
   and categories, 48–53
   comparing items, 159
   and completed listings, 178–81, 227
   Description Editor, 415–16, 423–29, 587, 647
   details of, 376–79
   and eBay Motors, 582
   and embedded images, 678–82
   formatting text, 423–29

   and gallery thumbnails, 107
   and horizontal rules, 645–48
   and HTML, 596–97
   and hyperlinks, 633
   and image hosting, 655
   and item number, 141
   and professionalism, 573
   and prohibited links, 689
   and restrictions on buyers, 275
   revising listings, 471–73
   and Safe Trading Checklist, 160, 164
   sample, 377
   and text editing, 416–17, 417–23, 597–609

K

Keller, Craig M., Sr., 8
keywords, 327
knockoff merchandise, 697–98, 700–701
Knouse, Craig, 86

L

labels, shipping, 499–506
Lamb, Barry, 492
land, 253–55
languages, 257–58, 263, 586
Lanzkron, Carolyn, 496
large items, 509–12
laws and legal issues, 276, 692, 694–95
Learning Center, 292
lending, 518
Letterman, David, 7
liability, 517–18
lighting, 339–41, 345
limits on purchases, 452
line breaks, 613–14
links, 627–28, 629–35, 689
Listing Designer, 396, 429–30
listing violations, 694–95
list tags, 620–21
Live Help, 290–91, 709–12
loans, 518
local buying, 264–65, 443, 445–46
location of merchandise, 131–32, 135, 171, 535–38
log-in name. *See* User IDs
logos, 634
lost auctions, 58
Luce, Heather, 316–17

M

Macintosh computers
  and digital images, 347
  and HTML, 592, 595, 600–605, 608–10
  and item descriptions, 374, 401
  and saving auctions, 241
  and sniping, 204
  and text editing, 415–29
managing auctions, 237–41, 546–56
manual sniping, 201–11
manufacturers, 529
Maracci, Sharon, 151
marketing, 5, 560–62
market niches, 522–26
market research, 524–26, 569–70
market values, 323
Mature Audience auctions, 435
mediation and arbitration, 279, 701
Meet the Seller, 52, 173, 175–76, 697
member profiles, 82–83, 143–44
messaging, 64
minus sign, 128, 129
MissionFish, 440
misspellings, 130
MoneyGram, 185, 442
Money Market Fund, 492–93
money orders, 184, 228, 235, 236, 397
movies, 247
multiple category listings, 393
multiple item listings, 137, 168–69,
    211–14
music, 247
mutually withdrawn feedback, 90
My eBay, 53–78
  and account information, 68–78
  and editing listings, 472
  and favorites, 65–67
  and help, 703–4
  and invoices, 482–84
  and managing bids, 237–41
  and My Messages, 64, 175, 286
  overview, 53–55
  and pending listings, 439, 470
  and personal information, 18
  and Picture Manager, 682–85
  sample page, 33
  and searches, 132–34
  and selling, 62, 307, 480
  and shipping labels, 499–506
  and spoof e-mails, 286
  and tracking listings, 546–47
  and Want It Now, 63
  watch lists, 59–61, 189
My Summary page, 54
My World page, 174

N

navigating eBay, 29–53. *See also* browsing
  and categories, 41–46, 46–48
  eBay home page, 38–39
  item description page, 48–53
  navigation bar, 29–36, 268
  sign-in page, 16–17, 36–37, 53, 225
  site map, 40
Netscape Navigator, 590, 648
new items, 100, 245
News section, 35
New Yorker, The 7
nonprofit organizations, 138
nonresponsive bidders, 476–77, 477–78,
    492
Notepad, 592, 648
notification preferences, 60–61, 72
number of items in listing, 168–69

O

obscenity, 692
office equipment, 538–39, 546
Omidyar, Pierre, xx–xxi, 4, 78, 303–4, 435,
    692
online auctions, 430, 431–35, 437–38
online payments, 189–90, 233. *See also*
    PayPal
on-site help, 702–3
organization, 538–39, 543–44, 563–67. *See
    also* file management
ownership delusion, 166

P

packing merchandise, 380–88, 499, 584,
    707–9
partnerships, 516
passwords
  changing, 19, 21
  choosing, 11, 13
  forgotten, 21, 37
  and links, 16
  and My Account page, 68–69

and security, 271–72
and the sign-in page, 36–37
paste feature, 416–17, 417–23
paying for purchases. *See also* PayPal
  accepted payments policy, 233
  and Buy It Now option, 217–20
  and completed listings, 227, 328–29
  and creating listings, 396
  and eBay Motors, 250–51
  escrow services, 186–87
  and HTML tags, 620–21
  immediate payment, 217–20, 442
  and international transactions, 583, 584
  and item description page, 378
  methods, 52, 76, 137, 183–87, 440–42
    (*see also specific forms of payment*)
  overview, 221–42
  payment details, 52
  payment instructions, 489–90
  payment policies, 185–86, 228, 229
  payment terms, 232–36
  Pay Now option, 57, 236
  personal checks, 184–85, 228, 235–36,
    311, 397
  and professionalism, 573
  and Safe Trading Checklist, 161
  and sample listing, 470
  and security, 189–90, 272
  timelines, 188
  unpaid items, 276
PayPal
  accessing, 75, 492–96
  background, 22
  and blocked buyers, 452–53
  business PayPal accounts, 317–22
  and buyer protection, 52, 696–97
  and completed listings, 223–28, 328–29
  and currency conversion, 261, 262
  Debit Cards, 493
  and difficult transactions, 281
  and eBay Stores, 556
  icon for, 107
  and international transactions, 583
  and invoicing buyers, 484–89, 491
  and Meet the Seller box, 173
  Money Market Fund, 492–93
  and My Account, 68
  and My eBay, 57–58
  opening an account, 22–27, 234

and payment terms, 184, 185, 440–42
phishing and spoof e-mails, 281–89
popularity of, 233
Premier and Business accounts, 317–22,
  495
and search options, 102, 155
and security, 189–90
and seller accounts, 76
and seller information, 176–77
and shipping, 152, 501–3
and tracking sales, 543–44
pending listings, 439, 467
permissions, 637
personal checks, 184–85, 228, 235–36, 311,
  397
personal information, 11, 18, 69
phishing e-mails, 64, 281–89, 635
phone support, 572–73
photographs and images, 331–71, 649–85
  advanced solutions, 649–55
  and AOL, 671–78
  and cameras, 333–34, 334–35, 341–42
  and comparing items, 157–58
  and completed listings, 241, 328
  copying, 680–81
  and copyright issues, 637
  cropping, 356–61, 412–13
  described, 331
  eBay Motors, 582
  eBay Picture Manager, 682–85
  eBay Picture Service, 401–5, 405–9,
    409–13, 471, 649–55
  editing, 346–55, 355–71, 409–13
  and embedding, 678–82
  featured items, 459
  and file management, 347–52, 368–71
  film photographs, 332, 333
  and flash photography, 342
  framing, 342–43
  and HTML tags, 635–37, 641–43, 679
  image hosting, 304, 649–85
  image options, 413, 414–15, 456–57, 471
  and Internet Explorer, 666–70
  and Item Description page, 178–81,
    181–82, 401–5, 405–9
  landscape format, 344
  lighting, 339–41
  and links, 634
  macro photography, 335, 342

photographs and images (*cont.*)
  managing, 682–85
  methods, 332–34
  options, 413
  of packing process, 380–81
  picture-taking tips, 345–46
  portrait images, 344
  resizing, 361–66, 413
  resolution, 334, 341–42, 345, 346,
    366–67, 370–71
  rotating, 355–56, 409–11
  scanning, 332, 333, 465, 538
  setting up for, 335–46
  SuperSize image option, 366, 413
  thumbnails, 106–7, 456
  troubleshooting, 471
  value of, 332
Picture Pack image option, 414–15
pictures. *See* photographs and images
Picture Show image option, 413–14
podcasts, 716
police auctions, 528–29
policies and procedures
  accepted payments policy, 233
  for buyers, 269
  customer policies, 228
  delivery policies, 229
  and feedback, 90–91
  listing violations, 694–95
  and Live Help, 710
  overview, 691–95
  payment policies, 185–86, 228, 229
  privacy policy, 9, 13
  return and refund policies, 378, 398, 427,
    453–54, 470
portal pages
  Buy portal, 31
  Category portal, 47
  Community portal, 34
  Help portal, 36
  Sell portal, 32
PowerSellers, 481–82, 530, 571–73,
  649
preferences, 60–61, 70–72
previewing listings, 462–65
pricing
  and advanced searching, 135
  Buy It Now prices, 433–34
  and completed listings, 327

and market research, 323
reserve prices, 161, 164–65, 165–66, 198,
  199, 433, 479–81
and search results, 128
sorting by, 101
starting prices, 327, 431–32
printing listings, 238–39, 538
Priority Mail, 383–84
privacy, 9, 11, 13, 277
private listings, 435
product lines, 523–24
product selection, 521–26, 527–28, 530
profanity, 88, 277, 692
professionalism, 491, 573–74, 575
prohibited items and activities
  avoiding, 272
  and feedback, 692
  import/export restrictions, 513–14
  and links, 634–35
  and listing violations, 694–95
  list of, 276
  overview, 688–91
  profanity, 88, 277, 692
  shill bidding, 692
promoting listings, 454–66, 568–69, 580
property, 253–55
property rights, 697–98
proxy bidding, 191–99, 199–211
psychology of auctions, 165–66
public offering of eBay, 7
public storage auctions, 529
punctuation, 128, 129, 400

Q

quantity of items in auctions, 434
questionable items and activities, 276–77,
  278. *See also* prohibited items and
  activities

R

radio programs, 714–17
random-access memory (RAM), 598
Rayner, Dave, 303–4
real estate, 253–55
receiving won items, 242
recent ratings, 81
record-keeping, 545–46, 563–67
recurring payments, 318
Reddick, Tom, 89

refreshing windows, 202, 209–10
refunds, 161, 187, 228–29, 329, 453, 574, 696
refusing purchases, 212
regional trading, 265
registration
    address, 70
    categories of accounts, 10
    confirming e-mail, 14–17
    and contact information, 17–19
    and My Account page, 68, 69
    and PayPal, 23–27
    process described, 9–13
    use agreement, 13
    and User IDs, 10
relisting items, 474–75
reminders, 56. *See also* alerts
repeat business, 81
reputation, 696. *See also* feedback
requirements for eBay use, 8
resale on eBay, 530
rescheduling auctions, 470
researching items for sale, 271, 323–30,
    569–70
Reseller Marketplace, 530
reserve price
    and bid increments, 198
    described, 433
    and proxy bids, 199
    and Safe Trading Checklist, 161, 164–65,
        165–66
    and Second Chance offers, 479–81
retracted bids, 272–74, 475–76
return business, 535
returns
    and buyer protection, 696
    and completed listings, 228, 229, 329
    and international transactions, 584
    and item descriptions, 52
    return policies, 378, 398, 427, 453–54,
        470
    and Safe Trading Checklist, 161, 187
Review and Confirm Bid, 195, 196, 207–10,
    220
reviews, 77
revising listings, 471–73
risk, 528
Rittel, Deanna, 299
rules, 267–79, 694–95. *See also* policies and
    procedures

S
Sachs, Robert, 480
Safari Web browser, 595
SafeHarbor Department, 688
Safe Trading Checklist
    and Buy It Now option, 166–68
    and completion of listings, 169–81
    and feedback, 161–63
    and number of items in listing, 168–69
    overview, 160–90
    and reserve prices, 165–66
    and shipping, 152
safety, 11, 270, 271–76. *See also* security
sales reports, 563–67
sales tax, 228, 519–20
sales volume, 572
scheduling auctions, 467, 470
searching
    advanced, 134–38, 258–60, 261
    and Buy It Now option, 214–15
    and categories, 102, 120–21, 123–24
    commands, 129–30
    completed listings, 323–30
    and currency options, 136, 261
    customizing, 103–5, 124–27
    for drop shippers, 531
    and eBay Motors, 250
    and eBay Stores, 110–18, 557
    and favorites, 65, 66
    and featured items, 105–8
    and hyperlinks, 630
    and international eBay sites, 258–60
    and keywords, 39, 327
    narrowing searches, 128, 129
    options, 110, 120
    overview, 118–50
    and payment options, 155
    and product finder, 108–10
    results, 100, 101, 121, 123, 128, 462
    smart search, 130–50
    titles, 120–29
    variety of items on eBay, 93–100
    Want It Now listings, 144–50
    wholesale products, 530
Second Chance offers, 435, 479–81
Secure Socket Layer (SSL), 189–90
security
    Buyer Trust and Safety Checklist, 270,
        271–76

security (*cont.*)
  and eBay Motors, 251–52
  and ID Verify, 315
  and Live Help, 710
  and My Messages, 64
  and passwords, 11, 21, 271–72
  and PayPal accounts, 22
  phishing and spoof e-mails, 281–89
  and Want It Now listings, 150
Security & Resolution Center, 39, 286–87,
    478, 479, 695, 697
Seller's Assistant. *See* Blackthorne (Basic
    and Pro)
selling
  account setup, 305–30
  All Selling page, 62
  asking questions, 72
  and bookkeeping, 539
  and categories, 390–94
  and eBay Motors, 253
  and favorites, 65, 66
  and fees, 310–11
  formats, 328, 430–38
  and ID Verify, 313–15
  and Inserts tool, 426–29
  and listing items, 467–70
  and negative feedback, 496–97
  policies, 229
  preference settings, 72
  premier PayPal accounts, 317–22
  rules for, 688–91
  sample invoice, 466
  sample listing, 468–70
  and searching, 135, 140
  seller accounts, 75–76, 306–15
  Seller Guides, 255
  seller information, 52
  Sell portal page, 32
  Sell Your Item form, 373–79, 388–470,
    585
  Show/Hide option, 395–99
  special requirements, 161, 188
  steps summarized, 305–6
  testimonials, 303–4, 316–17, 373, 480,
    481–82, 492, 532, 534–35, 587–88,
    649
  tools, 547, 551, 555–56
  troubleshooting, 471–80
Selling Manager (Basic and Pro), 551–54

shill bidding, 276, 692
shipping
  and advanced searching, 137
  and bidding on items, 151–52
  and blocking buyers, 451–53
  and community help, 707–9
  and comparing items, 159
  and completed listings, 227, 228, 230,
    329
  and customs, 263, 264, 512–13, 584
  and difficult transactions, 281
  domestic, 442–51
  and eBay Express, 245
  and feedback, 87
  free shipping offers, 480
  international, 262–63, 512–14, 583–84,
    585
  and international transactions, 584
  and item description page, 52, 378
  labels, 499–506
  methods, 506–7
  and My Account page, 69, 70
  options, 52, 187–88, 397, 442–51
  overview, 498–514
  and packaging, 381–82, 499
  policies, 229
  and professionalism, 573
  and promoting items, 480
  rate calculators, 230, 263, 380, 442–51,
    451–53, 507–8
  receiving won items, 242
  and restrictions on buyers, 275
  and Safe Trading Checklist, 161, 170
  and sample listing, 470
  and smoking households, 536
  and Terms of Service, 182
  timing of, 499
  and USPS materials, 383–84
Shipping Calculator, 230, 263, 380,
    442–51, 451–53, 507–8
Shipping Center, 511–12
shopping. *See* browsing; searching
Shosted, Keri Lyn, 373–74
Show/Hide option, 395–99
sign-in page, 16–17, 36–37, 53, 225
site map, 40
Skoll, Jeff, xxi
Skype, 72
Small Business Administration, 516

smart search, 130–50
smoking households, 387, 536
SMS text messages, 60–61
sniping, 200–211
sole proprietorships, 516, 517–18
Sovernet, 654, 657–66, 678
spam, 280, 575, 635
special characters, 626–29
Spell Check, 416
Spencer, Chris, 649
spoof e-mails, 64, 281–89
SquareTrade, 277, 279, 701
starting prices, 327, 431–32
starting time of listings, 169–70, 438–39, 465
state taxes, 398, 519–20
status of auctions, 58
storage, 537–38
stores. *See* eBay Stores
Streamlined Sales Tax Project, 520n
studios, photographic, 336–39
Styrofoam packaging, 381, 388
subcategories, 102, 123–24
subscriptions, 76, 318
subtitles, 400–401, 457, 582
SuperSize image option, 366, 413
symbols, 400

T
table tags, 638–43
tag sales, 528
tags (HTML), 610–26, 635–37, 638–43, 643–48, 652–55
tailoring searches, 124–27
taxes
    and bookkeeping, 539, 545–46
    and business structure, 516, 518–19
    and home businesses, 535–36
    income tax, 519–20
    and international purchases, 263
    and payment terms, 228
    state taxes, 398, 519–20
terms and conditions, 634
Terms of Service
    and completing transactions, 227
    and customs, 513
    and item description page, 378
    and payment terms, 236
    and privacy, 13
    and professionalism, 573–74
    and safe trading checklist, 161
    and shipping terms, 182
testimonials, 91–92
text editing
    and character entities, 626–29
    and formatting, 423–29, 458, 615–20, 623–26
    and HTML, 591–92, 597–609, 639–41, 648
    and item descriptions, 373–76, 415–29
    TextEdit, 374, 592
text messages, 60–61, 173
theft, 64
threats, 575
tie bids, 199
time-shares, 255
timing of listings
    and browsing, 100
    ending time, 103
    and payment, 188
    reference time for eBay auctions, 107
    and Safe Trading Checklist, 161
    and search filters, 128
    and shipping, 499
    starting time, 169–70, 438–39, 465
Tips & Advice link, 252–53
title of listings, 51–52, 106–7, 120–29, 130–38, 214–15, 327, 399–400
Tools Recommendations, 555–56
tracking listings, 513, 543–44, 546–47
trademarked merchandise, 697–98, 700–701
trade shows, 529
Trading Assistants, 144, 533–35
transferring funds, 493–95
translation services, 263, 586
transparency in eBay, 323
trends, 524–26, 569–70
troubleshooting, 312. *See also* Help
trust, 78. *See also* feedback
Trust & Safety Department, 278, 688, 689, 691, 694–95
Turbo Lister, 547–51, 552–54

U
unclaimed merchandise, 528
"Uncle Griff," xx, 35
United Parcel Service (UPS), 263, 506–7, 513, 514, 583

United States Postal Service (USPS), 383–84, 503–5, 506–7, 509, 513, 583
unpaid items, 276, 452, 478–79, 692–94
unwelcome buyers, 275
URLs (uniform resource locators), 631, 635–36, 651–55, 676, 678–82, 685
U.S. Customs & Border Protection, 264
used merchandise, 335
used packing materials, 387–88
User Agreement, 9, 13
User IDs
  changing, 19, 20
  choosing, 11–13
  and contacting bidders, 477
  and eBay stores, 117
  and e-mail alerts, 149–50
  and feedback, 79, 82, 175
  forgotten, 21, 37
  and image hosting, 659
  and invoicing, 485
  and My Account, 68, 69
  and My eBay, 55
  and My World, 174
  and password security, 272
  and private listings, 435
  and promotional options, 459
  and sign-in page, 16–17, 36–37
  and unpaid items, 693

V

value of items, 323
variety of items on eBay, 93–96, 94–95, 523–24, 532–33
Vehicle Protection Program, 251–52
vehicles, 139, 249–53. *See also* eBay Motors
Verify for Export page, 514
VeRO Program, 688, 698, 700–701, 710
video games, 247
Visitor Counter, 396, 430
volume of eBay listings, 44, 439, 547
vulgar language, 88, 277, 692

W

Wagner, Terry, 221–22
wanted items, 63, 144–50

watch lists, 52, 54, 59–61, 172, 189
Web browsers
  and HTML, 590, 594–96, 608–10
  and HTML tags, 610–26
  and hyperlinks, 633
  and images, 650–55
  and text formatting, 615–20
weddings, 95–96
Western Union, 185, 442
Whitman, Meg, 7
wholesalers, 530
wildcard searches, 128, 129
Windows operating system
  and ActiveX controls, 406
  and HTML, 593, 598–600, 605–8
  and image management, 347–52
  and item descriptions, 401
  and saving auctions, 240–41
  and text editing, 415–29
wireless e-mail, 69
wire transfers, 185, 235
withdrawing funds, 493–95
Withers, Pam, 150
Won Items, 56–57, 237–41
workshops, 294–96
World Wide Web
  and eBay's origins, 4
  and HTML, 588, 589–90
  and hyperlinks, 629–35
  and images, 650–55, 656–66
  Web servers, 655
  Web sites, 12, 580
WS_FTP, 656
WYSIWYG interfaces, 548

X

Xmission, 654, 678

Y

yard sales, 528

Z

zip codes, 131–32, 264–65, 380